SENTENCE ANALYSIS IN
MODERN MALAY

SENTENCE ANALYSIS
IN MODERN MALAY

by

M. BLANCHE LEWIS

formerly Senior Lecturer in Malay,
School of Oriental and African Studies,
University of London

WITH EXAMPLES DRAWN FROM
TWO PLAYS BY ZA'BA

CAMBRIDGE
AT THE UNIVERSITY PRESS
1969

Published by the Syndics of the Cambridge University Press
Bentley House, 200 Euston Road, London, N.W.1
American Branch: 32 East 57th Street, New York, N.Y.10022

© Cambridge University Press 1969

Library of Congress Catalogue Card Number: 69–10062
Standard Book Number: 521 05554 7

Printed in Great Britain
at the University Printing House, Cambridge
(Brooke Crutchley, University Printer)

CONTENTS

PREFACE

The material

I began this book as an attempt to formulate and synthesise the conclusions which I had reached on the subject of Malay syntax as the result of teaching the language for many years. The Malay language is growing apace, to meet the demands made upon it by the complexities of modern life, and in this process of growth the written language is adding some new designs to its stock of formal syntactic patterns. But those patterns nevertheless seem to remain substantially intact, and it is from the spoken language that they have grown. It is from the spoken language that the springs well up, through novelist, playwright and short-story writer, to keep the patterns alive and fresh and to ensure that established formality does not end in desiccation. It was therefore to the spoken language that I turned for my material in this preliminary study of the structure of the Malay sentence.

For a period of three years I had the satisfaction of working closely with Dato' Dr Haji Zainal-Abidin bin Ahmad (Za'ba) during the time when he was a visiting lecturer at the School of Oriental and African Studies, University of London, and it was to a couple of little plays, familiar plots gaily refurbished, which he wrote for student performance that my thoughts turned when I was in search of live material for analysis. With two very short narrative pieces by the same author they are now to be found on pp. 197–240 of this book (The Texts), where I hope their vitality will ensure their survival in spite of the indignity of numbered sentences, made necessary for reference purposes. I feel sure that the casts for whom they were written (now scattered about the world) will agree with me in declaring them excellent material for light-hearted end of term performance.

The occasional reference to intonation in the footnotes, always to justify a particular syntactic decision, is based on remembered cadences enjoined by the author himself during rehearsals.

I take this opportunity of tendering my sincere thanks to Dato' Za'ba for the gift of the plays, with permission to use them in any way that I might choose, and for the interest which he has shown in the progress of this present work.

The method

In 1964 there was submitted to the University of London a doctoral thesis entitled 'Basic Syntactic Structures in Standard Malay'.* The author, Dr E. M. F. Payne, very kindly lent me a copy, and after studying it for some time I decided that it was a challenge that I must accept, even if it meant surrendering some of my long-held theories. The analyses in this book are kept within the grammatical framework which I deduced from Dr Payne's thesis. By constantly being on my guard against pre-judged decisions, I have resisted the temptation to wander outside the prescribed confines of the basic structures set up in the thesis. Here and there I have found it necessary to allow myself a fairly liberal interpretation of possibilities within those structures in order to accommodate the lively colloquial style of Texts A and B, but wherever I have done so the accommodation has been noted, either in the text or in a footnote, and I alone am to be held responsible for such inter-pretations. In a few cases I have found it desirable to add to the sub-classes of the framework deduced. Such additions are placed within square brackets where they occur in Appendix I (The Conspectus) which sets out the framework in concise form for reference purposes.

I make no apology for the frequency of alternative analyses offered, nor for the occasional open-ended soliloquy which I have allowed myself in the footnotes. In a preliminary essay of this sort rigidity of decision would be out of place.

I record here my thanks to Dr Payne for permission to use the results of his research as a springboard for this attempt to analyse the Malay sentence in accordance with the principles of structural linguistics.

---

* Submitted for the degree of Doctor of Philosophy in the University of London by E. M. F. Payne, School of Oriental and African Studies. May 1964.

I am grateful also to Professor E. J. A. Henderson, and to Professor R. H. Robins, both of the Department of Phonetics and Linguistics, School of Oriental and African Studies, University of London, for advice and encouragement during the writing of the book.

The orthography

The spelling of the Texts has been retained*, except that the *pĕpĕt* to mark the neutral vowel [ə] has been omitted and, in compensation, the phoneme /e/ (covering all gradations from [e] to [ɛ]) is marked by an acute accent.

For the sake of uniformity the examples quoted from the thesis are given in the same spelling.

The purpose

The book has been written primarily as a working textbook for second-year university students reading Malay. But it is hoped that the provision of a glossary and translations for the Texts will bring it within the reach of students—and possibly others—who, though having little or no knowledge of Malay, may yet be interested in the application of a formal grammatical framework to the sentences of a language which belongs to the Austronesian family.

M. BLANCHE LEWIS

London, 1967

---

* This is the system used in most school textbooks, which remains officially acceptable pending the publication of the long-awaited revised scheme.
See *Dewan Bahasa,* October 1964.

SYMBOLS AND ABBREVIATIONS USED

A	Adjunct (an ELEMENT in clause structure)
adj.	adjective (Word Class II.2. (A.II.1a))
aux.	auxiliary (Word Class II.3)
C	Complement (an ELEMENT in clause structure)
c	co-ordinative particle (Word Class I.1(b)ii)
(c)	potentiality of a co-ordinative particle
|c|	non-initiating co-ordinative particle
Cl	clause (a STRUCTURE)
con.	connective particle (Word Class I.1(b))
co-ord.	co-ordinate
D	say, Determinant (an ELEMENT in noun phrase structure)
dei.	deictic (ref. Word Class II.1(a))
det.	determinative (Word Class II.1(a))
dir.	directive particle (Word Class I.1(a))
H	Head (an ELEMENT in noun phrase structure)
Hv.	Head verb (an ELEMENT in verb phrase structure)
incl.cl.	included clause (within clause, phrase or group structure)
M	say, Measurer (an ELEMENT in noun phrase structure)
N	noun (Word Class II.1(b))
n.grp.	noun group (a STRUCTURE)
NNQ	Non-numeral Quantifier (Word Class I.1(c))
nom.	nominal (Word Class II.1)
n.phr.	noun phrase (a STRUCTURE)
NP	noun phrase as an element in prep. phrase structure
num.	numeral (Word Class II.2.(A.II.1b))
P	Predicate (an ELEMENT in clause structure)
P_1	the first of two or more predicate elements linked, as the result of transformation, in the same clause

P₂   a second predicate element linked to another predicate element in the same clause as the result of transformation

P.. ..P   a discontinuous predicate element

pa.   passive

parat.   parataxis

part.   particle (Word Class I)

prep.phr.   prepositional phrase (a STRUCTURE)

Pr.   pronoun (subclass of II.1(b))

Q   say, Qualifier (an ELEMENT in noun phrase structure)

S   Subject (an ELEMENT in clause structure)

s   subordinative particle (Word Class I.1(b)i)

(s)   potentiality of a subordinative particle

|s| non-initiating subordinative particle

subord.   subordinate

tr./intr.   transitive/intransitive

vb.   verbal (Word Class II.2)

vb.phr.   verb phrase (a STRUCTURE)

voc.   a vocative piece

x(i)/(ii)   a pre-Hv. ELEMENT in verb phrase structure

              x(i) = an auxiliary

              x(ii) = a verb of Class A.II.3c operating as an auxiliary

Yg(a)/(b) the *yang*-piece

ø   zero, denoting absence of potential verbal prefix

.. ..   sign denoting discontinuity of an element or structure

⋮ ⋮   sign denoting an intrusive particle, element or structure

⌐‾‾⌐   sign denoting immediate relationship between words or expressions so braced

§1. INTRODUCTION

The material

The sentences analysed in this book are taken from the Texts (A–D, printed on pp. 197–240). They are analysed within the grammatical framework which is summarized in Appendix 1. This framework has been abstracted from the data presented in a doctoral thesis of the University of London, entitled 'Basic Structures in Standard Malay'.[1]

The definitions

Definitions which are direct quotations from the thesis are printed in angle brackets and are followed by 'decimal' references to the relevant chapter, paragraph and section, but, for economy of space, the dots are omitted: e.g. the reference (5731) refers to chapter 5, paragraph 7, section 3, subsection 1. In the few occurrences where the paragraph numeration runs into double figures the dots are retained, e.g. 7.12.1.

The footnotes provide the key to terms which are unavoidably used in advance of their definitions.

The definitions are the criteria by which decisions are to be made. They are grammatical definitions, not dependent on meaning, and have been reached by research methods. They may present themselves in any one of three forms, i.e. by listing, by prescribing a diagnostic test, or by exclusion.

All three types chance to be illustrated in the three classes into which Full Words are divided:

Class 3, the Auxiliaries, are listed.
Class 2, the Verbals, are required to satisfy the *yang* test.
Class 1, the Nominals, cover *all other* Full Words.

---

1 See Preface, p. x.

The order of presentation

Each unit of Malay syntax—the Word, the Phrase (and Group), the Sentence—is in turn defined and then illustrated briefly by examples given in the thesis.

From §4 onwards, i.e. for Phrase (and Group), Clause, and Sentence, each definition and exposition is followed by an abundance of examples from the Texts, analysed in accordance with the method prescribed in Appendix II.

References to the Texts are given thus: A. 126, i.e. Text A, sentence 126.

The procedure, from this point onwards

The STRUCTURE descriptions on the bars of the analyses (e.g. noun phrase, included clause) can be conveniently checked from Appendix I (Conspectus of the Grammatical Framework).

The symbols and abbreviations used to indicate the ELEMENTS of these STRUCTURES (e.g. S for subject), and for Word Classes (e.g. N for noun), are to be identified in the List of Symbols and Abbreviations on p. xiii.

The translation of the examples quoted from the Texts is, with intent, free and colloquial. This leaves the immediate constituency of the Malay words to be deduced directly from the information given in the successive steps of an analysis.

The Texts are given in full and thus provide a generous reservoir for practice. The student is advised to begin early, e.g. at the end of page 23, to go in pursuit of all the Noun Groups to be found on any one page of the Texts, opened at random. This exercise may be repeated with profit at the end of each group of Examples from the Texts as far as page 75 (i.e. to the end of the Simple Sentence), provided that the operator is content for the time being to deal with parts of sentences, without worrying unduly about the possibility of having to revise a decision here and there, when, at a later stage, a clause has to be fitted into a larger unit of utterance.

The remainder of §6 is concerned with the examination of the

Compound Sentence. It is presented under tabulated headings (e.g. 'i. Co-ordination with particle') and many of the compound sentences analysed are for this reason lifted from longer units of utterance, as shown by the dots which precede or follow them. It will probably be wiser therefore to work through the rest of the material, following the guiding lines offered, before accepting the challenge implicit in §10: to analyse any ten consecutive sentences in the Texts.

§2. THE UNITS OF MALAY SYNTAX

The units to be described are: sentence, clause, phrase (and group), word.

A sentence must consist of one or more clauses, a clause must consist of one or more words. Phrase and group are not obligatory units in the clause.

1. The sentence

The Malay sentence is of two types: (*a*) simple; (*b*) compound.

2. The clause

The Malay clause is of two types: (*a*) nominal; (*b*) verbal.

3. The phrase

A clause may, or may not, contain one or more phrases.

The Malay phrase is of three types: (*a*) the noun phrase; (*b*) the prepositional phrase; (*c*) the verb phrase.

4. The word

The Malay word is of two types: (*a*) the particle; (*b*) the full word.

§3. THE WORD

A. WORD TYPES

The Malay word is of two types:

I. Particles

⟨A particle is a word which cannot exist alone as a complete sentence. (421)⟩

II. Full words

A full word is a word which can exist alone as a complete sentence. A full word may be simple or composite. A simple word consists of a single free morpheme. A composite word may be complex or compound. A complex word consists of a simple full word with one or more affixes:

e.g. *perkataan* 'word' (*per-kata-an*).

A compound word consists of two forms, each of which may be a full word:

e.g. *surat-khabar* 'newspaper'.

B. WORD CLASSES

I. Particles.
II. Full words.

I. Particles

The particles are divided into three subclasses:

1. the prepositions,
2. the postpositions,
3. the adjunctival particles.

I. THE PREPOSITIONS

⟨The prepositions are those particles which stand before that grammatical constituent with which they are in immediate syntactic relation. (451)⟩

They are divided into three subclasses:

- (*a*) directives,
- (*b*) connectives,
- (*c*) non-numeral quantifiers.

(*a*) *Directives*

⟨Directive particles are those which form exocentric[2] constructions with noun phrases. (4511)⟩

---

2 Endocentric and exocentric constructions:

(*a*) Bloch and Trager, p. 76:

'If a phrase has the same function as one or more of its constituents it is an *endocentric phrase* and has an endocentric construction' [e.g. the phrase 'great pleasure' (adj., noun) has the same function as its head-constituent 'pleasure' (noun)].

'If a phrase has not the same function as any of its immediate constituents it is an *exocentric phrase* and has an exocentric construction' [e.g. 'with great pleasure' (prep., adj., noun) cannot be replaced by a preposition, or by an adjective, or by a noun. Cf. n. 64. *Pagi hari* is an endocentric expression; *Hari pagi* is an exocentric expression.]

(*b*) Robins, 2, p. 235:

'Endocentric groups are either co-ordinative or subordinative according to whether they are syntactically comparable to only one word...within them, or to more than one. Thus "men and women" (noun, conj., noun) is co-ordinative since it could be replaced by "men" or "women"...but "clever boys" (adj., noun) is subordinative, since it could be replaced by "boys" but not...by "clever"...The word or group sharing the syntactic functions of the whole subordinative construction is called the head and the other components are subordinate.'

They are:[3]

(i) ka-, di-, dari, ber-[4] with noun phrase (as in berbaju, berbaju puteh);

(ii) oléh;

(iii) dengan, akan, bagi, untok.

(b) Connectives

⟨Connective particles are those which connect units of comparable status structurally, establishing either a co-ordinate or a subordinate relation. (45112)⟩

They may be listed. Examples:

(i) *subordinating*

jikalau, kalau, jika, supaya, bila,[5] supaya jangan.

(ii) *co-ordinating*

dan, serta, tetapi, atau.

(c) Non-numeral quantifiers

⟨These form endocentric[6] constructions with noun phrases. They can in such structures be preceded by directive particles to form prepositional phrases. (45113)⟩

Examples of non-numeral quantifiers are:

semua,[7] segala, tiap-tiap.

---

3 For the significance of the subclasses (i, ii, iii), see pp. 28–29.

4 Note that *ber-* before a noun is described as a particle (prepositional), not as a prefix.

5 *bila* and *apabila* occur also in the list of Interrogative Nominals.

6 Endocentric: see n. 2.

7 Note that *banyak, semua*, etc., are described as non-numeral quantifiers only when they precede a noun, e.g. in *banyak orang* 'many people', *semua buah* 'all the fruit'. But in *Semua itu saya mahu* ('All that I want') *semua* is described as a noun; and in *Yang banyak itu orang China* ('The greater number are Chinese') *banyak* is described as a verb, i.e. of Class A.II.1a, the adjective. See p. 12.

Such words are termed 'grammatical neutrals': ⟨While there are

⟨The class also includes words which reflect a different attitude to quantification. Included will be (for formal reasons) *pada*, *bukan*, and *tiada*.[8]⟩

Examples:

Orang itu *bukan* ketua kampong.

That man is not the village headman (no village headman).

Buku itu *pada* saya.

The book is with me. (is 'in-the-sphere-of-me')

Dia mendengar kata saya dengan *tiada* memberi nasihat apa-apa.

He listened to what I had to say without giving any advice whatever. (with not-giving-advice of any kind)

Dia memberi buku ka*pada* kawan-nya.

He gave a book to (the person of) his friend.

2. THE POSTPOSITIONS

⟨The postpositions are those particles which stand after the grammatical constituent with which they are in immediate syntactic relation. (451)⟩

They are: -lah, -kah, -tah, pun.

---

many words which can easily and unambiguously be placed in a word class there are also many that must be allocated to more than one word class according to their syntactic behaviour...e.g. *kerja* may be 'to work' in which case it has potentiality of *ber-* as a verb. It may also be a noun forming a noun group in *kerja kampong*, 'village work'. (47)⟩

8 *tiada*: ⟨There are contexts in which *tiada* seems to alternate with *tidak*:

Example 1. dengan tiada menggunakan pisau

Example 2. dengan tidak menggunakan pisau

        'without using a knife'.

Example 1 suggests that *tiada* is a non-numeral quantifier with verb-noun *menggunakan*.

Example 2 suggests that the verb group *tidak menggunakan* is operating as a noun. Auxiliaries cannot do this, so *tidak* is not here performing auxiliary function. (45113)⟩

3. THE ADJUNCTIVAL PARTICLES

⟨The positionally free particles may be in immediate syntactic relation with a word, phrase, or clause. They are not restricted in position with relation to the grammatical element with which they are in immediate syntactic relation. (451)⟩

The most frequent are: sangat, amat, lagi, sahaja, belaka, langsong, juga, pula, selalu.

II. Full words

The full words are divided into three subclasses:

    1. the nominals,
    2. the verbals,
    3. the auxiliaries.

1. THE NOMINALS

⟨Nominals are full words which are not verbals as defined below or auxiliaries as listed. They can occupy the S, C or A[9] positions, according to their subclass, in a verbal clause. (4421)⟩

The nominals are divided into four subclasses:

(a) *The determinatives*, itu and ini.
    They may close a noun phrase.

    Example: orang yang datang *itu*...
             the person who comes...

If determinative function alone is to be performed (i.e. as in the above example) then *itu* is used.

    Both words may perform deictic (i.e. distinguishing) function.

    Examples: orang *itu*   that man
             orang *ini*   this man

Performing this function they may be exponents of S or C in a verbal clause; and of S or P in a nominal clause.

---

9 For these symbols, see p. xiii.

Examples:

Itu 'nak menyukakan hati orang sahaja. (S in verbal clause structure.)
    That is for pleasing people only.

Ini saya hendak. (C in verbal clause structure.)
    This I want.

Itu ketua kampong. (S in nominal clause structure.)
    That is the village headman.

Ketua kampong *itu*. (P in nominal clause structure.)
    The village headman is that one. (When spoken with appropriate
    intonation and pause.)

(b) *The noun*

The noun is defined as a word which collocates with *itu*. It may be head
of a noun phrase. It may be S or C in clause structure. The pronouns[10]
are a subclass of the noun.

---

10 i.e. the personal pronouns (*saya, aku, engkau, ia, dia,* and *-nya* when
    it is not a nominalising suffix.

    NOTE: The traditional 'possessive pronoun' *-nya* is described as:

    (*a*) a nominalising suffix, e.g. in *berani-nya*, which is assigned as a
        Complement in the example *Ahmad itu termashhor berani-nya*,
        with the (literal) translation: 'Ahmad is very famous in respect
        of bravery. Cf. *sakit perut*.' (6232).

    (*b*) An alternative form of the Complement in the passive clause
        construction.

    The traditional 'demonstrative pronouns' (*itu, ini*) are listed (above)
    as Determinatives. The traditional 'interrogative pronouns' (*apa,
    siapa,* etc.) are listed (below) as Interrogative Nominals. The tradi-
    tional 'conjunctive pronoun' (*yang*) is described as a subordinating
    particle, with fixed construction potential. See pp. 21–22. The tradi-
    tional 'indefinite pronouns' (e.g. *semua, tiap-tiap*) are listed as
    Non-numeral Quantifiers. See p. 7 (*c*).

(c) The adjuncts

⟨These words cannot be exponents of S or C in verbal clause structure or of S or P in nominal clause structure. They can be listed. Like the nouns, they collocate with *itu/ini* but they differ from the noun in not having potentiality of further expansion. There is a small lexically restricted group of nouns which can also operate as adjuncts. (4521)⟩

Example: *Sekarang* orang itu datang   Now the man comes.

(d) The interrogative nominals

⟨This is a small group of words which can operate as exponent of S or C in verbal clause structure or as exponent of S or P in nominal clause structure. They do not collocate with *itu* or *ini*. (4521)⟩

The more frequent are: apa—what? siapa—who? mana—where? berapa—how many? mengapa—why? kenapa—why? bila—when? apabila—when?

2. THE VERBALS

⟨Those full words are verbals which, preceded immediately by *yang*, can form a nominal piece which can function as exponent of S in verbal or nominal clause structure, or C in verbal clause structure, or as a second element in a noun group.[11] Verbals, subject to certain restrictions, operate as exponents of P in verbal clause structure or as exponent of Q in phrase structure.[12] The verb phrase also satisfies the condition for a verbal as do also certain prepositional phrases.[13] (4422)⟩

The verbals are presented in two classes:

A. *Non-derived forms*. These consist of one free morpheme.
B. *Derived forms*.[14] These verb forms are composite full words.

---

11 See p. 20.
12 See pp. 43 and 16.
13 See p. 28.
14 ⟨If a complex word is syntactically and for further morphological processes equivalent to a simple word, the complex word is said to

A. *Non-derived forms*

	Examples:
I. *Transitive*[15]	Orang yang *membacha* buku itu...
	The person who is reading...
	Buku yang *di-bacha*...
	The book which is read...

II. *Intransitive*[15]

Class 1 a. Adjectives[16]	...basikal yang *baharu*...
	...a new bicycle...
b. Numerals	...yang *satu* itu.
	...that single one.

Class 2 Forms having potentiality of *ber-*

a. Reciprocal	Orang yang *bertengkar* dengan Ahmad itu...
	The person who is quarrelling with Ahmad...
b. Reflexive	Orang yang *berchukor* itu...
	The person who is shaving...

---

be derived. If a complex word is not grammatically equivalent to any simple word in all the constructions where it occurs it is said to be inflected. (343 n. 1)⟩

Robins, 2, p. 257: 'Broadly speaking inflectional formations... are those which...restrict the grammatical functioning of the resultant word form, whereas derivational formations produce a form substantially the same for grammatical purposes as a root form...[e.g.] English noun plural formatives...are inflectional... [e.g. in *The horses eat*, the word *horses* cannot be replaced by *horse*].'

15 ⟨The terms transitive and intransitive apply to those verbs which can or cannot respectively have a *di-* form. (3521 n.)⟩

16 Class 1 a = ⟨those [intransitive verbs] which cannot collocate with *kena*. These are conveniently called adjectives. Most adjectives collocate with *sangat*. (4522)⟩

Class 3 Other intransitive verbs.
     These can be listed.[17]
     They cannot have *ber-* forms.
     Some may have *me-* forms.

     Three subclasses are set up:

     a. Non-predicating with *me-*
          Ex.: Orang yang *mendatang* itu...
                The people who are arrivals (immigrants)...
     b. Predicating[18] with *me-*
          Ex.: Bukit yang *menurun* ka-laut itu...
                The hill which runs down to the sea...
     c. A small subclass[19] of intransitive verbs which are
          capable also of operating as auxiliaries
          Ex.: Siapa *hendak* buah?   Saya yang *hendak.*
                Who wants fruit?   I want (some).

B. *Derived forms*[20]

   I. *Transitive*

                         Examples:

with suffix *-kan* or *-i,*   Orang yg. *menjalankan* keréta itu...
   or prefix *pe(r)-*, or   The person who is driving the car...
   duplication   Budak yang *di-susuï* oléh Aminah itu...
                               The child who is suckled by Aminah...

---

17 The list would include the *pergi/datang* type verbs.
18 ⟨The term 'predicating' indicates that the verb may be exponent of
     P in verbal clause structure. (431 n.)⟩
19 The list is given as: *tidak, sudah, habis, dapat, hendak, mahu, kena*
     and *boléh.*
20 (*a*) The derivational affixes are listed as: pe(∼)-, pe(r)-, ke-,
     me(∼)-, se-, te(r)-, ke...an, pe(∼)...an, pe(r)...an, be(r)...an,
     -kan, -i, -an, -nya, -wan.
     (*b*) The inflectional affixes are listed as: di-, te(r)-, ∅, pe(r)-. See n. 14.

II. *Intransitive*

i. ke + Vb.A.II.1a + an Yang *kematian*[21] anak...
                                  (He) who has-suffered-the-death of a
                                  child...

ii. ke + Vb.A.II.1b   ...hadiah yang *kedua*...
                                  ...second prize...

iii. $me(\sim)$ + noun   Ikan yang *melaut* itu...
                                  The fish which go out to sea...

iv. $me(\sim)$ + Vb.A.II.1a   Padi yang *mengijau* itu...
                                  The rice which is growing green...

v. $me(\sim)$ + Vb.A.II.3a   Orang yang *mendatang* itu...
                                  The immigrants...

vi. $me(\sim)$ + Vb.A.II.3b   Yang *menurun* itu jin-nya.
                                  That which comes down is his
                                  familiar spirit.

vii. $te(r)$ + Vb.A.II.1a   Gulai yang *termasin* itu...
                                  Oversalted curry...

viii. Vb.A.1 + an Jambatan yang *larangan* itu...
                                  The bridge which is forbidden-to-
                                  others...

ix. $pe(\sim)$ + Vb.A.II.1a   Anjing yang *penakut* itu...
                                  The dog which is cowardly...

x. sa + noun   Budak yang *sa-baya* dengan saya...
                                  The child who is the same age as I
                                  am...

xi. $be(r)$ + Vb.A.II.3 + an Orang yang *bepergian* anakberanak itu...
          or   People who travel with their families...
     $be(r)$ + Vb.A.II.1a + an ...orang yang *berkechilan*[22] hati.
                                  ...people who are discouraged.

---

21 ⟨Two forms are found in *ke...an* derived from transitive verbs...
   kelihatan, kedengaran... (431 n. 1)⟩
22 ⟨Duplication of the root is possible with intransitive verbs except
   B.II.v, vi, x (431 n. 2)⟩

3. THE AUXILIARIES

⟨This small class of words has special function in the verb phrase. The members may be listed. (443)⟩

The list is given thus:

akan	implying that something will be done
belum	not yet
maséh	still, e.g. *maséh kechil*—still young
pernah	ever
sedang	in the process of
ta' pernah	never
telah	implying completion, hence a sense of past

§4. PHRASES AND GROUPS

⟨Phrases are sequences of two or more words below the rank of clause, and among these words there obtain certain interior relationships. (122)⟩

        A. The noun phrase (and group).
        B. The prepositional phrase.
        C. The verb phrase.

A. THE NOUN PHRASE (AND GROUP)

The noun phrase has four potential ELEMENTS: the Measurer, the Head, the Qualifier and the Determinant, symbolised respectively as M, H, Q and D.[23]

Of these, the only obligatory element is the Head.[24]

Such elements as are present occur always in the given order.

Thus the Structure of a noun phrase is: (M) H (Q) (D).

Example:

      Semua rumah besar itu   All those large houses
        M   H   Q   D

---

23 In the thesis the three non-obligatory elements are designated as symbols only (M, Q, and D), but for a working textbook of this sort the suggested interpretations of the symbols (i.e. as Measurer, Qualifier and Determinant) will serve as pointers to their functions.

24 Since H is the only element of structure which must always be present, it follows that the noun phrase in its simplest form is a noun. Thus, the prep. phrase formed with the directive particle *ber-* (see n. 4) is described as 'ber-+noun phrase' even when there is no epithet attached to the noun, as in *orang berbaju* 'the man with a coat'.

[16]

Exponents of the structural elements M, H, Q, D

'M' MAY BE:

(i) a numeral[25] (symbolised as M(i));
(ii) a non-numeral quantifier (symbolised as M(ii)).

'H' MAY BE:

a noun or its syntactic equivalent.

The syntactic equivalents of a noun are:

(i)   a noun phrase;
(ii)   a noun group;

---

25 ⟨The numeral is treated as a subclass of the adjective. A numeral must always precede a noun. If it stands before a noun which is the head noun of a noun phrase it may be followed by a numeral coefficient or one of a small lexically restricted group of nouns of length, etc. This numeral coefficient is itself a noun but has limited distribution... The numeral is classified as a verb because it can satisfy the *yang* test. It cannot be exponent of Q in noun phrase or P in verbal clause. (551)⟩

The noun phrase *dua buah rumah itu* (those two houses) is analysed thus:

dua	buah rumah	itu
M	*n.grp.*	D

'in which the noun group consists of $N_1 + N_2$ in which N_1 is one of the nouns of restricted distribution.' For the noun group see p. 20.

The expression *rumah dua buah itu* is analysed thus:

N	*n.phr.*		
rumah	dua	buah	itu
	M	H	D

i.e. as a *noun group* consisting of a noun and a noun phrase.

(iii)   a verb-form as H of a noun phrase;[26]

---

26 ⟨...verb forms in Head position in a nominal phrase...are operating as nouns. (541)⟩

The forms that may so operate are listed. The list includes most of the verbal forms given on pages 12–14, but the following points should be noted:

(i) The forms most commonly found as H in noun phrase structure are the *me-* form of transitive, and the *ber-* form of intransitive verbs.

Examples:

Menchuri barang orang di-tegah agama.

   Stealing the goods of another is forbidden by religion.

Berlatéh itu guru yang sempurna.

   Practice is the surest teacher.

(ii) The *di-* and *ter-* forms are not found as H in noun phrase structure.

(iii) The following verb-forms require the nominalising suffix *-nya* when they are used as H in noun phrase structure:

1. The zero form of transitive verbs, and the zero form of A.II.2 verbs [i.e. *ber-* potential verbs when used without *ber-*].

Examples:

[*Tulis-nya* budak itu kurang baik.]

   That child's writing is not good.

Senam-nya budak sekolah dapat pujian.

   The drilling of the schoolboys received praise.

2. Verbs A.II.1a (i.e. adjectives) and A.II.3.

Examples:

Tinggi-nya pokok kelapa itu 50 kaki.

   The height of the coconut tree is 50 feet.

Tiba-nya buku itu...terléwat sadikit.

   The arrival of the book is somewhat delayed.

Habis-nya bulan puasa itu Hari Jumaat.

   The finish of the fasting month is on Friday.

3. Members of the subclasses of verbs of Class B.II. with the exception of numbers i and viii.

(iv) a *yang*-piece (i.e. Yg(a) or Yg(b));[27]
(v) a pronoun;
(vi) a deictic;
(vii) a downgraded (i.e. included) clause;[28]
[(viii) an interrogative nominal].

'Q' MAY BE:

(i) a verb-form,[29] the commonest being the adjective (i.e. Vb.A.II.1a);

---

27 For the *yang*-piece see p. 21.
28 For the included clause see pp. 62–65.
29 The examples (531) illustrating the verb-forms which may operate
    as Q in noun phrase structure include all the forms given on pp. 12–14
    except A.II.1b and B.II.vi, but the following points are to be noted:

    (i) The commonest is A.II.1a, i.e. the adjective.
         Ex.: Semua buku *mérah* itu..   All those red books..
    (ii) With the following verb forms the determinative *itu* is
          obligatory:
          (*a*) the *di-* and *ter-* forms of Vb.A.I:
          Exx.: Semua barang *di-churi* itu..
                    All the stolen property..
                    Semua harta *terkumpul* itu..
                    All the gathered-together property..
          (*b*) the *ber-* (potential) verbs of Class A.II.2:
          Exx.: Orang *berchukor* itu..
                    The man shaving himself..
                    Segala pisau *chukor* itu..
                    All shaving knives..
          (*c*) the verbs of Class A.II.3a and b:
          Ex.: Semua orang *datang* itu..
                    All the arriving people..
    (iii) All the verb forms of Class B.II are possible, except that B.II.i
           (i.e. *ke*+ adj.+ *an*) is used only with those verbs which do not

2-2

(ii) a prep. phrase beginning with *ka-*, *di-*, *dari*, or *ber-*;

(iii) an included clause (when the Head of the phrase is a time- or place-noun);[30]

(iv) an expanded verb-phrase[31] such as *baharu datang*.

'**D**' MUST BE:

a determinative (i.e. *itu* or *ini*).

The noun group

This is one of the syntactic equivalents of the noun. As such, it may operate as Head in noun phrase structure.

The noun group is of three forms:

1. NOUN+NOUN+NOUN+...

⟨in which the first noun is the Head and succeeding nouns are in subordinate relation to it. Any two or more of the nouns may form a head to a following subordinate noun and will within their own group be in head and subordinate relation to one another. (522)⟩

---

normally take a C element when used as P in verbal clause structure.

Ex.: Orang *kehujanan*..

The man who was caught in the rain..

30 The Head of such a noun phrase (i.e. one which has an included clause as its Q element) must be one of a limited group of nouns indicating time or place, e.g. *masa*, *tempat*.

Ex.: Hari ia sampai   The day he arrived.
     H   Q

31 The examples of ⟨expanded verb-phrase⟩ given (534) are:

Orang *belum masok* itu...

The those who have not yet entered...

Orang *sangat gemok* itu...

The very fat person...

Orang *baharu datang* itu...

The just-arrived person...

Example:

$$N_1 \qquad N_2 \qquad N_3 \qquad N_4$$
Penting-nya kedudokan bahasa kebangsaan (itu).
The importance of the position of the language
of the Nation.

2. NOUN+PRONOUN

Example: rumah saya   my house.

3. NOUN+YANG-PIECE

Example: rumah yang besar   the (a) house which is big.

Thus the possible Structures of a noun group are:

$$N_1+N_2+N_3+...; \quad N+Pr.; \quad \text{and} \quad N+Yg(a)/(b),$$

and, by definition, a second or succeeding noun is in subordinate relation to the noun which precedes it.

The yang-piece

This is one of the syntactic equivalents of the noun. It is found in two forms, namely:

(*a*) ⟨One in which *yang* is a subordinating particle to a verbal clause which must have as exponent of P the zero form of a transitive verb, and usually the zero form of verbs of A.II.2 or the *ber-* form of A.II.2 reciprocal subclass. (523)⟩

Example: Orang *yang saya lihat* itu datang dari Singapura.
The man that I see comes from Singapore.

(*b*) ⟨One in which *yang* replaces the S element in a simple verbal clause or is followed by verbs A.II.1b, or B.II.ii, or B.II.v, or B.II.viii;[32] or by a prepositional phrase with particles *ka-, di-, dari, ber-*. (523)⟩

---

32 Note that these are the verb forms which cannot operate as P in verbal clause structure, viz.: numerals (cardinal and ordinal); the *me*-form of verbs which are non-predicating with *me-*; and a transitive verb with suffix *-an*. See n. 52.

Examples:

i. Replacing S in a simple verbal clause:

Orang *yang membacha buku* itu adék saya.
   The person reading the book is my younger brother.

ii. With non-predicating verb-forms:

(A.II.1b)   Saya ambil *yang satu* itu.
              I will take that single one.

(B.II.ii)   Saya menerima hadiah *yang kedua* hari itu.
              I received the second prize that day.

(B.II.v)   Orang *yang mendatang* itu orang Siak.
              The immigrants are from Siak.

(B.II.viii)   Jambatan *yang larangan* itu jambatan saya.
              The bridge which is forbidden-to-others is mine.

iii. With the prepositional phrases (*ka-*, *di-*, *dari*, *ber-*):

Orang *yang ka-pasar* itu hendak membeli daging.
   The person going to the market is going to buy meat.
Budak *yang di-tepi sungai* itu Ali.
   The child at the river's edge is Ali.
Barang *yang dari Siam* itu mahal.
   The things from Thailand are costly.
Orang *yang berbaju Malayu* itu Ahmad.
   The person wearing Malay dress is Ahmad.

Examples from the Texts

NOTE. At this point the student is advised to read Appendix II, on the method adopted for indicating Immediate Constituency. The Conspectus (Appendix I) should be of help for the summarising of material *pari passu* with its presentation.

NOUN GROUPS

All Noun Groups are heavily underlined, with the plus sign used instead of the Structure-name on the bar. Noun Phrases are lightly underlined: and have the Structure-name on the bar.

1

kopi susu   coffee with milk
$\underline{N_1 + N_2}$

2

anak kawan[33]   my children
$\underline{N_1 + N_2}$

3

umor saya   my life-span
$\underline{N + Pr.}$

4

mata changkul   the blade of the hoe
$\underline{N_1 + N_2}$

5

rumpun rotan   a clump of rattan
$\underline{N_1 + N_2}$

6

kuéh kerépék   fritters[34]
$\underline{N_1 + N_2}$

7

urat benang kekabu   threads of the tree-cotton
$\underline{N_1 + N_2 + N_2}$

8

kuku jari-nya yang halus   its delicate claws
$\quad\;\; \underline{N + Pr.}$
$\underline{N_1 + \;\;\; N_2}$
$\quad\;\; \underline{N \quad + \quad Yg(b)}$

9

periok   sa-buah   one cooking pot
$\quad\;\; \underline{num. \;\; N}$
$\quad\;\; \underline{M(i) \; n.phr. \; H}$
$\underline{N_1 \quad + \quad N_2}$

10

waktu tengah hari   (at) midday
$\quad\;\; \underline{N_1 + N_2}$
$\underline{N_1 \quad + \quad N_2}$

---

33 A noun used as a pronoun.

34 Cf. *bunga ros* 'flowers, roses', *bandar Singapura* 'the city, Singapore'. Such generic + specific noun groups are characteristic of Malay. So, here, 'sweetmeats, fritters'.

11

tin	rokok	kosong	yang	sedia	kami	bawa

$N_1 + N_2$ Vb.A.II.1a

N   i.e. adj.

H   *n.phr.*   Q(i)

N   +   Yg(a)

an empty cigarette tin that we had brought with us

NOUN PHRASES

All Noun Phrases are heavily underlined. Noun Groups are lightly underlined.

1

tiga   orang   three people

num.   N

M(i) + H

2

suatu   lidi   kelapa   a coconut-frond midrib

N_1 *n.grp.* N_2

M(i) +   H

3

sa-tengah   jam   a half-hour

N_1 *n.grp.* N_2

M(i)   +   H

4

lima   enam   ékor   sepatong   five or six dragonflies

N_1 *n.grp.* N_2

M(i)   +   H

5

tiap-tiap   orang   everybody

NNQ   N

M(ii)   +   H

6

tiap-tiap   sa-orang   each person

M(i) + H

M(ii)   +   H

7

pada[35]   pikiran   kawan   in my opinion

NNQ N_1 *n.grp.* N_2

M(ii)   +   H

---

35 *pada* described as a Non-numeral Quantifier: see p. 8.

8

kekabu	putéh	
N	Vb.A.II.1a
H	+	Q(i)

white tree-cotton

9

binatang	terbang
N	Vb.A.II.3
H	+	Q(i)

a flying creature; an insect

10

musang	saya	'tu
N *n.grp.* Pr.	det.
H	+	D

that civet-cat of mine

11

urat-urat	benang	kekabu	itu
N_1 + N_2 + N_3	det.
n.grp.	
H	+	D

the threads of tree-cotton

12

suatu	tin	rokok	kosong
num.	N_1 *n.grp.* N_2	adj.
M(i) + H +	Q(i)

an empty cigarette tin

13

sa-	jenis	binatang	terbang[35a]
num.		N	Vb.A.II.3
		H	+ Q(i)
N_1	*n.grp.*	N_2
M(i)	+	H

a species of insect

14

kayu	kechil	yang ber-chabang	itu
N	adj.		det.
H	+ Q(i)		
N	*n.grp.*	Yg(b)
H	+	D

the little forked branch

35*a* An alternative analysis results in a Noun Group:

sa-	jenis	binatang	terbang
num.	N	N	Vb.A.II.3
M(i) *n.phr.* H		H *n.phr.* Q(i)
N_1	*n.grp.*	N_2

15

(lalu	mengemaskan)	chawan	di-	méja meréka	tadi[36]
		N	prep.(a)i	N n.grp. Pr.	Vb.A.II.1a

H	+	Q(i)

dir.(i) prep.phr. I(c)   NP

H	+	Q(ii)

(then collects) the cups on the table where they have been sitting (lit. their just-now table)

16

tempat	diam	a dwelling place
N	Vb.A.II.3	

H	+	Q(i)

17

perkara	bukan-bukan[37]	non-existent things
N	Vb.A.II.1a	

H	+	Q(i)

---

36 *tadi:* taken, here, to be operating as an adjective, i.e. a verbal. It complies with the *yang* test: *Yang mana?—Yang tadi itu* 'Which one?—The one I had just now.' Usually *tadi* operates as adjunct in clause structure and may be classified either as an adjunct (i.e. nom. (c), e.g. *sekarang*) or else as one of the 'small class of nouns such as *hari*' which can operate as A [iv.a]. Comparable with *tadi* are such words as *bésok, lusa, kemudian, dahulu, kelmarin*.

The analysis given above assigns the prep. phrase as a description of the cups, which were on-the-table-where-they-had-been-sitting. A different reading of the immediate constituency of the words in the sentence, taking 'on-the-table', etc., as referring not to the cups but to the collecting of them, would assign the prep. phrase as a transformational second predicate (prep.phr.i(b), see p. 31) as in the sentence *Dia mengambil sapu tangan [di-] dalam lachi.* 'He took a handkerchief from the drawer.' But here, too, the prep. phrase could be assigned as Q in noun phrase structure, with the meaning 'He took the handkerchief (which was) in the drawer'.

37 *bukan-bukan:* taken as an alternant for *kosong*, i.e. an adj.

18

Orang	tua	Pa'	Anjang	'tu		Old Pa' Anjang.[38]

Orang   tua   Pa' Anjang   'tu   Old Pa' Anjang.[38]
 N   adj.   N₁ *n.grp.* N₂   det.

$$\underline{\text{N} \quad \text{adj.}} \quad \underline{\text{N}_1 \; \textit{n.grp.} \; \text{N}_2} \quad \underline{\text{det.}}$$

H + Q(i)
   N   *n.grp.*   N
   H   +   D

19

Cherita   perempuan-perempuan   tua   'tu!   Those old-wives tales![39]
        N   +   adj.   det.
N₁   *n.grp.*   N₂
   H   +   D

20

(Dalam   hutan)   tempat   dia   lalu   sa-malam[40]
               N   Pr.   Hv.(A.II.3)   N
               S   P   A(iv.a)
              incl.cl.
       H   +   Q(iii)

In a part of the jungle which he came through yesterday..(lit. jungle, place he traversed..)

21

..waktu   dia   menarék   changkul   'tu..
   N   Pr.   Hv.(A.I)   N   det.
       S   P   C
     incl.cl.
H   +   Q(iii)   +   D

..as he was dragging his changkul along..(lit. time he dragged..)

---

38   This is the meaning required by the context (A.35). The same words could mean 'Pa' Anjang's father'. In that case, the immediate constituency analysis would result in a noun group, not a noun phrase, thus:

         orang   tua   Pa'   Anjang   'tu
         N *n.phr.* adj.   N₁ *n.grp.* N₂   det.
             H   *n.phr.*   D
           N₁   *n.grp.*   N₂

39   See the comment on Example 18 in the last note. If Example 19 is analysed in that way as a noun group, it gives the meaning 'the stories those old ladies told'. The analysis given above yields a meaning which satisfies the context. (A.82)

40   *sa-malam:* such nominal expressions are treated as extensions of 'the small class of nouns' which may operate as adjunct in clause structure. See n. 144 and n. 164(c).

22

..(pada) masa ia terhinggap di-rumput-rumput...[41]

N	Pr.	Hv.	prep.phr. i(b)
	S	P_1	P_2
		incl.cl.	
H	+	Q(iii)	

..at a time when it alights on grasses..

23

..ketika di-adakan isti'adat berpuar..

N	Hv.(pa.)		N_1 n.grp. N_2
	P	incl.cl.	S
H	+	Q(iii)	

..on the occasion of the exorcism ceremony..

B. THE PREPOSITIONAL PHRASE

⟨The prepositional phrase is an exocentric[42] construction which consists of a noun phrase preceded by a directive particle. (571)⟩

Thus, the ELEMENTS of a prepositional phrase are a directive particle and a noun phrase, in that order.

The Structure formula for a prepositional phrase is: dir.+NP.

The prepositional phrase may operate as Predicate (P), or Complement (C), in verbal clause structure, or as Adjunct (A) in nominal or verbal clause structure.

The prepositional phrase has three subclasses:

    (i)   with particles *ka-*, *dari*, *ber-*,

    (ii) with the particle *oléh*,

    (iii) with any other particle.

    (i) ⟨The particles *ka-*, *di-*, *dari* and *ber*(-) with a noun phrase form prepositional phrases which can operate as P in verbal clause structure. (5731)⟩

---

41 For this prep. phrase and dual predicate element see p. 31 (b).
42 See n. 2.

Examples:

Orang itu *ka-pasar*.	That person is going to market.
Ahmad *di-rumah*.	Ahmad is at home.
Ikan itu *dari laut*.	That fish is from the sea.
Dia *berbaju putéh*.	He is wearing a white coat.

⟨Prepositional phrases with *ka-*, *di-*, *dari* and *ber*(-) can also operate as exponent of Q in [noun] phrase structure. (5732)⟩
Examples:

Orang *ka-pasar* itu Ahmad.
   The person (who) is going to market is Ahmad.
Orang *berbaju putéh* itu pergi melihat anak-nya.
   The man wearing a white coat is going to see his child.
Guru *dari Seremban* itu pandai melukis.
   The teacher from Seremban is skilful at drawing.
Rumah *di-kemunchak bukit* itu istana lama.
   The building at the top of the hill is the old palace.

(ii) ⟨Prepositional phrases with *oléh* operate as C in clause structure in passive clauses. (574)⟩
Examples:

Kuching itu di-pukul *oléh budak jahat*.
   The cat was beaten by the bad boy.
Rumah itu tidak terdatang lagi *oléh saya*.
   That house cannot-be-come-to any more by me.

(iii) ⟨Prepositional phrases with particles other than those cited above operate as exponents of A in clause structure. (575)⟩
Examples:

Dia pukul budak *dengan kayu*.
   He struck the child with (a piece of) wood.
Dia membuat rumah *akan adék-nya*.
   He built a house for his younger brother.

Dia memberi wang itu *untok*[43] *membuat rumah abang-nya.*

He gave the money for the purpose of building a house for his elder brother.

Examples from the Texts

(i) Prepositional phrases beginning with one of the directive particles *ka-, di-, dari, ber-.*

(*a*) Operating as sole predicate in verbal clause structure:

1

(Dia	sangka)	saya	di-bendang.
		S	P

(She thinks) I am in the rice-field.

2

Rotan	itu...dua	batu	ka-dalam.[44]
S			P

The rattan is two miles in.

3

Anak	kawan...dalam	sekolah	inggeris.[45]
S		P	

My children are at the English school.

---

43 *untok:* ⟨The particle *untok* is frequently used with a noun phrase in which the Head is a verb-form: *Dia datang untok memberi salaam kapada datok-nya.* He came for-the-purpose-of giving salutation to his grandfather. (5751)⟩ So also for *dengan, dengan tiada,* and *bagi.*

44 *ka-dalam* 'to the-inside', directive particle + noun.

45 *dalam sekolah:* short for *di-dalam sekolah,* particle + noun group (*dalam* + *sekolah*—Noun$_1$ + Noun$_2$). So also for *atas, bawah, dekat,* etc.; but for the sake of brevity it may sometimes be convenient to describe any one of these words as, itself, operating as a directive preposition.

4
..tempat-tempat   yang   ber-rumput[46]   panjang.
                  (S)   P
..places where the grass is long.

5
..ber-macham-macham   pula   jenis-nya.
          P   S
..and they are of many sorts. (lit. their kinds are of many sorts)[47]

6
Bukan-kah   awak   ka-hutan   sa-malam?
             S   P
Didn't you go into the jungle yesterday?

(*b*) Operating, by conjunctive transformation, as second (or third) predicate preceded by a verb as first predicate:[48]

1
(Kawan   tahu)   awak   ada   di-sini.
                  S   P₁   P₂
I knew you were here.

2
Kasim   arah   ka-orang   ramai.
  S   P₁   P₂
Kasim is on the side nearest to the audience.

3
Kawan   singgah   chari   ka-rumah   awak   tadi.
  S   P₁   P₂   P₃
I called in at your house just now to look for you.

4
Dia   balék   dari   Kuala   Lui.
 S   P₁   P₂
He was on his way home from Kuala Lui.

---

46 *ber-rumput:* the hyphen is inserted in this example as a reminder that *ber-* in this context is described as a preposition, not as a verbal prefix.

47 But see n. 293 for an alternative analysis.

48 See p. 79.

(c) Operating as Qualifier (Q) in noun phrase structure:

(lalu mengemaskan) chawan di-méja meréka tadi.[49]

         H   Q(ii)

(then collects up) the cups-on-the-table-where-they-have-been-sitting.

(ii) Beginning with the directive particle *oléh*, and operating as Complement (C) in passive clause structure:

1

Di-junjong oléh Salim.

 P   C

Salim carries it on his head. (Lit. [It] is carried on the head by Salim.)

2

(Bulan ta' nampak sebab) terlindong oléh pokok-pokok hutan itu.

          P   C

(The moon was not visible because) it was hidden by the jungle trees.

3

..saya selalu di-suroh oléh emak saya..

 S A(iii) P   C

..I was often told by my mother (to go and catch..)

NOTE: In Texts A and B the particle *oléh* is not used to introduce the complement except in the stage directions. In the spoken sentences of the players the complement is usually placed immediately after the verb, without the pre-posed particle, as in:

Dia di-suroh Tuanku.

 S P C

He has been ordered by His Highness (to do it).

or else the colloquial particle *dék* is used, as in:

Ta' terpandang dék dia muka aku.

  P   C S

He couldn't bear to look me in the face. (Lit. was-not-able-to-be-looked-at by him my face.)

---

49 See n. 36.

(iii) Beginning with one of the directive particles *dengan*,[50] *akan, bagi, untok*, and operating as Adjunct (A) in clause structure:

1. [Dia] membacha ayat *dengan suara perlahan*.
   He recites sacred verses in a low voice.
2. *dengan suka*[51]
   with pleasure
3. Kita akan membuat pondok *untok tempat diam* dalam sa-minggu itu.
   We shall build a hut to live in during that week.

C. THE VERB PHRASE

⟨The verb phrase in its minimal form is a verb which can be exponent of P[52] in verb clause structure. (56)⟩

This predicating verb-form is symbolised as Hv. It may be preceded by one or more auxiliaries[53] and/or verbs of Class A.II.3c[54] operating as auxiliaries. These are symbolised respectively as x(i) and x(ii).

Thus the Structure formula for a verb-phrase is (x(i)/(ii))Hv.

---

50 But when *dengan* can be replaced by *dan* it is not a directive particle; it is then a co-ordinating connective particle as in *Masok Kasim dengan Musa*, which is a transform of *Masok Musa. Masok Kasim.* See p. 79. Similarly, a 'reciprocal transformation' has produced *Saya 'nak berpakat dengan orang rumah dahulu.* (A.63) (I must talk it over with my wife first) from *Saya 'nak berpakat. Orang rumah 'nak berpakat.*

51 *suka:* taken to be a verb operating as a noun. See n. 7.

52 Of the verb-forms listed on pp. 12–14 the only forms which cannot operate as predicate of a verbal clause are the following: A.II.1b (e.g. *dua*), B.II.ii (e.g. *kedua*), B.II.v (e.g. *menurun*), B.II.viii (e.g. *larangan*).

53 The auxiliaries are listed as: *akan, belum, maséh, pernah, sedang, ta' pernah, telah.*

54 The verbs of Class A.II.3c are listed as: *tidak, sudah, habis, dapat, hendak, mahu, kena, boléh.*

Example:

Dia belum pernah naik kapal terbang.
    x(i)   x(i)   Hv.

He has never yet travelled by aeroplane.

⟨The verb-phrase may be discontinuous, when the exponent of x may precede the S element in clause structure. (562)⟩

Example: Saya *belum membacha* buku itu.
         I have not yet read the book.

or *Belum* saya *membacha* buku itu.
      Not yet have I read the book.

⟨This latter order is more particularly found where the exponent of P in clause structure is a ∅ form.⟩

Example: *Belum* saya *bacha* buku.
       I have not yet got to reading books.

Examples from the Texts

(i) The verb-phrase with an auxiliary as x (symbolised as x(i)):

1

..sepatong yang telah   ber-rachun... itu..
            x(i)   Hv.(*prep.phr.*(*i*)a)

..the poisoned dragonflies..

2

..abang akan berjalan[55] pagi 'ni..
     x(i)   Hv.(A.II.3)

..(they know) that you are going away this morning..

3

..tempat yang akan di-lalui itu..
         x(i)   Hv.(pa.B.I)

..the place that we shall be passing through..

4

Emak ayah belum dapat khabar lagi.
         x(i)   Hv.(A.I)

My parents haven't heard about it yet.

---

55 *berjalan:* taken as a verb of Class A.II.3 (see p. 13). This seems preferable to assigning it to Class A.II.2b as 'reflexive', or to describing it as a prep. phrase, *ber-* + the noun *jalan*.

5

Saya   <u>tengah[56]</u>   berpikir.

      x(i)   Hv.(A.II.2)

I'm thinking it over.

6

Saléh   <u>maséh</u>   <u>terdiri</u>   dekat   pintu.

       x(i)   Hv.(A.II.2)

Saleh is still standing near the door.

    (ii) With a verb of Class A.II.3c as x (i.e. operating as an auxiliary), symbolised as x(ii):

1

Sekarang   <u>sudah</u>   <u>ada</u>   tiga   orang.

       x(ii)   Hv.(A.II.3)

Now there are three of us here.

2

. .saya <u>ada[57]</u>   juga   <u>berchampor</u>   dalam   permainan   itu.

     x(ii). .   . .Hv.(A.II.2a)

. .I *have* taken part in that sport.

3

Padi-nya   <u>'dah</u>   <u>kukoh.</u>

       x(ii)   Hv.(A.II.1a)

His rice crop is fine and ripe.

4

Semua-nya   <u>hendak</u>   <u>menangkap</u>   sepatong   juga.

        x(ii)   Hv.(A.I)

They were all of them out to catch dragonflies.

---

56 *tengah:* taken to be operating as an auxiliary, by analogy with *sedang.* Cf. n. 183, and contrast p. 101 Ex. 6, and p. 136 Ex. 1 where it is described as a noun.

57 *ada:* taken to be operating here as an auxiliary, comparable with *sudah* (aspect of completion); so *ada,* aspect of co-existence. If the sentence order were *Ada saya berchampor* (as it often is) it would be possible to take *ada* as Head verb with *saya berchampor* (included clause) as Subject. See n. 297 where this example is re-discussed.

5

Dia <u>mahu</u>   <u>pergi</u>   sama.
    x(ii)   Hv.(A.II.2)

He wants to go along too.

6

Kita <u>kena</u>   <u>dudok</u>   dalam hutan.
    x(ii)   Hv.(A.II.3)

We shall have to stay in the jungle.

7

..<u>tidak</u>   <u>di-perkenan</u>   oléh ahli-ahli   agama.
  x(ii)   Hv.(pa.B.I)

..it is not approved of by the religious authorities.

8

Di-mana <u>'nak</u>   <u>di-chari?</u>
      x(ii)   Hv.(pa.A.I)

Where am I to look for it?

9

Berapa-kah kita <u>boléh</u>   <u>dapat</u>   duit?
          x(ii)   Hv.(A.I)

How much money shall we be able to make?

10

Tetapi <u>tidak-lah</u>[58] pula ia <u>merosakkan</u> padi.
    x(ii)..   .. Hv.(B.I)

But they do not harm the rice plants.

(iii) With more than one x element:

1

Dia <u>belum</u>   <u>sudah</u>[59] <u>menuai.</u>
    (xi)   x(ii)   Hv.(A.I)

He hasn't finished cutting his rice yet.

---

58 An alternative would be to take *tidak* as Head verb, with *ia mero-sakkan padi* (included clause) as Subject. This would give greater weight to the two particles *lah* and *pula*: 'But, strangely enough, they do no harm to the plants.'

59 When the second x element is a verb of Class A.II.3c the thesis uses the term 'verb-group' to describe the combination of this element with the Head verb, and this combination is said to operate as 'a new Hv. element for the phrase' (561). Example: Dia telah *tidak di-terima* oléh Kerajaan 'He was-in-a-state-of not-being-accepted by

2

'Dah	'nak	malang..
x(ii)	x(ii)	Hv.(A.II.1a)

If it is decreed that you are in for a piece of bad luck..

3

Aku	ta'	boleh	tidak	kena	meninggalkan	engkau.
	x(ii)	x(ii)	x(ii)	x(ii)	Hv.(B.I.)	

I can't get out of having to leave you. (Lit. I cannot-not incur-leaving you.)

NOTE: Verbal sequences that contain more than one Head verb are not verb-phrases. They are to be resolved in various ways, e.g.:

By transformation,[60] conjunctive or subjunctive.
Examples:

Dia	pergi	menchari	musang	berjanggut.
	Hv.	Hv.		
S	P_1	P_2		C

He has gone to look for a bearded civet-cat.

Saya	berkira	'nak	pulang	ésok.
	Hv.	x(ii)	Hv.	
S	P_1		P_2	A

I'm planning to go home tomorrow.

By assigning the second Hv. as P in an included clause.
Example:

Ta'	patut	[awak]	pengechut.
x(ii)	Hv.(A.II.1a)		Hv.(A.II.1a)
		[S]	incl.cl. P
P			S

You've no business to be a coward. (Lit. Not seemly [you] being-a-coward.)

By assuming parataxis[61] between co-ordinate clauses.
Example:

..lalu	dudok	memandang	keliling.
	Hv.	Hv.	N
c	Cl_1	(c)	Cl_2

..and then sits up (and) looks around him.

the Government'. Except in one alternative analysis (n. 178), the term 'verb-group' is not used in the analyses from the Texts.

60 See p. 79.
61 See p. 77.3

§5. CLAUSES[62]

A. The nominal clause.
B. The verbal clause.

A. THE NOMINAL CLAUSE

⟨A nominal clause is one in which the P element in structure has as its exponent a noun or its syntactic equivalent. (61)⟩

It may be declarative or interrogative, but not imperative.

The ELEMENTS of a nominal clause are: Subject, Predicate and (Adjunct),[63] symbolised respectively as S, P and A.

Of these three elements subject and predicate are obligatory; the adjunct is optional.

Order of the elements

The subject always precedes the predicate.
The adjunct has freedom of position.

---

62 For the included clause see pp. 62–65.

63 A clause of either type (nominal or verbal) may contain a parenthetic Adjunct which is not an integrated component of the clause structure. ⟨There are a number of short phrases of the structure noun-*nya* which are of a parenthetic nature and have freedom of distribution in clause structure. They have potentiality of pause before and after and are usually on a level intonation contour. (65)⟩ Ex.: Dia tidak datang hari ini *agak-nya*. 'He will not come today, the guess is (I think)'.

To these well-established expressions has been added, for the sake of simplification in analysing the sentences of the Texts, a wider range of expressions which seem to justify a similar description, See the Conspectus (Appendix 1) under 'A.v.[b]'.

Thus, the potential Structures are:

S P (A),   (A) S P,   and   (less frequently)   S (A) P.

Exponents of the elements

S: the Subject must be a noun or a noun-equivalent.

P: the Predicate must be a noun or a noun-equivalent.

A: the Adjunct may be:

   (i) an adjunct (i.e. nominal (c));
   (ii) a prepositional phrase beginning with one of the directive particles *dengan, akan, bagi, untok*;
   (iii) an adjunctival particle.

Examples: Orang itu ketua kampong tahun ini.
               S   P   A

That man is village headman this year.

or:

Tahun ini orang itu ketua kampong.
     A   S   P

or:

Orang itu tahun ini ketua kampong.
    S   A   P

Examples of nominal clauses from the Texts

1
Hari pagi.
 N   N
 S   P

It is morning.[64] (The time-of-day is-morning.)

---

64 This analysis is based on the intonation pattern, which has medial pause. (See Text B.1.) If the words had been in reverse order it would have been a Minor-type sentence (as often in stage-directions), with no medial pause: *Pagi hari*, 'Morning' (the-early-part of-the-day, i.e. $N_1 + N_2$, a noun-group). Cf. B.164: *Tengah hari* 'Midday', and see p. 74.

2

Itu	lanting	Kasim.
dei.	N_1	$n.grp.$ N_2

N		N
S		P

That's Kasim's lantern.

3

Ini	'bang	Musa.
dei.	N_1	$n.grp.$ N_2

N		N
S		P

Here comes Musa. (lit. This is-Musa.)

4

Ini	dia	tahu. .
dei.	Pr.	Hv.

	S *incl.cl.* P

N		N
S		P

And now (I find) she knows![65] (lit. This-situation is-that-she-knows.)

5

Kedua-nya[66]	orang	raja.
Vb.B.II.ii + part.	N_1	$n.grp.$ N_2

N		N
S		P

They are both of royal birth.

6

To'	Laksamana	sa-orang		lagi.
N	$n.grp.$ N	num.	N	part.3

N		M(i)	H	

		N		
S		P		A(iii)

The Laksmana is another one.

---

65 Context (A.21), combined with intonation, demands this analysis. If the sentence had yielded the meaning 'She knows *this* (but not the other) bit of news', the sentence would have been a verbal clause, with the analysis

Ini	dia	tahu.
C	S	P

66 The nominalising particle *-nya* allows the verb form B.II.ii to operate here as a noun. But see also n. 68, and n. 136.

7

Apa	ikhtiar?
nom.(d)	N

N	
S	P

What's to be done? (What is-our-course?)

8

Apa	pula	susah-nya?
N	part.3	N
S	A(iii)	P

Why should it be a trouble? (lit. What, I ask you, is the trouble-in-the-case?)

9

Apa	pula	tidak-nya![67]
S	A(iii)	P

And why not? (lit. What, pray, is the not-ness?)

10

Ini-lah	masa-nya.[68]
dei.	N + Pr.

N	N
S	P

This is the time!

11

Siapa-nya	pula	'ni	agak-nya?
nom.(d) + Pr.	part.3	dei.	

N		N	
S	A(iii)	P	A(v.(a))

Now which of them is this, I wonder?

---

67 A bold use of the nominalising particle -*nya*; if, indeed, it is a particle. The alternative is to describe *tidak* here as a noun, and equate the -*nya* in this example with the *nya* in Ex. 10. This solution would allow the common expression *Mengapa tidak?* (Why not?) to be analysed as a nominal clause.

68 -*nya* attached to a noun is a pronoun, not a particle. In this non-specific context it relates the noun not to a particular person but to the relevant situation: 'the time-of-it', 'the time that concerns us'.

12

Semua[69]	'tu	sangka-sangka	kosong.
N	det.	N	Vb.A.ii.la
H *n.phr.* D		H *n.phr.*	Q(i)
S		P	

All that is just imagination.

13

Dia- lah	musang	berjanggut	yang	Raja	suroh	chari[70]	'tu..
Pr. + part.2	N	*prep.phr.i*(c)			Yg(a)		det.
N	H	*n.phr.* Q(ii)					
		N₁	*n.grp.*	N₂			
		H		*n.phr.*			D
				N			
S				P			

He shall be the bearded civet-cat that the Raja told me to go and find..

14

Apa	kata	Kasim?[71]
nom.(d)	N₁ *n.grp.* N₂	
N	N	
S	P	

What do you say, Kasim? (lit. What are the words of Kasim?)

---

69 *semua:* taken as a noun. See n. 7. On p. 134, Ex. 10, it is described as an adjective.

70 Since the *yang*-piece, by definition, consists of a particle followed by a verbal clause the intermediate step of analysing this particular type of included clause will as a rule be omitted.

71 Note that this sentence has to be analysed as a nominal clause. If it were analysed as a verbal clause it would produce the clause-element order *CPS, which is not among the 'structures found'. See n. 75. See also Ex. 4 on p. 131. But note that sentence B.761: *Apa Tengku fikir?* (What do you think, Tengku?) has the structure CSP and is therefore analysed as a verbal clause. The word *kata* is a grammatical neutral.

B. THE VERBAL CLAUSE

⟨A verbal clause is one in which the P element in clause structure is a verb or its syntactic equivalent. (61)⟩

It may be: I. active;[72] II. passive.

It may be declarative, interrogative or imperative.

I. The verbal clause active

  1. Declarative and interrogative.
  2. Imperative.

I. DECLARATIVE AND INTERROGATIVE

The ELEMENTS of structure are: (Subject),[73] Predicate, (Complement),[74] (Adjunct), symbolised respectively as S, P, C, A.

---

72 In the thesis the term ⟨non-passive⟩ is preferred (3522 n.).

73 The subject of a verbal clause is defined as ⟨that element which can stand alone with the predicate in a declarative sentence (simple) in structures SP and PS (6212)⟩.

Example:

Saya datang.   I come.   Datang dia.   He comes.
  S   P   P   S

It is further defined as ⟨that element which must immediately precede the predicate in a CSP structure⟩.

Example:

Ali Ahmad pukul.   Ahmad strikes Ali.
  C   S   P

74 The complement of a verbal clause is defined as ⟨the element other than the subject which must be a noun or its syntactic equivalent⟩. ⟨When S and C elements are both present and separated by the P element the element other than an adjunct which follows P is the complement. (6214)⟩

Of the four potential elements only P, the predicate, is obligatory. By inference, therefore, the predicate may be defined as that part of a verbal clause which can stand alone as a complete utterance.

The order of the elements

1. The subject may precede or follow the predicate, i.e. SP or PS.

2. The complement may precede or follow the predicate, i.e. CP or PC.

3. When the subject and the complement are separated by the predicate, the subject comes first, i.e. SPC.[75]

4. When subject and complement both precede the verb, the complement comes first, i.e. CSP.[76]

Example:

Ali memukul Ahmad.   Ali strikes Ahmad. (6212)
S   P   C

Note that by this definition the word *pisau* in *Tangan saya kena pisau* (I've cut my hand (with a knife)) is to be described as complement even though *kena*, since it does not have a *di-* form, is to be described as an intransitive verb. It must be remembered that the assignment of a clause element as complement, in accordance with the definition given above, has nothing to do with the transitiveness of any verb-form which may precede it as exponent of P.

75 ⟨If S and C elements are both present and are separated by the predicate then the first element which has as its exponent a noun or its syntactic equivalent is the subject. (6212)⟩

Example:

Ahmad memukul Ali.   Ahmad strikes Ali. [He strikes him]
S   P   C

[i.e. the structure *CPS is *not found* in verbal clause structure.]

76 ⟨In non-passive clauses when S and C are not separated by the P element the C element must precede the S element in sequence. (6214)⟩

5. When (very rarely) subject and complement both follow the verb, the complement comes first, i.e. PCS.[76]

6. The adjunct has freedom of position,[77] and different exponents may fill different places in the sequence of elements.[78]

Thus, the structures found in the verbal clause (active) are: SP, PS; CP, PC; SPC, CSP, and (rarely) PCS; with A in free position.

Examples:

Ali Ahmad pukul.   Ahmad strikes Ali. [Him he strikes.]
C   S   P

Memukul Ahmad Ali.   Strikes Ahmad—Ali.
    P   C   S

[= Ali strikes Ahmad = strikes him, He (rare).]

(6212)
[i.e. *SCP and *PSC structures are *not found*.]

It is noted (625) that in CSP structures where the predicate is a *me-* form verb (instead of the more usual zero form) there is potentiality of the affixation of the pronoun *-nya* to the verb (or of repetition of the complement itself).

Example:

Tahun ini sawah itu Ahmad menchangkul-nya.
     A   C   S   P   (C)
This year that field Ahmad   tills   (it)

Cf. CSP in passive clause structure. (See p. 49 Item 2.)

77 Except that when it is an adjunct (i.e. Word Class II.I.(c) Ex. *sekarang*) it cannot separate P and C. [When it is an adjunctival particle, its position is determined by its immediate constituency.]

78 Example: (6215)

Sekarang dia memukul kuching dengan kayu sahaja.
A[1]   S   P   C   A[2]   A[3]
adjunct   prep.phrase adjunctival
                                          particle
Now he strikes the cat with a stick only.

The exponents of the elements

S: the subject must be a noun or its syntactic equivalent.

P: the predicate must be a verb or its syntactic equivalent.
   The syntactic equivalents of a verb are:
   (i) a verb-phrase;
   (ii) a prepositional phrase beginning with one of the directive
        particles *ka-, di-, dari, ber-*.

C: the complement must be a noun or its syntactic equivalent.

A: the adjunct may be:
   (i) an adjunct;
   (ii) a prepositional phrase beginning with one of the directive
        particles *dengan, akan, bagi, untok*;[79]
   (iii) an adjunctival particle;
   (iv) (*a*) one of a small group of nouns or noun phrases indicative of
            position in time, e.g. *ésok, hari ini, hari dia datang,*
        [(*b*) one of a limited group of nominal expressions indicative of
            extent in time or space, e.g. *sa-jurus lama-nya, dua kaki
            panjang-nya*];
   (v) parenthetic expressions spoken on a level tone,
        (*a*) a number of short phrases of the structure noun+*nya*
            e.g. *agak-nya,*
        [(*b*) a number of interpolations such as *entah, mémang*. See
            n. 245].

---

79 Also, exceptionally, with *kapada*, when the prep. phrase replaces the
   2nd complement of a two-complement verb (see p. 50), and with
   dari (or *daripada*) when it can be translated 'than' after an adjective
   predicate.
   Example (5731):

Chara dia menulis itu	ganjil	dari biasa.
S	P	A

   The style in which he writes is more awkward than usual.

2. IMPERATIVE

The ELEMENTS of structure are: Predicate, (Complement), (Adjunct), symbolised respectively as P, C, A.

Of the three potential elements only P, the predicate, is obligatory.

Order of elements

The elements may occur in any sequence.

Exponents of elements

P: the predicate may be:
  (i) one of the following verb-forms: a transitive verb (i.e. Class A.I or Class B.I) in the zero form; any Class A.II verb except subclasses 1(b) and 3(c); a B.II verb of subclasses iii, vii, or ix;
  (ii) a prepositional phrase beginning with *ka-* or *ber-*.

C: the complement
    as for declarative clauses.

A: the adjunct.
    as for declarative clauses.

Examples:
  (i) *Verb forms*
  Angkat-lah! Lift (it).
      P
  Bacha buku itu. Buku itu bacha-lah.   Read that book.
   P   C   C   P
  Bacha sekarang ini.   Read now.
   P   A
  Jangan dia datang.   Let it not be—he comes.[80]
        S------P
    P   C

---

80 I.e. 'I hope he doesn't come!' The word *jangan* is assigned as verb class A.II.1a, and the complement *dia datang* is an included clause.

(ii) *Prepositional phrases*

Berkasut-lah!   Get your shoes on!
Ka-tepi-lah.   Move to one side.

II. The verbal clause passive

⟨The mark of the passive clause is the potentiality of a complement with
oléh and a verb in the *di-* or *ter-* form[81] as exponent of P in declarative
sentences or *per-* in imperative sentences. (624)⟩

Examples:

Ahmad di-pukul oléh Ali.   Ahmad was struck by Ali.
Ahmad terpukul oléh Ali.
     S   P   C

The elements of structure: as for verbal clauses active.

The order of the elements

As for active verbal clauses, with the addition of the structure PSC.

Example: *Tidak terdatang   rumah itu   oléh saya.*
                 P   S   C
Not-to-be-come-to (was)   that house   by me.
I could not visit that house.

---

81 ⟨The *di-* forms are possible only with transitive verbs while *ter-*
   passive forms are possible with both transitive and intransitive
   verbs. Not all classes of transitive verbs have a *ter-* passive. Although
   the adjectives have a *ter-* form this is a separate derivational forma-
   tion. (3521)⟩

   That is to say, the adjectival *ter-* is not inflectional, and has no
   syntactic significance (see n. 14); *termasin, terbesar*, etc., 'too salty',
   'very large' could be interchanged with their root forms *masin,
   besar* 'salty', 'large', without affecting the grammar of the phrase or
   clause in which they occur. It must be stated here, however, that in
   the analyses of sentences from the Texts it has sometimes been
   found necessary to describe a non-adjectival *ter-* form as non-passive.

Of the structures found in the active verbal clause (i.e. SP, PS; CP, PC; SPC, CSP, and (rarely) PCS, with freedom of position for A, there are the following points to be noted:

1. When there is no *oléh* before the complement, C follows immediately after P.

Example: Ahmad *di-pukul Ali* dengan kayu.
          S   P   C   A

Ahmad is struck by Ali with a stick.

2. In CSP structure the complement with *oléh* must be repeated after the P element, or else there must be *-nya* or *oléh-nya* after the verb:

Oléh Ahmad rumah itu di-beli-*nya* or *oléh-nya* or *oléh Ahmad.*
      C   S   P   C

By Ahmad that house was bought (by him).

3. CSP structure is not possible with a *ter-* verb.

4. In the structures SPC, PCS, and CSP there is potentiality of *akan* with the S element.

Example: *Akan surat itu* di-bacha oléh dia
            S   P   C

(As for) the letter it was read by him.

The exponents of the elements

S: the subject must be a noun or its syntactic equivalent.

P: the predicate may be the *di-* form or the *ter-* form of transitive verbs, or the *ter-* form of intransitive verbs, except subclass B.II.vii (i.e. *ter-*+adj., as *termasin*).

C: the complement must be a noun or its syntactic equivalent, with potentiality of the directive particle *oléh* in pre-position.
⟨When the exponent of P is a *ter-* verb then *oléh* is obligatory with the complement. (6243)⟩

A: as for active verbal clauses.

CLAUSES WITH TWO-COMPLEMENT VERBS

Two complements may occur with:

1. a verb of the 'giving'-type;
2. a transitive verb to which the 'benefactive' suffix -*kan* has been attached.

I. In active verbal clauses

1. WITH VERBS OF THE 'GIVING'-TYPE

⟨In verbal clauses with certain exponents of P (which can be listed), the element C may have two simultaneous exponents, which may be contiguous or may be interrupted. C_2 is optional and has potentiality of transformation to a prepositional phrase. This phrase has *ka-* in pre-position and the particle *pada* as exponent of M[82] in the noun phrase. (626)⟩

The prepositional phrase functions as adjunct in verbal clause structure.

Examples:

With two exponents of C,[83] labelled C_1 and C_2:

Dia memberi saya buku.   He gives me a book.
S   P C_2 C_1

Saya dia beri buku.   (To) me he gives books.
C_2 S   P C_1

With the prepositional phrase in place of C_2:

Dia memberi buku kapada saya.
S   P   C   A

He gives a book to (the person of)[82] me.

---

82 '*pada* as exponent of M': see p. 24 Ex. 7.

83 The only structures in which this is possible are given as: SP C_2 C_1 C_2 SP C_1, C_2 PC_1 S, C_1 SPC_2, C_1 C_2 SP, C_2 C_1 SP. In all other structures the prepositional phrase with *kapada* must be used.

2. VERBS WITH THE BENEFACTIVE SUFFIX -kan

⟨Two complements are possible when the exponent of P...is the benefactive transitive with -kan. (6262)⟩

With verbs of this type the alternative prepositional phrase begins with *akan*.

Examples:

With two exponents of C, labelled C_1 and C_2:

Dia membelikan saya buku.
S   P C_2 C_1
He bought-on-behalf-of me a book.
He bought me a book.

With the prepositional phrase in place of C_2:

Dia membelikan buku akan saya.
S   P   C   A
He bought-on-behalf a book for me.
He bought a book for me.

II. In passive verbal clauses

In a passive clause with a two-complement verb the recipient[84] is still counted as the second complement (C_2), regardless of its position. But the first complement of the active clause (C_1—the book) now becomes the subject (S), and C_1, as in all passive clauses, is the 'actor'[84] (here, the giver[84]) whether preceded by *oléh* or not.

Here, too, ⟨there is potentiality of transformation to a structure in

---

84 'Recipient', 'actor', 'giver': these notional terms are not used in the thesis, since its purpose is to present a scheme which describes the mechanics of the language without having recourse to considerations of meaning. They are used here as a bridge for the student seeking to equate values between traditional nomenclature and the labels used in this more scientific approach.

which C_2 has as exponent[85] a prepositional phrase with *pada* as exponent of M in the noun phrase. (6243)⟩

Examples:

With two exponents of C, labelled C_1 and C_2:

Saya di-beri buku oléh Ahmad.
$\quad C_2 \quad\quad P \quad\quad S \quad\quad C_1$
(To) me was given a book by Ahmad.
I was given a book by Ahmad.
Ahmad gave me a book.

With the prepositional phrase in place of C_2:

Kapada saya di-beri buku oléh Ahmad.
$\quad\quad A \quad\quad\quad P \quad\quad S \quad\quad C$
To me was given a book by Ahmad.
I was given a book by Ahmad.

EXAMPLES OF VERBAL CLAUSES FROM THE TEXTS

I. Non-passive

1. DECLARATORY OR INTERROGATIVE

1

Meréka berchabut.
 Pr. Hv.(A.II.2)
 —
 N
 —
 S P

They draw lots (lit. pull out [straws]).

2

Kepala-nya bulat...
N *n.grp.* Pr. Hv.(A.II.1a)
 —
 N
 —
 S P

Its head is round...

---

85 ⟨has as exponent⟩: the prepositional phrase with *kapada* is not specifically described here as 'adjunct', but in the analysis of sentences from the Texts it is so assigned.

3

Awak	pun	ma'alum...
Pr.	part.2	Hv.(A.II.2)

N
—
S   P

You know how it is...

4

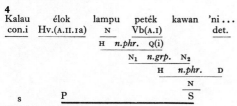

Kalau	élok	lampu	peték	kawan	'ni...
con.i	Hv.(A.II.1a)	N	Vb(A.I)		det.

H   *n.phr.*   Q(i)

N₁   *n.grp.*   N₂

H   *n.phr.*   D

N

s   P   S

If this torch of mine were working...

5

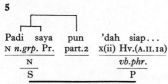

Padi	saya	pun	'dah	siap...
N *n.grp.* Pr.		part.2	x(ii)	Hv.(A.II.1a)

N   *vb.phr.*
—
S   P

And my harvest is in...

6

Orang	mengetok	pintu.
N	Hv.(A.I)	N
S	P	C

There is a knock at the door.

7

Sekarang	dia	ta'	dapat	berjalan	lagi.
nom.(c)	Pr.		x(ii) Hv.(A.II.2)		part.3

x(ii) *vb.phr.* Hv.

A(i)   S   P   A(iii)

Now he can't walk.

8

	Di-dalam	pak	itu	Tuan	Kadhi.
	N	det.		N₁ *n.grp.* N₂	

H *n.phr.* D   N

N₁ *n.grp.* N₂

dir.(a)i *prep.phr.*(i)a NP

P   S

Inside the chest is the Kadhi.

9

[Dia]	'Nak	buat	apa?
	x(ii)	Hv.(A.I)	nom.(d)
		vb.phr.	N
[S]		P	C

What is he going to do with it?

10

[Aku]	Chemburu	apa?[86]
	Hv.(A.II.1a)	nom.(d)
[S]	P	C

Jealous about what?

11

Dia	luka	kaki.[86]
Pr.	Hv.(A.II.1a)	N
S	P	C

He has hurt his foot (He is-foot-wounded).

12

Rotan	baik	harga[86]	sekarang.
N	Hv.(A.II.1a)	N	nom.(c)
S	P	C	A(i)

Rattan is fetching a good price just now (is-price-good).

13

. .luka[87]	itu	membengkak. .
N	det.	Hv.(A.II.3b)
H *n.phr.* D		
S		P

. .the wound swelled up. .

---

86 *apa, kaki, harga:* by definition, in non-passive clauses any noun which comes after the verb when the subject has preceded the verb, is to be accounted complement. (For the inserted subject see *Fragmentary Sentences* on p. 67.) So also for the 2nd member of such expressions as *sakit hati* (heart-hurt), *nipis telinga* ('ear-thin', touchy); but with well-established pairs such as these last it is simpler to count the whole expression as a compound word.

87 *luka:* described here as a noun. In Ex. 11 above the word is described as a verbal, 'be afflicted with a wound'. It is thus one of the words described as grammatical neutrals. Cf. *malam, malang, petang, demam,* etc.: *malam hari* (a noun group, $N_1 + N_2$) 'night time', but *Hari*

14

Empat	lima	hari	dahulu[88]	dia	balek	dari sawah..
num. + num.		N	N	Pr.	Hv.(A.II.3)	*prep.phr.i*(b)
M(i) *n.phr.*		H				
A(iv.b)			A(iv.a)	S	P_1	P_2

Four or five days ago, he was coming back from his rice-field..

15

Bulan	depan[89]	saya	'nak mengawinkan	anak.
H *n.phr.*	Q(ii)			
A(iv.a)		S	P	C

Next month I am getting my daughter married.

16

Masok	Temenggong.
P	S

Enter, the Temenggong.

17

Suami	terlalu	sugul	muka-nya.[90]
S	A(iii)	P	C

The husband looks very downcast.

sudah malam (a verbal clause, S P), 'Darkness had fallen' (lit. The day had become dark).

88 *dahulu*: described as a noun. See n. 36.

89 *depan*: a contraction of *di-hadapan*.

90 *muka-nya* as complement. See n. 86. But an exact parallel to those examples would be *sugul muka* 'sad of face' as in *puchat muka* 'pale (of face)'. See also n. 10(a) where *berani-nya* is accounted complement by virtue of the nominalising suffix *-nya*. But in Ex. 17 *muka* is already a noun. The construction is common with generic words such as *orang*, e.g. *TCE*, p. 150.6: *Dia 'tu pintar orang-nya* 'He's a wily one, he is!' *Saya ini penakut orang-nya* 'I'm a nervous sort of a chap'. *Bangsa baik baisekel-nya yang saya beli itu* 'It's a good make of bicycle, the one that I've bought'. And in Text B nos. 626/7: *Ulit benar orang-nya* 'She's a real slow-coach'. *Bukan main besar pula perempuan-nya, ia?* 'And yet she's a fine strapping woman, isn't she?' and B.885: *Raja Muda 'tu, ia, élok budak-nya, 'Bang?* 'The Raja Muda, he's a handsome young man, don't you think?'

But when the noun is specific, as in Ex. 17, the label C seems to be

18

Kita	baharu[91]	kahwin.
Pr.	part.3	Hv.(A.II.2a)
S	A(iii)	P

We're only just married.

19

Apa	kena	Ché' Kasim?[92]
nom.(d)	Hv.(A.II.3c)	N
S	P	C

What's the matter, Kasim?

20

..nampak-nya	kita	akan	berchenggang.
	Pr.	x(i)	Hv.(A.II.2a)
A(v.a)	S		P

It looks as if we are going to be parted.

21

Abang	ta'	boléh	tidak	pergi.[93]
N	x(ii)	x(ii)	x(ii)	Hv.(A.II.3)
S				P

I can't get out of going (lit. not-able not-to-go).

---

less apposite. It is tempting to take it as S, with -nya as pronoun not particle, and suami as a preliminary 'statement of topic':

Suami	/	sugul muka-nya.
T	/	P S

This, however, would introduce a new clause element, and is therefore not a legitimate solution within the framework set up. Cf. n. 151.

91 *baharu kahwin:* by position, *baharu* cannot be an adjective (unless it is taken to be P_1 by transformation, a solution which is 'intuitively' wrong); by definition, it cannot be described as x. In this context, it could not stand alone. It is therefore assigned as an adjunctival particle. See also n. 182.

92 *Ché' Kasim:* intonation makes it unlikely that *Ché' Kasim* is a vocative-piece, as in the English translation.

93 *pergi:* verbs such as *pergi, datang, dudok, terbang* which have no predicating *me-* form will be labelled simply 'A.II.3'.

22

Aku	kena	pergi	juga.
Pr.	x(ii)	Hv.	part.3
S		P	A(iii)

I shall just have to go (that's all there is to it).

23

Janggut-nya	mémang[94]	panjang.
S	A(v.b)	P

Its beard is long enough!

24

Bukan	aku[95]	membunoh	engkau.
NNQ	Pr.	Hv.(A.I)	Pr.
M(ii) *n.phr.* H			
S		P	C

It wasn't *I* who killed you.

25

Ini	semua[96]	karut.
dei.		Hv.(A.II.Ia)
N	N	
S_1	S_2	P

This is all quite ridiculous.

---

94 *mémang:* described as Adjunct v.(b). See n. 245.

95 This analysis presumes a rising tone on *aku*, followed by a pause. If *Bukan* has rising tone+pause (with the meaning 'I *didn't* kill you!') a possible analysis is to take '*Bukan* as a Head verb (see n. 113 for B.192). The S element would be the included clause *aku membunoh engkau*. Alternatively, if *Bukan* is still described as NNQ (as prescribed on p. 8) with the included clause as H in noun phrase structure, the result is a minor-type (nominal) sentence. See p. 74.

96 *Ini semua:* two separate sentence elements, not a noun group, since that description would imply that *semua* is subordinate to *ini*. Contrast *Semua 'tu* in Ex. 12 on p. 42 where *'tu* is used as a determinant, not as a deictic.

26

Bini abang 'ni   pelupa!
N₁ *n.grp.* N₂ det.   Hv.(B.II.ix)

$\underline{\text{N} \quad \textit{n.phr.} \quad \text{D}}$

$\underline{\text{S} \qquad\qquad \text{P}}$

I'm a forgetful creature, I am!

2. IMPERATIVE

27

$\overline{\text{Dudok-lah}}$ sa-bentar.
Hv.(A.II.3)   N

$\underline{\text{P} \qquad \text{A(iv.(b))}}$

Sit down for a few minutes.

28

  Masok   ka-dalam almari 'tu![97]
Hv.(A.II.3)   *prep.phr.(i)*b

$\underline{\text{P}_1 \qquad\qquad \text{P}_2}$

Go inside that cupboard!

29

Masok Tuan Kadhi ka-dalam pak 'ni!
 Hv.   N   *prep.phr.(i)*b

$\underline{\text{P}_1 \qquad \text{S} \qquad\qquad \text{P}_2}$

You get into this chest!

30

$\overline{\text{Masok-lah}}$ Ché' Yam.
 Hv.   N

$\underline{\text{P} \qquad \text{(voc.piece)}}$

Come in, Che' Yam.

31

Perdulikan kuéh 'tu!
 Hv.(B.I)   *n.phr.*

$\underline{\text{P} \qquad \text{C}}$

Bother those cakes!

---

97 For the dual (transformational) P element, see p. 129.

II. Passive

1

Changkul-nya	di-sérét-	nya.
N Pr.	Hv.(A.I.)	Pr.
S	P	C

He was dragging his hoe along, trailing it behind him.

2

Kalau	di-pikul	changkul	'tu...
	Hv(A.I.)		
s	P	S	

If he had carried the hoe on his shoulder...

3

..apabila	terpandang[98]	mata Salim mengerling dia...[99]
	Hv.(pa.)(A.I)	n.grp.? phr.?
s	P	S

..when she caught sight of Salim looking at her out of the corner of his eye...

---

98 *terpandang:* for the *ter-* forms as passive see n. 81. Verbs such as *termasin* (Class B.II.viii, i.e. adj.) are not passive. But there are some *ter-* forms which are difficult to classify, e.g. C. 4: *..sayap-nya sentiasa terhampar* 'its wings are always outspread'. It seems best to take *hampar* here as Vb.A.II.1a (i.e. adj.). Cf. *mati, hidup,* etc. (n. 144). The structure is then SAP in a non-passive clause.

Again, in B.816: *Kita ta' terbau apa-apa* '*I* can't smell anything', *ter-* is followed by a noun. A possible solution would be to take *terbau* as an alternant of *berbau* in a context where the latter is used not with its prep. phrase function (prep.phr.i(a)) as in *Kain ini ber-bau durian* (This cloth smells of durian) but with its verbal function as the equivalent of *mendapat bau.* This would satisfy the meaning and give a non-passive structure SPC.

Another possibility might be to regard *terbau* here as a two-complement verb 'to-give-a-smell-of something to somebody'. In the passive form the 'something' would become the subject and

4

..di-bungkus	-nya	sadikit[100]	nasi	dengan[101]	ikan	kering.
Hv.(B.I, zero 'kan')	Pr.	NNQ	N	part.I.b.ii	N	Vb.A.II.1a

$$\text{H } \textit{n.phr.} \quad \text{Q(i)}$$

$$\text{N}_1 \textit{ co-ord.} \quad \text{c} \quad \textit{n.grp.} \quad \text{N}_2$$

M(ii)   *n.phr.*   H

P   C   S

..she wraps up a little rice and some dried fish.

---

the 'somebody' would be assigned as the second complement, with no first complement expressed:

> Kita ta' terbau apa-apa.
> To-me is-not-given-to-smell anything-at-all.
> C_2 P   S

with possible transformation to the prep. phrase with *kapada*:

> Kapada kita ta' terbau apa-apa
>   A   P   S

NOTE: A simple analysis is possible if *Kita* is described as 'T'. See n. 90 and n. 161.

99   *mata Salim mengerling dia:* for further discussion see §9.

100 *sadikit:* described as NNQ, by analogy with *banyak*, when followed by a noun. See also n. 159.

101 *dengan:* taken here not as a directive particle (prep.(a)iii) but as a connective particle (prep.(b)ii) equivalent to *dan*, which is seldom used in the Texts.

A stricter analysis would treat the expression *sadikit...kering* as a conjunctive transformation of two underlying noun phrases, *sadikit nasi* and *sadikit ikan kering*. Similarly, a clause with a 'shared' subject such as *Mat dengan Saleh sudah sampai dengan selamat* (Mat and Saleh have arrived safely) would be resolved into its underlying clauses: (*a*) *Mat sudah sampai* and (*b*) *Saleh sudah sampai*. In the analyses it has been considered sufficient to mark the successive members of a composite element of this sort as S_1, S_2, etc. See p. 130 (4).

5

Sekarang ini	sudah[102]	jarang-jarang	di-adakan[102]	isti'adat menyémah itu...
adjunct + det.	x(ii)	part.3	Hv.(pa.B.I)	N₁ *n.grp.* N₂ + det.
A(i)	P. .	A(iii)	. .P	S

Nowadays it has become a rare thing for this ceremony of exorcism to be carried out...

6

. .sebab	tidak	di-perkenan	oléh	ahli-ahli agama.
con.(i)	x(ii)	Hv.(pa.B.I.)	dir.(ii)	N₁ *n.grp.* N₂
s		P		C

. .because the religious leaders do not approve of it.

7

Musang	ber-janggut[103]	di-mana	'nak	di-chari!
N	*prep.phr.i(c)*	dir.(i) nom.(d)	x(ii)	Hv.(pa.A.I)
H *n.phr.* Q(ii)		*prep.phr.i(b)*		
S		P₁		P₂

Where is one to look for a bearded civet-cat!

8

Apa	di-nanti [kan]	lagi?
nom.(d)	Hv.(pa.I.B. zero 'kan')	part.3
S	P	A(iii)

What are we waiting for?

---

102 X.. ..Hv.: the dots indicate a discontinuous clause-element.

103 *ber-janggut*: the hyphen is inserted as a reminder that *ber-*+noun is a prep. phrase. This saves one line in the analysis; strictly speaking, the description 'prep.phr.i(c)', i.e. a structure, should not appear on line 1 when all the other words on that line are merely assigned to their word categories. But such telescoping will be used, in moderation, when it is not likely to result in loss of clarity. The intermediate steps can be reconstructed if necessary from the given data, e.g. if the first line of information for *musang berjanggut* had read 'H *n.phr.* Q(ii)', these three items when 'looked up' in the Conspectus (Appendix 1) would fix *musang* as a noun, and *berjanggut* as a 'prep. phrase with *ka-*, *di-*, *dari* or *ber-*', i.e. 'prep.phr.i(c)' beginning with directive particle *ber-* in front of a noun.

9

Ta'	terbalas	saya	budi	tuan.
x(ii)	Hv.pa.(A.I)	Pr.	N_1 +	N_2

P	C	S

I cannot thank you enough for your kindness.

10

Kemudian[104]	di-kemaskan-nya	anyam-anyaman-nya	itu..
N	Hv.pa.(A.I) Pr.	N +	Pr. + det.

A(iv.a)	P C	S

Then she folds up her weaving.

11

Ta'	terpandang	dék[105]	dia	muka	aku.
x(ii)	Hv.pa.(A.I)	dir.(ii) + Pr.	N +	Pr.	

P	C	S

He couldn't bear to look me in the face.

12

Di-pilin-pilin-nya	misai-nya.
Hv.pa.(A.I) Pr.	N + Pr.

P	C	S

He keeps twisting and untwisting his moustaches.

THE INCLUDED CLAUSE

⟨A clause may occupy a place in structure of lower rank than that of place in sentence.[106] It may under certain circumstances fill the S and C positions in clause structure or it may fill the Q position in phrase structure. (64)⟩

Thus, the term 'included' is used for a clause which occurs within another clause or within a phrase, as an element of structure within that clause or phrase.

---

104 *Kemudian* as noun. See n. 36.

105 *dék*: see note, p. 32.

106 Such a clause is termed 'down-graded'; it will not appear in the sentence-pattern formula as clause 1, clause 2, etc., and the clause which contains it, if it stands alone, is described as a simple, not a compound, sentence.

The included clause may be either nominal or verbal. It is a syntactic equivalent of the noun.

Examples:
The included clause as subject:

    Orang itu berjalan[107] chepat.
        S-------P
         S   P

That man walks [or is-walking] fast (lit. that-man-walks is-fast).

The included clause as complement:

    Dia kata[108] Ahmad 'nak datang.
             S----------P
  S P   C

He said Ahmad would come.

---

107 This is analysed as an included clause because the potential pause comes after *berjalan*. But note that in the sentence *Orang itu chepat berjalan* (That man is a fast walker) the pause comes after *itu*, and *chepat berjalan* is analysed as a dual transformational predicate comparable to *suka bermain* (see p. 82(*b*)). In the sentence *Orang berjalan itu chepat* the pause comes after *itu*, but the verbal *berjalan* is Q in a noun phrase, with *orang* as H and *itu* as D: The-man-walking is-fast. See n. 29 (ii)*b*.

108 The included clause which operates as complement after such words as *kata* is described as ⟨a special case of subordination⟩. ⟨Verbs which in this context can be the exponent of the P element could be listed...This restricted class of verbs includes also the verb *hendak* when used alone, i.e. not as an auxiliary. (763)⟩ Example: *Dia hendak Ahmad datang melihat anak-nya* 'He wants Ahmad to come and see his children'.

    Note is taken of a ⟨modern transformation⟩ for such sentences by the insertion of one of the ⟨conjunctive particles⟩ *ia-itu*, *bahawa*, *yang*, symbolised as c_1. Example: *Dia kata (ia-itu) Ahmad mem-*

Jangan dia datang[109]
      S-----P
P   C

Let it not be—he comes.

Jangan membuat pekerjaan itu[110]
P   ------------C------------

Do not do that piece of work

Jangan dia ketua kampong.
      S-------P
P   C

Let it not be—he is village headman

Biar-lah dia ketua kampong.
      S-------P
P   C

Let it be—he is village headman.

The included clause as Q (say, qualifier) in noun phrase structure:

⟨This type of structure is limited to a small group of nouns indicating place and time. These could be listed. (533 n. 1)⟩

Waktu *ia sampai* saya pergi.
The time he arrived—I went.
When he arrived I went.

---

bacha buku (He says (that) Ahmad is going to read a book). $S_1 P_1 (S_2 P_2 C_2)$ being transformed to $S_1 P_1 c_1 S_2 P_2 C_2$, i.e. a compound sentence (Cl_1 c Cl_2), with no included clause.

An alternative solution for *ia-itu* (and *ia-lah*) is offered in n. 284.

109 A reminder: ⟨The Complement is the element other than the Subject which must be a noun or its syntactic equivalent.⟩ *Jangan* is described as a verb, and an included clause is a noun-equivalent.

110 From the context in which it occurs, this complement, too, is to be described as an included clause, of the pattern P C; but the omission of the clause-element symbols seems to indicate that it is being taken as a noun group.

⟨. . . the analysis of *waktu ia sampai* is as a complex adjunct in which the Head *waktu* is expanded by the down-graded clause *ia sampai*. (643)⟩

Tempat *biji durian di-tanam oléh Ali* semaian nama-nya.

The place where the durian seeds have been planted by Ali is called a nursery.

Dalam pada[111] *nasi di-jerangkan oléh Aminah* itu gulai pun sudah menggelegak pula.

When the rice was put on the fire by Aminah the curry was already bubbling.

NOTE: Since the included clause is not to be analysed as filling a place in sentence structure (see n. 106) an extended selection of examples from the Texts is postponed until the framework for sentence structure has been set up in §7.

---

111 *pada* is here H in noun phrase structure, and must therefore be described as a noun.

§6. SENTENCES

⟨The grammatical sentence is defined as that unit which has potentiality of indefinite silence both before and after it. It is grammatically complete... (711)⟩

A. SENTENCE CATEGORIES

Three sentence categories are set up:

I. The declarative sentence is one which is not marked as interrogative or imperative. The commonest form of the declarative sentence tune has two parts: (1) rising to suspense pause, (2) falling to final pause.

II. The interrogative sentence is marked by either or both of the following features:

    1. The postposition particle *-kah* or *-tah* added to any element of the clause.

    2. Final high tone.

III. The imperative sentence is marked by the following features:

    1. No S element.

    2. In general, a falling intonation tune.

B. SENTENCE TYPES

⟨The sentence may be simple or compound. The simple sentence contains only one clause. The compound sentence contains more than one clause. Clauses may be of two types, viz. verbal and nominal. (721)⟩

    I. The simple sentence.
    II. The compound sentence.

I. The simple sentence

Examples:

Dia ketua kampong.	—a nominal clause
He is village headman.	
Dia datang.	—a verbal clause
He comes.	
Dia di-rumah.	—a verbal clause
He is at home.	

Since a simple sentence contains only one clause it is not necessary to give here further examples of clause analysis from the Texts, except for the purpose of examining two special types of simple sentence:

1. The fragmentary sentence.
2. The minor-type sentence.

I. FRAGMENTARY SENTENCES

⟨Non-initiating utterances are fragmentary sentences of types already treated. Almost any part of the sentence may function in this way and is always replaceable by the complete (initiating) sentence of which the non-initiating fragmentary sentence then forms a part. (7.10)⟩

⟨[Fragmentary sentences] are contextually bound and can be expanded to a sentence of one of the types described. (712)⟩

Thus, a fragmentary sentence is a portion of a complete sentence which suffices to convey the speaker's (or writer's) meaning because the hearer (or reader) is already cognizant of the context in which it is spoken (or written) and can at will fashion for himself the complete sentence, by supplying the missing clause elements.

Examples:

Dia ada buku-kah?	Ada. (or: Dia ada buku.)
Has he a book?	(He) has.
Bila dia 'nak datang?	Bésok. (or: Dia 'nak datang bésok.)
When does he intend to come?	Tomorrow.

A non-initiating utterance may begin with a connective particle:
Example:

'Dah ajak dia ka-rumah?—'Dah. *Tetapi* dia ta' mahu datang.
Have you invited him home?—Yes. But he didn't want to come.

These fragmentary sentences occur frequently in Texts A and B, particularly in the stage-directions, but scarcely at all in the descriptive writing of Texts C and D.

Examples of fragmentary sentences from the Texts
(possible 'missing' clause elements in brackets)

1   (A.1)
[Meréka]   Di-kedai   kopi.
           prep.phr.i(a)
  [S]   P
[They are] In the coffee-shop.

2   (A.4)
[Kami   minta]   Dua   kopi   susu.
             n.phr.
  [S   P]   C
[We would like] Two white coffees.

3   (A.8)
[Ada]   Kuéh   sepit?
      n.phr.
  [P]   S
[Are there] Any wafers?

4   (A.35)
[Mentua   Che'   Lah]   Orang   tua   Pa'   Anjang   'tu.[112]
                        n.phr.
         [S]   P
[Che' Lah's father-in-law is] Old Pa' Anjang.

---

112 See the Text. The word *ia?* at the end of the sentence (omitted above) is itself a minor-type sentence. 'It is so?' See n. 113.

5 (A.37)

[Dia] Belum. [sudah menuai]
      x(i)   [Hv.]

[S]   P

Not yet. [has he cut his rice]

6 (A.77)

[Rumpun rotan itu] Bukan[113] jauh.
               x(ii) Hv.(adj.)

      [S]   P

Not very far. [is the clump of rattan]

7 (B.18)

Sekarang ini juga! [aku kena pergi]
  A(i)   (Aiii)   S   P

This very moment! [I must go]

---

113 *bukan* before a noun is described as a non-numeral quantifier (e.g. in B.844: *Bukan hadiah kahwin!*, 'No wedding-present, this!'). See p. 8. But it seems better in the present context, before a verbal, to count it as a variant of *tidak*, operating as an auxiliary. In B.192: *..bukan-kah bagitu?* (isn't that so?), with *bagitu* as a nominal, *bukan* is equivalent to *tidak* operating as Head verb, and the analysis is P S. So, also in A.289/290: *Bukan! Bukan saya 'nak mengambil.* 'Oh no! I wasn't going to *take* it!' A.289 is a minor-type sentence (verbal). See n. 126. In A.290 *Bukan* may be taken as a Head verb with the included clause which follows it as subject, or else as NNQ, with the included clause as H in noun phrase structure, the whole being a minor-type nominal sentence. See n. 233 for the analysis.

In B.100: *Dia 'tu, ia, manis sadikit bukan?* ('Oh him, he's rather nice, isn't he?') *ia* and *bukan* are both minor-type sentences (verbal). So also in A.489: *Bagus awak, ia, Ché' Saléh!* 'You're a fine one, aren't you, Che' Saleh!' Cf. n. 210.

On the other hand, in A.588: *Awak bukan-nya ada bersama-sama kawan masa itu!* (But *you* weren't with me at the time!) *bukan-nya* is a nominal predicate, with the discontinuous included clause *Awak...ada bersama-sama kawan masa itu* ($SP_1 P_2 A$(iv.a)) as the subject element.

8　　　　　　　　　　　　　　　　　　　　　　　　　　　　　　(A.95)

Wah![114]	Sampai[115]	[ka-]	sa-banyak[116]	'tu?	[untong kita]
	Hv.(A.III.3)		num.	N	det.	*n.grp.*
			M(i)	H	D	
				n.phr.		
		[dir.i]	*prep.phr.i(a)* NP		
	P₁		P₂		[S]

Whew! As much as that? [our profit]

9

(a)[117]	[Itu]	Ta'	mengapa.	or	(b)[117]	[Itu]	Ta'	mengapa
	dei.	x(ii)	Hv.(B.II.iii?)			dei.	neg.part. + nom.(d)
	[S]		P			N		N
						[S]		P

[That] Doesn't matter.　or　(in this context): Don't worry!

10　　　　　　　　　　　　　　　　　　　　　　　　　　　　　(A.120)

Saya	pun	[boléh]	bagitu[118]	pula.
Pr.	part.2	Hv.(A.II.3)	N	part.3
S		[P]	C	A(iii)

And so can I.

---

114 *Wah!* itself a minor-type sentence. See p. 75.

115 *sampai:* taken to be operating as a verb of Class A.II.3. (Cf. p. 134 Ex. 10), with [ka-]*sa-banyak itu* as secondary (transformational) predicate, as in *Ahmad datang ka-Kuala Lumpur* on p. 80. An alternative would be to take *sampai* itself as directive particle (i), replacing [*ka-*], in which case the fragment becomes the sole predicate as 'prep.phr.(i)a'.

116 *sa-banyak:* see n. 164 (*a*); but see also (*b*) iii (A.576) in the same footnote.

117 (*a*) or (*b*): In (*b*), *mengapa* is taken as a nominal. For *ta'* as a negative pre-posed particle cf. *ta' pernah*. In (*a*) *mengapa* is taken as a verb, 'not being-something', comparable with such verbs as *membukit*, *menanjong* in the examples: *Tanah sa-belah sana membukit-bukit.* 'The land in that direction is hilly' and *Pantai di-sana menanjong.* 'The shore-line at that spot runs out into a cape.' But it is possible that Ex. 9 should be described as a minor-type sentence rather than as a fragmentary sentence, i.e. that it should be taken as 'not contextually bound'. See n. 122.1.

118 *bagitu:* in this context it seems best to assign it as a noun (= *bagai*

11   (A.59)

Empat puloh ringgit [harga] sa-pikul, kata 'bang Musa?[119]

num.		N		num.	N	N		N

num.   N   num.   N   N   N

M(i)   *n.phr.* H   M(i) *n.phr.* H N_1 *n.grp.* N_2

      N   [N_1] *n.grp.* N_2 N

                      N

        S   P   A(v.b)

Forty dollars a pikul, you said?

12   (A.234)

[Kawan sakit di-] Sa-belah[120] kiri ini.

   N   Hv.(A.II.la)   num.   N   det.

   S *incl.cl.* P   M(i) *n.phr.* H

      N N_1 *n.grp.* N_2

                   H   *n.phr.* D

        [dir.(i)] *prep.phr.i(a)* NP

    [S]   P

[I feel the pain] Here on the left.

13   (A.221)

[Kawan] Sakit macham mana?[121]

   N   Hv.(A.II.la)   N   adj.

[S] *incl.cl.* P   S *incl.cl.* P

     N   N

     S   P

What sort of a pain? [have you got]

14   (A.232)

    Di- mana[121] [kawan] sakit?

    part.I(a)i   N   N   Hv.(A.II.la)

dir.(i) *prep.phr.i(a)* NP   [S] *incl.cl.* P

       P   S

Where [do you feel] the pain?

---

itu), and therefore, if the fragment has been correctly expanded, as the complement. In n. 275 *bagitu* is taken as a particle.

119 For this extended interpretation of the parenthetic adjunct see p. 46, and compare n. 202.

120 *sa-belah:* for *sa-*+verbal see n. 164 (*b*). But in this example *sa-* is described as a numeral because *belah* is taken to be operating as one of the 'nouns of limited distribution' referred to in n. 25. Cf. '*sa-potong dua*' for 'a couple of slices'.

121 *mana:* is listed as an interrogative nominal, but when it follows a noun (as in Ex. 13) it seems possible to take it as a verb of Class

15 (A.233)

[Kawan	sakit]		Di-sini-lah.		
N	adj.	part.1(a)i	N	part.2	

S *incl.cl.* P   dir.(i)   NP

N   *prep.phr.(i)a*

[S]   P

[I feel the pain] Here.

2. MINOR-TYPE SENTENCES

⟨All other sentences which are not of the favourite sentence type[122] dealt with [i.e. other than the fragmentary sentences] are minor-type sentences or minority patterns. (712)⟩

A.II.1a, i.e. an adjective. Alternatively, *macham+mana* could be described as a compound interrogative nominal (cf. *bagaimana*), and still analysed as a nominal predicate. The same result will be reached, too, if *mana* is described here as a nominal, except that the included clause is then a nominal, not a verbal, clause. A similar analysis is suggested for A.516: *Mana tahu?* 'Who knows?' (lit. How is one to know?):

[Macham] mana   [orang] tahu?
[S] *incl.cl.* P   [S] *incl.cl.* P
S   P

In Ex. 14, where *mana* follows a directive preposition, it is described as a noun. See n. 203.

122 Robins, 2, p. 232: 'The patterns common to large numbers of the sentences of a language may be called its *favourite sentence types*; and a basic syntactic structure is the simplest form of any favourite sentence type...Sentences are, however, found in all languages, that do not conform to and are not reducible to one of the basic syntactic structures...Sentences of this sort may be referred to as ...minority pattern sentences. They fall into two main classes:

1. Those that are not referable to a longer sentence, of which they may always form a part, are structurally independent of a previous sentence, and many initiate a discourse or conversation. Sentences of this sort are often exclamatory, e.g. *poor old John!*... Others may

Thus, a minor-type sentence is *not* a fragment. It cannot be expanded into a 'favourite type' sentence. Yet, by definition, it is to be accounted a sentence since it is a complete utterance with potential silence on either side of it.

A minor-type sentence is not contextually bound.

A minor-type sentence may be:
- (*a*) completive;
- (*b*) exclamatory;
- (*c*) aphoristic.

---

be gnomic, such as *the more the merrier*... Sentences of this type are lexically restricted in most cases, and little or no variation of their particular word content is normally permitted.

[These are the *minor-type sentences*.]

2. Sentences that are referable to longer sentences containing the same word or sequence of words. These are often non-initial in a discourse, and constitute responses to a previous utterance, particularly a question: (Where do you live?) *In Ashford.* But they need not be. Sentences like *Here! Fifteen all, Fourpence a pound*, can all be...understood irrespective of previous utterance, in an appropriate situation. What distinguishes them all from those of the first class is that each may be replaced in the situation by a longer and more explicit sentence (of a favourite type) serving the same purpose, and of which they may form a part: (*We live*) *in Ashford*, (*These cost*) *fourpence a pound*... [Hence] such short sentences are often called "incomplete" or "elliptical", and explained grammatically in terms of other elements being "understood".

[These are the *fragmentary sentences*.]

...Non-favourite sentences of class 1 [i.e. minor-type sentences] have no such referability to a longer sentence in which they may be incorporated. Their meaning must be explained directly by reference to the situation, or indirectly by a paraphrase.'

Examples:

(*a*) *Completive* (supplementing a situation):

> Yang itu.   That one.
> Siapa?   Who?
> Ia.   Yes.

(*b*) *Exclamatory* (including interjections and vocative forms):

> Chéh! Si-chelaka ini!   Bah! The knave.
> Ahmad![123]   (calling him)

(*c*) *Aphoristic*

> Mandi ta' basah.   Immersed but unwetted (immune)

Examples of minor-type sentences from the Texts

1. COMPLETIVE (i.e. arising out of a given situation)

> 1. Ia.[124]   Yes.
> 2. Entah.[125]   May be.
> 3. Baik-lah.   Very well.
> 4. Ma'alum-lah dalam chemas. (B.158)   No wonder! I'm all of a
>   dither.

---

123 *Ahmad!* ⟨A vocative piece may occur by itself as a minor sentence. [It] may comprise a noun phrase or noun group, but more usually a single noun or pronoun. Such a piece has potentiality of pause before it or after it or both before and after it according to its position in the sentence. (6272)⟩

124 This one-word sentence usually occurs in the Texts as a forerunner of a favourite-type clause, e.g. A.181: *Ia, saya datang.* 'All right. I'm coming.'

125 See n. 245 for *entah* described as a parenthetic adjunct. Since all parenthetic adjuncts have potentiality of pause before and after, they are themselves minor·type clauses.

5. ..pasal rotan 'ni..[126]   About this rattan..
6. Bagitu-lah. (A.370)   That's right.
7. Barangkali juga bagitu. (A.85) Perhaps so.
8. Dato' 'ni, mengada-ngada-nya! (B.237) The conceit of the man!
                                    (spoken playfully).
9. Baik-nya To' Laksamana. (B.847) How very kind of him.

2. EXCLAMATORY (including vocative pieces)

1. Hai nasib!   Just my luck!
2. He^nh!   Hmh! (So *you* think!)
3. Pura-pura wara'!   Sham saint!
5. 'Bang! 'Bang!   for: Salim! Salim!
6. Puh! Hantu!   Poof! Ghost, indeed! (Whatever next!)

II. The compound sentence

⟨Clauses in a compound sentence may be linked co-ordinatively or subordinatively...A co-ordinated pair will always make sense if reversed

---

126 Possibly a noun phrase:

$$\begin{array}{ccc} \text{pasal} & \text{rotan} & \text{'ni} \quad \text{'this rattan business'} \\ N_1 & \textit{n.grp.} & N_2 \\ \hline H & \textit{n.phr.} & D \end{array}$$

But it is doubtful if any useful purpose is served in seeking to
analyse these minor-type sentences. The printed sentence in this
case (A.51) continues with: *apa macham?* 'what about it?'. Unless
the minor-type sentence is to be taken as an extra-syntactic
'declaration of topic' (see n. 161) standing before this nominal
sentence, it can only be regarded as a nominative predicate
standing alone. Cf. B.359: *Sayang-nya!* 'The pity of it!' So also
for Exx. 6 and 7. Exx. 1, 2, and 3 are verbal predicates standing
alone. Ex. 4 is two verbal predicates in parataxis: 'There-is-
knowing' and 'In a state of anxiety'; [*di-*]*dalam chemas* is a
prep.phr.i(a). Ex. 8 is two nominal predicates in parataxis: 'This
Dato', the boastfulness of him!' and Ex. 9 is a noun group,: $N_1 + N_2$:
'The goodness of To' Laksamana!'.

but interchange of main and subordinate clause will not always result in a possible sentence. (721)⟩

Examples:

Dia membacha buku tetapi adék-nya mendengar radio. (co-ordinated)
He is reading a book but his brother is listening to the radio.
or:
Adék-nya mendengar radio tetapi dia membacha buku.

Dia datang bésok jikalau hari ta' hujan (main cl.+subordinate cl.).
He will come tomorrow if it is not a wet day.
but not:
*Hari ta' hujan jikalau dia ta' datang bésok.

⟨When two clauses are joined in subordinate relation one is the main clause and the other, preceded by the particle, is the subordinate clause. (7511)⟩

Thus, a compound sentence is a sentence which consists of more than one clause.

The clauses may be linked co-ordinatively or subordinatively.

The connective particle may be expressed or implied:

1. co-ordination with particle;
2. subordination with particle;
3. co-ordination without particle, i.e. by parataxis;[127]
4. subordination without particle.

NOTES.

1. Subordination which results from the inclusion of a downgraded clause after certain verbs gives a different sentence pattern. See n. 106 and n. 108.

2. Co-ordination (and occasionally subordination) which results from transformation gives a different sentence pattern. See p. 79.

---

127 Bloomfield, p. 185: '...free forms which are united by no other construction may be united by *parataxis*, the mere absence of a phonetic sentence final...'

Examples:

1. CO-ORDINATION WITH PARTICLE

Saya membacha buku dan dia mendengar radio. (co-ord. verbal clauses.)

I read a book and he listens to the radio.

Dia ketua kampong tetapi Ahmad soldadu. (co-ord. nominal clauses.)

He is village headman but Ahmad is a soldier.

2. SUBORDINATION WITH PARTICLE

Ayah saya selalu marah kalau saya tidak membacha buku. (main + subord.)

My father is always angry if I do not study my books.

or:

Kalau saya tidak membacha buku ayah saya selalu marah. (subord. + main.)

If I do not study my books, etc.

3. CO-ORDINATION WITHOUT PARTICLE, I.E. BY PARATAXIS

Dia menchangkul sawah orang, Ahmad menjual ikan, Aminah tukang jahit.[128]

He hoes someone's rice-field, Ahmad sells fish, Aminah is a seamstress.

Dia membacha buku, dia mendengar radio.[128]

He is reading a book but he is listening to the radio.

---

128 ⟨Each of these clauses is a simple sentence grammatically and can be used separately. With the appropriate intonation tune they form a compound sentence co-ordinated paratactically. (7412)⟩ The first sentence is described as being marked by the 'Listing' intonation, and the second by 'Antithetic' intonation.

4. SUBORDINATION WITHOUT PARTICLE

⟨Subordination without particle is only possible when the subordinate clause precedes the main clause except when the exponent of P in the main clause is *kata*[129] and certain other listable verbs. (752)⟩

　　Ada keréta dia pergi.
　　　　(If) there is a car, he will go.

⟨There is always the potentiality of the insertion of the particle.⟩
　　Kalau ada keréta dia pergi.

Co-ordinative parataxis and subordination without particle are combined in the following example:
　　Makan berlari kerja beréngsut.
　　　　If it's to eat, he runs, but if it's to work he creeps.

Clause-pattern formulae for Compound Sentences

The following symbols are used for defining the pattern of clauses in a compound sentence:

　　Cl_1 for the first clause encountered.
　　Cl_2 for the second clause encountered.
　　Cl_3 for the third clause encountered.
　　c　for a co-ordinative particle.
　　(c) for potentiality of a co-ordinative particle (i.e. it is an indication of parataxis).
　　s　for a subordinative particle.
　　(s) for potentiality of a subordinative particle.

The minimal possibilities of clause arrangement in a compound sentence are:

　　1.　　Cl_1 c Cl_2　　co-ordination with particle.
　　2.　　Cl_1 (c) Cl_2　　co-ordination without particle (parataxis).

---

129 *kata:* see n. 108.

3(i). Cl_1 s Cl_2 subordination with particle (main clause+subord. clause).

3(ii). s Cl_1 Cl_2 subordination with particle (subord. clause+main clause).

4. (s) Cl_1 Cl_2 subordination without particle (subord. clause+ main clause).

Thus the clause-pattern formula for the sentence given above (p. 78) would be:

(Kalau) makan berlari (tetapi) (kalau) kerja beréngsut.
{ (s) Cl_1 Cl_2 } (c) { (s) Cl_3 Cl_4 }

Interpretation of the formula:

The complete utterance is a compound sentence.

This compound sentence itself consists of two sentences joined paratactically, as shown by (c).

Each of these sentences is itself a compound sentence consisting of a subordinate clause without particle (as shown by (s)) followed by a main clause.

Co-ordination and subordination as the result of transformation.[130]

1. Conjunctive transformation.
2. Subjunctive transformation.

1. CONJUNCTIVE TRANSFORMATION

On p. 31, Ex. (b) 1, the symbol P_2 is used for a prepositional phrase which is described as a 'second predicate', preceded by a verb form as a 'first predicate' (P_1). The implication is that such a sentence represents the fusion of two underlying sentences:

| | (a) Awak ada. | You are present. |
| and | (b) Awak di-sini. | You are here. |

---

130 At this point the student is recommended to read Appendix III, A note on Transformational Grammar.

In Ex. (*b*)3 on the same page the underlying sentences would be:

(*a*) Kawan singgah.　　　　I called in.
(*b*) Kawan chari.　　　　　I looked for (you).
(*c*) Kawan ka-rumah awak.　I (went) to your house.

Three main types of conjunctive transformation are described:

(*a*) Resulting from the combination of a verbal P element with a prepositional-phrase P element.
(*b*) Resulting from a common S element.
(*c*) Resulting from 'paratactic co-ordination within the same intonation contour'.

(*a*) *With a prepositional phrase beginning with ka-, di-, dari or ber-as P_2.*

⟨In a compound[131] sentence a prepositional phrase may be the exponent of P in a co-ordinated clause with or without particle or with conjunctive transformation. (5731)⟩
Example:

Ahmad datang ka-Kuala Lumpur.[132]
　S　　P_1　　　P_2
Ahmad comes to Kuala Lumpur.

(*b*) *Resulting from a common S element*

⟨Compound declarative sentences which contain a clause without an S element may be considered as resulting from a conjunctive transformation. (7411)⟩

---

131 In the analyses of sentences from the Texts such sentences, although technically 'compound' are treated as simple sentences with dual (or triple, or multiple) sentence-elements resulting from transformation.

132 The symbols P_1 and P_2 have been substituted for the symbols P and P_1 in the thesis.

Example:

Dia membacha buku serta mengisap paip.

S   P$_1$ C$_1$ c   P$_2$ C$_2$

He is reading a book and smoking a pipe.

(*c*) *Resulting from paratactic co-ordination within the same intonation contour*

⟨Paratactic co-ordination within the same Intonation Contour is always accompanied by a transformation. (761)⟩

This is the description given to the very common Malay construction of the type *Dia pergi menchari...* (He goes and gets...) which presents two (or more) Head-verbs in succession. Such sequences are not verb phrases since each of the verbs is a predicating element although the S element is common to both.

Examples:

Dia berlari mengambil buah.

S   P$_1$ P$_2$ C

He runs and fetches fruit.

Dia naik bus mengikut orang lain.

S   P$_1$ C$_1$ P$_2$ C$_2$

He boards the bus, following the other people.

He follows the other people and boards the bus.

2. SUBJUNCTIVE TRANSFORMATION

(*a*) Resulting from a common S element.

(*b*) Resulting from paratactic subordination within the same intonation contour.

(*a*) *With a common S element*

⟨The subjunctive transformation is only possible when the two clauses have structures S P$_1$ C$_1$ and S P$_2$ C$_2$ which transform to S P$_1$ C$_1$ s P$_2$ C$_2$ or s P$_2$ C$_2$. S P$_1$ C$_1$. (7511)⟩

i.e. the main clause and the subordinate clause (of the presumed original sentence) must have a common subject, which is deleted in the

6

subordinate clause of the transformation whether that clause (with its particle) precedes or follows the main clause.

Example:

Ayah saya membeli ikan kalau ayah dapat duit.

    S P_1 C_1 s   S P_2 C_2

My father will buy fish if my father gets some money.

transforms to:

Ayah saya membeli ikan kalau dapat duit.

    S P_1 C_1 s P_2 C_2

My father will buy fish if (he) gets some money.

or:

Kalau dapat duit ayah saya membeli ikan.

    s P_2 C_2 S P_1 C_1

(b) Paratactic subordination within the same intonation contour

⟨With a small number of adjectives, Vb.A.II.1a (e.g. *pandai*, skilful; *suka, gemar*, like, enjoy; *segan*, shy; *malu*, shy, ashamed), constructions of the type exemplified below are possible. (5613)⟩

Examples:

Ia *pandai membacha* buku.   He is skilful at reading.

Ia *suka bermain*.   He likes playing.

Ia *malu bertanya*.   He is shy of asking.

The word *pandai* is analysed as ⟨Head verb of the clause *ia pandai*⟩, and *membacha buku* is analysed as ⟨Subordinate clause after subjunctive transformation.⟩

The pre-transformation sentences would be: (*a*) *Ia pandai.* (*b*) *Ia membacha buku*, but the second clause is described as dependent on the first clause.

Examples which exhibit transformation will occur sporadically throughout the analyses of selected sentences from the Texts which are set out below. Additional examples, grouped under specific headings, are to be found in §8.

Analyses of selected compound sentences from the Texts

I. CO-ORDINATION WITH PARTICLE

The pattern of clause arrangement, minimally stated, is: Cl_1 c Cl_2, i.e. the clauses are linked by a medial co-ordinative connecting particle.

Examples:

1   (B.11)

Kita	baharu[133]	kahwin	tetapi	nampak-nya[134]	kita	akan	berchenggang.
Pr.	part.3	Hv.(A.II.2a)	part.		Pr.	x(i)	Hv.(A.II.2a)
			l.b(ii)				
S	(A.iii)	P		A(v.a)	S		P
	Cl_1		c		Cl_2		

We are only just married, but it looks as if we are going to part.

Pattern: Cl_1 c Cl_2.

2   (C.4)

..ékor-nya	panjang	dan	sayap-nya	sentiasa	terhampar[135]..
N+Pr.	Hv.(adj.)	part.1.b.(ii)	N	part.3	Hv.(B.II.vii)
S	P		S	A(iii)	P
	Cl_1	c		Cl_2	

..it has a long tail and its wings are always spread wide..

Pattern: Cl_1 c Cl_2.

3   (A.123)

Meréka	ketiga[136]	pun	bangkit	lalu	[meréka]	keluar.
Pr.	N	part.2	Hv.(A.II.3)	part.1.b(ii)		Hv.(A.II.3)
N_1 *n.grp.* N_2						
S		P			[S]	P
	Cl_1		c		Cl_2	

The three of them get up and go out.

Pattern: Cl_1 c Cl_2.

---

133 *baharu:* taken as a particle. See n. 91. The overbrace indicates that it is in direct relationship with the Head verb.

134 *nampak-nya:* such parenthetic expressions will not be assigned to word-categories. But see n. 125.

135 *hampar:* taken as verb A.II.1a. See n. 98, and n. 155.

136 *ketiga:* described as a noun. On p. 14 the form *ke*+A.II.1b (Ex. *yang kedua*) is described as a verbal (B.II.ii). But *ketiga* in Ex. 3

4 (A.532)

[dia]	mengambil	chadar	dari tempat tidor[137]		lalu	di-selubongkan-nya	[chadar]
	Hv.	N	prep.phr.i(c)		part.1.b(ii)	Hv.(pa.)	Pr.
		H	n.phr.	Q(ii)			
(S)	P		C			P	C	[S]
	Cl₁				c	Cl₂..	→

	kapada kepala dan badan-nya[138]	sambil[139]	[ia]	keluar	balek.
	prep.phr.i(exception 2)	part.1.b.(ii)		Hv.1	Hv.2
	A (exception 2)		[S]	P₁	P₂
←	..Cl₂	c		Cl₃	

..he takes the sheet from the bed, throws it over his head and body, and comes out again.

Pattern: Cl₁ c Cl₂ c Cl₃.

---

could not be preceded by *yang* and is therefore not Vb.B.II.ii. Neither could it operate as M(i) to create a noun phrase with a noun group consisting of numeral coefficient + noun as H. It is therefore not Vb.A.II.1b. Such group-numerals are described in the analyses as nouns.

137 For the prep. phrase taken as Q in noun phrase structure, see p. 26, Ex. 15. The alternative, as in that case, is to take it as a second (transformational) predicate, but this description is more difficult to accept when the first predicate is not a verb of movement as it is in *Dia datang ka-Kuala Lumpur* (p. 80(a)), where the prep. phrase is capable of operating as sole predicate.

138 *kapada kepala dan badan-nya* described as adjunct: this implies that *selubongkan* is taken to be a two-complement verb 'to throw-as-a-veil something over somebody'. See p. 50 and n. 98 *ad fin.* Note that *dan* in this expression connects words, not clauses. The word seldom occurs as a clause-connective in the Texts.

139 *sambil:* taken to be operating as a co-ordinating connective. Cf. n. 164(b)iii, Sentence A.576, and p. 130, Ex. 3. But in both these examples it would be possible to treat *sambil* (with no inserted S element) as directive iii, forming a prep. phrase iii, with the following *me*-form (verb-noun) as NP.

2. SUBORDINATION WITH PARTICLE

The pattern of clause arrangement, minimally stated, is: Cl_1 s Cl_2 or s Cl_1 Cl_2. The clause which is not preceded by s is the main clause.

Examples:

1 (A.254)

Kalau	bagitu[140]	biar-lah	kawan	pergi.
part.1.(b)i	N	Hv.(A.1)	N	Hv.(A.II.3)

			S *incl.cl.* P

	P	P	C
s	Cl_1		Cl_2

If it's like that, then let me go.

Pattern: s Cl_1 Cl_2.

2 (c.16)

Maka[141]	sepatong itu[142]	apabila	di-lihat-nya	sahaja	kekabu...itu
(part.)	*n.phr.*	part.1.(b).i	Hv.pa.	Pr. part.3	*n.phr.*

	prelim. S of Cl_2	s	P	C	A(iii)	S
				Cl_1		

ia	pun[142]	datang	menyembar[143]...kekabu itu.
Pr.	part.	Hv.1	Hv.2 *n.phr.*
S		P_1	P_2 C

Cl_2

The dragonfly, the moment it saw the tree-cotton..., made a dive for it.

Pattern: s Cl_1 Cl_2.

NOTE: The main clause (i.e. Clause 2) has a preliminary subject-element in initial position before the opening of the subordinate clause (i.e. Clause 1).

---

140 *bagitu:* taken as a noun. See n. 118 and n. 126.

141 *maka:* since this traditional transition particle does not appear in the Conspectus it is not taken into account in the analysis. It occurs only in Texts C and D. It is to be described as a connective.

142 *sepatong itu...ia pun:* see n. 284.

143 *datang menyembar:* exactly parallel with *berlari mengambil,* on p. 81 (*c*), i.e. paratactic co-ordination under one intonation contour

3   (c.20)

Masa	itu	semua-nya	sepatong	itu	sudah	mati[144]
n.phr.		N	*n.phr.*		x(ii)	Hv.(A.II.1a)

N_1 *n.grp.* N_2

A(iv.a)   S   P

Cl_1

kerana	[dia]	bertutup[145]	di-dalam	chepu	itu	tadi.[146]
part.1.(b)i		Hv.(pa.A.I)	*prep.phr.(i)b*			N
	[S]	P_1	P_2			A(iv.a)

s Cl_2

By that time all the dragonflies were dead, because they had been shut up in the box.

Pattern: Cl_1 s Cl_2.

---

resulting from transformation. For further examples of this verbal arrangement, see pp. 127–129.

144 *mati:* in the analyses such words as *mati, hidup, siang, malam* which express states, and also such words as *suka, rasa*, which express states of mind, are usually described as adjectives (i.e. Vb.A.II.1a), but sometimes as nouns. For a study of data used in seeking to decide whether such words should be labelled adjective, verb or noun, see Teeuw, p. 417.

145 *bertutup:* Cf. *TCE*, p. 152.2: *Buah itu ta' berjual, di-biarkan busok.* 'The fruit is never sold, they just leave it to rot', and p. 180.16: *'Dah berpakai baju itu.* 'That coat has been worn (by somebody).' Although the complement with *oleh* does not occur with this verb form (see definition on p. 48) it seems reasonable to describe it as passive.

146 *tadi* taken as a noun: see n. 36. In Kedah *hak tadi* (N_1+N_2) is commonly used for 'the one we had just now', comparable with *hak kelmarin* 'yesterday's' (e.g. of a newspaper).

147 *bagini* taken as a noun: this gives a transformed predicate consisting of a verbal + a nominal element. But it seems to be the right solution since *bagini* could stand as sole predicate if *terantok* were deleted. The [S] element is deleted by subjunctive transformation. See p. 81.2(a).

148 *nyalang:* taken here as a subordinating connective (prep.(b)i). An

4 (A.306)

Kalau	[kepala aku]	selalu	terantok	bagini[147]	⎧ nyalang[148]	aku	keluar	sekarang
			Hv.(A.II.2a)	N	⎪		Hv.(A.II.3)	nom.(c)
	[S]	A(iii)	P₁	P₂	⎨	S	P	A(i)
s			Cl₁		⎩ s		Cl₂	

habis-lah	kepala aku	binchul-binchul.[149] ⎫
x(ii)..	n.grp.	..Hv.(A.II.1a) ⎬
P..	S	..P ⎭
	Cl₃	

If I go on crashing into trees like this, my head will be all over bumps and bruises by the time I get out.

Pattern: s Cl₁ (s Cl₂ Cl₃).

---

alternative would be to take it as a directive (prep.(a)iii) with an included clause as NP:

nyalang	aku	keluar	sekarang
		incl.cl.	
dir.iii	*prep.phr.iii*	NP	
	A(ii) in the main clause		

It would then be comparable with the modern use of the *me-* form in such initiating phrases as *Menurut sumber yang boléh di-perch-ayaï*.. 'According to a reliable source..' which have perhaps grown out of the traditional double predication (by transformation) in such expressions as *belayar menyusor pantai* 'to sail along the shore', *berjalan menerusi kebun bunga* 'to walk across the park'. For the meaning, cf. *TCE*, p. 155.4: *menjalang* or *menjelang*, usually pronounced *'nyalang* or *'nyelang* meaning 'by the time that', e.g. *'Nyalang dia tiba 'kang, nasi kita pun masak-lah*. 'By the time he arrives our rice will be cooked.'

149 This analysis, treating *habis...binchul-binchul* as a discontinuous verb-phrase with *kepala* as its subject, seems to be more satisfactory than to take *habis* as a main verb with *kepala aku binchul2* (whether as noun group or included clause) as its subject. Cf. B.562: *Habis seluar baju lawar-nya dengan destar baharu-nya itu kena arang*. 'His smart suit and his new turban are simply smothered with soot.'

A few such examples occur in *TCE*, p. 186.34: *Habis anak pokok*

5　　　　　　　　　　　　　　　　　　　　　　　　　　　　(A.272)

'Tapi[150] saya[151]	kalau	terchabut	péndék[152]	pun, biar-lah	hantu wéwér	juga.
Pr.		Hv.(pa.A.1)	N	Hv.(A.1)	N	
C		P	S	P	C	A(iii)
|c| Cl₁..	s	..Cl₁			Cl₂	

(table values: Hv.(pa.A.1) over P; N over S; Hv.(A.1) over P; N over C; A(iii); bottom row: |c| Cl$_1$.. , s , ..Cl$_1$, Cl$_2$)

But me, even if I do draw the shorter twig, let me have the flickering ghost all the same (rather than the corpse).

Pattern: |c| (s Cl$_1$ Cl$_2$).

NOTES: The subordinate clause is preceded by a non-initiating co-ordinating connective which introduces the main clause (Cl$_2$).

The complement of the passive subordinate clause (Cl$_1$) precedes the subordinating connective, and lacks the particle *oléh*. But see n. 151.

---

itu di-kerjakan kambing. 'Those seedlings have all been got at by the goats' and p. 214.32: *Habis segala chaching dan ulat-ulat ketakutan.* 'All the worms and the grubs were frightened out of their wits.'

In all of these examples an analysis showing a discontinuous verb-phrase offers a satisfactory solution.

150 *'Tapi:* for this connective particle used to introduce a non-initiating utterance (i.e. one that is linked in thought with a previous, possibly unexpressed, 'utterance'), see p. 68. Such particles are indicated by the symbols |c| and |s|.

151 *saya:* in this analysis the pronoun *saya* is taken to be the complement with the passive verb, brought to a position of prominence and with the pre-posed particle (*oléh*) dispensed with because deliberateness of utterance, and an ensuing pause, make the syntactic relationship clear. But see p. 49 under 'C'.

Two easier solutions suggest themselves but each of them falls outside the framework set up. They are: 1. To take *saya* as 'T', i.e. a preliminary statement of topic. Cf. n. 90 and see n. 161. 2. To take *terchabut* as non-passive, with *saya* as S, and [*yang*] *péndék* as C.

152 *péndék:* taken as colloquial brevity for *yang péndék*, i.e. Yg(b), a noun-equivalent.

6 (A.291)

Saya	'nak	betulkan	sumbu-nya	sahaja,	jangan[153]	bang Musa	ta' chukup	terang.[154]
Pr.	x(ii)	Hv.(B.I)	N	part.3	part.I.(b)i	N	part.3	Hv.(adj.)
S	P		C	A(iii)		S	A(iii)	P

Cl$_1$ s Cl$_2$

I was only going to trim the wick, so that you shouldn't be in half-darkness.

Pattern: Cl$_1$ s Cl$_2$.

7 (C.4)

..sayap-nya	sentiasa	terhampar[155]
N	part.3	Hv.(B.II.vii)
s	A(iii)	P

Cl$_1$

walau	pun	[?di-]	pada[156]	masa	ia	terhinggap[155]	di-rumput-rumput..
part.I(b)i		NNQ	N		Pr.	Hv.(B.II.vii)	prep.phr.i.b
					S	P$_1$	P$_2$
						incl.cl.	

				H	n.phr.	Q(iii)
		M(ii)	n.phr.	H		
	[dir.i]	prep.phr.i.a	NP			
		P				

s Cl$_2$

..the wings are always outspread, even (if) (at a time) when it alights on grasses..

Pattern: Cl$_1$ s Cl$_2$.

NOTE: The subordinate clause has one element only, P (a prepositional phrase of type i.a.), i.e. it is a fragment.

---

153 *jangan:* the intonation indicates that *jangan* is used here as a subordinating connective, not as an imperative verbal as it is in B.517: *Jangan-lah dia berjumpa kawan di-sini malam-malam buta 'ni!* (Don't let him find me here at this time of night! or, more literally, 'Let it not be that...'), where the included clause *dia...* '*ni* is the complement following the imperative predicate *Jangan*. In Ex. 6, above, *jangan* is a colloquial equivalent of *supaya jangan*, listed as particle I.(b)i.

154 *ta' chukup terang:* this may be counted a colloquial equivalent of, say, *kegelapan* (Vb.B.II.i) and is therefore an acceptable predicate expression for '*bang Musa* as subject; *ta' chukup* is taken as an

alternant for *kurang*, which might operate as an adjunctival particle by analogy with *sangat*. For the absorbtion of *ta'* as a negative particle, not a full word, cf. *ta' pernah* which is listed as one of the seven auxiliaries.

155 *hampar*, *hinggap*: both taken as Vb.A.II.Ia, 'be outspread', 'be poised'; not an altogether satisfying solution, but less uneasy than a passive description for these *ter*- forms.

156 *pada*: taken as NNQ. See p. 8. A noun phrase beginning with a non-numeral quantifier as M may be preceded by a directive particle to form a prep. phrase: Ex. *ka-semua kampong*. On p. 65 there occurs the following example with *pada*: *Dalam pada nasi dijerangkan oléh Aminah itu..* 'When the rice was put on the fire by Aminah..' In this sentence *dalam* (noun) = [*di-*]*dalam*, and *pada* itself is taken as H in noun phrase (with the included clause *nasi... Aminah* as Q). Example 7 above would be parallel with this sentence if the word *masa* were deleted. As the sentence stands, it is possible to retain *pada* as NNQ, with the directive particle [*di-*] in front of it. There has been speculation as to why [*di-*]*pada* is not found, side by side with *kapada* and *dari pada*. (In both these expressions the directive particle is sometimes omitted, e.g. B.868: *Dia mémang sukakan besar* [*ka*]*pada apa-apa pun.* 'He always likes his things to be on the large side', and the proverb: [*Dari*] *Pada putéh mata baik putéh tulang*. lit. 'Better whitened bones than whites of eyes', i.e. 'Death rather than cowardice').

The omission of the directive *di-* is postulated in this example as a trial solution for the clause structure presented. An alternative would be to describe the fragment as 'A(iv.a)', with the noun phrase *pada masa* (NNQ + N) as H, and the included clause as Q(iii). The example is re-discussed in n. 289.

The grammatical framework set out in the Conspectus (Appendix I) does not allow for the occurrence of an essentially subjectless Head-verb. (A subject-element deleted by transformation, as, e.g. in 2.(a) on p. 81, can be restored, and an imperative clause has an inherent, though unexpressed, subject-element.) But it is perhaps worth noting that in sentence A.453 (*Di-tangan Saléh, memegang suatu kayu kechil berchabang*. 'In his hand Saleh holds a small forked branch') the intonation indicated by the author of the play, with pause *after* '*Saleh*', not before it, made it clear that *tangan Saléh* was intended as a noun group ($N_1 + N_2$). The author was quite sure that he wanted the comma retained and that nothing was to be inserted after it. Similarly, in discussing sentence A.484a (*Dalam tangan-nya menjinjing lanting maséh terpasang*. 'In his hand he carried the lantern, still alight'), the author was equally insistent that no *dia* was to be 'understood' before *menjinjing*. Since the verb-form (as well as the meaning) precludes the assignment of *lanting* as S, there seems to be an indication here either of a subjectless predicate in a declaratory clause, or else of the use of the *me-* form of the verb as the S element in clause structure in a way that differs from the common verb-noun use exemplified by *menuai* in sentence A.32. (See p. 121, Ex. 29.)

In sentences B.776 and 775 a *ber-* form seems to fall into this same category: *Ini ta' ada bertandok*, in which the *ini* is likely to be a 'situational' deictic rather than a 'distinguishing' deictic, i.e. not 'This (creature) has no horns' but 'In this case (lit. This-is) there-are-no-horns', as a sequel to: *Kalau kerbau, bertandok*. '*A buffalo* has horns.' In these examples it would be simpler to describe *ber-tandok* as a noun:

B.776:	Ini	ta'	ada	bertandok.	B.775:	Kalau	kerbau,	bertandok.
			P	*incl.cl.* S			P(nom.)	P(nom.)
	S		P			s	Cl$_1$	Cl$_2$

But this necessitates taking a prep. phrase i (*ber-tandok*) as nominal.

For further discussion of this point (resulting in acceptance of B.775 as an example of the normal subjunctive transformation pattern with common S element) see n. 289 *ad fin*.

8   (A.66)

Sebab[157]	saya	pun	hendakkan	duit	juga[158]	sadikit.[159]
part.1.(b).i	Pr.	part.2	Hv.(B.I)	N	part.3	N
				N *n..*		*..grp.* N
	S		P	C..	A(iii)	..C
|s|				Cl₂		

$$\text{Cl}_2$$

Because I too want to make a bit of money.

Pattern: s Cl$_{(2)}$.

NOTE: This subordinate clause is labelled Cl$_{(2)}$ because it opens with a non-initiating subordinating connective which implies a preceding main clause as 'Cl$_1$'.[160]

---

157 *Sebab:* see n. 150.

158 *juga:* since the free-position particles (particles 3) frequently bear reference to the whole of an utterance, their immediate constituency is not as a rule indicated in the analyses. Where *pun* has already occurred in the utterance it is to be presumed that the particles *pun...juga* interlock to pick up the word which has been pinpointed by *pun*, with the resultant translation value of 'too', 'also'. Modern usage has transferred this function to *juga* alone, which may therefore sometimes be found in initial position. No examples of this occur in the Texts.

159 *sadikit:* described as a noun, when it follows a noun. When it precedes a noun it is described as NNQ. See n. 100.

160 For this decision see the Text. It might be said that sentence 65a: *Saya mémang tengah berpikir-pikir juga* ('I'm just turning it over in my mind') is itself the 'missing' main clause. But the deliberateness of the words used—the hesitation implied in the duplication, the 'braking' effect of *juga*, and the hint of remonstrance in *mémang* ('Don't press me. Give me time. I *am* considering the proposition') —all this suggests that the author's full-stop between the two sentences was not accidental, and that the main clause, probably a qualified assent, is represented by a pause between the two utterances. Cf. Eng. 'I'm all right, if only I could get rid of this cough', where the verb-form of the first sentence makes it clear that an intermediate main clause ('but I would be better') is implied.

9

Saya[161]	kalau	bagitu[162]	boléh-lah.
Pr.	part.1.(b).i	N	Hv.(A.11.3c)
S..		P	..P
Cl₂..	s	Cl₁	..Cl₂

In that case, I can manage it.

Pattern: s Cl₁ Cl₂.

NOTE: The subject of the main clause (Cl₂) precedes the subordinate clause (Cl₁), which is thus enclosed within the main clause. The subordinate clause consists of one element, a nominal predicate, and is therefore a fragment.[162]

---

161 *Saya:* cf. p. 88, Ex. 5. In both sentences the setting up of an extra-syntactic element 'T' (for 'topic announcement' or 'statement of topic') would restore the normal clause pattern but would leave a subjectless predicate in the main clause: 'As far as I'm concerned, if it's like that it will be possible.' See n. 156 *ad fin.*

In sentence A.397: *Kasim apa pasal?* 'What about Kasim?', spoken with continuous descending intonation (except for the 'up-down' on the last syllable) the remainder, if *Kasim* is described as 'T', would be a nominal clause S P.

In the sentence *Balai itu ada lantai* (*LTTM*, p. 105.21) 'Now the pavilion, in that there is flooring', the author's intonation, together with his indignant rebuttal of the suggestion that he was perhaps using *ada* as a transitive verb here, left no doubt that he intended *lantai* to be the subject element and was happy to have *Balai itu* described as 'statement of topic'.

Other possible examples are:

B.805:

Awak /	sa-kurang²-nya	tentu	ada	satu² pikiran yg putus.
T	A(iv.b)	A(iii)	P	S

You, at any rate, will surely have some definite opinion about it. (lit. You / ..there will surely be..)

B.867:

Dia /	tentu	besar	barang yg akan di-kirim-nya 'tu.
T	A(iii)	P	S

What ever *he* sends is sure to be big. (lit. He / ..the gift that he will send..)

A.366:   Makanan   tadi / entah   apa   salah-nya.
              T   A(v.b)   S   P

That food you ate, I wonder what was wrong with it?

B.907:   Wah!   Aku / ada   surat   'aja   sa-keping!
              T   P   S..   A(iii)   ..S

Did you ever! All that *I've* got is a letter! (lit. Me / ..there's only a letter)

B.809:   Fasal janggut / sah-lah   [janggut] ada,   Tuanku.
              N₁ *n.grp.* N₂   [S] *incl.cl.* P
              ———————————   ————————————————
                 T   P   S   voc. piece

As for a beard, yes, there's certainly a beard, Your Highness.

C.2:   Masa   itu umor   saya / ada-lah   kira-kira   lima   atau   enam   tahun
          A(iv.a)   T   P   A(iii.b)   S

At that time I was about five or six years old.

Here the description of *umor saya* as 'T' brings the sentence into
line with the sentence *Balai itu | ada lantai* quoted above. But in this
case there is the alternative of taking *umor saya* as the subject of a
discontinuous included clause operating as S in a verbal clause:

Masa   itu   umor   saya   ada-lah   lima   atau   enam   tahun.
                  ————————   —————————————
                      N   N
                  ————————   —————   —————————————
                  S *incl...*   *..cl.*   P
          A(iv.a)   S..   P   ..S

lit. . . .there existed (this state of affairs) my age was five or six years.

B.783:   Macham   mana   fikiran   Dato',   /   musang   saya   'tu?
              S *incl.cl.* P   N₁ *n.grp.* N₂   *n.phr.*
              ——————————   ————————————   —————————————
                    S   P   T

What do you think of that civet-cat of mine, Dato'? (lit. What is the Dato's
opinion / my civet-cat?)

The author's punctuation here seems to point to 'T' as the best
description of the noun phrase, even though it is postponed to the
end of the sentence.

Finally, there is that well-remembered sentence of long ago, so
baffling to the newly-arrived beginner, so homely-sounding to the
Malay child opening his primer at page 1: *Abang saya banyak buku.*
Set the scene, and tell the tale: 'My brother / many-are his books',
with the resultant analysis T P S.

162 *bagitu:* see n. 118 and n. 126.

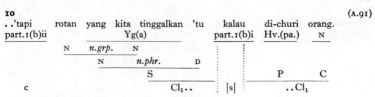

10 (A.91)

..'but what if the rattan we left there got stolen!

Pattern: ..c (s Cl$_1$ [Cl$_2$]).

NOTE: This is a fragment. The completing main clause, say, (by analogy with A.69) *alang-kah besar rugi-nya?* is fore-shadowed by the co-ordinating connective *'tapi* which links it to the preceding sentence. See the Text. The subject of the passive verb in the subordinate clause has been brought to initial position. But see n. 161.

11 (D.3)

..saya	suka	kerana	orang	ramai. .[163]
Pr.	Hv.(A.II.1a)	part.1(b)i	N	Hv.(A.II.1a)
S	P		S	P
Cl$_1$		s	Cl$_2$	

..I was happy, because there were crowds of people..

Pattern: Cl$_1$ s Cl$_2$.

---

163 *ramai:* nearly always predicative, 'be-in-large-numbers', and often in P S order:

Ramai orang di-situ.
　　　H *n.phr.* Q(ii)
P　　　　S
There were crowds of people there.

but *orang ramai*, when it means 'ordinary people', 'the man in the street', is to be described as a noun phrase (H + Q(i)); or else, more simply, as a compound word.

12

Sa-telah[164]	dapat[165]	kira-kira	tiga	empat[166]	puloh	penchuchok
part.1.(b)i	Hv.(A.II.3c)	part.3	num.		N	N
			M(i) *n.phr.*		H	
				M(i)	*n.phr.*	H
						N
	P	A(iii)				S
s			Cl$_1$			

di-bawa-lah	[penchuchok	itu][167]	ka-sawah.
Hv.pa.(A.I)			*prep.phr.(i)b*
P$_1$		[S]	P$_2$
		Cl$_2$	

When about thirty or forty spikes were ready, we would take them to the rice-fields.

Pattern: s Cl$_1$ Cl$_2$.

---

164 *sa-telah:* taken here as a subordinating connective. The question of the appropriate description for *sa*-compounds awaits further research. For the purpose of these analyses, the following tentative decisions have been taken:

(*a*) *sa-* as a numeral, in front of one of the numeral coefficients (themselves 'nouns of limited distribution') or one of the 'lexically restricted nouns of length, etc.' (See n. 25); described as M(i) in noun phrase structure.

e.g.	sa-	jenis binatang		[harga]	sa-	pikul
	num.	N$_1$ *n.grp.* N$_2$			num.	N
	M(i)	*n.phr.* H			M(i) *n.phr.* H	
					N$_1$ *n.grp.* N$_2$	

a species of creature   [the price] of a pikul

(*b*) *sa*+a verbal: this combination is taken to be basically nominal.

Some results of this decision:

(i) *sa-*+auxiliary (or Vb.A.II.3c)+*itu*:

e.g.	sa-sudah	itu..	Contrast:	Sudah	itu
	N	det.		Hv.	dei.
	H *n.phr.* D			P	S
				(s) Cl$_1$	

In clause analysis this noun phrase might qualify as 'A.(iv.a)' comparable with *ketika itu*.

(ii) *sa-*+auxiliary (or Vb.a.II.3c)+a clause (see Ex. 12 above). This is described as a subordinating connective. Cf. the use of the nouns *kerana* and *sebab* as connectives.

e.g.   (A.110)
Jadi sempat-lah kita sudah membuat pondok itu sa-belum masok matahari.
Hv.   Hv.(A.II.1a) S   P   C

               incl.cl.

P   P   S   P   S
Cl₁ (c)   Cl₂   s   Cl₃

And so we shall just have time to finish the hut before sunset.

(iii) *sa-*+Vb.A.II.1a (i.e. an adjective):

e.g. B.198: Serban sa-besar bakul, (hati ta' betul).
           N   N *n.grp.* N
           S   P

His turban is the size of a basket (but his heart is crooked).

The assignment of the resulting nominal expression sometimes presents difficulties, e.g.:

A.358: Hati-nya sedap sa-mula.
       S   P   A(iv.a)?

His heart is easy once more.

A.576:
sambil [ia] menggayakan dgn tangan-nya sa-banyak mana terangkat-nya.
                             N   adj.
                           S *incl.cl.* P
                               N   N
                               S   *incl.cl.*   P
c   [S]   P   A(ii)   C

'and he showed, with a gesture of his hand, how high he had lifted it'.

For *mana* see n. 121; but it is possible that *banyak*, here, should be taken as one of the 'restricted nouns of length, etc.' and that this example should be equated with those given under (*a*) above; alternatively, the *sa-* may be a relic of *sama* here, and not the numeral.

In the next three examples it is possible, by a generous interpretation of the idea of 'extent', to assign the (*sa*+verbal) nominal expression as 'A.(iv.b)' (cf. Ex. B.805 below):

A.148: Kita *sa-baik-baik* sempat 'aja menyudahkan pondok ini.
     We'll only just manage to get the hut finished in time.

B.882:   Tolong sampaikan *sa-penoh-penoh* terima kaseh..
Please convey our heartiest thanks..

C.3:   ..binatang yang *sa-akan-akan* kapal terbang rupa-nya..
..an insect that looks almost like an aeroplane..

(iv) *sa-* + adjective + *-nya*:

Since *sa-* and *-nya* are not simultaneous affixes (i.e. not *one* discontinuous affix) there is freedom of assignment between verbal and nominal according to whether the particular example is regarded as having arisen from: (*a*) *sa-* + (adj. + *nya*), i.e. *sa* + noun: (possibly verbal); or (*b*) (*sa-* + adj.) + *nya*, i.e. noun + *nya*: nominal.

Examples:

B.805:   Awak *sa-kurang-kurang-nya* tentu ada satu-satu pikiran yang putus..
You, at any rate, (putting it at the lowest estimate) surely have some definite opinion about it.. Nominal, say, 'A.(iv.b)'.

A.607:   Yang *sa-benar-nya* hantu itu semua angan-angan.
The truth is, ghosts are all moonshine. Verbal, as second member of 'Yg(b)'.

(*c*) *sa-* + a noun.

By definition, *sa* + noun is listed as a verbal (Class B.II.x. Ex. *budak yang sa-baya dengan saya*..). This, presumably, is *sa(ma)* + noun; an example would be *sa-umor* (i.e. *sama umor*) *dengan*. Contrast this with sentence A.100 below.

Of more frequent occurrence is the compound which arises from *sa-* (numeral) + noun, the result being nominal, and not differing essentially from the type described in (*a*) above.

Examples:

B.905:   Ini apa pula surat-nya *sa-chebis* 'ni? (N₂ in a noun group)
And what's this scrap of a note here?

B.442:   *Sa-kali ini* tahu-lah dia akan diri-nya! (A.(iv.a))
This time, they'll come to their senses!

B.246:   *Sa-kejap 'ni* juga kawan balék. (A.(iv.a))
I'll be back in the twinkling of an eye.

Perhaps also for:

A.100:   [Awak] 'Nak pegang tali dék bini *sa-umor hidup*? (A.(iv.b))
Are you going to have to hold on to your wife's apron-strings all your life long?

and for:

B.528:   *Sa-kadarkan* kurang sedap, Dato' kena menunggu sa-bentar. (A.(iv.b))
The only bother about it is (of this extent) that you will have to wait a bit. (*-kan = akan*?)

3. CO-ORDINATION WITHOUT PARTICLE, I.E. CO-ORDINATIVE PARATAXIS

The minimal pattern is: Cl_1 (c) Cl_2.

Examples:

1   (A.185)

Musa	ada,	Kasim	ada,	lanting	pun	berpasang.[168]
N	Hv.(A.II.3)	N	Hv.	N		Hv.pa.?(A.I.)
S	P	S	P	S		P
Cl_1	(c)	Cl_2	(c)	Cl_3		

Musa is there, Kasim is there, and the lantern is burning.

Pattern: Cl_1 (c) Cl_2 (c) Cl_3.

---

c.25: Ada pun nyanyi itu yang sa-benar-nya hanya-lah *sa-kadar* menyukakan hati kami. . (A.(iv.b))

As for the little song, all that it did was to keep us happy. .

(For *ada pun* see n. 283.)

165 *dapat:* a difficult verb to classify (when not operating as an auxiliary), but basically intransitive. Cf. sentence B.910: ..*kerana intan gemala yang sedia dapat kapada-nya itu lebéh mahal daripada segala emas intan dalam dunia.* '..because the lustrous jewel that is already his is more precious than all the gold and diamonds in the world'; and *TCE*, p. 190.32: *Dapat padi tahun ini?—Dapat-lah. Berzakat.* 'Did your padi do well this year?—Yes, I've paid my tithe.' With which may be compared sentence A.276: *Ha! Dapat-lah kehendak hati awak!* 'Ha! Your wish has come true!' But in Ex. 4 on p. 34 *dapat* is probably better described as transitive.

166 *tiga empat:* taken together for the sake of brevity; a paratactic transformation of: *tiga puloh penchuchok atau empat puloh penchuchok.*

167 [*penchuchok itu*]: since the *di*-form is categorically described as passive it is necessary always to presume the contextually derived S element if it is not present. It will not, however, always be inserted in the analyses. Moreover, the present writer is reluctant to surrender irrevocably the possibility of regarding this type of *di*-construction as an impersonal active statement. See *Teach Yourself Malay* §§115–116.

168 *berpasang:* see n. 145.

2 (A.184)

Ia	memandang	keliling,[169]	hati-nya	pun[170]	sedap.
Pr.	Hv.(A.I.)	N	N		Hv.(A.II.1a)
S	P	C	S		P

Cl_1 (c) Cl_2

He looks all round him (looks-at the-surroundings), and feels reassured.

Pattern: Cl_1 (c) Cl_2.

3 (A.161)

Di-ambil	-nya	lampu	peték	Musa	itu,	di-bélék	-nya.[171]
Hv.(pa.A.I)	Pr.	H *n.phr.* Q(i)				Hv.(pa.A.I)	Pr.

N_1 *n.grp.* N_2

H *n.phr.* D

N

P	C		S			P	C

Cl_1 (c) Cl_2

He picks up Musa's electric torch and has a good look at it.

Pattern: Cl_1 (c) Cl_2.

---

169 *keliling:* taken as a noun. This seems the best solution; perhaps comparable with the few existent *ke-* nouns, e.g. *ketagéh* craving, *kehendak* wish, *kekaséh* loved one, unless these are more correctly to be described as passive verbals. Text B shows (twice) the form *kedengar* but in each case functioning apparently as a non-passive verbal: B.581/582: *Patek ta' kedengar apa-apa—Kawan kedengar.* 'I can't hear anything—I can.' If the *ke-* form is taken to be passive in B.581, then *apa-apa* must be assigned as S, and *Paték* as C in initial position without *oléh*, and B.582 must be considered fragmentary, lacking the S element as well as the pre-complement prep. *oléh.* (But see n. 151, ref. 'T'.)

An article in *Indonesia* (Cornell Modern Indonesia Project) April 1966 quotes as an example of 'racy Djakarta colloquial' style the sentence *Ikan gedé ketangkap.* 'A big fish has been caught', and Text B.290a has the form *berkeputak* (? = *berkeputar*).

In n. 136 the group-numeral *ketiga* is described as a noun.

170 *pun:* when sentences are arranged paratactically the particle *pun* is of frequent occurrence in the second or third sentence when the object of the parataxis is to bring each sentence in turn into

4   (A.155)

Di-ambil-nya	lampu	peték-nya,	di-peték-nya[171]		ta'	menyala.
Hv.(pa.A.I) Pr.	N		Hv.(pa.A.I) Pr.		x(ii)	Hv.(A.II.3b)
P C	S		P C			P
Cl_1		(c)	Cl_2		(c)	Cl_3

He picks up the torch and switches it on, but it does not light up.

Pattern: Cl_1 (c) Cl_2 (c) Cl_3.

5   (A.213)

Ta'	ada	hantu,	hanya	Kasim	mengerang.[172]
x(ii)	Hv.(A.II.3)	N	part.3	N	Hv.(A.II.3b)
	P	S	A(iii)	S	P
	Cl_1	(c)		Cl_2	

There's no ghost, it's only Kasim groaning.

Pattern: Cl_1 (c) Cl_2.

6   (A.207)

Musa	arah	ka-dinding,	Kasim	arah	ka-orang	ramai,	Saléh	di-tengah-tengah
N	Hv.(A.II.3)	prep.phr.i(b)	N	Hv. prep.	N	Vb.A.II.1a	N	prep. N
					H n.phr. Q(i)			dir.(i) prep.phr.i(a) NP
				dir.(i)	prep.phr.i(b) NP			
S	P_1	P_2	S	P_1	P_2		S	P
	Cl_1		(c)		C_2		(c)	Cl_3

Musa is on the side nearest the wall, Kasim on the side nearest the audience, and Saleh in the middle.

Pattern: Cl_1 (c) Cl_2 (c) Cl_3.

---

dramatic relief. Such sentences would be spoken with the 'antithetic' intonation tune. See n. 128.

171   *di-bélék-nya, di-peték-nya:* see n. 167. The presumed S element here is *lampu itu*. An alternative analysis for Ex. 4 would be to take Clause 2 as subordinate to Clause 3, without particle (see p. 103): 'He picks up the torch, but when he presses the switch it does not light up.' The pattern would then be: Cl_1 (c) $\{(s)\ Cl_2\ Cl_3\}$.

172   *hanya Kasim mengerang:* an alternative analysis would be to describe this clause as a fragment, with [ada] as [P] and *Kasim mengerang* (as included clause) as S.

7   (A.212)

Saléh	terjaga[173]	lalu	dudok	memandang	keliling.[174]
N	Hv.(A.II.1a)	part.	Hv.(A.II.3)	Hv.(A.I)	N
		I.b.ii			
S	P		P	P	C
Cl$_1$		c	C$_2$	(c)	Cl$_3$

Saleh wakes up, then sits up and looks around.

Pattern: Cl$_1$ c Cl$_2$ (c) Cl$_3$.

> NOTE: The decision to analyse this sentence as three co-ordinate
> clauses, Cl$_2$ and Cl$_3$ being arranged paratactically, is based on the
> potential pause between the two verbs *dudok* and *memandang*.
> Contrast such a sentence as: *Sa-panjang hari dia dudok memandang
> arah ka-laut*, 'All day long he sat and gazed out to sea' where the
> two verbs are linked by conjunctive transformation (P$_1$ P$_2$) to form
> the predicate of a single clause.

8   (B.24)

Kerja	Raja	di-junjong,	kerja	sendiri	di-kélék.[175]
N	*n.grp.* N	Hv.(pa.A.I.)	N	*n.grp.* N	Hv.(pa.A.I)
S		P	S		P
Cl$_1$		(c)	Cl$_2$		

The Ruler's business we carry on the head, but our own we tuck under the arm.

Pattern: Cl$_1$ (c) Cl$_2$.

9   (B.10)

Malang	menimpa,	tuah	melambong	tinggi.
N	Hv.(A.I)	N	Hv.(A.II.3)	Hv.(A.II.1a)
S	P	S	P$_1$	P$_2$
Cl$_1$		(c)	Cl$_2$	

Misfortune crashes down upon us, luck soars above our heads.

Pattern: Cl$_1$ (c) Cl$_2$.

---

173 *jaga:* as Vb.A.II.1a 'be-awake'. Cf. *mati, hidup*, etc. See n. 144.
174 See n. 169.
175 Quoted in the play as a traditional saying; parataxis is common in
proverbial expressions.

4. SUBORDINATION WITHOUT PARTICLE

The subordinate clause always precedes the main clause.

Thus the minimal pattern is: (s) Cl_1 Cl_2.

It follows that, unlike clauses linked in co-ordinative parataxis, it is not possible to separate the clauses by putting a full-stop between them.

Examples:

1   (B.16)

'Dah	'tu,	'nak	di-apakan?[176]
Hv.(A.II.3c)	dei.	x(ii)	Hv.(pa.B.I)
P	S		P
(s)	Cl_1		Cl_2

Well, (if that's how it is) what's to be done?

Pattern: (s) Cl_1 Cl_2.

---

176 *di-apakan:* (i) See n. 167. But in this context it is difficult to assign an S element. See Text. It is tempting to describe the construction here as non-passive. (ii) For *apa* (a nominal) turned into a transitive verb by the suffix *-kan* cf. B.788:

'Dah 'tu,	di-apakan-nya	Temenggong?
	P C	S

'Well, what did it do to you then?'

and *TCE*, p. 190.25: *'Nak 'kau apakan peti itu?* 'What are you going to do with that box?' ? Cf. B.597: *Tudongkan seléndang 'ni ka-atas kepala.* 'Use this scarf to cover your head.'

This is perhaps the solution for the *ber*+noun+*kan* forms? E.g. *bersenjatakan sa-bilah parang* 'taking a parang to defend himself with' (*TCE*, p. 182.35); *dengan berpandukan keselurohan petékan ini, binchangkan..* 'using the whole passage (as your guide) discuss..' (from an examination paper). If the noun+*kan* is regarded as a transitive verb ('make into a weapon') such expressions can be compared with *berbuka* in *berbuka puasa* 'to break one's fast (with the evening meal)', the *ber* being regarded as reflexive.

2   (A.602)

'Dah	sudah	'tu	sudah-lah.[177]
x(ii)	Hv.(A.II.3c)	dei.	Hv.
	P	S	P
(s)		Cl$_1$	Cl$_2$

Well, since it did happen, it did. (and that's all there is to it) or perhaps; Now that it's over, it's over. (i.e. Let by-gones be by-gones)

    Pattern: (s) Cl$_1$ Cl$_2$.

3   (A.50)

'Dah	'nak	malang	'tu,	malang-lah.[178]
Hv.(A.II.3c)	x(ii)	Hv.(adj.)	det.	Hv.(adj.)
		vb.phr.		
	H	*n.phr.*	D	
	P		S	P
(s)		Cl$_1$		Cl$_2$

If it's decreed that you are in for a misfortune, in for it you are. (lit. If this about-to-be-unlucky state is already an existent decision, unlucky (you) will be.)

    Pattern: (s) Cl$_1$ Cl$_2$.

---

177 For an alternative analysis of Ex. 2 see n. 178.

178 *malang-lah:* not to be taken as a minor-type sentence such as *Baik-lah.* ('All right.') because the clause is contextually bound, but it is difficult to suggest a subject for the P element. See n. 156. The analysis of Ex. 3 given above is offered as an alternative for the decision taken in Ex. 2, an analysis which would give for Ex. 3 the following result:

'Dah	'nak	malang	'tu,
	x(ii)	Hv.(A.II.1a)	dei.
x(ii)		Hv.(*vb.group*)	
		P	S
(s)		Cl$_1$	

For the term 'verb-group', see n. 59.

    Conversely, Ex. 2, if analysed as Ex. 3, would give:

'Dah	sudah	'tu,	sudah-lah
Hv.(A.II.3c)	Vb.A.II.3c	det.	Hv.(A.II.3c)
	H *n.phr.* D		
	P	S	P
(s)		Cl$_1$	Cl$_2$

For verb-forms operating as Head in noun phrase structure see n. 26.

4 (A.84)

Hati	'dah	takut,	semua	di-sangka	hantu.[179]
N	x(ii)	Hv.(adj.)	N	Hv.pa.(A.I.)	N
			S		P
			$incl...$		$..cl.$
S		P	S..	P	..S
(s)		Cl$_1$		Cl$_2$	

Because you are frightened, you take everything to be a ghost.

Pattern: (s) Cl$_1$ Cl$_2$.

NOTE: In the main clause (Cl$_2$) the subject is a discontinuous included clause.

5 (A.337)

Ada	mayat	ta'ada	mayat	perut aku	lapar	juga.
Hv.(A.II.3)	N	x(ii)Hv.	N	N + Pr.	Hv.(adj.)	part.3
P	S	P	S	S	P	A(iii)
(s)	Cl$_1$	(c)	Cl$_2$		Cl$_3$	

Corpse or no corpse, I'm hungry, and that's a fact.

Pattern: (s) {Cl$_1$ (c) Cl$_2$} Cl$_3$.

NOTE: Clause 1 and Clause 2 are paratactically co-ordinate, and each of them is paratactically subordinate to the main clause (Cl$_3$).

---

179 This solution is based on a presumed non-passive clause such as:

Dia	sangka	semua	hantu
		N	N
		S $incl.cl.$	P
S	P	C	

'He thinks everything is a ghost.' Cf. p. 112. Ex.9, and n. 302.

A possible alternative would be to take *sangka hantu* as a compound expression = **hantukan* 'make into a ghost'. Cf. n. 176: *apakan*, 'make into what?' In that case *semua* alone would be S, and *di-sangka-hantu* would be P. This is perhaps the best solution for B.218: *Takut juga...'tapi siapa 'nak di-buat kawan?* 'Yes, I *am* a bit nervous..but who is to keep me company?' taken as a passive transform of: **Saya 'nak-buat-kawan siapa?*; and also for B.400: *Di-pandang orang pun 'aib* 'People would think it unseemly' from **Orang pandang-'aib[kelakuan itu]*.

6 (B.73)

Memandang-nya	pun[180]	Mah	meluat.
Hv.(A.I)	Pr. part.2	N	Hv.(A.II.3)
P	C	S	P
(s)	Cl₁		Cl₂

If I just look at him, I feel sick.

Pattern: (s) Cl₁ Cl₂.

7 (A.151)

Sekarang	'nak malam[181]	pun	malam-lah[181]
Nom.(c)	x(ii) Hv.(A.II.1a)	part.2	Hv.(A.II.1a) + part.2
A(i)..	P		..P
Cl₂..	(s) Cl₁		..Cl₂

Now, if it gets dark, it gets dark. (and that's that. Who cares?)

Pattern: (s) Cl₁ Cl₂.

NOTE: The main clause is discontinuous because the adjunct is brought to initial position, for emphasis.

8 (A.375)

Baharu[182]	ia	tengah[183]	membelitkan	tali itu	ka-lantai,[184]
adj.	Pr.	x(i)	Hv.(B.I)	N det.	prep.phr.i(exception 2)
	S		P	C	A
			incl.cl.		
P		S			
(s)		Cl₁			

mayat	itu	terangkat	balék
N	det.	Hv.₁(pa.A.I)	Hv.₂(A.II.3)
S		P₁	P₂
		Cl₂	

Just as he is tying the rope round the flooring laths, the corpse rises up again.

Pattern: (s) Cl₁ Cl₂.

---

180 *Memandang-nya pun:* this clause is not fragmentary; the omission of the S element is the result of subjunctive transformation. See p. 81.2(*a*).

181 *malam:* taken as a verbal. If an [S] element is to be presumed it would be *hari*, but a predicate of this type seems to merit the description of 'subjectless verb'. Cf. *malang-lah*, n. 178.

9   (A.338)

Makan	senja	tadi	kenyang[185]	'tapi	ini	[aku]	'dah	lapar	lagi.
Hv.(A.I)	N	N	Hv.(adj.)		dei.		x(ii)	Hv.(adj.)	part.3
						[S]		P	A(iii)
								incl.cl.	

					N		N	
P	A(iva)	A(iva)	P		S		P	
(s)	Cl$_1$		Cl$_2$	c		Cl$_3$		

When I had my meal last night, I was satisfied, but here I am, hungry again! (lit. This
is-I-am-still-hungry)

Pattern: $\{(s)\ Cl_1\ Cl_2\}\ c\ Cl_3$.

---

182 *Baharu:* taken as a verbal. It would be possible to take it as a
particle (A.iii) as in *baharu kahwin* (n. 133) but the order of words,
with the potential pause after *baharu*, favours the verbal interpretation, an interpretation which implies that there is a syntactic
distinction between *Saya baharu sampai* ('I've just arrived') and
Baharu saya sampai.. ('No sooner had I arrived than..').

183 *tengah:* taken to be operating as an auxiliary. See n. 56.

184 *ka-lantai:* Taken as A, rather than P$_2$. This description implies
that, by extension, *membelitkan* is being treated as a two-complement verb, with *lantai* as C$_2$, transformed to the prepositional
phrase. See n. 98, *ad fin* and cf. n. 138.

185 An alternative possibility would be to take *[Aku] makan senja tadi*
as an included clause, as in *Orang itu berjalan / chepat* (n. 107):

[Aku]	makan	senja	tadi	*kenyang*
[S]	P	A(1)	A(2)	
	incl.cl.			

S	P
Cl$_1$	

This eliminates the suggested subordination without particle since
the sentence is now analysed as two co-ordinate clauses linked by
particle, i.e. Cl_1 c Cl_2.

10   (A.164)

Ba'-lah[186]	saya	lanting	macham	ini	chukup-lah.
Hv.(A.I)	Pr.			det.	Hv.(A.II.1a)

$$\text{N} \quad n.phr. \quad \text{D}$$
$$\text{N}_1 \quad n.grp. \quad \text{N}_2$$

P	C_2		C_1		P
(s)	Cl_1				Cl_2

Give me a lantern like this one, and I'm satisfied. (i.e. If I have a lantern like this one, that's enough.)

Pattern: (s) Cl_1 Cl_2.

NOTE. This is taken as subordinative rather than co-ordinative parataxis because, if the order of the two clauses is reversed, it is necessary to insert the subordinating particle: *Chukup-lah kalau di-bagi*...

11   (A.288)

Dia	sudah	mati	awak	'nak	ambil	pula	harta-nya.
S		P	S		P	A(iii)	C
(s)	Cl_1				Cl_2		

He's dead—and you're going to help yourself to his possessions!

Pattern: (s) Cl_1 Cl_2.

NOTE. As in Ex. 10 above, this is taken as subordinative parataxis, not co-ordinative, because the clauses are not reversible without the insertion of a subordinating particle: *Awak 'nak ambil harta-nya kerana dia sudah mati.*

---

186 *Ba'* = *Bagi.* For the two-complement verb, see p. 50.

§7. FURTHER EXAMPLES OF
THE INCLUDED CLAUSE

Since the included clause is a noun-equivalent it may be expected to occur in any of the syntactic positions which may be filled by a noun, viz.:

1. as S in nominal or verbal clause structure;
2. as P in nominal clause stucture;
3. as C in verbal clause structure;
4. as H in noun phrase structure;
5. as N_1, N_2, etc., in noun group structure;
6. as NP in prepositional phrase structure.

Also, specifically,

7. as Q in noun phrase structure, when H is one of a limited number of nouns indicative of time or place.

All included Clauses are heavily underlined.

(A.208)

I

Musa	mendengkor[187]	perlahan-lahan.[188]
N	Hv.(A.II.3)	Hv.(?A.II.1a)
S	incl.cl. P	
S		P

Musa is snoring gently.

Occurrence of included clause: S in verbal clause structure, itself a verbal clause.

187 *Included clause as S*: comparable with *Orang itu berjalan | chepat* (n. 107). Contrast A.293: *Turun-lah lekas.* 'Go at once' (lit. Go down. Be quick), and B.645: *Berdiri tegak-tegak dekat orang tua betina 'tu.* 'Stand bolt upright, by the old woman.' Both sentences are double imperative clauses linked paratactically. Cf. n. 237.

188 *perlahan-lahan:* ⟨With the verb class, duplication is derivational (362)⟩. The word is therefore not strictly able to be described as a

2   (A.202)

Kita	rasa[189]	sama-sama.[190]
Pr.	Hv.(A.II.1a)	Hv.(A.II.1a)

S   *incl.cl.*   P

S   P

We'll share and share alike. (lit. We-experience is-alike)

Occurrence: S in a verbal clause, itself a verbal clause.

3   (A.247)

Dia	selimutkan	Kasim	baik-baik.[190]
Pr.	Hv.(B.I)	N	Hv.(A.II.1a)
S	P	C	

incl.cl.

S   P

He carefully wraps a blanket round Kasim.

Occurrence: S in a verbal clause, itself a verbal clause.

4   (B.619)

Orang tua itu	mengukor	bukan main[191]	chepat...
n.phr.	Hv.(A.I)	part.3	Hv.(A.II.1a)

S   *incl.cl.*   P

S   A(iii)   P

The old lady is rasping away at the coconut at a furious rate...

Occurrence: S in a verbal clause, itself a verbal clause.

Class A (i.e. non-derived) verbal. Moreover, the base-word itself, before duplication, has the appearance of being derived (perhaps with an infix rather than a prefix), not monomorphemic as the adjective class is required to be. The only alternative seems to be to describe *perlahan-lahan* as an adjunctival particle (comparable with *sangat*). In that case, the sentence elements are: S P A(iii), and there is no included clause.

189 *rasa* described as A.II.1a: see n. 144.

190 *sama-sama, baik-baik:* see n. 188.

191 *bukan main* as an adjunctival particle: taken to be a compound word, comparable with *sangat*. For an analysis of the whole sentence see n. 244.

5   (B.624)

Lama[192]	benar	pula	nampak-nya	dia	mengukor	nyior.
Hv.(A.II.1a)	part.3	part.3	(parenth.)	Pr.	Hv.(A.I)	N
					S incl... P ..cl. C	
P	A(iii)	A(iii)	A(v)		S	

She seems to be taking a terribly long time over rasping a coconut!

Occurrence: S in a verbal clause, itself a verbal clause.

6   (A.295)

Saya	'nak	turun-lah	'ni.
Pr.	x(ii)	Hv.(A.II.3)	dei.
S incl.cl. P			
N			N
S			P

I'm just going, this very minute! (lit. I-am-about-to-go is-this)

Occurrence: S in nominal clause structure, itself a verbal clause.

7   (A.242)

Ta'	sempat	di-buat	apa.
x(ii)	Hv.(A.II.1a)	Hv.pa.(A.I)	nom.(d)
		P inc.cl. S	
P		S	

There wasn't time to do anything about it.

Occurrence: S in a verbal clause, itself a verbal clause.

---

192 *lama:* assigned as a verbal, by definition [*pakaian yang lama*], with the result that *benar* is taken to be operating as an adjunctival particle. If, on the other hand, *lama* is taken to be operating as a noun, then the included clause becomes P in nominal clause structure, thus:

Lama	benar	dia	mengukor	nyior.
N	adj.	Pr.	Hv.	N
H *n.phr.* Q(i)		S incl... P ..cl.		C
N		N		
S		P		

Cf. *berapa lama*, n. 211.

8   (A.174)

Ta' patut	[awak]	pengechut.
x(ii) Hv.(A.II.1a)		Hv.(B.II.ix)
	[S] *incl.cl.*	P
P		S

(You're a man). You've no business to be a coward.

Occurrence: S in a verbal clause, itself a verbal clause.

9   (A.331)

Biar	di-sangka-nya	hantu	mayat	mengejar	dia.
			S	P	C
			incl.cl.(2)		
	P	C		S	
		incl.cl.(1)			
P		C			

Let him think that the ghost of the corpse is chasing him.

Occurrences: (1) an included clause (passive) as the complement of an imperative verb; (2) an included clause as subject of this (verbal) complement clause.

10   (A.317)

Baik	aku	balék	ajak	'bang	Musa	pergi	bersama.[193]
Hv.(adj.)	Pr.	Hv.(A.II.3)	Hv.(A.I)		*n.grp.?*	*n.phr.?*	
	S	P_1	P_2			C	
			incl.cl.				
P			S				

I had better go back and ask 'bang Musa to come with me.

Occurrence: S in a verbal clause, itself a verbal clause.

11   (A.53)

Itu-lah dei.	kawan	menchari	awak...
	N	Hv.(A.I)	Pr.
	S	P	C
		incl.cl.	
S		P	

That's why I've come to look for you... (lit. That-is I-come)

Occurrence: P in a nominal clause, itself a verbal clause.

---

193 *'bang Musa pergi bersama:* this is a possible case of the 'pivot noun phrase' suggested in §9.

194 *banyak* described as a verbal: see n. 7.

195 *apa:* listed as interrogative nominal, capable of acting as S, P or C in clause structure but not listed as a noun-equivalent, presumably

12 (C.24)

Dengan	jalan	ini	banyak-[194]lah	tikus	itu	mati.
part.I(a)iii	N	det.	Hv.(A.II.1a)	N	det.	Hv.(A.II.1a)

H *n.phr.* D   H *n.phr.* D

dir.iii *prep.phr.iii* NP   N

S *incl.cl.* P

N

A(ii)   P   S

In this way, the rats were killed in large numbers. (lit. Rats-died were-many. as in
Orang berjalan itu / chepat.)

Occurrence: S in a verbal clause, itself a verbal clause.

13 (B.324)

Ini	ta' ada	apa-apa[195]	yang siap.
dei.	x(ii) Hv.(A.II.3c)	nom.(d)	Yg(b)

N   N   *n.grp.*   N

N

P   *incl.cl.*   S

N

S   P

And here am I with not a thing ready! (lit. This is there-not-exists anything-ready.)

Occurrence: P in a nominal clause, itself a verbal clause.

14 (B.14)

Fasal	apa[196]	bercherai?[197]
N	N	Vb.A.II.2

S *incl.cl.* P   N

N

S   P

What's this about parting?

Occurrence: S in a nominal clause, itself a nominal clause.

---

because these words do not collocate with *itu*. In the analyses *apa*
is treated as a noun-equivalent. For a comment on *mengapa* see
n. 117; for *apakan* n. 176, and for *berapa* n. 211.

196 *Fasal apa:* taken as a nominal clause. An alternative would be to
treat *fasal apa* (*apa fasal*) as a compound nominal which has not
yet come to be written as one word, as has *apabila*. The included
clause then disappears and is replaced by N.

197 *bercherai:* operating as a noun. Verbs of Class A.II.2 have their
nominal forms in *ber-*, and there is therefore no need of the

15   (B.22)

Apa	fasal	[abang]	ta'	boléh	tidak?[198]
N	N	N	x(ii)	x(ii)	Hv.(A.II.3c)

S *incl.cl.*(1) P　　　[S]　*incl.cl.*(2)　　P

　　　N　　　　　　　　　　N
　　　S　　　　　　　　　　P

Why must you?

Occurrences: (1) S in a nominal clause, itself a nominal clause;
(2) P in a nominal clause,[199] itself a verbal clause.

16   (A.244)

Apa	bangsa[200]	sakit	perut-nya[201]	'ni!
N	N	N *n.grp.*	Pr.	det.

S *incl.cl.*　P　　　　H　　*n.phr.*　　D

　　N　　　　　　　　　N
　　S　　　　　　　　　P

What sort of stomach-ache is *this!*

Occurrence: S in a nominal clause, itself a nominal clause.

---

nominalising *-nya* which is required by such verbs when used
in the zero form before they can operate as nouns. See n. 26.iii.1.
An alternative would be to take *bercherai* as Head-verb to an
inserted S element [kita]. In that case, P becomes a second included
clause, as suggested in Ex. 15 above.

198 *tidak:* as Head-verb. Cf. n. 58.

199 When an included clause is labelled 'P' it must, by definition, be P
in nominal clause structure.

200 *Apa bangsa:* the possibility of taking this as a compound nominal,
the alternative suggested in n. 196 for *apa fasal* (and therefore for
apa sebab, apa macham, apa hal, etc.) seems less acceptable, but it
is grammatically the same structure.

201 *sakit perut:* taken here as a compound word, a noun. For the *-nya*
see n. 68.

202 *Saya pun terpikir:* the intonation (the whole expression being
spoken on a level tone) permits this verbal clause to be taken as
parenthetic. If, on the other hand, it is felt to be an integral part of
the sentence, then the whole of the rest of the sentence becomes an
included clause and is the exponent of the Complement, as on

17   (A.47)

Saya pun terpikir[202] macham mana-lah[203] dia 'nak menyudahkan menuai[204] kalau..

	N	adj.	Pr.	x(ii)	Hv.(B.I)	N(Vb.A.I)	con.(i)
	S	P	S		P		C
	incl.cl.(1)			*incl.cl.*(2)			
	N				N		
A(v.b.)	S				P		

I was just thinking, how is he going to do his reaping, if. . ?

Occurrences: (1) S in a nominal clause, itself a verbal clause; (2) P in a nominal clause, itself a verbal clause.

---

p. 121 Ex. 29, where the particle *-lah* highlights the initial verbal clause into significant intonation.

203 *macham mana:* this might have been treated as a single word, an interrogative nominal, by analogy with *bagaimana* which is traditionally written as one word. Cf. n. 196, where this possibility is suggested for *apa fasal*, etc.

With *mana*, however, two points of difficulty present themselves:

(1) the two 'nominals' cannot be reversed: *fasal apa, sebab apa,* and *hal apa* are all found, but not **mana macham,* **mana bagai.*

(2) *mana* seems to satisfy the diagnostic tests for a verbal (see p. 11): (*Yang*) *mana baik?* Which is the better? (S in clause structure); *Minta* (*yang*) *mana?* Which do you want? (C in clause structure); *Buku* (*yang*) *mana?* Which book? (2nd element in a noun group).

In these analyses, therefore, *mana* is described sometimes as a nominal, and sometimes as a verbal:

(*a*) As a nominal when it forms a prepositional phrase (or an abbreviation of such a phrase) with a directive preposition, as in (*di-*)*mana?* where? *dari mana?* whence? (*ka-*)*mana?* whither? *ka-mana-mana* to anywhere at all. (In B.48, quoted in n. 246, *mana-mana* and *tempat yang tentu* may be taken as N_1 and N_2 of a noun group.)

(*b*) As a verbal of Class A.II.1a (i.e. an adjective) when it follows a noun. Cf. n. 121.

204 *menuai:* as Complement, i.e. operating as a noun. Cf. the *me-* form of a transitive verb operating as Head of a noun phrase. See n. 26.i.

18 (A.535)

Mari ikut,[205] boléh kita téngok macham mana[206] rupa-nya[207] Musa ta'perchayakan hantu.

```
N   Hv.   x(ii)..: Pr. : ..Hv.   N     adj.                N    x(ii) Hv.(B.I)   N
                               ---   ---                  ---  --------------  ---
                                S     P                    S         P          C
                               inc.cl.(1)                       incl.cl.(2)
                                                       N1       n.grp.      N2
                                N                              N
                               ---                            ---
                                S          incl.cl.(3)         P
P    P    P..  :  S  :  ..P                    C
---  ---  ------------------------------------------
Cl1  Cl2                      Cl3
```

Come along, we'll just see how Musa doesn't believe in ghosts!

Pattern: Cl_1 (c) Cl_2 (c) Cl_3 (i.e. three co-ordinate clauses arranged paratactically). Clause 3 has a discontinuous P element.

Occurrences of included clauses: (1) S in a nominal clause, itself a verbal clause; (2) N_2 in a noun group; (3) C in a verbal clause, itself a nominal clause with included clause (1) as S.

19 (B.71)

Macham 'nak di-makan-nya Mah[208]

```
  N     x(ii)  Hv.(pa.A.I)  Pr.    N
 ---    ------------------  ---   ---
                P            C     S
                   incl.cl.
                      N
                     ---
  S                   P
```

It was as if he wanted to eat you.

Occurrence: P in a nominal clause.

---

205 *Mari ikut:* lit. 'Hither! Follow!' *Mari* is taken to be a noun, comparable with *sana* / *sini* (cf. *ka-sana ka-mari* 'thither and hither'). Here it is an abbreviation of the predicating prep. phrase i.a [*ka-*]*mari*, used imperatively. Clause 1 is therefore, strictly speaking, a verbal clause.

206 *macham mana:* see n. 203.

207 *rupa-nya:* by intonation and context clearly not a parenthetic adjunct in this sentence.

208 Exx. 19 and 20. Each example has been analysed as a nominal clause. Another possibility would be to take such an utterance as

20   (B.401)

Macham	Pa' Pandir	'nak	melawak.[208]
N	N	x(ii)	Hv.(A.II.3)

$$\underline{\quad\text{S}\quad\quad\quad\quad\quad\text{incl.cl.}\quad\quad\quad\text{P}\quad}$$

$$\text{N}$$
$$\overline{\quad\quad\quad\quad\quad\quad\text{P}\quad\quad\quad\quad\quad\quad}$$

S

It would be like Pa' Pandir trying to be funny.

Occurrence: P in a nominal clause.

21   (A.46)

Saya	pun	ada[209]	dengar	pasal	Pa'A.	luka	kaki	kena	changul	'tu /
Pr.	part.2	x(ii)	Hv.(A.I)		N	Hv.	N	Hv.	N	det.
					S	P_1	C_1	P_2	C_2	
							inclcl.			

$$\text{N}$$
$$\text{H}\qquad\qquad\qquad\textit{n.phr.}\qquad\qquad\qquad\text{D}$$

| | | N_1 | *n.grp.* | N_2 |

S   P   C

Yes, I heard about Pa' Anjang cutting his foot on his changkul.

Occurrence: H in noun phrase structure.

---

a minor-type sentence consisting of a noun group (cf. Ex. 18 above, incl.cl. 2) thus:

Macham	Pa' Pandir	'nak	melawak
		incl.cl.	
N_1	*n.grp.*	N_2	

Since *macham* in such sentences can always be replaced by *bagai* or *saperti* these two words also must be taken as nouns, thus:

                                                                       (A.410)

Suara-nya	makin	nyaring	saperti	orang	menjerit.
N	part.3	adj.	N	N	Hv.(A.II.3)
S	A(iii)	P		S	*incl.cl.*(3) P
	incl.cl.(1)			N	
			S	*incl.cl.*(2) P	
S			P		

His voice becomes shriller and shriller, like a scream.

Result: a nominal sentence with three included clauses. For (1) as S of the sentence cf. n. 187; (2), as P of the sentence, is an alternative for the noun group of Ex. 18.

209 *ada* taken to be operating as an auxiliary: see n. 57.

22   (A.24)

Apa	hal	'bang	Musa	menchari	Saleh	'ni?
nom.(d)	N	N		Hv.(A.I.)	N	det.
S	P	S		P	C	
incl.cl.(1)				incl.cl.(2)		

		H	n.phr.	D
			N	
			S	

N		
S		
		P

Why are you looking for Saleh? (lit. What is-the-business is this you-seek-Saleh)

Occurrences: (1) S in a nominal clause (but see n. 196); (2) H in a noun phrase.

23   (A.390)

'Tapi	dia	pergi	'tu	ta'	lama	bukan?[210]
	Pr.	Hv.	det.	x(ii)	Hv.(adj.)	Hv.(A.II.3c)
	S incl.cl.	P				

H	n.phr.	D
	N	
	S	

S		P	P

|c|	Cl₁	(c)	Cl₂

But he won't be away very long, will he?

Occurrence: H in a noun phrase.

24   (A.395)

(Apa 'ni!	Apa hal!)	Apa	pasal	awak	balék	tengah-tengah	malam	'ni?
S P	S P	nom.(d)	N	Pr.	Hv.(A.II.3)	N	N	det.
nom.cl.	nom.cl.					N₁ n.grp. N₂		
						A(iv.a)		
		S	P	S	P			
		incl.cl.(1)			incl.cl.(2)			
						H	n.phr.	D
			N				N	
(A.393)	(A.394)		S				P	

What's the trouble, that you've come home in the middle of the night like this?

Occurrences: (1) S in nominal clause, itself a nominal clause; (2) H in nominal phrase, itself a verbal clause.

---

210 *bukan?* Clause 2 is a minor-type verbal sentence attached paratactically to Clause 1. Cf. n. 113, sentence B.100.

25 (A.70)

Berapa	lama[211]	agak-nya	kita	kena	dudok	di-hutan	'tu?
NNQ	N	(parenth.)	Pr.	x(ii)	Hv.(A.II.3)	prep.phr.i(b)	det.
M(ii) n.phr. H			S	P₁		P₂	
N				incl.cl.			
				H		n.phr.	D
						N	
S		A(v)					P

How many nights, do you think, should we have to stay in the jungle?

Occurrence: H in noun phrase, itself a verbal clause.

26 (A.379)

...ebab[212]	kuat-nya	dia	terbangkit	itu	hingga[213]	terantok	muka-nya	ka-	pada[214]	dahi Musa
...part.		Pr.	Hv.(A.II.3)	det.	Hv.	Hv.(pa.?)	N		NNQ	N₁ + N₂
I.a		S incl.cl. P			(A.II.3)	(A.II.2a)			M(ii) n.phr. H	
		H n.phr. D						dir.(i) + NP	
	N₁	n.grp.	N₂					prep.phr.i(b)	
...ir.iii	prep.phr.(iii)	NP								
A(ii)					P₁	P₂	S		P₃	

He came up with such force that his face collided with Musa's forehead.

Occurrence: Head of noun phrase.

---

211 *berapa lama:* see n. 192. But if *lama* is described as a verbal in this
example (P in clause structure, with the noun phrase *kita...'tu* as
S) it will be necessary to describe *berapa* as an adjunctival particle.

If *lama* is taken to be operating as a noun, then *berapa* can be
described as a non-numeral quantifier (by analogy with *Berapa
hari?—Tiga hari*).

If *berapa* is retained as a nominal as listed on p. 11(d), the
expression becomes a noun group, N₁ + N₂.

Another possibility is to take *ber-apa* as a predicating prep.
phrase(i(a)), making the expression *Berapa lama* a verbal clause, of
structure P S.

The same possibilities are open for *berapa banyak* in sentence
B.764: *Ta' terhabis buat ubat walau berapa banyak pun kelurut
Tuanku.* ('It will last forever for ointment-making, no matter how
many carbuncles His Highness may have.') according to whether
banyak is analysed as nominal S (with *kelurut* as nominal P), or as
verbal P (with *kelurut* as S).

27   (A.64)

Awak[215]	Ché'Kasim	macham	mana[216]	[awak][215]	pikir?
Pr.	N	N	adj.	Pr.	Hv.

S *incl.cl.*(1) P   [S] *incl.cl.*(2) P

      N   N

voc.	voc.				
		S			P

You, Che'Kasim, what do you think about it?

Occurrences: (1) S in a nominal clause, itself a verbal clause; (2) P in a nominal clause, itself a verbal clause.

---

212 *sebab:* taken as a directive preposition, comparable with *dengan.* Cf. *kerana* in the prov. *Mati semut kerana gula.* But see also n. 213.

213 *hingga:* taken as Head-verb. Cf. *sampai* in n. 115, and see n. 305. An alternative analysis, still taking *hingga* as Hv. would be:

Sebab	kuat-nya	dia	terbangkit itu	hingga	[ka]	terantok	muka-nya	kpd. dahi Musa
N_1 +	N_2 +		N_3	Hv.	Hv.	N		*prep.phr.i.(b)*

          n.grp. P_1 S P_2

               N   *incl.cl.*

                            [dir.(i)] *prep.phr.i(b)* NP

        S P_1 P_2

lit. 'The-affair-of-the-force-of-his-uprising went-right-up-to his-face-bumping-into-Musa's forehead.'

214 *ka pada:* for resolution into prep. + NNQ see p. 8.

215 *Awak...[awak]:* it is not possible to take the first pronoun as subject, with *pikir* as predicate, because that would result in the unacceptable structure *SCP (see n. 76) since *macham mana,* whether described as a noun group, noun phrase, or included clause, is undoubtedly nominal. Perhaps it will be found defensible after further research to make one more addition to the adjunct possibilities, viz.: 'A[iv.c]—a small number of nominal expressions such as *bagaimana, macham mana* which have modal content.' If *pikir* is taken to be operating as N (see n. 71), it becomes the nominal predicate element, and the included clause, with its inter-polated S element, disappears.

216 *mana:* see n. 203.

217 *Tengku 'dah ada:* taken as P in a nominal clause (Cl_1) which is subordinated paratactically to the main clause (Cl_2). This solution

28   (B.609)

```
'Tapi   ini    Tengku         'dah   ada[217]       [paték]   'dah   suka         rasa-nya.[218]
        dei.   N              x(ii) Hv.(A.II.3)     N         x(ii) Hv.(A.II.1a)   N
        N      S              incl.cl.       P
                              N
                              P
        S                     P                      [S]       P                   C
 |c|   (s)     Cl₁                                              Cl₂
```

Now that you are here, I feel happy.

Occurrence: P in a nominal clause itself a verbal clause.

29   (A.32)

```
Awak   pun    tahu-lah[219]   menuai[220]   'tu    empat  lima[221]   hari   pun   ta'    sudah.
Pr.           Hv.(A.I)        N(Vb.A.1)     det.   NNQ                N            x(ii)  Hv.
                              H    n.phr.    D      M(i)   n.phr.      H
                              N
                              S                     A(iv.b)                              P
                                                    incl.cl.
S      P                                            C
```

You know well that harvesting your rice is a business that takes more than four or five days.

Occurrence: C in a verbal clause, itself a verbal clause.

---

is offered with some hesitation, as being the simplest, but it would be possible to analyse the words as a noun group:

```
ini    T.    'dah   ada
dei.         incl.cl.
N₁     n.grp.        N₂
```

In that case, however, it would be difficult to assign it satisfactorily as a clause element.

218 *rasa-nya:* it seems better to take it as C here, rather than as parenthetic A. Another possibility would be to take it as S in a P S clause, with no interpolation.

219 *tahu:* assigned as a transitive verb although it does not strictly answer the diagnostic test since, when *di-* is prefixed, it is the derived form *ketahui* that is used. An alternative would be to take the utterance as two co-ordinate verbal clauses linked paratactically. See n. 202.

220 *menuai:* for the *me-*form of the verb as H in noun phrase structure see n. 26(i).

221 *empat lima:* taken together as one NNQ for the sake of brevity;

30 (B.599)

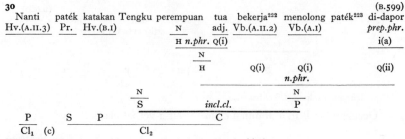

I'll say that you are an old woman who helps me in the kitchen.

Occurrence: C in a verbal clause, itself a nominal clause.

NOTE: The clause in which the included clause occurs (Cl_2) is linked in paratactic co-ordination with the one-word imperative clause (Cl_1) which precedes it.

31 (A.166)

[Ia]	Masok	terlompat[224] macham	orang	chemas,[225]	lalu	[ia]	menutup	rapat-rapat.
Pr.	Hv.	Hv.(A.II.3?)		N	Hv.(A.II.1a)	con.	Hv.(A.I)	Hv.(A.II.1a)
S *incl.cl.*(1) P		Hv.(A.II.3?)		S *incl.cl.*(2) P		[S] *incl.cl.*(3) P		

$$S \quad\quad P_1 \quad\quad N_1 \; n.grp. \; N_2 \quad\quad\quad S \quad\quad P$$
$$Cl_1 \quad\quad\quad\quad P_2 \quad\quad\quad\quad c \quad\quad\quad Cl_2$$

He leaps into the hut like somebody in a panic, and shuts the door tight.

---

strictly speaking, a paratactic transform of *empat hari ta'sudah, lima hari ta'sudah.*

222 *bekerja:* for the verb-forms which may operate as Q in noun phrase see n. 29.

223 *menolong paték:* the complement is counted as one unit with the verb, forming the second of these three transformational qualifiers.

224 *terlompat:* see n. 98. If *lompat* could be accepted as a nominal, *terlompat* might be compared with *terbau* but it seems more likely that it is verbal, and non-passive.

225 *macham orang chemas:* see pp. 116–117, Exx. 19 and 20. For the present example the footnote alternative (i.e. as noun group) has been chosen. If on the other hand the first alternative is followed, then another included clause (nominal) must be recorded, replacing the

Occurrences: (1) S in a verbal and (by transformation) nominal clause (Cl$_1$), itself a verbal clause; (2) N$_2$ in a noun group, itself a verbal clause; (3) S in a verbal clause (Cl$_2$), itself a verbal clause.

NOTE. Note 225 indicates the possible occurrence of two more included clauses.

32   (A.573)

Betul-kah	saya	ada	bangkit	dudok[226]	sa-belum	dari	pada	itu.[227]
Hv.(adj.)	Pr.	x(ii)	Hv.$_1$	Hv.$_2$	N	part.1(a)	NNQ	dei.
							M(ii) *n.phr.* H	
						dir.i. *prep.phr.i.a* NP		
					H	*n.phr.* Q(ii)		
	S	P$_1$	P$_2$			A(iv.a)		
			incl.cl.					
P			S					

Had I really sat up before that?

Occurrence: S in a verbal clause, itself a verbal clause.

---

noun group and described as P in a nominal clause. Yet another included clause (verbal) is created if *[Ia] masok terlompat* is taken as S of Clause 1, and *macham orang chemas* (however analysed) as the sole predicate element, thus:

[Ia]	masok	terlompat	macham	orang	chemas.
[S] *incl.cl.* P					
S	*incl.cl.*	P	a nominal piece		
S			P		

226 *ada bangkit dudok:* for convenience, the symbols P$_1$ and P$_2$ are placed under the Head-verbs only, but the x element belongs to both verbs: *ada bangkit, ada dudok*. For *ada* described as an auxiliary cf. n. 57.

227 *sa-belum daripada itu:* this somewhat tortuous analysis does produce a practicable result, i.e. a nominal expression which it is possible to assign as A(iv.a). For *pada* as NNQ see p. 8. For *sa*-compounds see n. 164.

The same solution seems possible (and less tortuous) for the quoted example on p. 65, where *pada* is clearly a noun:

33   (A.19)

Ahli   awak   katakan[228]   awak   tentu[229]   ada   di-sini.
                              S   A(v.b)   P₁   P₂

Ahli   awak   katakan[228]   awak   tentu[229]   ada   di-sini.
                             S   A(v.b) P_1 P_2
                                    incl.cl.

  S   P   C

Your wife said that you were sure to be here.

Occurrence: C in a verbal clause, itself a verbal clause.

34   (B.617)

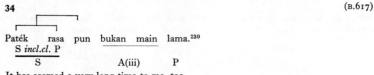

Paték   rasa   pun   bukan   main   lama.[230]
S *incl.cl.* P

  S   A(iii)   P

It has seemed a very long time to me, too.

Occurrence: S in a verbal clause, itself a verbal clause.

Dalam   pada   nasi   di-jerangkan   oléh   Aminah   itu,   ...
                      incl.cl.
         H   Q(iii)   D
N_1 *n.grp.* N_2
        A(iv.a)

If *pada* is described as a noun in Ex. 32 the same result is reached, but the last two words are analysed thus:

        pada   itu
      N *n.phr.*   det.

228 *-kan:* here a 'benefactive' suffix.

229 *tentu:* described as a parenthetic Adjunct: see n. 245.

230 *lama* described as a verb: see n. 192.

§8. FURTHER EXAMPLES OF TRANSFORMATION

1. OF THE TYPE DESCRIBED ON P. 82(b) AS PARATACTIC SUB-ORDINATION WITHIN THE SAME INTONATION CONTOUR, POSSIBLE WITH A SMALL NUMBER OF ADJECTIVES. (Example: *pandai membacha*.)

1 (B.230)

'Dah	chanték	⌐*pandai*	pula	*menganyam.*
x(ii)	Hv.(adj.)	Hv.(adj.)		Hv.(A.I)
P		P_1		P_2
Cl_1		(c)		Cl_2

Beautiful to look at, and good at weaving too!

NOTE: Clause 2 has for predicate a verb sequence of two Head-verbs resulting from the absorbtion, by transformation, of a subordinate verbal clause.

2 (A.86)

'Tapi	ia^{231}	$tidak^{231}$	pun,	saya	*ta'*	*suka*	juga	*'nak*	*berjumpa*	hantu
	Hv.	Hv.		Pr.	x(ii)	Hv.(A.II.1a)		x(ii)	Hv.(A.II.2)	N
	P	P		S		P_1			P_2	C
|c|	Cl_1	(c) Cl_2		S		Cl_3				

But, either way, I'm just not anxious to run into a ghost.

Pattern: $|c| \{(s) (Cl_1 (c) Cl_2) Cl_3\}$.

I.e.: this compound sentence is linked by a non-initiating co-ordinating connective (*'Tapi*) to a previous situation. The main clause (Cl_3) is preceded, without subordinating particle, by two subordinate clauses (Cl_1 and Cl_2) which are paratactically co-ordinate the one with the other.

---

231 *ia, tidak:* each taken as a minor-type clause. See p. 72.

3   (A.55)

Kawan	kok	dapat	*suka*	benar	*'nak*	*menambah-nambah*	jalan	duit	sadikit.
N	Hv.	Hv.	part.3	x(ii)		Hv.(A.1)		*n.grp.*	N

$$N_1 \quad n.grp. \quad N_2$$
$$N$$

S..			P	..P_1			..P_2		C
Cl_2..	s		Cl_1				..Cl_2		

I should be delighted to make a bit of extra money if there's any chance of it.

Pattern: s Cl_1 Cl_2.

NOTE: The main clause (Cl_2) is discontinuous because the subject is brought to initial position for the sake of emphasis, with the result that the subordinate clause is intrusive.

Further examples of 'subjunctive transformation without particle':

4   (A.128)

Kami semua *léka berchakap, ta' ingat*[232] *'nak bayar.*

We were all so busy talking that we forgot about paying the bill.

Pattern: Cl_1 (c) Cl_2 or, perhaps,   (s) Cl_1 Cl_2.

5   (A.239)

Saléh maséh terdiri dekat pintu, [dia] *takut hendak turun.*

Saleh is still standing near the door. He is afraid to go outside.

Pattern: Cl_1 (c) Cl_2.

NOTE: It is not possible to take the second clause as subordinate without particle because of its position. See p. 103.

6   (B.727)

Bukan[233] patek *susah-susah menchari.*

It wasn't that I had to go to the trouble of looking for it.

---

232 *ingat* taken as a verb of Class A.II.1a, 'be mindful': it accepts the suffixes *-i* and *-kan* to become transitive.

233 *Bukan:* the translation given implies that *Bukan* is to be taken as the exponent of P (i.e. Hv.A.II.3c) with *paték susah2 menchari* as S (included clause). Cf. A.290 in n. 113. If the description of *bukan* as a non-numeral quantifier is retained the whole utterance is a nominal minor-type sentence to be analysed as a noun phrase:

Bukan	paték	susah2	menchari
NNQ		*incl.cl.*	
M(ii)		*n.phr.*	H

7 (A.57)

Di-mana-lah 'nak kawan chabutkan duit, kok ta' *kerékéh menchari?*[234]

Where am I to get hold of the money, if I don't keep my eyes open for any chance that comes along?

Pattern: Cl_1 s Cl_2.

8 (A.584)

Geli benar *hati*[235] saya *menéngok*-nya.

I chuckled at the sight of it.

9 (A.341)

Musa terkemamar, mata-nya terbeliak, mulut-nya *ternganga*[236] *memandang* mayat itu.

Musa is dumbfounded, his eyes start out of his head, his mouth drops open as he gazes at the corpse.

Pattern: Cl_1 (c) Cl_2 (c) Cl_3.

10 (B.534)

Kawan pun *pandai* juga *membuat* kuéh.

I can make cakes, too.

2. OF THE TYPE DESCRIBED ON P. 81(c) AS 'PARATACTIC CO-ORDINATION WITHIN THE SAME INTONATION CONTOUR'. (Example: *berlari mengambil*.)

1 (A.381)

Saleh...*berlari*...*mengikut* Musa...
  S P_1 P_2 C

Saleh runs after Musa.

2 (A.44)

Itu-lah 'bang 'Lah dua laki bini *'nak pergi menolong* dia.
          S P_1 P_2 C
                          incl.cl.
S   P

That's why 'bang Lah and his wife are going to help him.

---

234 *kok ta' kerékéh menchari:* such a subordinate clause, lacking its subject (*kawan*), is itself described as a 'subjunctive transformation' on p. 81.2(*a*), but in the analyses the subject has usually been inserted in square brackets.

235 *geli...hati:* taken to be a compound word. See n. 86.

236 *ternganga:* the *ter*- derivative is taken to be adjectival.

3   (A.236)

Saléh	bangkit[237]	[dia]	pergi[237]	'nak	[mem]bakar	batu.
S	P	[S]	P_1		P_2	C

| Cl_1 | | (c) | | Cl_2 | |

Saleh gets up, and goes off to heat a stone.

4   (A.18)

Kawan	singgah	[men]chari...
S	P_1	P_2

I called in to look for you...

5   (A.214)

Saléh	baring	balék
S	P_1	P_2

Saleh lies down again.

6   (A.391)

Musa	menerja	masok...
S	P_1	P_2

Musa bursts into the room...

7   (D.3)

..dan	semua-nya	berjalan	mengharong	sawah	dengan	rioh-rendah-nya..
						prep.phr.iii
c	S	P_1	P_2	C		A(ii)

..and they all went wading across the rice-fields with uproarious merriment..

237 In most contexts *bangkit pergi* would itself be 'paratactic co-ordination within the same intonation contour', but in this example there
is likely to be a pause after *bangkit*, indicating a new clause, not a
transformation resulting from the fusion of two underlying clauses,
i.e. the co-ordinative parataxis is *not* 'within the same intonation
contour'. Cf. B.654: *Salmah berdiri mengélak*. ('Salmah stands up,
and slips away from him'.) Contrast with these the verb-sequence
in B.758: *Chuba Bendahara pergi téngok*. ('You go and have a look,
will you, Bendahara') which is to be analysed as three paratactic
imperative clauses. So also with the verb sequences in A.235:
Saléh pergi hidupkan api. ('You go and blow the fire up, Saleh')
and A.389: *Buka-lah pintu lekas!* ('Open the door! Be quick!').

238 *sambil..sambil:* it is difficult to offer any suggestion which would
present the two words as correlatives, performing the same function.
For the first occurrence it is possible to accept *berjalan itu* as a noun

8 (D.3)

..sambil[238] berjalan itu sambil[238] [dia]*ber-sengkéta melechutkan* batang keladi..
  H *n.phr.* D

dir.iii *prep.phr.iii* NP

A(ii)	A(iii)	[S]	P$_1$	P$_2$		C

..and as they went, they let fly their *keladi* spikes at each other..

3. OF THE TYPE RESULTING IN A DUAL PREDICATE CONSISTING OF A PREPOSITIONAL PHRASE BEGINNING WITH *ka-*, *di-*, *dari*, ACCOMPANYING A VERB.[239] (Example: *datang ka-Kuala Lumpur*.)

1 (A.381)

Saléh *keluar dari bawah rumah* berlari pula *mengikut* Musa *dari belakang.*
             prep.phr.i(b)   *prep.phr.i(b)*

S	P$_1$	P$_2$		P$_1$	A(iii)	P$_2$	C	P
	Cl$_1$		(c)			Cl$_2$		

Saleh comes out from under the house and runs after Musa.

---

phrase (n. 26(i)), with *sambil* as prep.(a)iii, the equivalent of *dengan*. Cf. B.113: *sambil mengerutkan muka serta menunjokkan misai Bendahara yang merundok ka-bawah itu.* 'screwing up her face and showing how the Bendahara's moustache sweeps downward'. Here the two *me-* verb-forms may be taken as H in noun phrase structure. See n. 43, ref. *untok.* See also n. 304.

The result would be the same if *dia* were inserted to provide a subject element for an included clause (as H for the noun phrase).

For the second occurrence the simplest solution is to assign *sambil* as adjunctival particle, i.e. A(iii) in clause structure; *ber-sengkéta* is to be described as a predicating prep. phrase (*sengkéta* or *singkéta*—a contest). So, too, for A.52: *'Bang Musa ber-kira 'nak pergi-kah?* 'Are you thinking of going, Musa?', and A.31: ..*dia sudah ber-janji 'nak pergi..* 'He has promised to go..', and perhaps also for A.102: *Saya ta' [ber-]kuasa 'nak bergadoh.* 'I can't bear arguing'. These are all transformational double predicates.

For *sambil* taken as a co-ordinating connective see n. 139 and p. 130 Ex. 3.

239 See p. 80.

9

2   (A.18)

Kawan   singgah   [*men*]*chari*   *ka-rumah*   *awak*   tadi.

                            $\overline{\text{prep.phr.}i(b)}$

S   P$_1$ P$_2$ P$_3$ A(iv.a)

I called at your house looking for you just now.

3   (B.165)

Salmah   *dudok*[240]   *di-atas   lantai*   sambil   [*dia*]   menganyam   tikar.

                    $\overline{\text{prep.phr.}i(b)}$

   S   P$_1$ P$_2$ [S]   P   C

   $\overline{\qquad\quad\text{Cl}_1\qquad\quad}$ c $\overline{\text{Cl}_2}$

Salmah is sitting on the floor and weaving a mat.

4. TRANSFORMATION OF THE TYPE RESULTING IN COMPOSITE CLAUSE ELEMENTS. (Example: *membacha buku serta mengisap paip.*[241])

1   (A.247)

Musa   dan   Saléh   selimutkan   mayat   Kasim...
S$_1$ c   S$_2$ P   C

Musa and Saleh cover up Kasim's corpse...

2   (A.391)

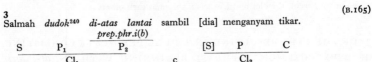

Musa bursts into the room, dithering with fright.

3   (A.65)

Hendak   ta',   pergi?

Do you intend going, or not?

The underlying sentences are: (*a*) Hendak pergi? (*b*) Ta' hendak pergi?

---

240 In a context which required rising intonation on *dudok*, followed by a pause, *Salmah dudok* would be an included clause, exponent of S, with *di-atas lantai* as sole exponent of P.

241 See p. 81.

242 *dengan:* taken as a preposition. In the context, this is an easier solution than to take it as a connective, the equivalent of *dan*, as in n. 101.

A first transformation would be:

Hendak atau ta' hendak pergi?
x(ii)   c   x(ii)   Hv.

In this, the composite element is the x element of the verb-phrase. The paratactic sentence of the Text is a further transformation in which the co-ordinating connective is deleted, and the second x element is reduced to its negative prefix:

Hendak ta', pergi?
x(ii)   x(ii) Hv.

4   (B.227)

Apa fikir Dato' tikar yang saya anyam 'ni, élok ta'?

What do you think of this mat that I am weaving, Dato'? Do you like it?

If this example is regarded as one utterance the analysis presents difficulties.

The first three words, *Apa fikir Dato'*, must be analysed as a nominal clause, since to analyse them as a verbal clause would result in the unacceptable structure *CPS. See n. 75. In the nominal clause *Apa* is S, with the noun group *fikir Dato'* as P.[243] This analysis implies a

---

243 But Asmah Haji Omar (*Dewan Bahasa*, April 1964, p. 161) considers the sentence *Apa makan dia?* to be ordered *Pelengkap—Perbuatan—Pelaku* (i.e. CPS), though admitting that it is 'somewhat jarring on the ear' (*agak janggal*). It, and the frequently occurring *Apa kata dia?* are taken to be transformations of the kernel-type sentences (*kalimat inti*): *Dia makan apa? Dia kata apa?*

Moreover, it is difficult to apply the solution given above to such a sentence as B.540: *Apa fikir Che' Mah detar baharu yang kawan pakai 'ni?* ('What do you think of this new turban that I'm wearing?') The pendent question, in this case, occurs two sentences later, B.542: *Sajak rupa-nya kawan pakai, bukan?* ('I look smart in it, don't I?').

If B.540 is to be analysed as in Ex. 4 above, then *detar...'ni?* must be taken as a fragment (S) requiring, say, *élok* (as P) for its completion, but the intonation, falling to sentence-final, does not suggest this. The same may be said of sentence B.785: *Apa fikir*

sentence-final intonation for *Dato'*, followed by a new sentence opening with *tikar:*

Tikar	yang	saya	anyam	'ni,	*élok*	*ta'*?
N		Yg(a)		det.	Hv.	x(ii)

S P_1 P_2

(Is this mat which I am weaving beautiful, or is it not?)

The double transformation, resulting in a composite predicate element, is the same as for Example 3 above.

Examples 3 and 4 above are exactly parallel with the quoted example, except that the paratactic arrangement indicates that a double transformation has taken place.

Examples 5 to 12 below, on the other hand, are of a somewhat different type.

The occurrence of successive predicate elements, each able to be attached independently to the shared subject, justifies their inclusion under the heading 'transformation'. But the 'echo' intonation of such predicates, each falling to sentence-final tone, indicates that they are not co-acting co-ordinates (as in *Musa dan Saléh*) nor mutually exclusive co-ordinates (as in *élok [atau] ta'?*), but corroborative alternatives, between which no connective particle is appropriate. By this they can be distinguished from such a sentences as Ex. 1 on p. 99,

---

Temenggong musang 'tu? ('What do you think of the civet-cat, Temenggong?').

A possible solution would be to take *musang 'tu*, and the corresponding word groups in the other examples, as 'T', in this case in post-position. See n. 161.

244 Contrast also such a sentence as B.619, where parataxis occurs between two independent clauses, each with its own complete sentence-tune.

Orang tua ita	mengukor	bukan main	chepat,	macham	'nak patah	kukoran	itu.
S *incl.cl.* P				P	*incl.cl.*		S

N   N

S   A(iii)   P   S   P

Cl_1 (c) Cl_2

The old lady is shredding her coconut at a furious rate; it seems as if the rasper will surely snap off.

where the paratactic arrangement is between co-ordinate simple sentences which are dramatically juxtaposed:[244]

5   (B.12)

Harus	entah[245]	[kita]	langsong	bercherai,	ta'	berjumpa	lagi.
Hv.A.II.1a				Hv.(A.II.2a)	x(ii)	Hv.A.II.2a	
		[S]	A(iii)	P_1		P_2	A(iii)

incl.cl.

P	A(v.b)			S

Perhaps, who knows, we may have to part forever, never meet again.

6   (A.327)

Dia	kata	dia	ta'	takut,	ta'	perchayakan	hantu!
		S		P_1		P_2	C

incl.cl.

S	P		C

He says he isn't afraid, doesn't believe in ghosts!

7   (A.493)

Kawan	péngsan	ta'	sedarkan	diri.
S	P_1		P_2	

I fainted, passed right out.

8   (B.40)

Yg aku tahu	pagi 'ni juga	[aku]	di-suroh-nya	pergi[246]	[aku]	ta'	boléh	léngah	lagi.
Yg(a)									
	A(iv.a) A(iii)	[C_2]	P	C_1	S	[S]		P	A(iii)

incl.cl.(1)   incl.cl.(2)

N		N		N
S		P_1		P_2

All I know is that I've been told to get away this very morning, that I can't hang about any longer.

---

245 *entah:* taken as parenthetic because of potential pause before and after. See n. 125. This description is convenient when a word such as *entah, mémang, tentu* is embedded in a sentence as a speaker's comment, comparable with the *agak-nya* type of comment which is labelled A(v.a) in the Conspectus. But there are many sentences in which such a word is the sole predicate, e.g. B.751: *Entah-lah, Tuanku.* 'I really don't know, Your Highness.' (lit. 'It is a matter of uncertainty.')

246 *[aku] di-suroh-nya pergi:* the suggested analysis treats *suroh* as a two-complement verb, assuming the non-passive analysis to be

Dia	suroh	aku	pergi.
S	P	C_2	C_1

9   (B.148)

Kemudian kalau dia berjumpa *abang ada di-rumah lagi, belum juga pergi,* masok angin-lah kita![247]

Then, if they find you still here, not yet gone, the game will be up.

Further possible examples of echo-intonation are:

10   (B.859)

Jangan	sampai	*pechah,*	*tahu*	*orang*	*semua.*[248]
Hv.	Hv.	verb-noun		*incl.cl.*	
	P	S_1		S_2	
		incl.cl.			
P			C		

The story mustn't be allowed to leak out, with everybody getting to know about it. (lit. Let it not be that breaking-out (of the news) comes to pass, that everybody-knowing comes to pass.)

A similar analysis might be offered for:

(B.175)

Dia..	di-suroh	Tuanku	menchari	musang	berjanggut!
				n.grp.	
C_2	P	C_1		S	

The Raja has told him to go and find a bearded civet-cat!

But a similar analysis for B.48 would necessitate taking a directive prep. phrase as a noun-equivalent, a contingency which is not provided for in the framework:

Dia	bukan	'nak	menyuroh	aku	ka-mana-mana	tempat	yg	tentu.
						prep.phr.(i)		
S		P		C_2		C_1		

He isn't ordering me to any particular place.

A way out of this difficulty would be to take *aku...tentu* as an example of the 'pivot-noun phrase' suggested in §9.

247 For the analysis of the echo-complements of the subordinate clause in this example see p. 142 Ex. 12. The predicate of the main clause (*masok angin*) is taken to be a compound word.

248 *tahu orang semua:* the translation of the clause indicates that *semua* is to be described as an adjective (structure: P S). It is not possible to take it as a noun ('and that people should know everything') because this meaning would give the order of elements as *PSC, a structure which is not found. See n. 76.

11 (A.546)

Kedua meréka *kelu, ta' dapat berchakap apa-apa.*

The pair of them are struck dumb, they can't get a word out.

12 (A.470)

Habis,[249] apa pasal *Che' Léh pula ikut datang sama, di-tinggalkan bang Chim di-hutan?*

Hv.	incl.cl.		incl.cl.	
P	S		P_1	P_2
(s) Cl_1		Cl_2		

Well? Why did you have to come too? and 'bang Chim left all alone in the jungle!

A few further examples will serve to show that in the analyses the term 'transformation' has been extended to cover any sequence of two or more predicating verbals, when that sequence can be resolved in such a way that each verb-phrase or verb-equivalent in it can be attached separately to the exponent of S in the clause. See Example 1 below.

It is sometimes difficult to decide whether such sequences can be described as 'within the same intonation contour' or are to be collated with such sentences as Example 1 on page 99, where the paratactic arrangement is between independent clauses and is merely a stylistic device.

A more delicate analysis would seek to indicate specific relationship between transformational elements, e.g. in Example 1 the prepositional phrase, when resolved, is easily seen to be attachable directly to the common S element, whereas in Example 2 the prepositional phrase has an immediate relationship with the second P element *arah*. Even before 'resolution' it is clear that $P_1 P_2 P_3$ in Example 2 on p. 140 are successively linked.[250]

---

249 *Habis:* taken as a subordinate clause without particle, 'Since that was the resultant position'.

250 Relationships which could be indicated by over-bracing, e.g.:

sudah berjanji	'nak pergi	menolong mentua-nya menuai.
P_1	P_2	P_3

By definition (see pp. 125 and 127), the first link is subordinative and the second link co-ordinative.

Nevertheless, as an interim tool, enabling the student to use a reasonably consistent (if not linguistically perfect) formula for the description of this very common type of Malay sentence, the technique of presuming 'transformation' is likely to prove helpful. Further research will no doubt indicate desirable adjustments in the application of the technique.

Examples showing multiple sentence-elements resulting from 'Transformation'.

1   (A.206)

Orang	bertiga	itu	tidor[251]	dekat-dekat	melintang	di-tengah-tengah	bilék.
n.phr.			Hv.(A.II.3)	Hv.(A.II.1a)	Hv.(A.II.3b)	N_1	*n.grp.* N_2
S	*incl.cl.*	P				dir.i	*prep.phr.i(b)* NP
	S			P_1	P_2		P_3

The three men are sleeping side by side, across the middle of the room.

The pre-transformation clauses would be:

(*a*) [Dia][252] dekat-dekat.   They are close together.

(*b*) [Dia] melintang.   They are lying transversely across the stage.

(*c*) [Dia] di-tengah2 bilék.   They are in the middle of the room.

2   (A.283)

Musa	pun	dudok[253]	jauh	sadikit	[meng]arah	ka-kanan	mayat	itu.
N		Hv.	Hv.(A.II.1a)	N	Hv.(A.II.3b)		N	+ det.
S	*incl.cl.*	P				N_1	*n.grp.*	N_2
	N					dir.i	*prep.phr.i(b)*	NP
	S		P_1	A(iv.b)	P_2		P_3	

Musa is sitting a little further away, on the right of the corpse.

---

251 *tidor:* assigned as Vb.A.II.3, but it would be possible to take it as Vb.A.II.1a (i.e. adjective) 'be asleep'. Cf. n. 144.

252 *Dia:* the pronoun is substituted for the included clause (as S) for the sake of brevity. If the process of de-transforming were continued the included clause itself would be 'resolved'. For examples of complete resolution see Asmah Haji Omar, *Dewan Bahasa*, March/April 1964.

253 See n. 240.

3   (B.629)

Dia	*chuba*	*hendak*	*mengechilkan*[254]	badan-nya.
Pr.	Hv.(A.I)		x(ii) Hv.(B.I)	N
S	P_1		P_2	C

He tries to make himself small.

4   (A.215)

Kasim	mengerang	*bertambah*[255]	*kuat*	lagi.
	Hv.(A.II.3)	Hv.(A.II.2)	Hv.(A.II.1a)	
S *incl.cl.* P				
S		P_1	P_2	A(iii)

Kasim's groans get louder and louder.

5   (A.121)

Kalau	bagitu[256]	baik	kita	*pulang*	*lekas*	sekarang	*bersiap.*
			S	P_1	P_2	A(i)	P_3
					incl.cl.		
	P	P			S		
s	Cl_1			Cl_2			

In that case we had better go home at once now and get ready.

6   (A.380)

Musa	terpekék	besar	lalu	[dia]	*bangun*	*lari*	*meluru*	*keluar*
S	P	A(iii)		[S]	P_1	P_2	P_1	P_2
	Cl_1		c		Cl_2		(c)	Cl_3

terus	*menuju*	jalan	ka-kampong.
P_1	P_2		C
(c)		Cl_3	

Musa gives a wild shriek, then stands up and rushes out, heading straight for the village.
(lit. gets up and runs off, rushes forward and goes out, goes straight on and heads for
the road to the village.)

---

254 A passive version of such a sentence, however, presents a difficulty,
e.g. B.497: *Di-chuba-nya hendak memelok pinggang Salmah.* ('He
tries to put his arm round Salmah's waist.') Here it is not possible
to find a common subject-element for the two predicate elements.
This perhaps indicates that Ex. 3 should not be described as a
transformation. The alternative is to take *hendak mengechilkan badan*
as C (a verb-noun complex). In the passive sentence the corresponding word-group would then be described as S.

255 *bertambah:* as Vb.A.II.2; or perhaps as prep. phrase (i): *ber-tambah.*

256 *bagitu:* taken as a nominal predicate. Cf. n. 118.

7   (B.445)

Mata-nya *memandang-mandang* *sérong* *ka-pintu.*[257]
　　S　　　　　P₁　　　　　　　P₂　　　　P₃

She keeps giving side-long glances towards the door.

---

257 *ka-pintu* described as P_3: see n. 137 *ad fin*. But there is no question, here, of the prep. phrase being Q in a noun phrase.

An alternative analysis, taking *Mata-nya memandang* as included clause (as in Ex. 2), would give S P_1 P_2. Similarly, in Clause 1 of Ex. 6, the first clause could be analysed with *Musa terpekék* as S, and *besar* as P.

§9. A PIVOT-NOUN PHRASE?

In the thesis (762) a noun-group complement is indicated for the following sentence:

Dia melihat Ahmad menchangkul sawah.[258]

                  n.grp.

S   P   C

He sees Ahmad hoeing the rice-field.

The same decision has been made, with some hesitation, in one or two analyses of sentences from the Texts, e.g.:

---

258 The construction is perhaps to be compared with Chomsky's 'noun-phrase object' (p. 82) in sentence A: 'John found the boy studying in the library', to be contrasted with sentence B: 'John knew the boy studying in the library'. It is 'intuitively obvious', it is stated, that the two sentences have different grammatical structure as can be seen, for instance, by trying to add to sentence B the words 'not running about the street'. A linguistic proof of the difference in immediate constituency is adduced from the fact that sentence A is a transformation of the underlying 'string' 'John—found studying in the library—the boy' whereas sentence B is not a transformation of a similar string.

In the same way, sentence A.317 could be re-ordered:

          ...*ajak pergi bersama—Musa*

whereas such a re-ordering is not possible for sentence A.327:

Dia kata dia ta' takut..

            S *incl.cl.* P

S   P   C

(a) Ex. 10, p. 112:

Baik   aku   balék   ajak   'bang   Musa   pergi   bersama.

                                n.grp.?

    S P_1 P_2 C

              incl.cl.

P   S

I had better go back and ask 'bang Musa to go with me.

(b) Ex. 3, p. 59:

..apabila   terpandang   mata   Salim   mengerling   dia..

                               n.grp.?

  s   P   S

..when she catches sight of Salim giving her a sidelong look..

In Ex. (a): *'bang Musa* is at once the complement of *ajak* and at the same time the Head-noun of the 'noun-group'; and the second 'noun' is a predicating verb-form.

In Ex. (b): *mata Salim* is at once the subject of *terpandang* and the Head-noun of the 'noun-group'; and the second 'noun' is a predicating verb-form.

SOME FURTHER EXAMPLES FOR CONSIDERATION:

1   (A.419)

Tolong   aku   menahankan   dia..

               n.grp.?   *phr.?*

   P   C

Help me keep him back!

2   (A.31)

'Tapi   sayang   dia   sudah   berjanji   'nak   pergi   menolong   mentua-nya   menuai.

                                                    n.grp.?   *phr.?*

  c   A(v.b)   S P_1 P_2 P_3 C

But unfortunately he has promised to go and help his father-in-law get his rice harvested.

3   (A.30)

Kata-nya   dia   teringat   'nak   'ngajak   saya   pergi   barang   dua   tiga   hari

                                           n.grp.?   *phr.?*..   ⟶

                                              C..

                                         mengambil   rotan   itu.

                                           ..*n.grp.?*   *phr.?*

   A(v.b)   S P_1 P_2 ⟶   ..C

He says it occurred to him that he might ask me to go with him for a few days to collect the rattan.

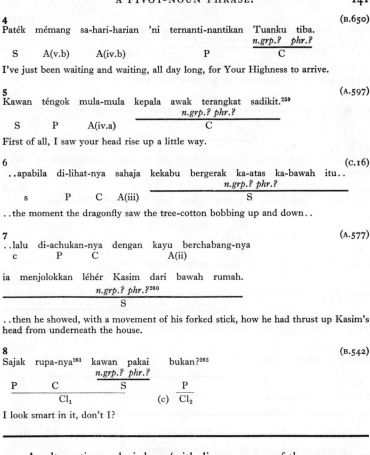

4   (B.650)
Paték mémang sa-hari-harian 'ni ternanti-nantikan Tuanku tiba.
                                                n.grp.?   phr.?
S   A(v.b)   A(iv.b)   P   C
I've just been waiting and waiting, all day long, for Your Highness to arrive.

5   (A.597)
Kawan téngok mula-mula kepala awak terangkat sadikit.[259]
                            n.grp.?   phr.?
S   P   A(iv.a)   C
First of all, I saw your head rise up a little way.

6   (C.16)
..apabila di-lihat-nya sahaja kekabu bergerak ka-atas ka-bawah itu..
                            n.grp.?   phr.?
s   P   C   A(iii)   S
..the moment the dragonfly saw the tree-cotton bobbing up and down..

7   (A.577)
..lalu di-achukan-nya dengan kayu berchabang-nya
  c   P   C   A(ii)

ia menjolokkan léhér Kasim dari bawah rumah.
                n.grp.?   phr.?[260]
                        S
..then he showed, with a movement of his forked stick, how he had thrust up Kasim's
head from underneath the house.

8   (B.542)
Sajak rupa-nya[261] kawan pakai   bukan?[262]
                n.grp.?   phr.?
P   C   S   P
          Cl₁   (c)   Cl₂
I look smart in it, don't I?

---

259 An alternative analysis here (with disappearance of the noun-group
     or -phrase) might be:

      Kawan téngok mula2 kepala awak terangkat sadikit.
      A(v.b)   A(iv.a)   S   P   A(iv.b)
      First of all, your head rose up a little way, so it appeared to me.

260 Or included clause? See p. 144.

261 *rupa-nya:* taken as C, as for *berani-nya* in n. 10(a). But the result

9   (B.712)

Nanti   aku   bawa   dia   mengadap   ka-istana   ésok.
                               n.grp.? phr.?

 P   S   P   C   A(iv.a)
Cl_1 (c) Cl_2

I'll take him to pay his respects at the palace tomorrow.

10   (B.74)

[Aku]   Benchi   menéngok   kelakuan-nya   mengada2   kebesar2an   ta'[ber]ketahuan   arah.
                                N   Vb.(A.II)   Vb.(B.II.i)   Vb.(B.II.ix)
                                                          n.grp.?   phr.?

[S] P_1 P_2 C

I hate to see the way he carries on, showing off, and boasting, with no sense of what is fit
and proper.

11   (B.92)

Mah   minta   jangan-lah   ada   orang   lain   lagi   hendakkan   Mah   juga.
                                               n.grp.?   phr.?[263]

                          P   *incl.cl.(1)*   S
                    P   *incl.cl.(2)*   C
S   P   C

I was only praying that there wasn't anybody else after me!

12   (B.148)

Kemudian   kalau   dia   berjumpa   abang   ada   di-rumah   lagi,   [abang]   belum   juga   pergi..
                                    n.grp.?   phr.?   *n.grp.?   phr.?*

A(iv.a)   s   S   P C_1 C_2

Then, if they find you still at home, not yet gone..

13   (B.491)

Aléh-aléh   kawan   nampak   Che'   Mah   menjengok   keluar   dari   tingkap.
                                           n.grp.?   phr.?

A(iv.a)   S   P   C

Suddenly, I caught sight of you looking out of the window.

---

is the 'rare' structure PCS (p. 45). See also p. 144. The alternative is to take it as N of a noun-group:

Sajak   rupa-nya   kawan   pakai
                   S *incl.cl.* P
        N   *n.grp.*   N
P   S

Cf. n. 207.

262 *bukan?*: as a separate clause: see n. 210.

263 Or included clause? See p. 144, but see also n. 271.

14 (B.471)

Kadhi dudok terkelip-kelip menanti[kan] Salmah belum juga sudah-sudah.

				n.grp.? phr.?
S	P₁	P₂	P₃	C

The kadhi sits there blinking, waiting for Salmah who is still not *quite* through (with her cake-making).

15 (B.827)

Tolong-lah bawa balék[264] tawanan awak 'ni pulang.

P		P₁	P₂	*n.grp.? phr.?*
Cl₁	(c)			C
				Cl₂

Will you please take this captive of yours back home with you.

In the above examples there seem to be two common factors:

(i) The first member of the 'noun-group' is a noun (or pronoun) which has dual function. It operates twice. It is a pivot.

(ii) The second member of the 'noun-group' is a predicating verb, often accompanied by a complement. The first member of the group is the notional subject of this verb.

When the 'noun-group' is the exponent of C in clause structure there is the possibility of re-ordering the sentence in such a way that the main P element and this second member of the 'noun-group' are brought together under one intonation contour, with the first member of the 'noun-group' following them in terminal position.

e.g. Ex. 1: Tolong menahankan dia—aku.

Ex. 9: ..bawa mengadap—dia.

---

264 *bawa balék* taken as dual predicate elements by transformation 'within the same intonation contour' (p. 81 *berlari mengambil*). If this description is correct it applies also to:

(a) Bawa pergi méja ini. Take this table away.

P₁	P₂	C

but: (b) Pergi bawa méja kechil itu. Go and get the small table.

P	P	C
Cl₁	(c)	Cl₂

and (as in Ex. 15): (c) Bawa budak ini pulang. Take this child home.

	n.phr.
P	C

This rearrangement, however, is less convincing when the 'noun-group' is exponent of S

e.g. Ex. 8: Kawan—sajak pakai.

   Ex. 7: Ia—di-achukan menjolokkan léhér Kasim..

   Ex. 11: orang lain lagi—ada hendakkan Mah.

This is a possible sentence, but with changed meaning, i.e. it is a different sentence.

   Ex. 6: kekabu—di-lihat-nya bergerak ka-atas..

Here the determinant *itu* is lost, and the sentence is therefore not the same sentence. This indicates, perhaps, that in Ex. 6 *kekabu bergerak itu* is a noun-phrase in which the second member is a verb-form used as an epithet, not as a predicate: 'saw the bobbing tree-cotton' not 'saw the tree-cotton bobbing'.

It will perhaps be advisable then to regard this 'pivot-noun' construction as restricted to examples in which the noun-group or phrase is operating as C in clause structure.

This leaves the relevant expression in Example 6 to be described simply as a noun-phrase with a verb-form as Q (as in Ex. 30 on p. 122), and those in Exx. 7, 8, and 11 as included clauses.[265]

It is the dual function of the opening member of the group that distinguishes it from an included clause.

In the quoted example on p. 139, the second member of the group (*menchangkul*) is described as a noun, Head of the 'second noun-group' *menchangkul sawah*. In these contexts this is a difficult conception. Moreover, it does not suggest the 'hinge' function of the first noun.

If further research establishes this construction as being grammatically distinguishable from an included clause in similar sentence position, it will be more helpful to describe it as a noun-phrase of fixed composition (H being always a pivot-noun, and Q a predicating verb-form or a predicating prepositional phrase), operating as C in clause structure.

In the sentences analysed in §10 the construction is described as 'pivot-noun phrase'.

---

265 But see n. 271.

§10. SHORT ANALYSES OF CONSECUTIVE SENTENCES FROM THE TEXTS, WITH TABULATED RESULTS

Ten sentences from Text A (nos. 497–506) Exx. 1–10, pp. 145–154.
Ten sentences from Text B (nos. 269–278) Exx. 11–20, pp. 154–161.
Five sentences from Text C (nos. 3–7) Exx. 21–25, pp. 161–170.
Five sentences from Text D (nos. 1–5) Exx. 26–30, pp. 171–180.

SENTENCES 1–10 (FROM TEXT A, NOS. 497–506)

Example 1

Itu	pun[266]	baik	juga	awak	terpikir[267]	meninggalkan[268]	kawan	makanan	awak
				S	P_1	P_2	C_2		C_1
						incl.cl.			

P		P	A(iii)			S			
(s) Cl_1				Cl_2					

All the same, it was a good thing you thought of leaving me your food.

---

266 *itu pun* taken as a minor-type (nominal) sentence. This decision is based on remembered intonation—level tones for *itu*, with the up-down final tone on *pun*. With a different intonation pattern—rising tones on *itu* and level, non-final tone on *pun*—it would be a preliminary subject, with the meaning 'But that was a good idea of yours, to leave me your food'. For an interesting set of pitch-contour variations played on *itu/ini* see Asmah Haji Omar, *Dewan Bahasa* (Dec. 1962).

267 *terpikir*: see note on *terlompat* in n. 224. Here, too, it is difficult to avoid accepting *terpikir* as verbal but non-passive. To describe it as passive it would be necessary to describe *awak* as C in pre-predicate position without *oléh*, and *meninggalkan...awak* as S.

268 *meninggalkan*: it is possible that the suffix here represents a fusion

TABULATION

Length: 8 full-words + 2 particles.

The particles: *pun*   postposition
               juga adjunctive

Type of sentence: Compound.

Clause pattern: (s) Cl_1 Cl_2

Clause descriptions:

Clause 1 (subordinate)

Nominal. Minor-type. Without subordinating particle.[269]
Elements: P (a deictic).

Clause 2 (main)

Verbal
Elements: P S.
   S is an included clause (verbal).
   Elements: S P_1 P_2 C_2 C_1.
   P_1 and P_2 are the result of transformation.
   C_1 and C_2 are the two complements of a benefactive verb-form.

---

of two separate suffixes: (*a*) -*kan* which turns the intransitive verb *tinggal* ('be left', 'remain') into the transitive verb *tinggalkan* ('cause to be left') , 'leave behind' and (*b*) the benefactive -*kan* which creates the two-complement verb *tinggalkan* 'leave something for somebody'.

269 'without subordinating particle': but it is difficult to suggest an appropriate particle to insert. Perhaps 'co-ordinate without particle' (i.e. Cl_1 (c) Cl_2) would be better a description, taking the minor-type sentence to be the equivalent of '*Sunggoh pun bagitu*. See n. 306.

Example 2

Bila[270] kawan tersedar itu kawan téngok bakul makanan ada dekat kawan.

N *incl.cl.* det. pivot-noun phrase

---- ---------- ---- ----------------------------

H Q(iii) D

n.phr.

A(iv.a) S P C

When I came to myself I saw the basket of food, there beside me. (lit. 'being-there'.)

TABULATION

Length: 11 full-words.

Type of sentence: Simple.

Clause description:

Verbal.

Elements: A S P C.

---

270 *Bila:* taken as a noun, an extension of its description as an interrogative nominal. It is the presence of the determinant *itu* that necessitates this assignment. Without it, *Bila kawan tersedar* would be a subordinate clause (s S P) and the sentence would be labelled 'compound' (s Cl_1 Cl_2). The fact that *bila* is a time-noun makes the solution offered just possible here. But if the 'subordinating connective' had been *sebab* it would not have been possible. The result in that case might be described as a noun-group:

Sebab kawan tersedar itu

S *incl.cl.* P

H *n.phr.* D

N_1 + N_2

----

but only if the rest of the sentence provided a predicate for this noun-group as S. Otherwise it might be described as a prep. phrase iii (operating as A(ii) in clause structure), with *sebab* described as directive iii, as in Example 26 on page 119. There is need for further investigation into the part played by *itu*, both as determinant and as deictic, in Malay syntax. For the licence taken in printing 'N' and 'included clause' (i.e. word category and structure) on the same line, see n. 103.

A is a noun-phrase.

Elements: H is a time-word; Q is an included clause.

C is a pivot-noun phrase.

Example 3

Kawan buka, [*kawan*] *téngok ada lagi sadikit nasi...tinggal di-dalam bakul 'tu.*

				S	incl.cl.[271]	P

			P	A(iii)		S

incl.cl.

S	P	[S]	P	C
Cl$_1$	(c)			Cl$_2$

I opened it and saw that there was still a little rice...left in the basket.

TABULATION

Length: 12 full-words + 4 particles (see full sentence A.499).

The particles: *lagi*   adjunctive;

sadikit   (as 1(c), by analogy with *banyak*) NNQ;

dengan   (as 1(b)ii) connective between co-ordinate nouns resulting from transformation. (See p. 60 Ex. 4);

di-   directive (i).

---

271 For this decision see p. 144. But it is possible that in such sentences the noun that comes between *ada* and the predicate of the so-called included clause is indeed a pivot-word, with the difference (compared with a pivot-noun which is Head of a C element) that its two functions are identical: the noun-group *sadikit nasi dengan lauk sambal udang* is operating as S to the verb *ada* and also as S to the verb *tinggal*. Cf. B.475: *Ada orang bunyi-nya berjalan di-luar 'tu* (*bunyi-nya* taken as A(v.a)). 'It sounds as if there's somebody walking about outside'.

These sentences seem at first sight to be comparable with the English ballad-type sentence 'There is a willow grows aslant a brook'. But in the English sentence the second predication is a close-knit form of the 'additive' relative clause 'which grows'

Type of sentence: Compound.

Clause pattern: Cl₁ (c) Cl₂.

Clause descriptions:

   Clause 1

   Verbal (paratactically co-ordinate with Cl₂).
   Elements: S P.

   Clause 2

   Verbal (paratactically co-ordinate with Cl₁).
   Elements: [S] P C.
   C is an included clause (verbal).
      Elements: P A S.
      S is an incl. clause[271] (verbal).
         Elements: S P.

Example 4

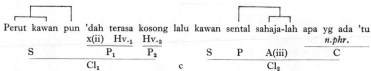

Perut kawan pun	'dah	terasa	kosong	lalu	kawan	sental	sahaja-lah	apa yg ada 'tu
		x(ii)	Hv.₁	Hv.₂				*n.phr.*
S		P₁	P₂		S	P	A(iii)	C
	Cl₁			c		Cl₂		

I was feeling empty by that time, and I just polished off the whole lot.

TABULATION

Length: 10 full-words + 5 particles.

   The particles: *pun*   postposition;
                   lalu (as 1.b.ii) co-ordinating connective (between
                           clauses);
                   sahaja adjunctive;
                   lah   postposition;
                   yang

___

meaning 'and it grows', i.e. the sentence is compound, whereas in
the Malay sentence, as here analysed, the second verb (*tinggal,*
berjalan) is part of a sentence-element in a simple sentence.

Type of sentence: Compound.

Clause pattern: Cl_1 c Cl_2.

Clause descriptions:

Clause 1

Verbal (co-ordinate with Cl_2).
Elements: S P_1 P_2 (by transformation).

Clause 2

Verbal (co-ordinate with Cl_1).
Elements: S P A C.
C is a noun-phrase.
    Elements: H D.
    H is a noun-group.
        Elements: N + Yg(b).

Example 5

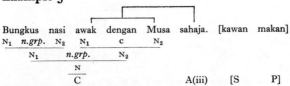

Bungkus	nasi	awak	dengan	Musa	sahaja.	[kawan	makan]
N_1	*n.grp.*	N_2	N_1	c	N_2		

N_1 *n.grp.* N_2

N

C   A(iii)   [S   P]

Only your package of rice, and Musa's.

TABULATION

Length: 4 full-words + 2 particles.

    The particles: *dengan*   (as 1.b.ii) connective between co-ordinate nouns, resulting from transformation.

                sahaja   adjunctive.

Type of sentence: A fragment.

    Elements: C A.

Example 6

Bungkus nasi kawan kawan champakkan sebab
    n.grp.

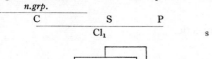

| C | S | P |

Cl_1 s

kawan ingat[272] makanan kawan 'tu-lah agak-nya yg menjadikan kawan sakit perut[273] tadi.
    n.phr.   Yg(b)

        N   N

A(v.b)   S   A(v.a)   P

            Cl_2

My own rice I threw away because, I thought, it was that perhaps that had given me the stomach pains.

TABULATION

Length: 16 full-words + 4 particles.

The particles: *sebab* (1(b)i) subordinating connective;
                 lah   postposition;
                 nya   nominalising;
                 yang

Type of sentence: Compound.

Clause pattern: Cl_1 s Cl_2.

Clause descriptions:

  Clause 1 (main).

  Verbal.

  Elements: C S P.

---

272 *kawan ingat:* it would be easy to take this as S P of the subordinate clause, with the nominal clause *makanan...tadi* as C, but the words were probably spoken on an even tone and the result, when they are taken as parenthetic, has a more idiomatic ring. Cf. n. 202.

273 *sakit perut:* to be taken as a compound word, probably adjectival in this context, with the result that *kawan sakit perut tadi* becomes a verbal incl.cl. as C of *menjadikan*.

Clause 2 (subordinate).

Nominal.

Elements: A(1) S A(2) P.

P is a *yang*-piece.

A(1) and A(2) are both parenthetic.

Example 7

Entah apa salah-nya makanan yang di-bekalkan dék Ché' Yam sa-malam?

				Yg(b)		
		N_1		*n.grp.*		N_2
	N_1		*n.grp.*		N_2	
	N			N		
A(v.b)	S			P		

Now what was wrong with that food that you put up for me yesterday, I wonder?

TABULATION

Length: 7 full-words + 3 particles.

The particles: *nya* nominalising;

    yang

    dék (as 1(a)ii) directive.

Type of sentence: Simple.

Clause description:

Nominal.

Elements: A S P.

P is a noun-group.

A is parenthetic.

Example 8

'Bang Chim champakkan?

   S P

You threw it away?

TABULATION

Length: 3 full-words.

Type of sentence: Simple.

Clause description:
Verbal.
Elements: S P.

Example 9

Alang-kah[274]   membuang-buang!
Hv.(A.II.1a)   N
‾‾‾‾‾‾‾‾‾   ‾‾‾
P   S

What a shocking waste! (*Lit.* Was the wastage a light matter?)

TABULATION

Length: 2 full-words + 1 particle.

The particle: *kah*   postposition.

Type of sentence: Simple.

Clause description:
Verbal.
Elements: P S.
S is a verb-form operating as a noun.

Example 10

Makanan   yang   bagitu[275]   bagus!   [awak   champakkan]
                      Yg(b)
                   ‾‾‾‾‾‾‾‾
  N   *n.grp.*   N
         ‾‾‾‾‾‾‾‾‾‾‾‾‾‾‾‾
              N
         ‾‾‾‾‾‾‾‾‾‾‾‾‾‾‾‾
             C   [S   P]

Good food like that! [you threw away].

---

274 *Alang-kah:* taken as a predicating Head-verb, 'being just-medium'.
    If it is taken as a crystal, operating as an adjunctival particle, then
    membuang-buang becomes a minor-type sentence consisting of a
    nominal predicate. For the *me-* form operating as a noun, cf. p. 115,
    Ex. 17, and p. 121, Ex. 29.

275 *bagitu:* the word has usually been described as a noun (see nn. 118
    and 140) but in this context it seems to be operating as an adjunc-
    tival particle. So also in sentence A.148: *Kawan ta' sangka sampai
    bagitu léchéh kerja-nya membuat pondok.* 'I didn't think that putting

TABULATION

Length: 2 full-words + 2 particles.

The particles: *yang*

bagitu   (as 3, comparable with *sangat*[275]) adjunctive,
forming with *bagus* an 'expanded verb phrase'
(see n. 31).

Type of sentence: A fragment.

Element: C, consisting of a noun-group.

SENTENCES 11–20 (FROM TEXT B, NOS. 269–78)

Example 11

Masok Temenggong berlénggang-lénggang menjinjing dua biji durian berikat tali.[276]

			num.	N_1 *n.grp.* N_2	*prep.phr.i.c*
			M(i)	H	Q(ii)
				n.phr.	
P_1	S	P_2	P_3	C	

The Temenggong enters, with an affected swaying gait, a couple of durians tied together dangling from his fingers.

up the hut would be such a long drawn out business', and sentence B.788: *'Dah 'tu, di-apakan-nya Temenggong sampai terlompat ka-belakang bagitu jauh?* 'Well then what did it do to you, to make you jump back so far?'

In sentence A.495: *Apa pasal-nya awak lari tinggalkan kawan bagitu?* 'What made you run off and leave me like that?' it is possible to take *bagitu* as a noun, described as a second (transformational) predicate element:

Apa pasal-nya	awak lari	tinggalkan kawan	bagitu
incl.cl.		*incl.cl.*	N
S		P_1	P_2

276 *berikat tali:* taken as a prep. phrase. This seems the simplest solution here, but see n. 145. In sentence D.7 the prep. + noun construction is more easily acceptable: *Batang keladi itu di-sedia-kan berikat-ikat.* 'The *keladi* stalks were made ready beforehand, in bundles.'

TABULATION

Length: 9 full-words.

Type of sentence: Simple (with multiple predicate element).

Description of clause:

Verbal.

Elements: P_1 S P_2 P_3 C.

P_1, P_2 and P_3 are co-ordinate by transformation, arranged paratactically.

C is a noun-phrase.

Elements: M H Q.

Q is a predicating prep. phrase.

Example 12

Ini	sadikit	hadiah	buat[277]	menyuka-nyukakan hati[278]	Salmah tinggal sa-orang.
dei.	NNQ	N	Hv.	Hv.	pivot-noun phrase
	M(ii) *n.phr.*	H			N
	N				
S	P_1	P_2		P_3	C

Here's a little present, to cheer you up now that you are left alone.

277 *buat:* see n. 43. If it is thought that *buat menyukakan hati* should be taken as parallel with *untok memberi salaam*, i.e. that *buat* should be described here as a preposition, the multiple predicate elements disappear and the pattern becomes S P A, thus:

...buat	menyukakan-hati	Salmah tinggal sa-orang
part.1.a.(iii)	verb-noun	pivot-noun phrase
	N_1	*n.grp.*	N_2
dir.iii	*prep.phr.iii*	NP
	A(ii)	

This analysis has the merit of avoiding the necessity of yoking together nominal and verbal elements as transformational predicates. It certainly seems the best solution for Example 25 below. A third possibility would be to retain *buat* as a verbal, with the noun-group *menyukakan hati...sa-orang* as complement.

278 *menyukakan hati:* taken as a compound word. Cf. *suka hati, sakit*

TABULATION

Length: 8 full-words + 1 particle.

The particle: *sadikit*   (as 1(c)) NNQ.

Type of sentence: Simple (with multiple predicate element).

Clause description:

Nominal/Verbal (by transformation. But see n. 277 for alternatives.)

Elements: S P_1 P_2 P_3 C.

P_1 is nominal.

P_2 and P_3 are verbal.

C is a pivot-noun phrase.

Example 13

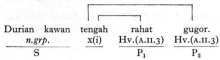

Durian kawan	tengah	rahat	gugor.
n.grp.	x(i)	Hv.(A.II.3)	Hv.(A.II.3)
S		P_1	P_2

My durians are all coming tumbling down.

TABULATION

Length: 5 full-words.

Type of sentence: Simple (with dual predicate element).

Clause description:

Verbal.

Elements: S P_1 P_2.

P_1 and P_2 are linked by co-ordinative transformation within the same intonation contour.

---

hati. If, on the other hand, *hati* is labelled C, then the pivot-noun phrase becomes N_2 in a noun-group, with *hati* as N_1. Contrast Example 15 below, where *Salim* is not a pivot-word as *Salmah* is in this example.

Example 14

Ini-lah	kawan	bawakan	dua biji,	kawan	pilehkan	durian	tembaga	yg	baik sa-kali.
dei.	S	P	C			*n.grp.*			Yg(b)

Ini-lah kawan bawakan dua biji, kawan pilehkan durian tembaga yg baik sa-kali.

dei.   S   P   C   *n.grp.*   Yg(b)

N   *incl.cl.* N_1 *n.grp.* N_2

               N   N

S   P   S   P   C

     Cl_1 (c) Cl_2

So I've brought you a couple. I picked out my very best golden durians.

TABULATION

Length: 11 full-words + 2 particles.

The particles: *lah*   postposition;
                yang

Type of sentence: Compound.[279]

Clause pattern: Cl_1 (c) Cl_2.

Clause descriptions:

   Clause 1

Nominal (paratactically[279] co-ordinate with Cl_2).
Elements: S P.
P is an included clause.
    Elements: S P C.

---

279 Cf. n. 244. But there is not, in this example, the same contextually close connection between the two co-ordinate clauses, and it might perhaps be better to ignore the comma and to analyse the utterance as two simple sentences.

On the other hand, if the author intended Clause 2 to echo the intonation of the included clause in Clause 1, Clause 2 should be assigned as P_2 (an included clause) and the whole utterance should then be described as a simple sentence. (See Exx. 5 and 6 on p. 133). But this does not seem likely.

Clause 2

Verbal (paratactically co-ordinate with Cl₁).

Elements: S P C.

C is a noun-group.

Example 15

Kawan	dengar	khabar	Salim	ta'	ada.
			S	*incl.cl.*	P
		N₁	*n.grp.*		N₂
S	P		C		

I hear that Salim is away.

TABULATION

Length: 6 full-words.

Type of sentence: Simple.

Clause description:

Verbal.

Elements: S P C.

C is a noun-group, N₁ + N₂.

N₂ is an included clause.

Example 16

Itu-lah	kawan	datang	menéngok	Salmah.
dei.	S	P₁	P₂	C
N			*incl.cl.*	
			N	
S			P	

That's why I have come to see you.

TABULATION

Length: 5 full-words + 1 particle.

The particle: *lah* postposition.

Type of sentence: Simple.

Clause description:

Nominal.

Elements: S P.

P is an included clause.

Elements: S P_1 P_2 C.

P_1 and P_2 are the result of co-ordinative transformation within the same intonation contour.

Example 17

Terhutang budi[280] saya, Dato'.

      P   S   voc.

I'm very grateful to you, Dato'.

TABULATION

Length: 4 full-words.

Type of sentence: Simple.

Clause description:

  Verbal.

  Elements: P S (+vocative piece).

Example 18

Baik kita belah sekarang, kita makan sama-sama.

      S   P   A(i)   S   P

      incl.cl.   *incl.cl.*

         N   N

P   S   S   P

  Cl_1 (c) Cl_2

We had better split them at once, and then we'll eat them together.

---

280 *terhutang budi:* *hutang budi* is taken to be a compound word, operating as Vb.A.II.Ia. This seems to be the simplest solution. For comment on another *ter-*+noun-form (*terbau*) see n. 98. If *ter-hutang* in this example is treated in the same way, i.e. as a two-complement verb in the passive, the analysis would be:

                Terhutang budi saya Dato'

                    P   S C_1 C_2

'Kindness is-a-debt-to-be-paid by me to you.' But since the author's comma indicates that *Dato'* is to be taken as a vocative piece, this solution is clearly not the right one.

TABULATION

Length: 7 full-words.

Type of sentence: Compound.[281]

Clause pattern: Cl_1 (c) Cl_2.

Clause descriptions:

Clause 1

Verbal (paratactically co-ordinate with Cl_2).
Elements: P S.
S is an included clause.
 Elements: S P A.

Clause 2

Verbal (paratactically co-ordinate with Cl_1).
Elements: S P.
S is an included clause.
 Elements: S P.

Example 19

Biar	kawan	belahkan
	S *incl.cl.*	P
P	C	

Let me split them for you.

TABULATION

Length: 3 full-words.

Type of sentence: Simple.

---

281 See n. 279. The same alternatives suggest themselves for this example, i.e. to analyse it as two separate clauses, or to take Clause 2 as an included clause, with echo-intonation of the included clause in Clause 1, and therefore to be described as S_2 in a simple sentence.

Clause description:
   Verbal (imperative).
   Elements: P C.
   C is an included clause.
       Elements: S P.

Example 20

[Di-] Mana[282]   parang?
    N   N
prep.phr.i.a
    P   S
Where's your chopper?

TABULATION

Length: 2 full-words.

Type of sentence: Simple (fragmentary).

Clause description:
   Verbal.
   Elements: P S.

SENTENCES 21–25 (FROM TEXT C, NOS. 3–7)

Example 21

Ada pun yang di-katakan sepatong itu ia-lah sa-jenis binatang terbang yang sa-akan-akan kapal terbang rupa-nya.

Now this creature that is called *sepatong*, it is a species of insect that looks something like an aeroplane.

SKELETON ANALYSIS

is-existent   this-insect-is-like-an-aeroplane
                     incl.cl.
   P   S

---

282 *Mana*: see n. 203.

DETAILED ANALYSIS

Ada pun[283] yg di-katakan s. itu ia-lah[284] sa-j. bin. terb. yg sa-akan2[285] k.t. rupa-nya.

```
Hv.(A.II.3)      Yg(b)      det. Pr.        n.phr.               Yg(b)
                 ─────────────              ─────────────────────────
                 N  n.phr. D                N₁     n.grp.      N₂
                 ──────                             ───
                 N                                   N
                 ─────                               ─
                 S (1)      S (2)                    P
                            ─────
                            incl.cl.
                 ──────────────────────────────────────────
     P                              S
```

283 *Ada pun:* taken as P in a simple sentence: an alternative would be to describe *Ada pun* as Clause 1, arranged in co-ordinate parataxis with Clause 2; but it is *not* possible to relegate *Ada pun* to the position of a parenthetic adjunct (A.v(b)), since it would not be spoken on level tones. Moreover, it is a statement of fact, not of opinion. (Contrast n. 202.)

284 *ia-lah:* taken as a repetitive sentence-element. (Cf. *ia pun* in Ex. 2 on p. 85.) This use of *ia-lah* is sometimes described as the insertion of a copula, probably because it can be translated so easily by an English copula; and in n. 108 *ia-itu* is described as ⟨a modern conjunctive particle⟩. But it seems preferable, in most contexts, to describe both expressions as noun-phrases (*ia-lah* as pronoun+particle, and *ia-itu* as pronoun+determinant) which repeat, in more succinct form, a longer nominal expression which immediately precedes this noun-phrase: 'what is called a dragonfly, *it* is..'. As such portmanteau repetitions the two expressions perform a useful service of clarification (and hence are increasingly used in the written language) without violating Malay idiom. In Example 24 below, *ia-itu* occurs as the sole S element (or perhaps as 'T'?). See also n. 298.

285 *sa-akan-akan:* perhaps to be described as a 'nominal expression of extent' which would qualify as 'A(iv.b)'. See n. 164(*b*)iii. For an example of *akan* used as an adjective, see *TCE*, p. 174.28: *Itu semua perkara akan.* 'Time will tell.' (lit. 'All that is an affair of-the-future'.)

TABULATION

Length: 12 full-words + 4 particles.

The particles: *pun*   postposition;

              yang   (twice);

              lah   postposition.

Type of sentence: Simple.

Clause description:

Verbal.

Elements: P S.

S is an included clause (nominal).

    Elements: S(1) S(2) P.

    S(1) is a noun-phrase, consisting of H (a Yg-piece) + D.

    S(2) is repetitive.

    P is a noun-group, consisting of N_1 (a noun-phrase) + N_2 (a Yg-piece).

Example 22

; kepala-nya bulat penoh dengan mata saperti mata lalat, badan-nya bujor, ékor-nya panjang dan sayap-nya sentiasa terhampar walau pun pada masa ia hinggap di-rumput-rumput dan di-pokok-pokok padi itu.

; its head is round, and full of eyes[286] like the eyes of a fly, it has an oval body and a long tail and its wings are always outspread, even when it alights on grasses and paddy stalks.

SKELETON ANALYSIS

Its head is round,		its body oval,		its tail long,		its wings spread,		even if...stalks
Cl_1	(c)	Cl_2	(c)	Cl_3	c	Cl_4	s	Cl_5

---

286 If *-nya* is inserted after *mata*, then *dengan* becomes a co-ordinating connective ('and its eyes are...') making six clauses; *penoh* becomes Particle 3. See p. 281.

DETAILED ANALYSIS

; kepala-nya bulat penoh dengan mata saperti[287] mata lalat,

$$N_1 \; n.grp. \; N_2$$

$$N_1 \quad n.grp. \quad N_2$$

$$N_1 \quad n.grp. \quad N_2$$

dir.iii *prep.phr.iii* NP

S	P_1	P_2	A(ii)

Cl_1

badan-nya bujor,   ékor-nya panjang

	S	P		S	P
(c)		Cl_2	(c)		Cl_3

dan sayap-nya sentiasa terhampar[288]

	S	A(iii)	P
c		Cl_4	

walau pun[289] [di-] pada masa ia hinggap di-rumput2 dan di-pokok2 padi itu.

prep.phr.i(a)

P

s	Cl_5

287 *saperti:* taken as a noun. See n. 208.
288 *terhampar:* for detailed analysis of Cl_3 and Cl_4 see p. 83 Ex. 2.
289 *walau pun:* for detailed analysis of Cl_4 and Cl_5 see p. 89 Ex. 7.

In that analysis Clause 5 is described as being subordinate to Clause 4 and consisting of one element only, the predicate.

But Clause 4 is 'intuitively' not a main clause in this context; it is an independent sentence, and Clause 5 is an additional statement.

Should *wa-lau* perhaps be analysed (in accordance with its origin) as a double connective, the first syllable being a *co-ordinating* connective between Clause 4 and an unexpressed main clause (say, 'Clause 6') to which Clause 5 is subordinate? i.e.: 'The wings are always outspread, and [the wings are outspread] if...'

The S element of such a subordinate clause (deleted by transformation) should be identical with the S element of the main clause (see p. 81.2 (a)), i.e.: *Sayap-nya sentiasa terhampar* (Cl_4) *wa sayap-nya terhampar* (say, Cl_6) *(ka)lau sayap-nya* [*di-*] *pada masa ia hinggap di-...pokok2 padi.* (Cl_5.) This leaves Clause 5 still to be described as a fragmentary subordinate clause consisting of the P element only, that element being a predicating prepositional phrase.

An alternative, already suggested in n. 156, is to take *pada masa ia hinggap* as 'A(iv.a)', i.e. as a noun-phrase of the *hari dia datang* type:

walau pun [binatang itu di-pandang] pada masa...padi itu.
     s   [S   P]   A(iv.a)
even if [the insects are watched] at-the-time they alight...

There is the possibility, too, of comparing this *kalau*+noun-phrase with a type of subordinate clause consisting of *kalau*+nominal predicate which does not lend itself to the description of 'transformation by deletion of S element', as shown on p. 81.2 (*a*), e.g.

A.95a: Kalau bagitu   bagus-lah.
                N   Hv.(adj.)
               —   —
               P   P
     s   Cl$_1$ Cl$_2$
If it's like that, that's fine.

Cf. the following examples from *TCE*:

p. 172.1 *Saya suka kalau bunga biru.*
          I like *blue* flowers best.
          Kalau budak baik dia ta' menangis.
          A *good* little boy doesn't cry!
          Saya suka kalau wayang bangsawan.
          I like the *live* theatre (not the cinema).

Similar to these examples are:

B.775: *Kalau kerbau, bertandok.*
        A *buffalo* has horns.
D.6:   *Jika budak2 ada yang menangis oléh sakit...*
        Children, indeed, would sometimes cry with the pain...

Perhaps it is necessary to accept such conditional clauses as examples of the normal subordinative transformation which results

TABULATION

Length: 20 full-words+9 particles.

The particles: *dengan*   directive iii;
dan (twice)   co-ordinating connective;
sentiasa   adjunctive;
walau   subordinating connective;
pun   postposition;
pada   non-numeral quantifier;
di- (twice)   directive i.

Type of sentence: Compound.

Clause pattern: Cl_1 (c) Cl_2 (c) Cl_3 c (Cl_4 s Cl_5).

Clause descriptions:

Clause 1

Verbal (linked by co-ordinative parataxis with Cl_2).
Elements: S P_1 P_2 A.
P_1 and P_2 are transformational.

---

in deletion of the S element in the subordinate clause when it is common to both clauses. In fact it is difficult to avoid this conclusion in the second example from *TCE* given above, since the S element (*dia*) is present in the main clause. In B.775, too, it is possible to take the main clause as fragmentary for: *Kalau kerbau [dia] bertandok*. But in the other examples it is difficult to suggest an S element that would satisfy both clauses.

In the *TCE* examples, however, the difficulty vanishes if the subordinate clause is taken to be verbal: *kalau bunga biru* 'if flowers are blue', i.e. sSP.

It may be worth noting that the fragmentary sentence on p. 95 (Ex. 10: *'tapi rotan...kalau di-churi orang.* A.91) was spoken with sentence-final intonation. Is *rotan di churi orang* perhaps to be taken as an included clause, i.e. a noun-equivalent?

Clause 2

Verbal (linked by co-ordinative parataxis with Cl_1 and Cl_3).

Elements: S P.

Clause 3

Verbal (linked by co-ordinative parataxis with Cl_2 and by co-ordinating connective with Cl_4).

Elements: S P.

Clause 4 (main).

Verbal (linked by co-ordinating connective with Cl_3 and by sub-ordinating connective with Cl_5).

Elements: S A P.

Clause 5 (subordinate)

Verbal (fragmentary).

Element: P.

P is a predicating prepositional phrase.

Example 23

Binatang ini selalu di-dapati terlalu banyak [di-]dalam sawah kerana ia suka diam di-tempat-tempat yang berrumput panjang dan berayer.

These insects are always found in large numbers in the rice-fields because they like to live in places where there is long grass and water.

Binatang	ini	selalu	di-dapati	terlalu	banyak[290]	[di-]dalam sawah
N +	det.	part.3	Hv.(pa)	part.3	Hv.(adj.)	*prep.phr.i(b)*
S		A(iii)	P_1	A(iii)	P_2	P_3

Cl_1

kerana	ia	suka	diam	di-tempat2 yang ber-rumput panjang dan ber-ayer.
part.1(b)i				*prep.phr.i.b*
	S	P_1	P_2	P_3
s				

Cl_2

290 *banyak* as a predicating verb-form. Cf. n. 194.

TABULATION

Length: 15 full-words + 5 particles.

The particles: *selalu*   adjunctive;

     terlalu   adjunctive;

     kerana   subordinating connective;

     yang

     dan   co-ordinating connective (linking, in transformation, two Yg-pieces).

Type of sentence: Compound.

Clause pattern: Cl_1 s Cl_2.

Clause descriptions:

Clause 1 (main)

Verbal.

Elements: S A(1) P_1 A(2) P_2 P_3.

P_1 is a passive Head-verb.

P_2 is a non-passive Head-verb of Class A.II.1a.

P_3 is a predicating prepositional phrase.

Clause 2 (subordinate)

Verbal.

Elements: S P_1 P_2 P_3.

P_1 is Hv. (Class A.II.1a).

P_2 is Hv. (Class A.II.3).

P_3 is a predicating prepositional phrase.

---

291 *Maka:* see n. 141.

292 *ia-itu:* see n. 284.

293 *jenis-nya, warna-nya:* taken as Complement with the predicating prep. phrase *bermacham-macham*. But see n. 90.

Example 24

Maka[291]	ia-itu[292]	ber-macham2 pula jenis-nya,[293]	ada	yang besar,
part.	Pr. det.	*prep.phr.i(a)*	Hv.	Yg(b)

n.phr.

S   P   A.II.3

      Cl₁   (c)   P   S

                                                  Cl₂

ada	yg kechil	serta	[ia-itu]	ber-macham2 warna-nya.[293]
Hv.(A.II.3)	Yg(b)			*prep.phr.i(a)*
P	S		[S]	P
(c)	Cl₃	c		Cl₄

They are of many kinds; there are some that are large and some that are small, and they are of various different colours.

TABULATION

Length: 9 full-words + 5 particles.

The particles: *maka*   connective;
                     pula   adjunctive;
                     yang (twice)
                     serta   co-ordinating connective (linking clauses).

Type of sentence: Compound.

Clause pattern: Cl₁ (c) Cl₂ (c) Cl₃ c Cl₄.

Clause descriptions:

Clause 1

Verbal (linked in paratactic co-ordination with Cl₂).
Elements: S P.
P is a predicating prepositional phrase.

Clause 2

Verbal (linked in paratactic co-ordination with Cl₁ and Cl₃).
Elements: P S.
S is a *yang*-piece.

Clause 3

Verbal (linked in paratactic co-ordination with Cl_2 and linked by co-ordinating particle with Cl_4).

Elements: P S.

S is a *yang*-piece.

Clause 4

Verbal (linked by co-ordinating particle with Cl_3).

Elements: [S] P.

P is a predicating prepositional phrase.

Example 25

Tetapi jenis yg besar itu-lah yang di-kehendakkan buat[294] umpan merachun tikus.

	N	Yg(b)	det.				H	*n.phr.*	Q(i)
	N_1	*n.grp.*	N_2				*dir.iii*	*prep.phr.iii*	NP
	H	*n.phr.*	D	(for S)		P		A(ii)	
		N					Yg(b)		
							N		
|c|		S				P		

But it is the large sort that you need for rat-bait.

TABULATION

Length: 7 full-words + 5 particles.

The particles: *tetapi*   co-ordinating connective (non-initiating).[295]

yang (twice)

lah   postposition;

buat   (as 1(a)iii, by analogy with *untok*) directive iii.

---

294 *buat* described as a preposition; see n. 277.

yang...tikus: the *yang*-piece has here been analysed in order to investigate the function of *buat*. 'Yg(b)' is the form of the *yang*-piece in which *yang* is said to 'replace' the S element. See p. 21(*b*).

295 'non-initiating': i.e. it links this sentence with a (possible) preceding clause which would be co-ordinate with it, e.g. *Sunggoh pun bagitu, tetapi..* See p. 67.

Type of sentence: Simple.

Clause description:
  Nominal.
  Elements: S P.
  S is a noun-phrase.
  P is a *yang*-piece.

SENTENCES 26–30 (FROM TEXT D, NOS. 1–5)

Example 26

Masa saya budak-budak saya ada juga berchampor dalam permainan 'bersengkéta batang keladi' itu ketika di-adakan isti'adat berpuar di-kampong saya ia-itu kampong Jempul, jajahan Kuala Pilah, Negeri Sembilan.

Long ago, when I was a child, I myself have taken part in the game of *keladi*-stalk fighting at a time when the ceremony of *berpuar* was carried out in my own village, that is to say, the village of Jempul in the Kuala Pilah district of Negeri Sembilan.

SKELETON ANALYSIS

Long ago, I took part, (was) in this game, when it happened in Jempul.
  A(iv.a)   S P_1 P_2 A(iv.a)

i.e. a simple sentence.

DETAILED ANALYSIS

Masa	saya	budak2	dahulu[296]	saya	ada		juga	berchampor[297]
N	Pr.	N	N	Pr.	x(ii)		part.3	Hv.(A.II.2.a)
	S	P	A(iv.a)					
		incl.cl.						
H	*n.phr.*	Q(iii)						
	A(iv.a)			S	P_1 ..		A(iii)	.. P_1

---

296 *dahulu:* see n. 36.

297 *ada juga berchampor:* see n. 57. The position of *juga* suggests that
    ada should perhaps be taken as Head-verb, with *saya berchampor*

[di-]	dalam	permainan	'ber-sengkéta	batang	keladi'	itu.
		N		prep.phr.i(c)		det.
		H		Q(ii)		D
				n.phr.		
	N$_1$		n.grp.		N$_2$	
[dir.(i)]	prep.phr.i(b)	NP				
	P$_2$					

ketika	di-adakan	ist.	ber-puar	di-kg. saya	ia-itu[298]	kg.	Jmpl.	jaj.	KP	Neg.	Semb.[299]
N	Hv.(pa.B.I)	N	prep.phr.i.c	N + Pr.	Pr. + det.	N$_1$ + N$_2$	N$_1$+N$_2$		N$_1$+N$_2$		
		H n.phr.	Q(ii)	N$_1$ +	N$_2$ +	N$_3$ +	N$_4$ +		N$_5$		
		N				n.grp.					
				dir.i	prep.phr.i.b		NP				
	P$_1$	S			P$_2$						
			incl.cl.								
H		n.phr.	Q(iii)								
		A(iv.a)									

(included clause) as S, but the position of *saya* (unless it is taken as 'Topic' declaration) weakens the suggestion. Another possibility is to take *ada* and *berchampor* as transformational dual predicate elements, P$_1$ and P$_2$, but the position of *juga* (putting a 'brake' on *ada*) does not favour this solution.

298 *ia-itu*: see n. 284. In this example it is a re-statement of *kampong saya* and becomes item 2 in the series of nominals that make up the noun-group. When it is used in this way, it is usually a 'gloss' on the nominal expression which precedes it, introducing an amplification of some sort (whereas the nominal expression which follows *ia-lah* is usually a predicate). Consequently, *ia-itu* may often be translated as 'i.e.' An example in *TCE* (p. 175.3, 5) illustrates this frequently-made distinction, which is a question of usage not of syntax: *Malam Mi'raj ia-itu malam Nabi kita mimpi naik ka-langit ia-lah malam 27 Rejab.* 'The night of *Mi'raj*, that is to say the night when our Prophet dreamed that he ascended to Heaven, (it) is the night of 27 Rejab.'

299 *Negeri Sembilan:* by definition (see n. 25) the numeral, although classed as an adjective, may not follow the noun except when it operates as M in a noun-phrase of structure M H, of which the H element is a numeral coefficient, e.g.

TABULATION

Length: 25 full-words[300] + 2 particles.
The particles: *juga*   adjunctive;
     di   directive i.

Type of sentence: Simple.[301]

Clause description:
Verbal.
Elements: A(1) S P_1 .. A(2) .. P_1 P_2 A(3).
P_1 is discontinuous and consists of x(ii) + Hv.
P_2 is a predicating prepositional phrase.
The first and third adjuncts are noun-phrases. Each has a time-word as Head, and an included clause as Q. (But see n. 301.)

---

rumah	dua	buah
	M *n.phr.* H	
N_1	*n.grp.*	N_2

The state name here is therefore taken to be an abbreviation of *Negeri Sembilan Buah* and analysed as a noun-group.

300 '25 full-words': but note that of this number eight words are in the nature of a 'specification' to identify a particular locality.

301 'Simple': if the Head-noun of such time-expressions as *Masa...dahulu* and *ketika...Negeri Sembilan* comes to be regarded as a subordinating connective (as has happened with *bila*) the first and third adjuncts become subordinate clauses, and the sentence is then to be described as 'Compound', with Clause pattern: s Cl_1 (Cl_2 s Cl_3).

Example 27

Tetapi	di-sana	isti'adat itu	di-sebut	orang	menyémah.[302]
	dir.i+N	N + det.	Hv.(pa.A.I)	N	verb-noun
	prep.phr.i.b	N			N
		S			P
		incl...			*..cl.*
|c|	P_1	S..	P_2	C	..S

But there the ceremony is called *menyémah*.

TABULATION

Length: 6 full-words + 2 particles.

The particles: *Tetapi*   co-ordinating connective (non-initiating).

                    di   directive i.b.

Type of sentence: Simple (with dual predicate element).

Clause description:

Verbal.

Elements: P_1 S.. P_2 C ..S.

P_1 is a predicating prepositional phrase.

P_2 is a passive Head-verb.

S is discontinuous and is an included clause (nominal).

Example 28

Pada masa itu saya ta'mengerti apa tujuan isti'adat itu, hanya saya suka
kerana orang ramai dan semua-nya berjalan mengharong sawah dengan

---

302 This analysis presumes the sentence to be a passive transform of
the active sentence:

Orang	sebut	isti'adat	itu	menyémah.
		N		N
		S	*incl.cl.*	P
S	P		C	

People say that the ceremony is a-propitiating-of-the-spirits.

See n. 179 for a similar example, with *sangka* as Head-verb. But
in Ex. 27 above, this contrived solution seems to leave the prep.
phrase *di-sana* as an unusually unconvincing transformational predicate for the included clause subject-element.

rioh rendah-nya sambil berjalan itu sambil bersengkéta melechutkan batang keladi sa-besar-besar lengan ka-atas belakang kawan-kawan dengan sa-kuat-kuat hati hingga bersepai-sepai batang keladi itu.

At that time I did not understand what the purpose of the ceremony was; I was just delighted because there were crowds of people about, and because they went wading through the rice-fields shouting at the tops of their voices. As they went along they shot arm-long *keladi*-stalks at each other's backs as hard as ever they could, so that at last the spikes broke into bits. (or: until at last...).

SKELETON ANALYSIS

I didn't understand,		I was happy
Cl_1	(c)	Cl_2

because	(there were crowds	and	they waded)
s	Cl_3	c	Cl_4

	they fought with stalks		at last the stalks broke.
(c)	Cl_5	(c)	Cl_6

DETAILED ANALYSIS

Pada	masa	itu	saya	ta'	mengerti	apa	tujuan	isti'adat	itu,
NNQ	N	det.						N	det.
M(ii)	H	D						H *n.phr.*	D
	n.phr.						N_1	*n.grp.*	N_2
							N		N
							S	*incl.cl.*	P
A(iv.a)		S		P				C	
					Cl_1				

hanya	saya	suka	kerana	orang	ramai[303]	dan	semua-nya	berjalan	mengharong
A(iii)	S	P		S	P		S	P_1	P_2
(c)	Cl_2		s	Cl_3		c	Cl_4 ..		→

sawah	dengan	rioh-rendah-nya		sambil[304]	berjalan	itu
	dir.iii	*prep.phr.iii* NP		N	*n.phr.*	D
→ C		A(ii)		dir.iii	*prep.phr.iii* NP	
	.. Cl_4				A(ii)	
			(c)		Cl_5 ..	→

_____

303 *ramai*: cf. n. 163.

sambil[304] [dia] ber-sengkéta melechutkan batang keladi sa-besar2 lengan

				N_1 *n.grp.* N_2		N_1 *n.grp.* N_2

N_1 *n.grp.* N_2

→ A(iii) [S] P_1 P_2 C

..Cl$_5$..
→

ka-atas belakang kawan2 dengan sa-kuat-kuat hati

N_1 + N_2 + N_3 N_1 + N_2

dir.i *prep.phr.i(b)* NP   dir.iii *prep.phr.iii* NP

P_3 A(ii)

→   ..Cl$_5$
→

hingga[305] bersepai2 batang keladi itu.

Hv.$_1$ Hv.$_2$ *n.phr.*

P_1 P_2 S

(c)   Cl$_6$

TABULATION

Length: 37 full-words + 9 particles.

The particles:	*pada*	non-numeral quantifier;
	hanya	(as 3) adjunctive;
	kerana	subordinating connective, 1(b)i;
	dan (twice)	co-ordinating connective (between clauses), 1(b)ii;
	dengan	directive 1(a)iii;
	nya	as a nominalising particle (A(ii) in Cl. 4);
	sambil	(as 1(a)iii) directive;
	sambil	(as 3) adjunctive;

304 *sambil...sambil:* see n. 238. If it were not for the determinant *itu* it would be possible to divide Clause 5 into two co-ordinate clauses, with *sambil* described as an adjunctive particle (comparable with *selalu*) in each case: *sambil [dia] berjalan sambil [dia] ber-sengkéta...* as in the proverbial expression *Sambil menyelam sambil minum ayer,* 'diving and drinking at the same time'. But *itu* fixes the first expression (*berjalan itu*) as nominal, either as a noun-phrase (as in the analysis) with a verb-form as Head, or as an included clause with [*dia*] as S.

305 *hingga:* taken as Hv. There are contexts in which it is easy to

Type of sentence: Compound.

Clause pattern (but see note on p. 178):
  Cl_1 (c) Cl_2 s (Cl_3 c Cl_4) (c) Cl_5 (c) Cl_6.

Clause descriptions:

Clause 1

Verbal (paratactically co-ordinate with Cl_2).
Elements: A S P C.
C is an included clause (nominal).
  Elements: S P.

Clause 2 (main)

Verbal (paratactically co-ordinate with Cl_1, and Cl_5 and linked by subordinative particle with Cl_3).
Elements: A S P.

Clause 3 (subordinate)

Verbal (linked by subordinative particle with Cl_2 and by co-ordinative particle with Cl_4).
Elements: S P.

Clause 4 (subordinate to Cl_2).

Verbal (linked by co-ordinative particle with Cl_3).
Elements: S P_1 P_2 C A.
P_1 and P_2 are the result of co-ordinative transformation under one intonation contour.

---

describe *hingga* and *sampai* as directive prepositions, operating in place of the dropped *ka-* or *di-*, but there are other contexts in which it is clear that they are functioning as verbs (see n. 213). If *hingga* is taken as a preposition in this example, then *bersepai2 batang keladi itu* becomes an included clause and the whole expression must be assigned as P_4 (prep.phrase i(b)) in Clause 5.

Clause 5

Verbal (linked in paratactic co-ordination with Cl_2 and with Cl_6.
Elements: $A(1)$ $A(2)$ P_1 P_2 C P_3 $A(3)$.
P_1 and P_2 are the result of co-ordinative transformation under one intonation contour.

Clause 6

Verbal (linked in paratactic co-ordination with Cl_5).
Elements: P_1 P_2 S.

NOTE: It is possible that the author intended not only Clauses 3 and 4 but also Clauses 5 and 6 to be introduced by the subordinating connective *kerana*, thus:

$$Cl_1 \text{ (c) } Cl_2 \text{ s } (Cl_3 \text{ c } Cl_4 \text{ (c) } Cl_5 \text{ (c) } Cl_6).$$

Example 29

Maka	sunggoh	pun[306]	batang	keladi	itu	tidak	keras	saperti[307]	kayu
part.	Hv.(adj.)		*n.phr.*			x(ii) Hv.(adj.)		N *n.grp.*	N
									N
				S		P_1			P_2
						incl.cl.			
	P						S		
			Cl_1						

tetapi	[orang]	sakit	juga	oléh	-nya.[308]
part.1(b)ii		Hv.(adj.)		*prep.(a)iii*	Pr.
				dir.iii prep.phr.iii NP	
	[S]	P	A(iii)	A(ii)	
c			Cl_2		

Although the calladium stalks were not rigid, like wood, nevertheless they hurt quite a bit. (lit. It is true...but...)

306 *sunggoh pun:* usually translated as 'although', but the fact that the next clause almost invariably begins with the co-ordinating connective *tetapi* indicates that it is not itself a subordinating connective; when it is described as an adjective accompanied by an adjunctive particle it becomes P in the first of a pair of co-ordinate clauses.

307 *saperti* taken as a noun: see n. 208. The resulting noun-group gives a nominal predicate, to be paired (transformationally) with a

TABULATION

Length: 10 full-words + 4 particles.

The particles: *Maka*   connective;
     pun postposition;
     tetapi co-ordinative connective (linking clauses);
     juga adjunctive.

Type of sentence: Compound.

Clause pattern: Cl$_1$ c Cl$_2$.

Clause descriptions:

 Clause 1

 Verbal (co-ordinate with Cl$_2$ and linked to it by particle).
 Elements: P S.
 S is an included clause.
  Elements: S P$_1$ P$_2$.
  P$_1$ is verbal; P$_2$ is nominal.

---

verbal predicate. Nevertheless it seems to be the best solution. Cf. Ex. 12 on p. 155.

308 *oléh-nya:* described as 'A(ii)'. In a sentence such as A.265: [*Dia*] *menggeletar oléh ketakutan.* ('He is gibbering with fright') it is possible to take *oléh* either as directive iii (equivalent to *dengan, kerana, sebab*) with *ketakutan* operating as a noun, the result being prep. phrase iii (A(ii) in clause structure—'by-means-of fright', 'because of fright') or else as a subordinating connective (equivalent to *kerana, sebab*) with *ketakutan* as Hv.(B.II.i):

oléh [*dia*] *ketakutan* 'because he is-frightened'.
 s [S] P

In the analysis of Ex. 29 the first alternative has been accepted: *sakit oléh-nya* 'hurt by-means-of it'.

On the other hand it is possible that *oléh-nya* could justifiably be described in the usual way (as C) even here, although it does not accompany a passive verb-form (*di-* or *ter-*), the implication being that the existence of an agent is inherent in the word *sakit* used in such a context, 'being-hurt (by somebody or something)'.

Clause 2

Verbal (co-ordinate with Cl_1 and linked to it by particle).

Elements: S P A (1) A (2).

A (1) is an adjunctive particle.

A (2) is a prep. phrase iii.

Example 30

Tiap-tiap	orang	yang	kena	itu	membalas	pula.
NNQ		Yg(b)		det.	Hv.	part.3

| | N_1 | *n.grp.* | N_2 | | | |
| M(ii) | | H | | D | | |

n.phr.

N

S   P   A(iii)

Everyone who got a hit, hit back at his attacker.

TABULATION

Length: 4 full-words + 3 particles.

The particles: *tiap-tiap*   non-numeral quantifier;

yang

pula   adjunctive.

Type of sentence: Simple.

Clause description:

Verbal.

Elements: S P A.

Summary of the foregoing analyses taken at their face value

I. SENTENCE TYPES

Simple sentences   17

Compound sentences   11

Fragmentary sentences   2

Ratio of simple sentences to compound sentences: say, 65% to 35%.

2. CLAUSE PATTERNS IN THE COMPOUND SENTENCES

  (i) Co-ordination with particle
          Number of occurrences of the symbol 'c'   5
 (ii) Subordination with particle
          Number of occurrences of the symbol 's'   4
(iii) Co-ordination without particle (parataxis)
          Number of occurrences of the symbol '(c)'   10
 (iv) Subordination without particle
          Number of occurrences of the symbol '(s)'   1

3. NUMBER OF INCLUDED CLAUSES

(i.e. down-graded clauses, not shown in the clause-pattern formulae.)

As S in clause structure	7
As P in clause structure	2
As C in clause structure	3
As N in noun-group	1
As Q in noun-phrase	3
Total	16

(Number of clauses recorded in the clause-pattern formulae: 48.)

4. RATIO OF VERBAL CLAUSES TO NOMINAL CLAUSES

(including the included clauses, but excluding the inherent verbal predicates in the sentence-element labelled [A(v.b)], and in the noun-equivalent labelled *yang*-piece.)

   Number of verbal clauses: 53 (52+two 'halves')
   Number of nominal clauses: 11 (10+two 'halves').

NOTE: the 'halves' refer to Examples 12 and 29 in each of which, for want of a better solution, a transformational predicate has been presumed to combine a verbal with a nominal element.

   Ratio of verbal clauses to nominal clauses: say, 80% to 20%.

5. NUMBER OF VERBAL CLAUSES WITH TRANSFORMATIONAL PREDICATES

With two or more verb-forms	11
With a verb-form and a prepositional phrase	2
With a verb-form and a nominal phrase	2
Total	15

6. LENGTH OF SENTENCES

10 words or fewer (including particles)	17
11 to 20 words	10
Over 20 words	3

Comments on the foregoing summary

The summary offers nothing more than a rough quantitative estimate of a very small area of the material used in the book. Any attempt to base firm conclusions on it would be of little value.

Nor, indeed, would a similar summary of the whole of the material used afford a valid basis for such conclusions, since the apparently definitive results recorded reflect many tentative decisions. For instance:

Item 1. The ratio between simple and compound sentences would be altered if, as in the thesis, all sentences with a multiple transformational element were to be described as 'compound'; or if on the other hand, not in line with the thesis, all sentences containing an included clause were to be so described.

Item 2. The ratio between nominal and verbal clauses would be altered if word sequences of the type *apa macham, apa fasal* were to be analysed not as nominal clauses but as compound words.

Item 3. The incidence of the symbol (c) marking co-ordination without particle (parataxis), and of the symbol (s) marking subordination without particle, is necessarily based on judgement rather than fact.

Item 4. The figures recording sentence-length would be higher if the directive particles *ka-* and *di-* were included in the count; and in the long sentences the figures might be reduced if punctuation changes were considered.

To provide additional data for items 1 and 2 of the observations recorded below, two further counts have been made:

(*a*) Of the clause-types indicated in the sentences analysed in §6.

(*b*) Of the clause-types and sentence-types occurring in Act II, sc. 2 of Text B.

Observations on Malay syntax

(based on the colloquial and narrative style of the Texts examined.)

1. The simple sentence predominates.

NOTE: The additional data (see (*b*) above) confirm the proportion of, say, 65% simple sentences to 35% compound sentences.

2. The verbal clause predominates.

NOTE: The additional data (see (*a*) and (*b*) above) produce a figure of 84% verbal clauses to 16% nominal clauses.

3. The compound sentence without expressed connective particle, whether co-ordinative or subordinative, is of frequent occurrence.

NOTE: The frequency of this paratactic arrangement is an indication that sequence of presentation is an important pointer to syntactic structure. It follows from this that Malay syntax does not exhibit complexity of structure.

4. The included clause, functioning as a noun-equivalent in clause and phrase structure, is of frequent occurrence.

5. In verbal clauses the multiple predicate element which consists of two or more predicating verb-forms contained within one intonation contour is of frequent occurrence.

NOTE: It is described as resulting, by the process of 'transformation', from the merging of separate and successive predicates which have identical subjects.

6. Narrative style (as exemplified in Texts C and D and in the continuous passages of the stage-directions in Texts A and B) does not show any marked difference from colloquial style (as exemplified in Texts A and B), except that the sentences tend to be longer, abbreviated word forms are rare, and parataxis is less frequent.

7. It is possible that the setting up of a 'T-piece' as an extra-syntactic element of sentence-structure would result in a simpler analysis pattern for a certain number of Malay sentences. (See n. 161.) The symbol 'T' would indicate a free-standing noun, or noun-piece, which announces the 'topic' of the complete sentence that follows it, or, occasionally, sums up the 'topic' of the complete sentence which precedes it.

CONSPECTUS OF THE GRAMMATICAL FRAMEWORK

===

STRUCTURES

Sentences

    (a) Simple.

    (b) Compound.

        Patterns: Cl_1 (c) Cl_2; Cl_1 s Cl_2;   (s) Cl_1 Cl_2.

Clauses

    (a) Nominal.

        Elements: S P (A)   Order: S P.

    (b) Verbal.

        Elements: (S) P (C) (A).

        Order: P, SP, PS, PC, CP, SPC, PCS (rare), CSP, PSC (passive only).

        NOTE: *Not found* are **CPS* and **SCP*.

Phrases

    (a) Noun.

    (b) Prepositional.

    (c) Verb.

        (For elements see below.)

WORD CLASSES AND ELEMENTS OF STRUCTURES

(in alphabetic order)

NOTE: Except for items within square brackets all the examples given are quoted from the thesis.

'A' (the Adjunct): an ELEMENT in nominal and verbal clause structure

    (i) An adjunct (Noms.(c)). Ex: *sekarang*.

    (ii) A prep.phr. with *dengan, akan, bagi, untok*.

    (iii) An adjunctival particle. Exx.: *belaka, pula, juga*.

    (iv) [(*a*)] A small number of nouns (Ex. *hari*) with limited expansion possibilities, Ex. *tahun ini* [position in time].

        ⌈(*b*) A small number of nominal expressions (e.g. *sa-jurus lama-*⌉
        ⌊   *nya*) indicative of extent in time or space.   ⌋

    (v) Parenthetic expressions.

        [(*a*)] Of the structure noun *-nya*. Ex. *agak-nya*.

        ⌈(*b*) An interpolated (or juxtaposed) predication of opinion,⌉
        ⌊   e.g. *entah, mémang, kata orang, perasaan saya*.   ⌋

NOTE: See also under prep.phr.i (exceptions).

Auxiliaries, The: (Word Class II.3).

        akan, belum, maséh, pernah, sedang, ta' pernah, telah.

    Potential auxiliaries (A.II.3c verbs)

        tidak, sudah, habis, dapat, hendak, mahu, kena, boléh.

'C' (the Complement): an ELEMENT in verbal clause structure.

    (i) A noun, or the syntactic equivalent of a noun.

    (ii) An interrogative nominal.

'D' (say, the Determinant): an ELEMENT in noun phrase structure.
A determinative (i.e. *itu* or *ini*).

'H' (the Head): an ELEMENT in noun phrase structure.
A noun or the syntactic equivalent of a noun.

Hv (Head-verb): an ELEMENT in verb phrase structure.
A verb.

'M' (say, the Measurer): an ELEMENT in noun phrase structure.

    (i) A numeral.

    (ii) A non-numeral quantifier.

Nominals, The: (Word Class II.I).

(*a*) The determinatives, i.e. *itu*/*ini*. When deictic [i.e. distinguishing] may be S or C; or P in nominal clause.

(*b*) Nouns, including pronouns. Diagnostic tests: can collate with *itu*; can be H in noun-phrase; can be S or C in clause structure.

> *Noun equivalents* are:
>   (i)   a noun-phrase;
>   (ii) a noun-group;
>   (iii) a verb as H of noun-phrase;
>   (iv) a *yang*-piece:
>   Yg(a): with *yang* as subordinating particle to a verb clause.
>   Ex.: *yang saya lihat*;
>   Yg(b): with *yang* replacing S in a verb clause. Exx.: *yang membacha*; *yang kedua*;
>   (v)   a pronoun;
>   (vi) a deictic;
>   (vii) a downgraded (i.e. included) clause.
>   N O T E: the affixes *-nya* and *sa-* are sometimes nominalising particles.

(*c*) The adjuncts. Ex. *sekarang*. Diagnostic tests: can collocate with *itu*; cannot be S, P or C in clause structure.

(*d*) The interrogative nominals. Exx. apa, siapa, mana, berapa, mengapa, kenapa, bila, apabila. Can operate as S or C in verb clause, and as S or P in nominal clause.

> N O T E: see Index to Footnotes which suggest variant assignments for some of the interrogative nominals.

Noun Group, The: a STRUCTURE.

Elements: $N_1 + N_2 + N_3$ etc.

Noun Phrase, The: a STRUCTURE (the nominal phrase with a noun as H).

Elements: (M) H (Q) (D) in that order. Minimal exponent, a noun.

'P' (the Predicate): an ELEMENT in clause structure.

> (*a*) In a nominal clause:
>   (i) a noun or its syntactic equivalent;
>   (ii) an interrogative nominal.

(*b*) In a verbal clause:

    (i) a verb-phrase (minimal exponent, a verb);

    (ii) a prepositional phrase with *ka-, di-, dari, ber-*.

Particles, The: (Word Class I).

1. Prepositions.

    (*a*) Directives:

        (i) *ka-, di-, dari, ber-*;

        (ii) *oléh*;

        (iii) *dengan, akan, bagi, untok*.

    (*b*) Connectives:

        (i) subordinative. Ex. *kalau*;

        (ii) co-ordinative. Ex. *dan*.

    (*c*) Non-numeral quantifiers.

        Exx. *semua, tiap-tiap*.

2. Postpositions:

    -lah, -kah, -tah, pun.

3. Adjunctival particles.

    Exx. *sangat, juga, pula, lagi*.

NOTES: (*a*) *yang*, since it cannot occur in isolation, must be considered a (connective) particle in a class of its own.

(*b*) *-nya* is sometimes a nominalising particle (and sometimes a postposition pronoun).

(*c*) *sa-* may sometimes be a nominalising particle.

Prepositional Phrase, The: a STRUCTURE.

Elements: a pre-posed particle + a noun phrase.

    (i) beginning with *ka-, di-, dari, ber-*:

        (*a*) as sole P in verbal clause structure;

        (*b*) as second (or third) predicate, by transformation, in verbal clause structure, i.e. $P_2 P_3$ etc.

        (*c*) as Q in noun phrase structure.

        NOTE: Exceptions are:

           1. (*dari* + NP) as A, when P is an adjective.

           2. *kapada-nya* as A with a two-complement verb.

   (ii) Beginning with *oléh*:
       as C in a clause with a passive verb.
  (iii) Beginning with *dengan, akan, bagi, untok*:
       as A(ii) in clause structure.

'Q' (say, the Qualifier): an ELEMENT in noun phrase structure.

   (i) a verb-form (some with obligatory *itu*);
  (ii) a prepositional phrase with *ka-, di-, dari, ber-*;
  (iii) an included clause with a time/place noun as H;
  (iv) an expanded verb-phrase. Exx. orang *belum masok* itu..., orang *baharu datang* itu...

'S' (the Subject): an ELEMENT in clause structure.

   (i) a noun or its syntactical equivalent;
  (ii) an interrogative nominal.

Verbals, The: (Word Class II.2).

A *Non-derived forms*	B *Derived forms*

I. Transitive
   Ex. *bacha*
	I. Transitive
	   with *-kan*, *-i* or duplication
	   Exx. *menjalankan, susui*

II. Intransitive
   1.a. Adjectives
       Ex. *mérah*
     b. Numerals
       Ex. *dua*
 	
   2.a. Reciprocal
       Ex. (*ber*)*tengkar*
     b. Reflexive
       Ex. (*ber*)*chukor*
 	
   3. Other intransitives
      a./b. Exx. *datang/turun*
      c. Verbs which may also
        operate as auxiliaries
        Ex. *boléh*
	II. Intransitive (examples only)
	   (i) ..kematian..
	  (ii) ..kedua..
	  (iii) ..melaut..
	  (iv) ..mengijau..
	  (v) ..mendatang..
	  (vi) ..menurun..
	  (vii) ..termasin..
	  (viii) ..larangan..
	  (ix) ..penakut..
	  (x) ..sa-baya (dengan)..
	  (xi) ..berpergian..
	       or
	      ..berkechilan hati..

A note on two-complement verbs (i.e. (i) 'giving' verbs, (ii) verbs with the 'benefactive *-kan*' affixed).

Description of sentence elements:

(*a*) in the active clause:
　　the donor is　　S
　　the gift is　　　C_1
　　the recipient is C_2
(or a prep.phr. with *kapada*)

(*b*) in the passive clause:
　　the donor is　　　C_1
　　the gift is　　　　S
　　the recipient is C_2
(or a prep.phr. with *kapada*)

Verb Phrase, The: a STRUCTURE

Elements: $x(i)/(ii) + Hv$.

Word Classes, The:

　I. Particles.
　II. Full words:
　　　1. Nominals.
　　　2. Verbals.
　　　3. Auxiliaries.

'X': an ELEMENT in verb phrase structure.

x(i): an auxiliary.
x(ii): a verb of Class A.II.3c operating as an auxiliary.

Yang-piece, The: see nominals (*b*) (iv).

APPENDIX II

A NOTE ON THE INDICATION OF IMMEDIATE CONSTITUENCY

The noun-group in the first example on p. 139 is analysed thus in the thesis:

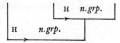
```
...   Ahmad   menchangkul   sawah
                          H    n.grp.
           H    n.grp.
```

The immediate constituency (i.e. the interrelation of parts) is indicated by the symbol H for the Head constituent with an arrow pointing towards the subordinate constituent within each brace.

Since the accepted word-order in Malay is progressive, with Attribute following Head, whereas in English it is regressive, with Attribute preceding Head, the arrows in a Malay diagram will usually point to the right and those in an English diagram to the left.

Examples:

(a) rumah besar

(b) large house

(a) tin rokok kosong
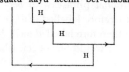

(b) empty cigarette tin

(a) suatu kayu kechil ber-chabang

(b) a little forked stick

The left-pointing arrow on the third brace in (a) is due to the fact that the numeral in Malay, unlike the attributive adjective, precedes the noun.

The first and second braces in (a) show that to the Malay ear the idea presents itself as a little stick, with a forked end; in (b) they show that to English ears it is a forked stick, a little one.

But for the analysis of whole sentences such a system of successive bracing is inconvenient. In the analyses of sentences from the Texts immediate constituency is expressed in terms of function within a structure. When a full line-by-line analysis is given, the first line gives the category of each word and the second line gives, or begins to give, the constituent-grouping within the structures set up in the framework.

For the symbols used see p. xiii.

For the categories and structures referred to see the Conspectus on pp. 185–90.

Example 1:

	rumah	besar	
line 1	N	Vb.(A.II.1a)	= categories: a noun, an adjective
line 2	H	n.phr. Q(i)	= a structure: a noun-phrase, consisting of Head (by definition a noun) and a qualifier which is a verb-form

Example 2:

	suatu	kayu	kechil	ber-	chabang
line 1	num.	N	adj.	part. 1(a)i	N
line 2		H n.phr. Q(i)		dir.(i) prep.phr.i(c) NP	
line 3		N			
line 4		H	n.phr.	Q(ii)	
line 5			N		
line 6	M(i)	n.phr.	H		

Explanation:

line 3 : the noun-phrase of line 2, being a noun-equivalent, is evaluated as N.

line 4 : the Q element here is a prepositional phrase with *ber-* (not a verb-form as in line 2) and is therefore labelled Q(ii).

line 6 : the M element is a numeral and is therefore labelled M(i). If the phrase had been *semua kayu kechil* it would have been labelled M(ii).

The example given in n. 25 could be set out thus:

	dua	buah	rumah	itu
line 1	num.	N	N	det.
line 2		N_1 *n.grp.* N_2		
line 3			N	
line 4	M(i)		H	D
line 5		*n.phr.*		

NOTE. Lines 1 and 2: as a short cut, since no ambiguity would result, these two lines might be combined as in the next example below.

In the analysis of a phrase or a group the last line records the elements of the phrase or group which are present:

> e.g. for a noun-phrase, some selection from (M) H (Q) (D);
> for a noun-group, a minimum of $N_1 + N_2$;
> for a prepositional phrase, an identification of the particle, and an indication of the noun phrase (NP) which follows it,

and, on the bar between them (or else on a separate bar below them), an identification of the resultant prepositional phrase

> e.g. in Example 2 above, for *ber-chabang*:

line 2: *chabang* is the noun-phrase (minimal form, a noun). *ber-* is 'directive i'. See the Conspectus under Particles. The resultant prepositional phrase must therefore be either an exponent of a predicate element in verbal clause structure (i.e. i(a) or i(b)), or else it must be an exponent of Q in noun phrase structure (i.e.i(c)). See the Conspectus under Prepositional Phrase.

Since the context marks the prepositional phrase here as a qualifier for the noun-equivalent *kayu kechil*, the appropriate description for the phrase is 'prep.phr.i.(c)'.

line 4: a 'Q' element which consists of a prepositional phrase beginning with one of the prepositions *ka-*, *di-*, *dari*, *ber-* (i.e. particles 1(a)i, or, more succinctly, directives i) is to be labelled 'Q(ii)'. See the Conspectus under 'Q'.

N.B.: When a structure has more than two elements, the name of the structure is usually given on a separate line. See line 5 above

In the analysis of a clause, the last line records the clause elements:

Examples:

(*a*) Dua buah rumah itu kosong.
num. N_1 *n.grp.* N_2 det. Hv.(A.II.1a)

N

M(i) H D

n.phr.

N

S clause P

Those two houses are empty.

NOTE: This is a verbal clause, because the predicate is labelled Hv. (Head verb).

(*b*) Rumah itu tempat mengaji.
N det. N Vb.(A.I.)

H *n.phr.* D H *n.phr.* Q(i)

N N

S clause P

That building is used as a school.

NOTE: This is a nominal clause, because the predicate is labelled N. If *mengaji* is described as a verb-noun the result is the same, but P is a noun-group ($N_1 + N_2$) instead of a noun-phrase.

N.B.: In the analyses, immediate constituency is occasionally indicated by over-bracing:

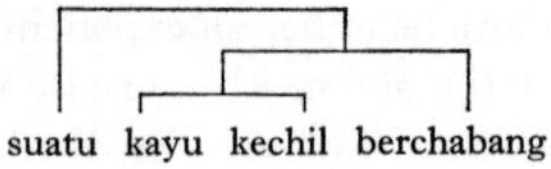
suatu kayu kechil berchabang

APPENDIX III

A NOTE ON
TRANSFORMATIONAL GRAMMAR

Modern linguistic analysis is based on formal criteria applied to the syntactic structures of the sentences of the language which is being examined. It is not based on the meaning* of the individual words or word-groups encountered in those sentences. Such an analysis results in a framework of basic sentence-types from which all longer sentences in the language may be evolved by expansion of the basic elements postulated in setting up the framework.

But this method has been supplemented in recent years by a technique which is based on a process known as 'transformation'.† Transformational grammar constructs rules, expressible in formulae, by which related sentences may be generated from the basic types already established. For example, from the basic sentence *He writes*, the 'tied' sentences *He does not write, Does he write? Does he not write?* would be brought into being, step by step, by the application of the relevant transformational 'rules'. It is a technique that has always been used by language teachers, if in

---

* N. Chomsky, *Syntactic Structures*, p. 100: 'It is, of course, impossible to prove that semantic notions are of no use in grammar, just as it is impossible to prove the irrelevance of any other given set of notions. An investigation of such proposals, however, invariably seems to lead to the conclusion that only a purely formal basis can provide a firm and productive foundation for the construction of grammatical theory.'

† R. H. Robins, (2), p. 241: 'At the present time the full value and the place of transformation cannot be definitely assessed, either as part of the theory of grammar or as an analytical procedure, but henceforward any serious consideration of language in general and the structural analysis of sentences in languages must take it into account.'

For an application of the theory of transformation to Malay sentence-structure see articles in *Dewan Bahasa* by Asmah Haji Omar (March/April 1964) and A. Bakar Hamid (July 1964).

piecemeal and unscientific fashion, in such *ad hoc* reminders as that 'after a historic leading verb, a future perfect of *Oratio Recta* must become pluperfect subjunctive in *Oratio Obliqua*', and it is taken for granted in the familiar type of exercise: 'Put the following sentences into the plural.'

This is the aspect of transformational grammar which is of importance in the synthesis of a language; in the analysis of the sentences of a language, where the processes are reversed, its usefulness lies in the formulae which it provides for the resolution of sentences which, superficially, do not seem to fit into the basic framework. That is how it has been used in these analyses, where it has been found helpful as a solvent for those groups of contiguous verbals which are so marked a characteristic of the Malay sentence.

TEXT A

HANTU BUNGKUS

Lakunan I

Pertunjokan 1

[¹*Di-kedai kopi Malabari.* ²*Masok Kasim dengan Saléh lalu dudok.*]
MALABARI: Kopi enché?
KASIM: ³Ia. ⁴Dua kopi susu. ⁵Taroh lebéh sadikit gula, ia, kaka?
MALABARI: Baik. Apa mahu makan? Roti? Biskut? Kuéh?
SALÉH: ⁶Apa kuéh ada? ⁷Ada kerépék? ⁸Kuéh sepit?
MALABARI: Ada. Baharu punya. Saya punya bini baharu bawa dari
   rumah. Lagi panas.
[*masok Musa*]
KASIM: Ha! ⁹Ini 'Bang Musa. ¹⁰Mari kita minum kopi, 'Bang Musa.
   [*kapada Malabari*] ¹¹Éh, kaka, bikin tiga kopi, ia? ¹²Sekarang sudah ada
   tiga orang. ¹³Bawa-lah kuéh kerépék itu banyak-banyak sadikit.
MALABARI [¹⁴*sambil pergi membuat kopi*] ¹⁴ᵃBaik.‡

---

‡ 14*a*: No significance is to be attached to the duplicate numbering. Some
originally unnumbered sentences have been so marked. Those still left
unmarked are mainly fragmentary repetitions or deliberately incoherent
utterances.

MUSA [*kapada Saléh*] [15]Kawan tahu awak ada di-sini, Saléh. [16]Itu sebab kawan chari ka-sini.

SALÉH: [17]Macham mana 'bang Musa tahu?

MUSA: [18]Kawan singgah chari ka-rumah awak tadi. [19]Ahli awak katakan awak tentu ada di-sini.

SALÉH: O—o—o! [20]Saya harap-harap tadi orang rumah saya sangka saya di-bendang juga lagi. [21]Ini dia tahu saya ada di-kedai kopi pula. [21a]Saya ta' boléh léngah lagi 'ni. [22]Sudah janji 'nak pulang lekas. [23]Dia minta tolong jolokkan kelapa.

KASIM: [24]Apa hal 'Bang Musa menchari Ché Saléh 'ni, 'Bang Musa?

SALÉH: [25]Ia, apa hal?

MUSA: [26]Anu—kawan saya Ché Lah baharu balék dari Kuala Lui. [27]Dalam hutan tempat dia lalu sa-malam kata-nya dia terjumpa rumpun rotan bukan main banyak. [28]Bukan jauh. [29]Chuma kira-kira dua batu sahaja ka-dalam dari jalan raya arah ka-sebelah sini. [30]Kata-nya dia teringat 'nak 'ngajak saya pergi barang dua tiga hari mengambil rotan 'tu. [31]Tapi sayang dia sudah berjanji 'nak pergi menolong mentua-nya menuai di-Simpang Tiga. [32]Awak pun tahu-lah menuai 'tu empat lima hari pun ta' sudah. [33]Tapi rotan 'tu kalau lambat pergi takut di-ambil dék orang lain.

KASIM: [34]Siapa mentua-nya Ché Lah? Oh! [35]Orang tua Pa' Anjang 'tu, ia? [36]Apa, dia belum sudah menuai lagi?

MUSA: [37]Belum. [38]Dia luka kaki. [39]Empat lima hari dahulu dia balék dari sawah, changkul-nya di-sérét-nya. [40]Entah macham mana waktu dia menarék changkul 'tu mata changkul 'tu hinggap ka-tumit-nya, luka menganga dekat 'nak putus urat keting-nya. [41]Sudah itu luka itu membengkak naik kelurut. [42]Sekarang dia ta' dapat berjalan lagi. [43]Macham mana 'nak menuai? [44]Itu-lah 'Bang Lah dua laki bini 'nak pergi menolong dia. [45]Padi-nya pun 'dah kukoh benar.

KASIM: [46]Ia, saya pun ada mendengar pasal Pa' Anjang luka kaki kena changkul 'tu. [47]Saya pun terpikir macham mana-lah dia 'nak menyudah-kan menuai kalau kaki luka bagitu. [48]Pelék juga, 'dah tua menyérét changkul macham budak-budak. [49]Kalau di-pikul changkul 'tu apa-lah salah-nya?

SALÉH: [50]Dah 'nak malang 'tu, malang-lah. [51]Tapi pasal rotan 'ni apa macham, 'Bang Musa? [52]Bang Musa berkira 'nak pergi-kah men-gambil-nya?

MUSA: Ia. [53]Itu-lah kawan menchari awak kalau mahu pergi sama. [54]Rotan baik harga sekarang, awak tahu, empat puloh ringgit sa-pikul. [55]Kawan kok dapat suka benar 'nak menambah-nambah jalan duit sadikit. [56]Awak pun ma'alum, anak kawan tiga orang dalam sekolah inggeris, semua-nya hendak belanja, makan minum, basikal, buku-buku, kain baju. [57]Di-mana-lah 'nak kawan chabutkan duit kok ta' kerékéh menchari?

SALÉH [[58]*sambil tundok berfikir*] [59]Empat puloh ringgit sa-pikul, kata 'Bang Musa?

MUSA: Ia. [60]Kawan terpikir barangkali awak mahu pergi sama, boléh kita berkongsi.

SALÉH: [61]Mahu juga menchuba, apa salah-nya? [62]Padi saya pun 'dah siap masok kepok. [63]"Tapi saya 'nak berpakat dengan orang rumah dahulu, apa kata dia.

MUSA [*kapada Kasim*]: [64]Awak, Ché' Kasim, macham mana pikir? [65]Hendak ta', pergi?

KASIM: [66a]Saya mémang tengah berpikir-pikir juga. [66]Sebab saya pun hendakkan duit juga sadikit. [67]Bulan depan saya 'nak mengawinkan anak, kena juga belanja sa-ratus dua, habis kurang-nya. [68]Kalau kita dapat lima enam pikul rotan 'tu sa-orang bukan-kah bagus juga? [69]Lima pikul sudah dua ratus ringgit, alang-kah besar pertolongan-nya? [70]Berapa lama agak-nya kita kena dudok dalam hutan?

MUSA: [71]Habis lama-nya sa-minggu. [72]Itu chukup-lah.

SALÉH: Hmh!

MUSA: [73]Mengapa, awak berkata 'Hmh!', Saléh?

SALÉH: [74]Saya ta' berapa sedap rasa-nya berpikir kena bermalam di-hutan 'tu. [75]'Bang Mat Zain dahulu berjumpa hantu kopék masa bermalam di-hutan bagitu-lah. [76]Ta' boléh-kah kita pulang ka-rumah tiap-tiap petang? [77]Bukan jauh. [78]Kata 'Bang Musa tadi kadar dua batu sahaja dari jalan besar.

MUSA: [79]Chus! [80]Mengarut! [81]Kawan pun hairan menéngok awak 'ni perchayakan perkara bukan-bukan macham itu semua. [82]Cherita perempuan-perempuan tua 'tu! [83]Awak ta' tahu-kah cherita hantu semua pembohong? [84]Hati 'dah takut, semua di-sangka hantu.

SALÉH: [85]Barangkali juga bagitu. [86]"Tapi ia tidak pun saya ta' suka juga 'nak berjumpa hantu.

MUSA: [87]Ta' mengapa. [88]Ta' kan ada hantu. [89]Lagi pun apa-lah di-takutkan? [90]Kita akan membuat pondok untuk tempat diam dalam sa-minggu itu. ⁹¹Awak kata pulang tiap-tiap petang itu pun boléh juga, 'tapi rotan yang kita tinggalkan itu kalau di-churi orang.

KASIM: ⁹²Kata-lah kita bermalam di-hutan 'tu sampai sa-minggu. ⁹³Berapa-lah agak-nya kita boléh dapat duit?

MUSA: ⁹⁴Senang-senang boléh dapat dua ratus ringgit tiap-tiap sa-orang, pada pikiran kawan-lah.

KASIM: ⁹⁵Wah! Sampai sa-banyak 'tu? ⁹⁵ᵃKalau bagitu bagus-lah.

MUSA: ⁹⁶Saléh apa macham pula?

SALÉH: ⁹⁷Saya pun suka pergi — ia-lah, saya kena tanya orang rumah saya dahulu, mahu-kah dia membenarkan.

MUSA: Aa–i–ih! ⁹⁸Awak ta' dapat-kah putuskan sendiri? ⁹⁹Bila-kah masa-nya awak 'ni boléh berjalan sendiri, Saléh? ¹⁰⁰'Nak kena pegang tali dék bini sa-umor hidup?

SALÉH: ¹⁰¹Bukan bagitu, 'Bang Musa. ¹⁰²Saya ta' kuasa 'nak bergadoh. ¹⁰³Bising-lah kalau ta' di-tanya dia.

MUSA: ¹⁰⁴Baik-lah. ¹⁰⁵Tanya-lah orang rumah awak, Saléh. ¹⁰⁶'Tapi jangan sampai tersangkut ta' dapat pergi pula.

SALÉH: ¹⁰⁷Dapat. ¹⁰⁸Bila agak-nya kita 'nak pergi 'tu, 'Bang Musa?

MUSA: ¹⁰⁹Kawan kira kita boléh bertolak agak-agak waktu tengah hari ésok. ¹¹⁰Jadi sempat-lah kita sudah membuat pondok 'tu sa-belum masok matahari.

KASIM: ¹¹¹Saya kalau bagitu boléh-lah.

MUSA: ¹¹²Awak, Saléh, macham mana? ¹¹³Boléh-kah bagitu?

SALÉH: ¹¹⁴Boléh-lah. [¹¹⁵*kemudian macham berbisék*] ¹¹⁶Kalau di-lepaskan-lah dék orang rumah.

MUSA: Bagus. ¹¹⁷Kita berjumpa di-muka simpang dekat kedai Ché' Manap 'tu, ia? ¹¹⁸Lepas sembahyang lohor ésok?

KASIM: Ia. ¹¹⁹Tentu saya boléh-lah 'tu.

SALÉH: ¹²⁰Saya pun bagitu pula.

MUSA: ¹²¹Kalau bagitu baik kita pulang lekas sekarang bersiap. ¹²²Kita tentu hendak bawa parang, tali besar, sigai, beras sadikit, ikan kering sadikit buat bekal, periok sa-buah.

[¹²³*Meréka ketiga pun bangkit lalu keluar.* ¹²⁴*Ketika itu Malabari taukéh kedai itu berkejar di-belakang meréka.*]

MALABARI: Hai! 'Nché', belum bayar! Siapa mahu bayar itu kopi, kuéh kerépék, kuéh sepit?

[¹²⁵*Orang bertiga itu masok balék sambil meminta ma'af*]

MUSA: ¹²⁶Minta ma'af. ¹²⁷Terlupa.

SALÉH: [128]Kami semua léka berchakap, ta' ingat 'nak bayar.

KASIM: [129]Berapa semua, kaka?

MALABARI: Tiga kopi sa-puloh sén satu, tiga puloh sén. Kuéh berapa banyak enché' makan? [*Memandang kuéh*] Oh. Sa-keping pun enché' ta' makan. Enché' léngah berchakap-chakap sahaja, buat kira mahu jadi kaya chari rotan. Saya tentu ta' boléh jadi kaya kalau orang minum kopi sa-kali sa-kali dapat tiga puloh sén ini macham.

KASIM [*membayar*]: [130]Ini wang, kaka.

MUSA: [131]Kaka ta' usah susah hati. [132]Kita tiga orang tentu datang selalu minum kopi di-sini. [133]Kalau kita untong, nanti kita panggil kawan ramai-ramai belanja kopi di-kedai kaka.

MALABARI: Saya harap itu macham-lah. Jangan lupa datang enché'. [*sambil orang bertiga itu berjalan keluar*] 'Salam Aleikum. Nasib baik boléh untong. Saya harap enché' jangan berjumpa hantu!

MUSA: [134]Puh! Hantu! Ia, hantu! [135]Sekarang sudah tahun sa-ribu sembilan ratus empat puloh sembilan, tahu. [136]Kita ta' pakai hantu lagi, sudah buang.

[[137]*Ketiga-nya keluar.* [138]*Malabari itu menganggok-nganggokkan kepala macham ta' perchayakan chakap Musa itu, lalu mengemaskan chawan-chawan dan kuéh-kuéh di-méja meréka tadi.*]

Pertunjokan 2

[[139]*Dalam pondok.* [140]*Petang ésok-nya.* [141]*Kasim berdiri membelakang kapada orang ramai.* [142]*Dia menerék-nerékkan tali pengikat dinding pondok itu.* [143]*Sa-buah lanting terpasang terletak di-tengah-tengah bilék itu.*]

KASIM [[144]*menerék ikatan*]: Ha! [145]Itu dia. [146]Itu 'dah chukup kuat 'dah 'tu.

MUSA [[147]*naik ka-pondok itu seraya menchampakkan parang-nya*]: [148]Kita sa-baik-baik sempat 'aja menyudahkan pondok ini. [148a]Kawan ta' sangka sampai bagitu léchéh kerja-nya membuat pondok. [149]Semua pasal susah dapat akar pengikat di-sini. [149a]Tapi sekarang sudah siap juga, sudah-lah.

KASIM: Ia. [150]Macham mana pun pondok kita sudah siap. [151]Sekarang 'nak malam pun malam-lah. [152]Kita ta' susah lagi pasal tempat 'nak tidor.

MUSA: [153]Kawan bukan pula ta' suka bekerja malam-malam. [154]Kalau élok lampu peték kawan 'ni malam pun kawan boléh bekerja. [[155]*Di-ambil-nya lampu peték-nya, di-peték-nya ta' menyala*] [156]Téngok-lah 'tu.

Buatan lepas perang. [157]Kawan beli tiga ringgit harga-nya 'ni di-kedai
Ché' Manap. [[158]*Di-lémparkan-nya lampu peték itu ka-tanah.*] [159]Saléh
pula kata-nya lupa membawa lampu peték-nya!

KASIM: [160]Saya ta' perchaya barang-barang perbuatan baharu sekarang
'ni. [[161]*Di-ambil-nya lampu peték Musa itu, di-bélék-nya.* [162]*Ta' suka dia
nampak-nya lalu di-lémparkan-nya.*] [163]Saya pun bila-bila pun lebéh
suka lanting. [164]Ba'-lah saya lanting macham ini, chukup-lah. [[165]*Di-
ambil-nya lanting yang sedia di-bawa-nya, di-berséhkan-nya sumbu-nya.*]

SALÉH: [[166]*masok terlompat macham orang chemas, lalu menutup pintu
rapat-rapat.*] *Ya Allah!* [167]Perasaan saya saya nampak dua biji mata
mengikut saya dari belakang. [168]Mata hantu wéwér agak-nya? [169]Dalam
hutan bagini selalu ada bermacham-macham hantu. [170]Hantu raya,
hantu wéwér, hantu pemburu, hantu menjangan, langsuir pontianak,
jin tanah, macham-macham lagi.

MUSA [[171]*menepok belakang Saléh macham orang tua memujok chuchu-
nya*]: [172]Sudah-lah Saléh, ta' usah bodoh, mudah perchaya perkara
karut-karut bagini. [172a]Di-mana ada hantu dalam dunia. [173]Awak
jantan. [174]Ta' patut pengechut. [175]Hantu wéwér kata awak? [176]Semua 'tu
sangka-sangka kosong. Perut awak kosong. [177]Itu sebab terbit perasaan
kosong macham-macham bagitu. [178]Mari kita makan kenyang-kenyang.
[179]Kawan pun bukan main lapar rasa-nya. [180]Apa kata Kasim?

KASIM [*menerékkan suatu ikatan lagi*]: [181]Ia, saya datang. [[182]*Di-ambil-nya
bungkus barang-barang-nya di-hujong lantai pondok itu lalu dudok 'nak
makan bersama-sama Musa dengan Saléh. [183]Saléh mengambil nasi
bungkus-nya pula lalu dudok. [185]Ia memandang keliling, hati-nya pun
sedap. [185]Musa ada, Kasim ada, lanting pun berpasang.*]

SALÉH: [186]Sedap dudok di-sini dekat lanting Ché' Kasim, ia? [[187]*membuka
nasi bungkus*] [188]Biar saya téngok apa lauk di-buatkan dék orang rumah
saya dalam nasi bungkus saya 'ni, agak-nya.

MUSA: [189]Sadikit 'aja nampak-nya 'tu. [190]Apa, pasal makan pun dia sekat
juga-kah awak?

SALÉH: [191]Sadikit, sama sadikit kita. [192]Hati gajah sama di-lapah, hati
kuman sama di-chechah, bukan-kah bagitu? [193]Ambil-lah 'bang Musa,
Ché' Kasim.

MUSA: [194]Terima kaséh. [195]Ta' usah-lah. [196]Bekal awak 'tu sedikit 'aja.
[197]Baik awak ambil kawan punya dengan Kasim punya 'ni sadikit.
[[198]*Membuka nasi bungkus-nya*] [199]Ini bekal kawan. [200]Awak ambil-lah
pula. [201]Kasim pun sila-lah.

KASIM: Terima kaséh. [*Membuka nasi bungkus-nya*] ^{201a}Ini bekal saya. ²⁰²Ambil-lah 'Bang Musa, Ché' Saléh. ²⁰³Kita rasa sama-sama.

MUSA ⎱
SALÉH ⎰ Terima kaséh.

[*Meréka pun makan*]

Lakunan II

Pertunjokan 1

[^{203a}*Dalam pondok itu juga.* ²⁰⁴*Tiga jam kemudian.* ²⁰⁵*Lanting maséh menyala.* ²⁰⁶*Orang bertiga itu tidor dekat-dekat melintang di-tengah-tengah bilék.* ²⁰⁷*Musa arah ka-dinding, Kasim arah ka-orang ramai, Saléh di-tengah-tengah.* ²⁰⁸*Musa mendengkor perlahan-lahan.* ²⁰⁹*Kasim mulaï mengerang.* ²¹⁰*Saléh beraléh.* ²¹¹*Makin kuat mengerang.* ²¹²*Saléh terjaga lalu dudok memandang keliling.* ²¹³*Ta' ada hantu, hanya Kasim mengerang.* ²¹⁴*Saléh baring balék.* ²¹⁵*Kasim mengerang bertambah kuat lagi.*]

SALÉH [²¹⁶*dudok memandang kapada Kasim*]: Hai! ²¹⁷Apa kena Ché' Kasim?

KASIM: ²¹⁸Perut kawan sakit-lah. [²¹⁹*Mengerang macham orang kesakitan sangat.* ²²⁰*Musa mendengar dalam tidor-nya sambil beraléh*] Adohi!

SALÉH: ²²¹Sakit macham mana? ²²²Memulas-mulas-kah? ²²³Angin agak-nya?

[²²⁴*Kasim bangkit dudok, baring balék, bangkit lagi, baring balék beberapa kali sambil menekan perut-nya menahan sakit.*]

KASIM: Wah! ²²⁵Chika agak-nya. ²²⁶Bukan main sakit-lah. Adohi! Adohi! Allah! Allah!

MUSA [²²⁷*terjaga lalu dudok memandang kapada Kasim*]: ²²⁸Apa pasal?

KASIM [²²⁹*berguling-guling oléh kesakitan*]: *Allah!* ²³⁰Sakit benar.

MUSA: ²³¹Sakit apa ini? ²³²Di-mana sakit?

KASIM [*menekan perut-nya*]: ²³³Di-sini-lah. ²³⁴Sa-belah kiri ini.

MUSA [*menggosok-gosok perut Kasim; kapada Saléh*]: ²³⁵Saléh pergi hidupkan api, bakar batu boléh di-tuam.

[²³⁶*Saléh bangkit pergi 'nak bakar batu.* ²³⁷*Kasim golék-gelentang di-atas lantai dengan kesakitan yang amat sangat saperti orang kena pagut ular tedong.* ²³⁸*Sa-ketika lagi ia pun péngsan lalu diam ta' bergerak-gerak macham orang mati. Musa memanggil Saléh.* ²³⁹*Saléh maséh terdiri dekat pintu, takut hendak turun.*] ²⁴⁰Kasim 'dah habis, Saléh. ²⁴¹'Dah habis. ²⁴²Ta' sempat di-buat apa. ²⁴³Kaséhan! ²⁴⁴Apa bangsa sakit perut-nya 'ni?

SALÉH [²⁴⁵*datang balék terkejar-kejar*. ²⁴⁶*Memandang kapada Kasim dengan muka duka chita*]: Ia. 'Dah habis. *Inna lillah wa inna ilayhi raji'un!* [²⁴⁷*Musa dan Saléh selimutkan 'mayat' Kasim baik-baik*.]

MUSA: ²⁴⁸Salah sa-orang kita mesti-lah keluar ka-kampong pergi memberi tahu orang rumah Kasim.

SALÉH: Ia. ²⁴⁹Salah sa-orang antara kita mesti pergi.

MUSA: ²⁵⁰Siapa 'nak pergi? ²⁵¹Awak hendak?

SALÉH: ²⁵²Saya tidak-lah. ²⁵³Saya takut hantu wéwér tadi.

MUSA [*mendengus*]: Hantu wéwér! ²⁵⁴Kalau bagitu biar-lah kawan pergi. ²⁵⁵Awak tunggu mayat 'ni.

SALÉH [²⁵⁶*menjawab dengan lebéh ketakutan lagi*]: ²⁵⁷Tidak, 'Bang Musa. ²⁵⁸Ta' boléh bagitu. ²⁵⁹Itu lagi dahshat. ²⁶⁰Saya takut benar hantu orang mati.

MUSA: Baik-lah. ²⁶¹Tetapkan hati awak. ²⁶²Yang mana awak lebéh berani? ²⁶³Kawan ta' peduli. ²⁶⁴Hantu wéwér, hantu orang mati, biar kawan hadap.

SALÉH [²⁶⁵*menggeletar oléh ketakutan*]: Hantu wéwér, hantu orang mati. (²⁶⁶*macham orang menimbang yang mana lebéh dahshat*) Hantu wéwér, hantu orang mati. [²⁶⁷*Menegok ayer lior lalu memutuskan pikiran*] ²⁶⁸Biar-lah hantu wéwér. ²⁶⁹Kalau di-kejar-nya saya lari kuat-kuat.

MUSA: Baik-lah. [*Berubah suara*] ²⁷⁰"Tapi 'nak menyenangkan hati awak mari kita berchabut undi. ²⁷¹Siapa chabut panjang dia-lah pergi.

SALÉH: Baik-lah. ²⁷²"Tapi saya kalau terchabut péndék pun, biar-lah hantu wéwér juga.

[²⁷³*Meréka berchabut*. ²⁷⁴*Nasib baik Saléh terchabut yang panjang*. ²⁷⁵*Jadi dia-lah pergi*.]

MUSA: Ha! ²⁷⁶Dapat-lah kehendak hati awak. ²⁷⁷Ta' usah-lah gentar. ²⁷⁸Serahkan diri kapada Tuhan. ²⁷⁹Pergi-lah lekas. ²⁸⁰Mudah-mudahan semua selamat. ²⁸¹Bulan pun ta' berapa gelap boléh awak nampak jalan. ²⁸²Kawan tunggu di-sini.

[²⁸³*Musa pun dudok jauh sadikit arah ka-kanan mayat itu*. ^{283a}*Saléh menuju ka-pintu*]

SALÉH [²⁸⁴*berpaling diri pintu, berjalan berjéngkét-jéngkét hendak menchapai lanting buat suloh*]: ²⁸⁵Lanting ini terang-kah?

MUSA: Aih! ²⁸⁶Ta' usah-lah! ²⁸⁷Itu lanting Kasim. ²⁸⁸Dia sudah mati awak 'nak ambil pula harta dia.

SALÉH [*pura-pura memeréksa sumbu lanting*]: ²⁸⁹Bukan! ²⁹⁰Bukan saya 'nak mengambil. ²⁹¹Saya 'nak betulkan sumbu-nya sahaja, jangan 'Bang Musa ta' chukup terang.

MUSA (*mengéjék*): Ia. [292]'Nak betulkan sumbu. (*Mengubah suara*) [293]'Turun-lah lekas. [294]Jangan léngah lagi.

SALÉH: Ia. [295]Saya 'nak turun-lah 'ni. [[296]*Turun, hati-nya berdebar-debar sangat takut.*]

Pertunjokan 2

[[297]*Di-luar pondok.* [298]*Sa-jurus kemudian.* [299]*Saléh telah berjalan kira-kira tiga rantai dari pondok.* [300]*Hati-nya sangat takut.* [301]*Bulan baharu terbit tetapi ta' nampak sebab terlindong oléh pokok-pokok hutan itu.*]
SALÉH [[302]*Terluru-luru hendak lekas oléh ketakutan.* [303]*Terantok kepala-nya kapada suatu pokok*]: *Allah!* [304]'Terantok pula kepala-ku. [[305]*Terantok kepala-nya lagi sa-kali*] *Allah!* Terantok lagi. Wah! [306]Kalau selalu terantok bagini 'nyalang aku keluar sekarang habis-lah kepala aku binchul-binchul. [[307]*Kedengaran bunyi ranting patah*] [308]Apa pula nama-nya 'tu? — [309]Ta' ada-lah. — [310]Ini ta' boléh jadi 'ni! [311]Aku mesti-lah lekas dari sini. [[312]*Pada perasaan-nya suatu benda saperti orang ber-selubong kain putéh lalu menggésél-gésél dia. Dia terpekék.*] *La ilaha illa 'llah!* Hantu wéwér-kah agak-nya. *La ilaha illa 'llah!* [[313]*Suatu benda lain saperti orang berselubong kain hitam pula pada perasaan-nya lalu menggésél dia.* [314]*Terpekék lagi.*] *La ilaha illa 'llah!* Hantu kopék agak-nya. *Ya Allah!* [315]Tolong aku! [316]Macham ini ta' tahan-lah. [317]Baik aku balék ajak 'Bang Musa pergi bersama. [[318]*Terlari-lari ta' tentu arah, kemudian berhenti.*] [319]'Tapi kalau aku balék ajak dia tentu di-ketawakan-nya aku, di-kata-nya aku penakut. [[320]*Ia terdiam sambil berfikir.* [321]*Sa-ketika itu dia nampak batang kayu kechil dekat tempat ia berdiri itu berchabang dua*] Ha! [322]Berchabang kayu ini! [323]Aku dapat satu pikiran. [324]*Mulaï menetak pokok kechil itu dengan parang-nya.*] [325]Nanti-lah aku dayakan juga Musa. [326]Macham mana pun dia tentu lari turun dari dalam pondok itu. [327]Dia kata dia ta' takut, ta' perchayakan hantu! Nanti-lah! [328]Aku téngok sampai ka-mana benar berani-nya. [329]Ber-taroh apa pun aku mahu dia tentu lari keluar, lari ta' berhenti-henti sampai keluar ka-kampong. [330]Aku boléh ikut dia dari belakang sahaja. [331]Biar di-sangka-nya hantu mayat Kasim mengejar dia. [[332]*Berjalan balék ka-pondok*].

Pertunjokan 3

[[333]*Balék dalam pondok.* [334]*Sa-jurus lepas itu. Musa dudok di-sebelah 'mayat' Kasim membacha Qul huwa 'llah ta' berhenti-henti.* [335]*Kemudian berhenti membacha lalu menghulorkan tangan menchapai bakul tempat lebéh-lebéh nasi bungkus tadi.*]

MUSA: [336]Sudah-lah. [337]Ada mayat ta' ada mayat perut aku lapar juga. [338]Makan senja tadi kenyang, 'tapi ini 'dah lapar lagi. [*Membuka bakul*] [339]Ada tinggal nasi lagi agak-nya. [*Mula menyuap.* [340]*Kepala 'mayat' itu bergerak, di-changkah oléh Saléh dari bawah rumah lalu terangkat ka-atas, kadar dua inchi.* [341]*Musa terkemamar, mata-nya terbeliak, mulut-nya ternganga memandang mayat itu.* [342]*Tangan-nya terhenti di-antara bakul dengan mulut-nya.*] *Astaghfiru'llah!* [343]Bergerak kapala 'tu? [344]Aku nampak macham bergerak. [[345]*Di-renong-nya 'mayat' itu baik-baik sa-jurus.* [346]*Ta' bergerak.*] Chéh! [347]Chuma angan-angan aku agak-nya. [348]Aku sudah jadi macham Saléh pula sekarang! [[349]*Geli hati-nya*] [350]Saléh macham mana-lah hal-nya 'ni? [351]Aku jamin dia kechut keta-kutan berjalan sa-orang diri dalam gelap dalam hutan 'ni. [[352]*Di-masokkan-nya nasi yang di-suap-nya itu ka-mulut, di-telan-nya.*] Hantu! Merapék! [[353]*Kepala 'mayat' itu terangkat lagi, lebéh tinggi daripada tadi.*] *La ilaha illa 'llah!* Bergerak lagi? — Tidak! Ai! [354]Aku mesti beranikan hati aku. [355]Ini semua karut! [[356]*Di-renong-nya dekat-dekat ka-muka 'mayat' itu.* [357]*Dudok balék.* [358]*Hati-nya sedap sa-mula.* [359]*Ia menyuap lagi.* [360]*Kebetulan masa hendak membawa suap-nya itu ka-mulut, mayat itu bangkit hingga kira-kira sa-paroh dudok, lalu tetap di-situ.* [361]*Musa memandang dengan terlalu dahshat, mata-nya buntang.* [362]*Ber-chakap kapada mayat*]: [363]Baring balék! Baring! [364]Aku tidak salah! [365]Bukan aku membunoh engkau. [366]Makanan tadi entah apa salah-nya. [367]Baring-lah balék. [[368]*Badan 'mayat' itu rebah sa-mula.*] Hu-uh! [[369]*sambil mengipas-ngipas badan-nya*] Ha! [370]Bagitu-lah. [Kapada 'mayat']: [371]Baring diam-diam di-situ. [372]Jangan bergerak-gerak lagi. [[373]*Memandang keliling nampak sa-helai tali kasar, di-ambil-nya.*] [374]Nanti aku paksa. [375]Aku ikat engkau. [[376]*Pergi mengikat tali itu kapada 'mayat'.* [377]*Dia membongkok.* [378]*Baharu ia tengah membelitkan tali itu ka-lantai 'mayat' itu terangkat balék sampai dudok betul.* [379]*Sebab kuat-nya dia terbangkit itu hingga terantok muka-nya kapada dahi Musa.* [380]*Musa terpekék besar lalu bangun lari meluru keluar terus menuju jalan ka-kampong.* [381]*Saléh keluar dari bawah rumah berlari pula mengikut Musa dari belakang.*]

Lakunan III

Pertunjokan 1

[³⁸²*Di-rumah Musa.* ³⁸³*Sa-tengah jam kemudian.* ³⁸⁴*Dalam bilék di-rumah Musa Fatimah isteri Musa tengah tidor.* ³⁸⁵*Musa mengetok pintu rumah-nya macham 'nak roboh bunyi-nya.*]

FATIMAH [³⁸⁶*bangkit pisat-pisatan*]: ³⁸⁷Siapa itu?

MUSA: ³⁸⁸Aku Musa. ³⁸⁹Buka-lah pintu lekas!

[³⁹⁰*Fatimah membuka pintu.* ³⁹¹*Musa menerja masok dengan terlalu chemas dan ketakutan, lalu tersungkor di-hadapan Fatimah menchungap-chungap.*]

FATIMAH [³⁹²*terperanjat besar*]: *Ya Allah!* ³⁹³Apa 'ni? ³⁹⁴Apa hal? ³⁹⁵Apa pasal awak balék tengah-tengah malam 'ni? Rimau-kah?

MUSA [³⁹⁶*menchungap menarék nafas sambil menunjok ka-pintu*]: Kasim!

FATIMAH: ³⁹⁷Kasim apa pasal? ³⁹⁸Dia ada datang sama?

MUSA: Ia! ³⁹⁹Eh — bukan! ⁴⁰⁰Kasim 'dah mati — ⁴⁰¹'Tapi dia mengejar aku. ⁴⁰²Ada dia di-luar 'tu.

FATIMAH: ⁴⁰³Kasim mengejar awak? ⁴⁰⁴Apa awak 'ni berchakap ta' ketahuan? ⁴⁰⁵'Tapi kata tadi Kasim 'dah mati. ⁴⁰⁶Di-mana di-tinggalkan dia?

MUSA: Dalam pondok — Eh! — Tidak! — ⁴⁰⁷Di-luar 'tu.

FATIMAH: ⁴⁰⁸Kalau dia ada di-luar baik di-suroh masok. [⁴⁰⁹*Pergi ka-pintu.*]

MUSA [⁴¹⁰*suara-nya makin nyaring saperti orang menjerit*]: Jangan! Jangan! ⁴¹¹Jangan suroh masok! — ⁴¹²Bukan Kasim di-luar 'tu. ⁴¹³Hantu mayat Kasim.

FATIMAH [⁴¹⁴*dengan terperanjat*]: Hantu mayat? Hu-h. Hu-h. Hu-h. [⁴¹⁵*mengubah suara*] ⁴¹⁶'Tapi awak kata dahulu ta' perchayakan hantu.

MUSA [⁴¹⁷*ta' sabar*]: ⁴¹⁸Usah-lah peduli apa kata aku dahulu 'tu. ⁴¹⁹Tolong aku menahankan dia jangan dapat masok.

[⁴²⁰*Mula membacha ayat al-kursi serta bermacham-macham do'a yang dia tahu buat menghalau hantu shaitan.* ⁴²¹*Kumat-kamit mulut-nya.*]

FATIMAH: ⁴²²Nanti saya tutup pintu. [⁴²³*Pergi 'nak menutup pintu.*]

MUSA: ⁴²⁴Itu ta' berguna. ⁴²⁵Tutup pintu pun hantu lepas masok. ⁴²⁶Biar dia terbuka. ⁴²⁷Kalau ia masok senang kita lari keluar. ⁴²⁸Mari-lah berdiri dekat pintu 'ni, bacha apa-apa yang awak tahu. ⁴²⁹Menguchap kuat-kuat, sergahkan kapada muka-nya kalau dia 'nak masok. [⁴³⁰*Kedua-*

*dua-nya berdiri di-kiri kanan pintu lalu membacha-bacha ayat dengan
suara perlahan tetapi chepat.* [431]*Kedua-nya siap 'nak menyergahkan La
ilaha illa 'llah kalau hantu Kasim itu chuba hendak masok.* [432]*Sa-bentar
lagi Fatimah sudah makin lambat bachaan-nya.* [433]*Musa suroh bacha
chepat-chepat lagi.*] [434]Chepat-chepat, macham aku 'ni. [435]Kalau berhenti tentu dia masok. [[436]*Kedua-nya pun makin bertambah kenchang
bachaan-nya serta memandang keluar hendak menyergah hantu Kasim
dengan kalimah La ilaha illa 'llah sa-kira-nya dia 'nak masok juga.*]

Pertunjokan 2

[*Rumah Kasim.* [437]*Sa-jurus kemudian.* [438]*Dalam bilék rumah Kasim isteri
Kasim bernama Meriam tengah tidor pula.* [439]*Bunyi orang mengetok pintu
kemudian bunyi suara orang memanggil saperti berbisék.*]

SALÉH: Ché' Yam! Ché' Yam!

MERIAM [[440]*membuka mata tetapi badan-nya ta' bergerak*]: Hee-h?

SALÉH: Ché Yam! Ché Yam!

MERIAM [[441]*beraléh antara tidor dengan jaga*]: [442]Belum siang lagi 'Bang
Chim. [443]Mengapa lekas benar 'nak bangun?

[[444]*Kemudian terjaga betul.* [445]*Baharu dia teringat suami-nya tidak ada
bersama-sama.* [446]*Dia bangkit dudok sambil berkelip-kelip mata-nya lalu
mendengar baik-baik betul-kah ada orang memanggil atau tidak.*]

SALÉH: Ché' Yam! Ché' Yam!

MERIAM: [447]Siapa 'tu?

SALÉH: [448]Saya Saléh. [449]Buka pintu. [450]Saya Saléh datang 'nak memberi
khabar.

[[451]*Meriam bangun dari tempat tidor lalu pergi membukakan pintu.* [452]*Di-
lihat-nya Saléh terdiri di-pintu.* [453]*Di-tangan Saléh, memegang suatu kayu
kechil berchabang.*]

MERIAM: Aih! Ché' Léh! [454]Apa pasal balék tengah-tengah malam 'ni?
[455]Bukan-kah awak ka-hutan sa-malam sama-sama 'bang Chim dengan
'Bang Musa? [456]Di-mana 'Bang Chim sama 'Bang Musa 'ni? [457]Ada-kah
apa-apa hal?

SALÉH: Ia. [458]Ada kemalangan sadikit. Ché' Kasim 'dah — 'dah —

MERIAM: [459]'Dah apa? [460]Di-mana dia 'ni?

SALÉH: [461]Dia tinggal dalam pondok, tempat kami tidor di-hutan 'tu.

MERIAM: [462]Tinggal sama 'Bang Musa?

SALÉH: Tidak. [463]'Bang Musa 'dah pulang ka-rumah-nya.

MERIAM: 'Dah pulang? [464]Apa pasal? [465]Apa hal?

SALÉH: ⁴⁶⁶Entah-lah. ⁴⁶⁷Saya pun kurang peréksa apa pasal. ⁴⁶⁸Dia ta'
kata apa-apa 'tapi dia pulang dengan gopoh-gopoh benar. ⁴⁶⁹Agak-nya
'nak mengambil entah apa-apa barang tinggal.

MERIAM: ⁴⁷⁰Habis, apa pasal Ché' Léh pula ikut datang sama, di-tinggalkan 'Bang Chim di-hutan?

SALÉH: ⁴⁷¹Saya takut kalau-lalau 'bang Musa terjumpa bahaya apa-apa
malam-malam 'ni, berjalan sa-orang diri dalam hutan malam-malam
bagini. ⁴⁷²Sebab itu saya turut dia.

MERIAM: ⁴⁷³'Dah 'tu, 'Bang Chim tinggal sa-orang-orang diri-lah dalam
hutan 'tu? ⁴⁷⁴Itu ta' ada bahaya? ⁴⁷⁴ᵃKalau sa-kira-nya dia kena bahaya
apa-apa, apa kata Ché' Léh?

SALÉH: ⁴⁷⁵Ché' Kasim selamat, chukup selamat. ⁴⁷⁶Ta'ada apa-apa lagi
boléh di-takutkan. ⁴⁷⁷Satu bahaya pun dia ta' boléh kena lagi sekarang.
⁴⁷⁸Dia sudah selamat betul.

MERIAM: ⁴⁷⁹Apa erti chakap Ché' Léh 'ni? ⁴⁸⁰Mana tahu entah 'rimau
mengendapkan dia tinggal sa-orang-orang bagitu!

SALÉH: ⁴⁸¹'Rimau pun ta' mengapa.

MERIAM: Ta' mengapa? ⁴⁸²Apa chakap awak 'ni, Ché' Léh?

SALÉH: Apa pula? ⁴⁸³Saya berchakap benar 'aja. Dia 'dah — dia — dia
sudah —

[⁴⁸⁴*Pada sa'at ini Kasim pun tiba terkejar-kejar sangat gopoh laku-nya.*
⁴⁸⁴ᵃ*Dalam tangan-nya menjinjing lanting maséh| terpasang.* ⁴⁸⁵*Saléh
terchengang besar, lalu menchuba hendak menyembunyikan diri di-balék
pokok bunga dekat pintu itu.*]

MERIAM: Ha! ⁴⁸⁶Ini pun 'Bang Chim! ⁴⁸⁷Ia-lah selamat? ⁴⁸⁸Shukor
kapada Tuhan!

KASIM [*kapada Saléh*]: ⁴⁸⁹Bagus awak, ia, Ché' Saléh! ⁴⁹⁰Awak tinggalkan
kawan sa-orang diri dalam pondok, di-tengah hutan 'tu. ⁴⁹¹Apa sudah
jadi? ⁴⁹²Kawan ta' teringat satu apa lepas kawan kena sakit perut terok
tadi.

SALÉH: Saya berdua dengan 'Bang Musa sangkakan Ché' Kasim — Kami
téngok Ché' Kasim betul macham orang —

KASIM: ⁴⁹³Kawan péngsan ta' sedarkan diri. ⁴⁹⁴Bila kawan sedarkan balék
kawan téngok kawan tinggal sa-orang. ⁴⁹⁵Apa pasal-nya awak lari
tinggalkan kawan bagitu?

SALÉH: ⁴⁹⁶Saya berdua dengan 'bang Musa sangkakan Ché' Kasim —

KASIM: ⁴⁹⁷Itu pun baik juga awak terpikir meninggalkan kawan makanan
awak. ⁴⁹⁸Bila kawan tersedar itu kawan téngok bakul makanan ada dekat

kawan. [499]Kawan buka, téngok ada lagi sadikit nasi dengan lauk sambal udang tinggal di-dalam bakul 'tu. [500]Perut kawan pun 'dah terasa kosong lalu kawan sental sahaja-lah apa yang ada 'tu. [501]Bungkus nasi awak dengan Musa sahaja. [502]Bungkus nasi kawan kawan champakkan sebab kawan ingat makanan kawan 'tu-lah agak-nya yang menjadikan kawan sakit perut tadi. [503]Entah apa salah-nya makanan yang di-bekalkan dék Ché' Yam sa-malam?

MERIAM [[503a]*menjeling pura-pura marah*]: [504]'Bang Chim champakkan? [505]Alang-kah membuang-buang! [506]Makanan yang bagitu bagus. [507]Dalam masa serba susah serba mahal sekarang pula 'tu.

KASIM [*mengéjék*]: Ia, makanan bagus! [508]Chemas-chemas mati aku di-buat-nya dék memakan makanan yang Yam bekalkan 'tu. [509]Apa Yam buboh?

MERIAM [[510]*berfikir sa-bentar*]: [510a]Éh, apa pula agak-nya? [511]Jangan kok sebab ikan kering 'tu busok sadikit sa-malam? [512]Yam pun terpikir, 'tapi 'dah selalu kita makan ikan busok bagitu, ta' apa-apa. [513]Lagi pun 'Bang Chim ta' ingat-kah pantun orang tua-tua?

> 'Tikar puchok, tikar mengkuang,
> Alas nikah raja Melayu.
> Ikan busok jangan di-buang,
> Buat perenchah si-daun kayu.

KASIM: [514]Ah, ta'usah-lah berpantun-pantun pula. [515]Jaga 'aja-lah lain-lain kali kalau ikan busok buangkan, usah di-ambil. [516]Mana tahu? [517]Nasib 'nak malang, barangkali entah ada termasok benda-benda bisa maka dia jadi busok 'tu. [518]Kali ini nasib baik juga, ajal aku belum sampai shukor-lah kapada Tuhan. [[519]*berpaling kapada Saléh*] [520]'Tapi 'Bang Musa di-mana dia 'ni?

SALÉH: [521]Dia 'dah pulang ka-rumah-nya. [522]Dia pun macham saya juga menyangkakan Ché' Kasim 'dah mati.

KASIM: Ia? *Subhan Allah!* [523]Rupa-nya aku 'ni 'dah mati hidup balék!

SALÉH: [524]Ia, sebab di-sangkakan-nya 'dah mati 'tu-lah dia berlari pulang bukan main chepat. [525]Di-téngok daripada chemas-nya ia berlari 'tu saya nampak macham dia terpandang-pandang hantu mayat Ché' Kasim mengejar dia.

KASIM: Ha! Ha! Ha! [526]Bagitu-kah? [527]Geli hati kawan mendengar-nya. [528]Kawan sangkakan dahulu dia betul-betul ta' perchayakan hantu. [[529]*Teringat serta-merta*] [530]Oh, ia, kawan terpikir! [531]Mari kita usék dia.

[532*Meluru ka-dalam mengambil chadar dari tempat tidor lalu di-selu-bongkan-nya kapada kepala dan badan-nya sambil keluar balék*] 533Kawan 'nak tunjokkan penakut-nya 'tu, biar dia sedarkan diri. [534*Berjalan arah ka-rumah Musa, kemudian berpaling kapada Saléh dengan Meriam*] 535Mari ikut, boléh kita téngok macham mana rupa-nya 'Bang Musa ta' perchayakan hantu! [536*Berjalan terus.* 537*Meriam dengan Saléh ikut.*]

Pertunjokan 3

[*Di-rumah Musa. Sa-jurus kemudian.* 538*Pintu rumah Musa mémang terbuka.* 539*Musa dengan Fatimah ada di-sebelah dalam di-kiri kanan pintu sedang membacha-bacha serta menanti-nanti kalau-kalau hantu Kasim masok.*]

MUSA } [*berulang-ulang*]: La ilaha illa 'llah.
FATIMAH

[540*Nampak sa-kelibat suatu benda macham kain putéh di-tepi pintu. Musa dengan Fatimah terkejut.* 541*Terus membacha-bacha dan menguchap-nguchap lagi makin chepat.* 542*Sa-bentar lagi nampak rupa saperti sayap putéh menggerbang-gerbang dari luar pintu.* 543*Musa dengan Fatimah puchat lalu terhenti membacha-bacha oléh sebab ketakutan.* 544*Sa-bentar itu Kasim dengan selubong-nya masok.* 545*Sampai ka-tepi dinding sa-belah mengadap Musa dengan Fatimah seraya menganggok-nganggokkan kepala kapada meréka.* 546*Kedua meréka kelu ta' dapat berchakap apa-apa.* 547*Kasim angkat tangan kanan-nya perlahan-lahan dalam kain putéh itu serta menunjok kapada Musa sambil menganggok-nganggok sa-olah-olah menyalahkan Musa.* 548*Musa memandang buntang mata-nya.*]

MUSA [549*terchungap-chungap dengan ketakutan.* 550*Mulut-nya kumat-kamit sa-mula, suara-nya kedengaran macham orang berbisék*]: Ya Allah! Ya Allah! Tolong-lah! Tolong-lah! La ilahi illa 'llah.

[551*Fatimah maséh kelu.* 552*Kasim dengan serta merta berjalan merapat kapada Musa.* 552a*Musa undor ta' berani mengaléh mata-nya daripada 'hantu' itu takut kalau-kalau ia melompat menerkam dia.* 553*Kasim ikut dia barang ka-mana dia undor dalam bilék itu.* 554*Sa-telah Musa terasak pada suatu penjuru Kasim buat-buat macham 'nak memelok dia.* 555*Musa meraung dengan ketakutan, tetapi Kasim tidak jadi memelok, hanya di-lémparkan-nya kain chadar yang di-buat-nya kain selubong itu ka-atas kepala Musa.* 556*Musa hempas pulas hendak melepaskan diri daripada kain itu sa-hingga ia terdengar suara Kasim mengéjék dia.* 557*Sementara itu Fatimah lekat terpaku pada lantai itu, ta' berdaya hendak berbuat apa-*]

apa. [558]*Tetapi sa-ketika lagi ia tersedar benda yang di-sangka-nya hantu
itu dengan sa-kunyong-kunyong sudah beraléh rupa ia-itu tiada berubah
lain hanya Kasim betul dengan sa-benar-benar-nya.* [559]*Dia pun menepi
pergi berdiri dekat suami-nya.* [560]*Pada sa'at itu Saléh dengan Meriam pun
masok lalu tertawa bersama-sama melihat hal yang terjadi itu.*]

KASIM: [561]'Bang Musa pikir saya 'dah mati, ia, 'Bang Musa?

MUSA [[562]*melepaskan kepala daripada kain selubong itu, kemudian terdiri
memandang kapada Kasim dengan ta' dapat berkata apa-apa*]:
e—e—e.

KASIM: [563]Tidak! [564]Saya belum mati. [565]'Tapi sampai hati 'Bang Musa
tinggalkan saya sa-orang diri dalam hutan bagitu!

MUSA [[566]*dapat berchakap sa-mula*]: [567]Awak takut-takutkan kawan.
[568]Awak bangun dudok masa awak terbujor macham mayat 'tu.

KASIM [[569]*berasa pelék ta' mengerti*]: [570]Bila pula saya bangun dudok? [571]Ia-
kah saya bangkit dudok? [572]Saya ta' ingat apa-apa sampai tersedar, saya
dapati 'bang Musa dengan Ché' Léh ta' ada lagi di-situ. [573]Betul-kah
saya ada bangkit dudok sa-belum daripada itu?

MUSA: [574]Betul ada. [575]Kawan téngok mula-mula kepala awak terangkat
sadikit [[576]*sambil menggayakan dengan tangan-nya sa-banyak mana
terangkat-nya.* [577]*Saléh di-sebelah belakang memandang dengan tersenyum-
senyum lalu di-achukan-nya dengan kayu berchabang-nya itu ia menjolakkan léhér Kasim dari bawah rumah.*] [578]Kemudian turun balék lalu
senyap. [579]Kemudian terangkat lagi lebéh tinggi daripada tadi. [579a]Kawan
pun mula terasa seram-seram. [580]Kawan ambil tali hendak ikatkan awak
ka-lantai biar jangan dapat bangkit lagi. [581]Tengah-tengah kawan 'nak
mengikat 'tu tiba-tiba kepala dengan badan awak terangkat bukan main
kuat sampai terdudok betul. [582]Muka awak terantok kapada dahi kawan
[*meraba dahi-nya*]. [583]Ada lagi binchul-nya di-dahi kawan 'ni.

SALÉH [*tertawa*]: [583a]Ia, itu betul! Saya nampak. [584]Geli benar hati saya
menéngok-nya. [585]Kalau Ché' Kasim sendiri ada memandang tentu
pechah perut ketawa.

MUSA [[586]*berpaling serta-merta kapada Saléh*]: Saléh! [587]Apa awak tahu
pasal ini? [588]Awak bukan-nya ada bersama-sama kawan masa itu!

SALÉH: [589]Apa pula ta' ada-nya? [590]Saya mémang ada di-situ. [591]'Bang
Musa yang ta' nampak.

MUSA: [592]Di-mana awak masa itu?

SALÉH: [593]Di-bawah pondok itu. [[594]*Di-achukan-nya kayu berchabang-nya
itu kapada léhér Kasim menunjokkan dia menjolakkan kepala Kasim*

sampai terangkat bagitu kuat. Kasim tertawa. ⁵⁹⁵*Musa menggéléng-géléngkan kepala dengan malu rupa-nya.*]

KASIM: ⁵⁹⁶Rugi betul saya ta' dapat memandang sama hal kejadian itu! MUSA: *Astaghfiru'llah!* ⁵⁹⁷Betul-kah awak 'ni Saléh? ⁵⁹⁸Awak kena-kenakan kawan. ⁵⁹⁹Kawan pun bodoh benar. ⁶⁰⁰Bagitu senang dapat awak main-mainkan kawan. [*Maséh menggéléng-géléngkan kapala*] ⁶⁰¹Ia-lah, apa 'nak di-katakan? ⁶⁰²'Dah sudah 'tu, sudah-lah. [⁶⁰³*Menchuba hendak menghilangkan malu-nya dengan meluruskan muka-nya saperti gaya berani.*] ⁶⁰⁴'Tapi macham mana pun betul juga kawan. ⁶⁰⁵Mana ada hantu? ⁶⁰⁶Chuma Ché' Kasim 'aja yang ada. ⁶⁰⁷Yang sa-benar-nya hantu itu semua angan-angan. ⁶⁰⁸Bila hati takut waktu kita sa-orang diri di-situ-lah terbit macham-macham pikiran yang mengatakan hantu ⁶⁰⁹Kalau kita dapat menahan takut 'tu hilang-lah hantu-hantu 'tu semua-nya. [⁶¹⁰*Kasim membuat-buat saperti 'nak berselubong balék dengan chadar itu tetapi di-tahan oléh Musa.*] Ta' usah! Ta' usah! ⁶¹¹Kawan belum puléh betul semangat kawan lagi. [*Mengubah chakap-nya.*] ⁶¹²Ini semua pasal perut belum masok apa-apa. ⁶¹³Hari 'dah tinggi. [*Kapada isteri-nya.*] ⁶¹⁴Pergi-lah Ché' Mah jerangkan ayer panas, buat kopi dengan roti chanai sadikit, boléh kita makan.

FATIMAH: ⁶¹⁵Ia, biar saya pergi siapkan. [*Kapada Ché' Meriam.*] Masok-lah Ché' Yam.

MERIAM: Ia-lah. ⁶¹⁶Saya pun boléh tolong Ché' Mah ka-dapor.

[⁶¹⁷*Kedua perempuan itu masok terus ka-dapor*]

MUSA [⁶¹⁸*kapada Kasim dengan Saléh sambil menggayakan tangan-nya suroh meréka dudok*]: ⁶¹⁹Mari-lah dudok Kasim, Saléh, boléh kita berbual-bual pasal lain sementara Ché' Mah buat roti 'tu.

[⁶²⁰*Orang laki-laki bertiga itu dudok berbual-bual mengisap rokok sambil tertawa gelak-gelak.*]

MUSANG BERJANGGUT

Lakunan I

Pertunjokan 1

[¹*Hari pagi.* ²*Dua orang laki isteri muda-muda dudok di-atas tikar di-rumah.* ³*Kedua-dua-nya orang raja baharu kahwin.* ⁴*Isteri-nya sangat chanték, riang.* ⁵*Suami terlalu sugul muka-nya.*]

SALMAH: ⁶Abang 'ni apa fasal Mah téngok susah 'aja rupa muka abang? ⁷Macham orang kematian!

SALIM: ⁸Hai, entah-lah! ⁹Aku pun ta' tahu 'nak chakap. ¹⁰Malang menimpa, tuah melambong tinggi. ¹¹Kita baharu kahwin, tetapi nampak-nya kita akan berchenggang. ¹²Harus entah langsong bercherai, ta' berjumpa lagi...

SALMAH: ¹³Bercherai! ¹⁴Fasal apa bercherai? ¹⁵Belum sampai sa-bulan kahwin!

SALIM: ¹⁶'Dah 'tu 'nak di-apakan? ¹⁷Aku kena pergi juga, ta' boléh tidak meninggalkan engkau. ¹⁸Sekarang 'ni juga. ¹⁹Hai nasib! ²⁰Kalau emak aku ta' beranakkan aku kelmarin lagi baik!

SALMAH: ²¹Kena pergi ka-mana? ²²Apa fasal ta' boléh tidak?

SALIM: ²³Titah Raja menyurohkan, macham mana 'nak mengélak! ²⁴Kata orang tua-tua Kerja Raja di-junjong, kerja sendiri di-kélék.

SALMAH: [*terperanjat*] ²⁵Titah Raja! ²⁶Kalau bagitu ia-lah, abang ta' boléh tidak pergi. ²⁷Tetapi tentu ta' lama? ²⁸Habis lama-nya sa-minggu?

SALIM: [29]Sa-minggu. [30]Heⁿh! Engkau ta' tahu!

SALMAH: [31]Kok ta' pun, sa-bulan?

SALIM: [*mengéjék*] Ia! Sa-bulan!

SALMAH: Sa-tahun?

SALIM: [32]Engkau merépék! [33]Sa-lama-lama-nya, tahu? [34]Sampai mati ta' boléh balék-balék. [35]Apa boléh buat, langit menimpa kepala!

SALMAH: [36]Macham mana 'ni? [37]Mah ta' mengerti, 'Bang. [38]Abang 'nak ka-mana sampai bagitu lama?

SALIM: [39]Aku pun ta' tahu ka-mana. [40]Yang aku tahu pagi 'ni juga di-suroh-nya pergi ta' boléh léngah lagi.

SALMAH: [40a]Abang ta' tahu! [41]Usah-lah main-main 'Bang! [42]Abang tentu tahu. [43]Ta' kan Raja ta' khabarkan kapada abang ka-mana 'nak di-suroh-nya. [44]Macham mana pun dia sendiri tentu tahu 'nak di-suroh-nya ka-mana. [45]Kalau abang ta' tahu mangapa ta' di-tanya?

SALIM: [46]Mana pula! [47]Dia sendiri pun ta' tahu. [48]Dia bukan 'nak menyuroh aku ka-mana-mana tempat yang tentu!

SALMAH: [49]Héh! Karut kerja 'ni!

SALIM: [50]Dia 'nak suroh aku pergi menchari...

SALMAH: [51]Menchari apa?

SALIM: [52]Menchari musang berjanggut.

SALMAH: Musang berjanggut! [53]Di-mana ada musang berjanggut dalam dunia? [54]Kalau ia bagitu, nyata-lah Raja 'ni gila!

SALIM: [55]Sunggoh-lah dia gila. [56]Itu-lah sebab aku kena pergi juga menchari-nya.

SALMAH: [57]"Tapi apa fasal dia hendakkan musang berjanggut? [58]'Nak buat apa?

SALIM: [59]Dia bukan hendakkan musang berjanggut. [60]Yang betul-nya dia hendakkan engkau.

SALMAH: Apa? Hendakkan Mah? Chis! Mengarut! [61]Sudah-lah 'Bang. [62]Ta' usah berchakap lagi! [63]Abang jangan pergi. [64]Kalau pergi bawa Mah. [65]Jangan tinggalkan Mah!

SALIM: [66]Mah tahu, bukan Raja sahaja hendakkan Mah 'tu. [67]Semua orang besar-besar-nya pun tergila-gila hendakkan Mah belaka.

SALMAH: Chus! 'Aib! Gila! Merapék!

SALIM: [68]Dengar-lah! [69]Dato' Temenggong sa-orang yang hendakkan Mah. [70]Aku téngok mata-nya bulat memandang Mah sahaja masa kita bersanding kelmarin. [71]Macham 'nak di-makan-nya Mah.

SALMAH [[72]*dengan muka benchi*]: Hah! Berok tua sial 'tu! [73]Memandang-

nya pun Mah meluat. [74]Benchi menéngok kelakuan-nya mengada-
ngada kebesar-besaran ta' ketahuan arah.

SALIM: [75]To' Laksamana sa-orang lagi; [76]gila hendakkan Mah juga.

SALMAH: [[77]*suka sadikit rupa-nya*]: To' Laksamana? Hʰa! [78]Dia 'tu
élok-lah sadikit rupa-nya. [79]Misai-nya berdenting, macham dawai
melenték ka-atas, bukan main hébat! [[80]*sambil menunjokkan misai dengan
tangan-nya.*]

SALIM [[81]*rupa chemburu*]: [82]Mah! Aku rasa ta' élok engkau memuji-muji
To' Laksamana macham itu. [[83]*sambil mengurut-ngurut misai-nya
sendiri yang meranting ta' lebat.*]

SALMAH [[84]*macham rupa orang mengaku salah*]: Ah. [85]Abang ta' usah-
susah-lah fasal itu. [86]Mah mémang lebéh gemar misai ta' lebat. [87]Mah
kata misai macham To' Laksamana 'tu élok pada orang jadi laksamana
'aja.

SALIM [[88]*rupa kechil hati*]: [89]Ha, bagitu!

SALMAH [*dengan suka*]: [90]Siapa lagi? [[91]*sambil mengubah suara-nya apabila
terpandang mata Salim mengerling dia macham orang kechil hati.*]
[92]Mah minta jangan-lah ada orang lain lagi hendakkan Mah juga...

SALIM: [93]Apa pula tidak-nya! [94]Itu Tuan Kadhi 'tu, 'nak di-kemanakan?
[94a]Pura-pura wara'! 'Alim pelesu! [95]Dia pun tergila-gila hendakkan Mah.

SALMAH: Siapa? Tuan Kadhi! *Astaghfiru'llah!* [96]Betul-lah kata pantun,

Imam kadhi lagi berdosa,
Konon pula saya yang jahil.

[97]'Dah 'tu ada lagi?

SALIM: [98]'Tu Raja Muda ta' berguna 'tu. Dia pun...

SALMAH: Apa? Raja Muda? *La ilahi!* [[99]*sambil senyum-senyum kulum*].
[100]Dia 'tu, ia, manis sadikit bukan? [101]Kelakuan-nya pun macham budak
mentah. [102]Mah gemar juga menéngok dia 'tu.

SALIM [*rupa kechil hati*]: [103]Engkau 'ni, betul-lah Mah! [104]Kalau bagitu-
lah dalam hati engkau, baik-lah aku pergi, ta' usah balék-balék lagi.

SALMAH [[105]*sa-laku minta ma'af*]: 'Bang! 'Bang! [106]Ta' usah-lah ambil
hati, 'Bang. [107]Bukan betul-betul Mah kata bagitu. [108]Mah chuma suka
kalau dia jadi adék Mah.

SALIM [*dengan suara mengéjék*]: Ia, adék Mah! [109]Pergi-lah! [110]Ada sa-
orang lagi...Tengku Bendahara. [111]Itu pun agak-nya Mah suka 'nak
buat adék juga!

SALMAH: Tengku Bendahara? *Ya Allah!* [112]Selamatkan aku! Orang tua
ganyut agut-agut 'tu! [[113]*sambil mengerutkan muka serta menunjokkan*

misai Bendahara yang merundok ka-bawah itu.] [114]Rupa muka-nya pun chukup membuat hati kita ingatkan kubor 'aja.

SALIM: Baik-lah. [115]Sudah-lah 'tu. [116]Sekarang apa kita 'nak buat? [117]Apa ikhtiar? [118]Chari juga musang berjanggut 'tu-kah? [119]Ada-kah pernah Mah dengar fasal musang berjanggut? [120]Yang betul-nya tujuan Raja 'tu 'nak suroh aku pergi ta' usah balék-balék lagi, biar senang dia berkira dengan Mah. [120a]Itu sudah terang.

SALMAH: Haih! [121]Macham mana 'nak kita buat 'ni? [122]Apa akal? [[123]*menangis hempas-hempas terésak-ésak.* [124]*Sa-kunyong-kunyong berhenti menangis;* [125]*berkata dengan riang*]: [126]Mah dapat satu akal...

SALIM [[127]*tegak telinga-nya*]: [128]Apa dia?

SALMAH [[129]*sambil menganggok-nganggokkan kepala*]: [130]Serahkan sahaja-lah kapada Mah. [131]Mah tahu-lah buat. [132]Dia semua tahu abang akan berjalan pagi 'ni? [*bangkit dengan serta-merta*]: [133]Mari-lah 'Bang. [134]Siapkan bungkus-bungkus. [135]'Dah 'tu pergi-lah lekas!

SALIM [[136]*macham orang putus harap*]: [137]Pergi ka-mana? [138]Ka-mana aku 'nak pergi?

SALMAH: [139]Ka-balék Bukit Qaf! [140]Ka-mana-mana pun abang suka. [*Kemudian, dengan senyum simpul*]: [141]'Tapi ingat, mesti balék dalam pukul sa-belas malam 'ni.

SALIM: [142]'Tapi macham mana yang Mah 'nak buat 'ni? [143]Chuba-lah katakan, aku 'nak dengar...

SALMAH: [144]'Ta' payah. [145]'Ta' usah Mah katakan. [145a]Mah tahu-lah buat. [146]'Ta' ada témpoh 'nak berchakap panjang-panjang lagi. [147]Kalau dia semua tahu abang mesti pergi pagi ini juga, tentu ta' lama lagi datang-lah dia masing-masing 'tu ka-sini. [148]Kemudian kalau dia berjumpa abang ada di-rumah lagi, belum juga pergi, masok angin-lah kita! [149]Lekas-lah 'Bang. [150]Ini dia bungkusan. [151]Turun-lah chepat!

SALIM [[152]*mengambil bungkusan lalu turun, kemudian berpaling balék*]: [153]Baik aku bawa makanan sadikit. [154]Kalau 'kan sampai pukul sa-belas malam aku terlata-lata ta' tentu arah, atau bersembunyi dalam semak, tentu lapar.

SALMAH: [155]Ia pula! [156]Mah ta' ingat fasal itu. [157]Bini abang 'ni pelupa! [158]Ma'alum-lah dalam chemas. [[159]*Pergi ka-para, di-bungkus-nya sadikit nasi dengan ikan kering.*] [160]Ini dia. [161]Ada sadikit nasi sejok malam tadi, lauk ikan kering.

SALIM: [162]Terima kaséh. [[163]*Ambil bungkus nasi, turun lalu berjalan.*]

Pertunjokan 2

[¹⁶⁴*Tengah hari.* ¹⁶⁵*Salmah dudok di-atas lantai sambil menganyam tikar.* ¹⁶⁶*Terlalu susah rupa muka-nya.* ¹⁶⁷*Tiba Tuan Kadhi.* ¹⁶⁸*Salmah pura-pura ta' nampak.*]

KADHI: ¹⁶⁹Boléh-kah kawan masok? ¹⁷⁰Awak tinggal sa-orang sahaja-kah?

SALMAH: Éh! Tuan Kadhi! ¹⁷¹Sila-lah masok, Tuan. ¹⁷²Ia saya tinggal sa-orang. ¹⁷³Abang Salim ta' ada.

KADI: Hⁿa! ¹⁷⁴Ka-mana dia?

SALMAH: ¹⁷⁵Dia 'dah pergi, di-suroh Tuanku menchari 'musang ber-janggut'!

KADHI: Musang berjanggut! ¹⁷⁶Di-mana ada musang berjanggut! ¹⁷⁷Pelék pula! ¹⁷⁸Apa 'nak di-buat dék Tuanku agak-nya?

SALMAH: ¹⁷⁹Entah-lah saya pun ta' tahu apa erti-nya.

KADHI: ¹⁸⁰Haih, ia ganjil-lah! ¹⁸¹'Dah 'tu, Ché' Salmah ta 'takut tinggal sa-orang?

SALMAH: ¹⁸²Siang-siang 'ni ta' takut-lah saya. ¹⁸³"Tapi malam 'karang entah apa-lah hal saya!

KADHI: ¹⁸⁴Kalau bagitu biar-lah kawan dudok di-sini menemankan awak, menghibor-ngiborkan hati awak, pada tinggal sa-orang bagini. ¹⁸⁵Kok sampai malam 'karang pun kawan menemankan awak ta' apa!

SALMAH: ¹⁸⁶Terima kaséh, Tuan, banyak-banyak. ¹⁸⁷Ta' terbalas saya budi Tuan. ¹⁸⁸Tetapi sementara hari siang 'ni minta ma'af-lah saya. ¹⁸⁹Orang pandang ta' baik. ¹⁹⁰Saya pun ta' takut, kerana hari siang. ¹⁹¹Kalau Tuan 'nak datang, datang-lah malam 'karang agak-agak pukul 'lapan.

KADHI: ¹⁹²Ia ta' ia pula, orang pandang ta' baik. ¹⁹³Ta' usah-lah kawan masok dahulu. ¹⁹⁴Malam 'ni kira-kira pukul 'lapan kawan datang balék. ¹⁹⁵Tinggal-lah dahulu, ia? [¹⁹⁶*Ia turun pulang.* ¹⁹⁷*Salmah tertawa dalam hati-nya.*]

SALMAH: Malim kuching! ¹⁹⁸Serban sa-besar bakul, hati ta' betul! ¹⁹⁹'Kau 'tu-lah aku jadikan 'musang berjanggut' malam 'ni. ²⁰⁰Janggut 'kau pun chukup panjang! [²⁰¹*Terhenti berchakap.*] ²⁰²Lepas ini siapa pula agak-nya?

[²⁰³*Sa-bentar lagi kedengaran bunyi kaki orang berjalan.* ²⁰⁴*Salmah balék menganyam.* ²⁰⁵*Orang mengetok pintu.* ²⁰⁶*Masok Dato' Laksamana bukan main bergaya.*]

LAKS.: *As-salam alaikum*, tuan rumah.

SALMAH: Éh! To' Laksamana! [207]Terperanjat saya! [208]Perasan hati saya siapa tadi!

LAKS.: [209]Kawan lalu di-sini. [210]Teringat kawan élok singgah sa-kejap menéngok orang baharu kahwin 'ni. [211]Salim mana?

SALMAH [*pura-pura hiba*]: [211a]Abang Salim ta' ada. [212]Dia 'dah pergi di-suroh Tuanku mencharikan musang berjanggut. [213]Entah bila dia balék pun ta' tentu. [214]Saya tinggal sa-orang 'aja.

LAKS.: Kaséhan! [215]Musang berjanggut di-mana 'nak di-chari? [216]Kok ta' dapat tentu dia ta' balék, takut Tuanku murka! [217]Habis, Ché' Mah ta' takut-kah tinggal sa-orang?

SALMAH: [218]Takut juga... 'tapi siapa 'nak di-buat kawan? [219]Emak ayah belum dapat khabar lagi.

LAKS.: [220]Kalau bagitu biar-lah kawan 'aja menemankan awak. Sayang! [221]Bagini chanték, bagini muda, tinggal sa-orang!

SALMAH: [221a]Ta' payah-lah Dato'. [222]Ta' kan orang jantan pula 'nak menemankan orang betina! [223]Apa kata orang! [224]Lagi pun siang-siang 'ni saya ta' takut. [225]Saya pun ada kerja. [226]Téngok-lah 'ni. [227]Apa fikir Dato' tikar yang saya anyam 'ni, élok ta'?

LAKS.: [*memandang anyaman*]: [228]Elok benar. [229]Padan-lah dengan rupa tukang-nya pula! [230]'Dah chanték, pandai pula menganyam. [231]Ini tentang kelarai yang ini apa nama anyam-nya? [*Laksamana menunjok.*]

SALMAH: [232]Itu kelarai beras goring nama-nya.

LAKS.: [233]Nampak-nya mengkuang Ché' Mah sudah 'nak habis 'ni! [234]Ada-kah mengkuang lagi yang sudah siap-nya di-mana-mana? [235]Biar kawan tolong ambilkan. [236]Kalau tidak pun boléh kawan pergi tetakkan mengkuang, tolong layorkan, jangkakan, jemorkan, angkitkan. Boléh?

SALMAH: *Allah!* [237]Dato' 'ni, mengada-ngada-nya! Ta' usah-lah Dato'. Ta' payah. [238]Saya boléh buat sendiri.

LAKS.: [239]Kawan suka 'nak tolong pula. [240]Kawan ta' suka tangan Ché' Mah yang bagitu lembut bersusah-susah bekerja. [241]Biar kawan pergi ambilkan, ia? [[242]*mengachu 'nak pergi.*]

SALMAH: Ta' usah, Dato'! [243]Kalau 'nak ambilkan mengkuang pun ta' usah-lah sekarang. [244]Membuat susah!

LAKS.: [245]Apa pula susah-nya? [249]Sa-kejap 'ni juga kawan balék.

SALMAH: [247]Minta-lah saya Dato' ta' usah. [248]Nanti, kalau hendak juga boléh bawakan petang. [243]Sekarang 'ni saya 'nak pergi ka-rumah Ma'

Téh menéngok anak-nya demam; [250]'dah berjanji sa-malam. [251]Petang baharu saya balék. [[252]*berkemas-kemas macham orang 'nak berjalan.*]

LAKS.: [253]Oh bagitu! [254]Baik-lah! [255]Kawan pulang dahulu. [256]Petang 'karang kawan datang bawakan mengkuang, ia? [257]Pukul berapa éloknya?

SALMAH: [258]Kata-lah lepas makan. [259]Pukul 'lapan sa-tengah. [260]Siapa tahu, entah saya terléngah balék...

LAKS.: H[n]a, ia-lah, pukul 'lapan sa-tengah. [261]Jangan ta' nanti, ia? [261a]Selamat tinggal.

SALMAH: [262]Nanti. [262a]Ta' kan-lah ta' nanti! Selamat jalan. [[263]*Laksamana keluar lalu berjalan.* [264]*Salmah tersenyum sambil berfikir dalam hatinya*]: [265]Sampai masa-nya 'karang tahu-lah engkau 'kan diri! [[266]*Sajurus kedengaran bunyi orang berjalan.* [267]*Salmah mengangkat kening*] [268]Siapa-nya pula 'ni agak-nya? [*Orang mengetok pintu. Salmah membukakan pintu.*] Eh! Dato' Temenggong! Masok-lah.

[[269]*Masok Temenggong berlénggang-lénggang menjinjing dua biji durian berikat tali.*]

TEMENGG.: [270]Ini sadikit hadiah buat menyuka-nyukakan hati Salmah tinggal sa-orang. [271]Durian kawan tengah rahat gugor. [272]Ini-lah kawan bawakan dua biji, kawan piléhkan durian tembaga yang baik sa-kali. [273]Kawan dengar khabar Salim ta' ada. [274]Itu-lah kawan datang menéngok Salmah.

SALMAH: [275]Terhutang budi saya Dato'. Terima kaséh.

TEMENGG.: [276]Baik kita belah sekarang, kita makan sama-sama. [277]Biar kawan belahkan. [278]Mana parang? [[279]*Memandang berkeliling.*]

SALMAH: [280]Usah-lah jam ini juga. [281]Nanti malam. [282]Sekarang 'ni saya 'nak pergi ka-rumah Ma' Téh menéngok anak-nya sakit. [283]Sila Dato' datang malam 'ni. [284]Agak pukul sembilan balék-lah saya.

TEMENGG.: Oh! [285]Kalau bagitu ia-lah. [286]Pukul sembilan ada-lah kawan balék di-sini. [287]Nanti kawan! [288]Jangan belah dahulu durian 'tu, ia? [289]Nanti sampai kawan datang.

SALMAH: [290]Ta' kan-lah saya burok makan sampai bagitu! [[290a]*Temenggong keluar lalu pergi, sambil mengibar-ngibarkan tangan-nya berkeputak memberi selamat tinggal. Salmah membilang-bilang jari-nya*]: Satu, dua, tiga. Kadhi, Laksamana, Temenggong. [291]'Dah bertiga. [292]Tinggal bertiga lagi. [[293]*Sa-bentar itu kedengaran bunyi kaki orang berjalan menghentak.* [294]*Salmah menggéndéngkan kepala-nya mendengar*]: Tengku Bendahara tua ganyut 'tu! [294a]Ta' sedarkan diri! [295]Tua-tua keladi!

[296*Masok Bendahara termengah-mengah kepenatan.*]

BEND.: Hⁿa! 297Apa khabar?

SALMAH: 298Khabar baik, Tengku.

BEND.: Salim mana?

SALMAH: 'Bang Salim ta' ada. Dia 'dah pergi.

BEND.: 299'Dah pergi? 300Ka-mana?

SALMAH: 301Entah. 301ᵃPaték pun ta' tahu. 302Dia ta' kata ka-mana. 303'Tapi kata-nya pergi lama.

BEND.: 304Salmah ta' tahu? Ehem.

SALMAH: Ta' tahu, Tengku. 305Tengku 'nak berjumpa dia-kah?

BEND.: 306Tidak. 307Kawan bukan 'nak berjumpa dia. [*Terhenti*] Kawan 'nak berjumpa awak.

SALMAH: *Allah!* 308Besar hati paték mendengar-nya. 309Tengku sa-orang berpangkat besar bagini, sudi datang menéngok paték. [310*Sambil pura-pura berkemas menyimpan anyaman-nya macham orang 'nak turun berjalan.*]: 311'Tapi itu-lah paték tengah 'nak turun sangat benar. 312Ta' dapat-lah paték lama menahan Tengku.

BEND.: 313'Nak ka-mana? 314Apa fasal?

SALMAH: 315Paték kena panggil ka-baroh, ka-rumah Ma' Téh, mengata-kan si-Ajit anak-nya yang demam 'tu 'dah sangat benar. 316Itu-lah paték 'nak pergi menéngok-nya.

BEND.: Sayang! 317Ta' boléh-kah Salmah tanggohkan?

SALMAH: 318Macham mana pula 'nak di-tanggohkan Tengku? 319Orang sakit. 320Entah ta' dapat berjumpa lagi! 321'Tapi Tengku tentu boléh datang balék malam 'ni sekarang? 322Paték balék agak-agak pukul sembilan. 323Sila-lah Tengku datang agak pukul sembilan sa-tengah, boléh paték siap. 324Ini ta' ada apa-apa yang siap.

BEND.: Pukul sembilan?

SALMAH: Tidak. Pukul sembilan sa-tengah. 325Beri-lah paték témpoh sa-tengah jam. 326Paték pun 'nak bersiap-siap juga menanti Tengku. 327'Nak mandi, bersikat, bersalin baju, jerangkan ayer, macham-macham. 328Ta' kan paték 'nak biarkan Tengku kering 'aja!

BEND.: Hⁿa, élok-lah bagitu. 329Kawan pun gemar menéngok Salmah pakai chanték-chanték, bersanggul lawar-lawar. 330Pukul sembilan sa-tengah malam 'ni kawan datang balék. 331Sekarang biar kawan pulang dahulu, ia? Tinggal-lah.

SALMAH: Tengku. 332Paték pun 'nak turun 'ni. [333*Bendahara turun lalu pulang.* 334*Salmah pura-pura berkemas lagi sa-belum keluar*] 335Jelak aku rasa-nya. ³³⁶Siapa tinggal lagi? [*Membilang*] Kadhi, Laksamana, Temenggong Bendahara. Tinggal berdua lagi. ³³⁷Siapa akan tiba dahulu agaknya, bapa-kah, anak? [³³⁸*Sa-jurus terdengar bunyi orang berjalan perlahan-lahan.* ³³⁸ᵃ*Salmah meninjau.* ³³⁹*Nampak sa-orang muda berumor kira-kira delapan-belas tahun*]: Oh, anak-nya.

RAJA MUDA [³⁴⁰*Terintai-intai dari chelah pintu*]: ³⁴¹Ayah ta' ada di-sini-kah? Oh, ta' ada. ³⁴²Boléh masok-kah?

SALMAH: Aih! ³⁴³Tengku 'dah masok pun, buat-buat minta kebenaran pula! [³⁴⁴*Kedua-nya tertawa.*]

R. MUDA: ³⁴⁵Ia ta' ia-nya! ³⁴⁶'Dah masok, ta' perasan.

SALMAH: ³⁴⁷Mengapa? ³⁴⁸Tengku tiba-tiba bertanyakan ayahanda ada di-sini-kah, tidak, tadi? Mengapa?

R. MUDA: ³⁴⁹Sebab saya dengar dia menyebut kata 'nak datang menéngok Ché' Mah tadi. ³⁵⁰Saya nampak dia berangkat keluar dari istana. ³⁵¹Perasaan saya tentu-lah dia 'dah sampai ka-sini.

SALMAH: Ia-kah? ³⁵²Tuanku 'nak berangkat ka-rumah paték? Mustahil!

R. MUDA: Ia. ³⁵³Saya tahu ayah ada hati kapada Ché' Mah. ³⁵⁴Dia keluar tadi sa-orang 'aja, ta' ada siapa mengiring. ³⁵⁵Itu menunjokkan dia 'nak bersulit-sulit. ³⁵⁶Harus agak-nya sa-kejap lagi tiba-lah dia 'tu. ³⁵⁷Tapi kalau ayah ada hati, saya pun ada hati juga. ³⁵⁸Siapa Ché Mah piléh?

SALMAH: Chéh! ³⁵⁹Sayang-nya. ³⁶⁰Kalau dia ta' berangkat ka-mari alang-kah sedap-nya kita berdua dapat berbual puas-puas? ³⁶¹Paték mémang 'dah lama ingin 'nak berchakap panjang dengan Tengku.

R. MUDA: ³⁶²Ah 'tu, apa di-nanti lagi? ³⁶³Ini-lah masa-nya. ³⁶⁴Usah perdulikan orang tua 'tu. ³⁶⁵Mari kita dudok dekat-dekat bergébang bermain-main sampai malam.

SALMAH: Eh! ³⁶⁶Ta' boléh Tengku! Bahaya-nya besar. [³⁶⁷*Membuat pura-pura macham orang terlintas suatu fikiran*] ³⁶⁸Paték terfikir satu jalan. ³⁶⁹Tengku pulang dahulu. [³⁷⁰*Raja Muda nampak susah hati.*] ³⁷¹Tapi datang balék malam ni, pukul sa-puloh. ³⁷²Paték siap menanti masa itu. [³⁷³*Kedengaran bunyi kaki orang berjalan, bukan main kuat hentak-nya.*]

R. MUDA: *Ya Allah!* Itu pun ayah! ³⁷⁴Biar saya keluar jalan sini. [³⁷⁵*Lalu keluar dari pintu belakang dengan berbisék*]: Pukul sa-puloh, ia?

SALMAH [*menjawab dengan bisék juga*]: Ia, pukul sa-puloh. ³⁷⁶Keluar-lah lekas! [³⁷⁷*Bunyi ketok kuat bertalu-talu di-pintu.* ³⁷⁸*Salmah pergi mem-bukakan.* ³⁷⁹*Terhadap kapada Raja.* ³⁸⁰*Pura-pura terperanjat benar*]: Ya Allah! ³⁸¹Tuanku rupa-nya. ³⁸²Bertuah besar paték, Tuanku sudi

berangkat berchemar duli ka-pondok burok paték 'ni. [383]Harap di-
ampun, sila masok Tuanku. [*Raja masok.*]

RAJA: [384]Aku datang sa-kejap sahaja 'ni. [385]Orang besar-besar semua
tengah menanti di-Déwan. [386]"Tapi aku datang juga, 'nak mengatakan
kapada engkau fasal aku susah hati benar kena menyuroh Salim pergi
membuat . . . . . ada satu kerja. [387]Kalau aku salah, ma'af 'aja-lah. [388]Usah
susah pula.

SALMAH: [389]Ampun Tuanku. [390]"Tapi dia pergi 'tu ta' lama, bukan?

RAJA: [*macham ia-ia benar*]: Tidak! [391]Apa pula guna lama-lama?
[392]Chuma suatu kerja kechil aku surohkan dia. [393]Engkau tahu Salmah?
[394]Aku kena kelurut pada ibu kaki kanan. [395]Kata bomor yang mengubat
'tu, kelurut aku 'tu ta' boléh baik kalau ta' di-sapukan minyak yang di-
masak dari-pada janggut musang jebat. [396]Itu-lah sebab-nya aku
hendakkan musang berjanggut 'tu.

SALMAH: [397]Sunggoh-lah Tuanku, macham titah 'tu.

RAJA: [398]Ta' élok benar rupa-nya sa-orang raja macham aku 'ni ter-
témpang-témpang berjalan, sebab kena kelurut, élok-kah?

SALMAH: [399]Tentu-lah ta' élok, Tuanku. [400]Di-pandang orang pun 'aib.
[401]Macham Pa' Pandir 'nak melawak.

RAJA: [402]Hⁿa, itu-lah. [403]Jadi, mahu ta' mahu kena-láh aku suroh siapa-
siapa pergi mencharikan musang berjanggut 'tu. [404]"Tapi aku ta'
nampak orang lain yang boléh di-harap fasal itu melainkan Salim.
[405]Aku tahu ta' ada orang lain dalam negeri ini lebéh cherdék daripada
dia. [406]Itu sebab aku suroh dia.

SALMAH: Tuanku.

RAJA: [407]Itu satu kerja kechil kapada Salim, aku tahu. [408]Macham mana
pun dalam sa-hari dua 'ni balék-lah dia membawa musang berjanggut
'tu. [409]Sa-belum dia pergi aku 'dah katakan dia ta' usah susah fasal
engkau sa-peninggal-nya ini. [410]Aku sendiri akan menjaga engkau baik-
baik, kata aku.

SALMAH: Terima kaséh, Tuanku. [411]Lémpah kurnia Tuanku 'tu ter-
junjong di-atas batu kepala paték.

RAJA: [412]Baik-lah sekarang 'ni aku 'nak balék lekas. [413]Orang banyak
menanti. [414]"Tapi malam 'ni aku datang lagi menéngok engkau. [415]Kira-
kira lepas makan agak pukul sembilan ada-lah aku di-sini balék. [416]Siap,
ia?

SALMAH: [417]Harap di-ampun, Tuanku. [418]Pukul sembilan paték belum
ada di-rumah. [419]Paték 'dah berjanji 'nak pergi menolong-nolong di-

rumah orang kahwin di-baroh 'tu. [420]Sampai pukul sa-puloh baharu paték balék agak-nya.

RAJA: [421]Baik-lah, pukul sa-puloh-lah aku datang.

SALMAH: Pukul sa-puloh sa-tengah-lah, Tuanku. [422]Sampai ka-rumah ta' kan paték ta' 'nak bersiap-siap pula sadikit untok menyambut Tuanku. [423]Paték besar hati benar Tuanku 'nak berangkat datang 'tu. [424]Kechil tapak tangan, nyiru paték tadahkan.

RAJA: Ha, baik-lah. Pukul sa-puloh sa-tengah.

[*Raja keluar.* [425]*Salmah menggenggam tangan, di-achukan-nya penumbok-nya ka-balakang Raja.* [426]*Kemudian di-kemaskan-nya anyam-anyaman-nya itu lalu pergi ka-dapor.*]

SALMAH [[427]*merungut sambil berjalan ka-dapor itu, bibir-nya di-chemékkan-nya*]: He[n]h! [428]'Nak menjaga aku! [429]Nanti-lah, aku ajar malam 'ni!

Lakunan II

Pertunjokan 1

[*Di-dapor. Ada tungku, anglo, méja, bangku, lampu, pinggan mangkok, periok belanga, sa-buah kukor nyior yang berupa kuda, sa-buah pak besar.*]

SALMAH [[430]*membanchoh tepong dalam mangkok.* [431]*Macham orang ter-nanti-nanti rupa-nya.*]: [432]Sudah dekat pukul 'lapan 'ni. [433]Tuan Kadhi sa-kejap lagi tentu-lah tiba. [434]Aku minta masing-masing 'tu biar-lah tiba ikut gilir waktu-nya yang betul dalam janji. [435]Kalau tidak, kachau aku! [436]Nanti, aku ingatkan siapa-siapa pukul-pukul berapa: pukul 'lapan Kadhi, pukul 'lapan sa-tengah Laksamana, pukul sembilan Temenggong, pukul sembilan sa-tengah — siapa? [*termenong sa-kejap*] Oh, ia. [*dengan suara macham orang tua susah*] Bendahara! [437]Lepas 'tu pukul sa-puloh Raja Muda. [[438]*Tersenyum sadikit waktu menyebut ' Raja Muda' itu.*] [439]Aku mesti jaga betul-betul menyorokkan dia di-tempat yang selamat sa-belum ayah-nya tiba. [440]Aku ta' hendak dia susah apa-apa. [441]Raja tiba pukul sa-puloh sa-tengah. Baik-lah. Aku nanti! [441a]Aku buat-buat bekerja. [442]Sa-kali ini tahu-lah dia semua akan diri-nya! [[443]*Terdengar gong berbunyi pukul 'lapan.* [444]*Salmah menganggok-nganggokkan kepala sambil mengetap-ngetapkan bibir mendengar gong itu.* [445]*Mata-nya memandang-mandang sérong ka-pintu.* [446]*Kedengaran bunyi kaki orang naik dekat pintu.*] H[n]a! [447]Itu Tuan Kadhi agak-nya. [448]Kadhi mengeladi! [449]Dia belum tahu siapa Salmah! [[450]*Pergi membukakan pintu.* [451]*Masok Tuan Kadhi.*]

KADHI: Ha. [452]Apa khabar Ché' Muda? [453]Kawan tiba betul-betul ikut janji, ia? [454]Sadikit pun ta' léwat.

SALMAH: Ia! [455]Terlampau benar pula mengikut jam. [456]Sa-minit pun ta' seliséh.

KADHI: [457]Macham mana pula di-kata 'terlampau'? [458]Kalau pukul 'lapan tepat, pukul 'lapan-lah, ta' lebéh ta' kurang. [459]Yang betul-nya kawan mémang membilang tiap-tiap minit semenjak dari pukul tujoh sa-tengah tadi. [[460]*Salmah memandang kapada-nya macham rupa orang dahshat.*] [461]Sebab kawan khuatir benar mengenangkan awak tinggal sa-orang 'ni.

SALMAH: H[n]a.

KADHI: [462]Mari-lah dudok, kita berchakap-chakap sadikit. [[463]*Di-chuba-nya menarék Salmah ka-atas bangku.*] Ta' mahu?

SALMAH: Nanti! Belum lagi! [464]Téngok-lah 'ni, saya tengah 'nak mem-buatkan kuéh jemput-jemput sadikit untok tuan. [[465]*Mula membanchoh tepong dengan pisang masak.*]

KADHI: [466]Pandai betul Ché' Mah 'ni membuat kerja rumah. [467]Biar kawan tolong, ia?

SALMAH: Ta'usah. [468]Saya ta' terbayang pun dalam hati 'nak menyuroh tuan menolong. [469]Dudok-lah dahulu. [470]Saya sa-kejap 'aja 'ni. [[471]*Kadhi dudok terkelip-kelip menanti Salmah belum juga sudah-sudah.* [472]*Terdengar bunyi orang berjalan pergi balék di-luar.* [473]*Kadhi terperanjat lalu bangkit.*]

KADHI: [474]Apa 'tu? [475]Ada orang bunyi-nya berjalan di-luar 'tu. [476]Wah! Apa kawan 'nak buat 'ni. [477]Kalau orang terjumpa kawan di-sini malam-malam 'ni — kachau!

SALMAH [[478]*Pura-pura ketakutan.* [479]*Ia memandang keluar dari tinggap.*] Ya Allah! [480]Ia, ada orang-lah pula! [[481]*Menunjok kapada sa-buah pak besar.*] [482]Masok Tuan Kadhi ka-dalam pak 'ni!

[[483]*Kadhi masok ka-dalam pak.* [484]*Salmah tutup, kemudian letakkan barang-barang di-atas-nya. Masok Laksamana.* [485]*Terketék-keték bukan main suka laku-nya.*]

LAKS.: [486]Ha! Ché' Mah 'dah balék pun, ia? [487]Bagitu-lah orang berjanji, Ché' Sayang. [488]Kawan 'ni terlekas sadikit tiba. [489]Itu sebab kawan berjalan pergi balék di-luar tadi. [490]Di-sangkakan Ché' Mah belum balék. [491]Aléh-aléh kawan nampak Ché' Mah menjengok keluar dari tingkap.

SALMAH: Ia. [492]Saya teringat jangan pula To' Lak terdahulu sampai! [493]Jadi saya balék lekas.

LAKS.: Ia-kah bagitu? [494]Itu tanda hati kita sama hendak, bukan? [495]Kita berlumba masing-masing 'nak dahulu sampai. [496]Menang Ché' Mah. [[497]*Di-chuba-nya hendak memelok pinggang Salmah.*]

SALMAH: Belum lagi! [498]Sabar-lah sadikit! [499]Téngok saya tengah 'nak memasak kuéh 'nak menjamu To' Lak. [500]Biar-lah siap kuéh saya 'ni dahulu. [501]Dudok-lah sa-bentar. [502]Saya ta' lama 'ni. [503]Apa-apa 'nak buat pun, kita minum ayer dahulu baharu sedap. [*Laksamana dudok.*]

LAKS.: [504]Ada-kah siapa-siapa orang lain datang menéngok awak hari ini, Ché' Mah?

SALMAH: Ta' ada. Siapa pula? [505]To' Lak-lah sa-orang. [506]Saya ta' ingin ada orang-orang lain datang. [507]Tapi To' Lak bukan macham orang lain. [508]To' Lak sepésal!

LAKS. [[509]*Bangun berdiri pergi dekat kapada Salmah.* [510]*Di-chuba-nya hendak memelok léhér Salmah.*] Mari-lah dudok. [511]Perdulikan kuéh 'tu!

SALMAH [*menolakkan Laksamana*]: Sabar! Sabar! [512]To' Lak 'ni ta' sabar. [[513]*Laksamana berjalan arah ka-tingkap.* [514]*Memandang keluar. Teranjat.*]

LAKS.: [515]Éh! Nampak-nya — Oh, bukan, mana pula! — éh! ia, rupa-rupa-nya macham Temenggong datang 'tu! — Ia, dia! Ia! Wah! Lekas-lah! Lekas-lah! [516]Ka-mana kawan 'nak lari 'ni? Tolong kawan! Ia, Temenggong 'tu! [517]Jangan-lah dia berjumpa kawan di-sini malam-malam buta 'ni!

SALMAH: [518]Sini! [519]Masok ka-dalam almari 'tu. [520]Dudok diam-diam di-situ. [521]Matikan diri!

[[522]*Laksamana masok ka-dalam almari, berdiri macham batang di-situ.* [523]*Masok Temenggong, bukan main menghébat.*]

TEMENGG.: [524]Kawan 'ni terlekas sadikit sampai. [525]Usah-lah pula Ché' Mah marah, ia?

SALMAH: [526]Apa pula marah-nya? [527]Saya mémang suka To' Temenggong datang lekas 'ni. [528]Sa-kadarkan kurang sedap, Dato' kena menunggu sa-bentar. [529]Saya tengah membuat kuéh sadikit, 'nak memberi Dato' minum ayer. [530]Tapi belum siap lagi.

TEMENGG.: [531]Oh, itu ta' apa. [532]Élok-lah membuat kuéh 'tu. [533]Kawan boléh menolong. [534]Kawan pun pandai juga membuat kuéh.

SALMAH: Ah! [535]Ta' usah-lah Dato' menolong pula. [536]Saya ta' gemar menéngok baju Dato' chanték-chanték 'ni kena palit-palit dék tepong, kena arang, semua. Dudok-lah dahulu. [537]Sa-kejap lagi sudah-lah saya.

[*Temenggong dudok.* [538]*Di-pilin-pilin-nya misai-nya.* [539]*Di bélék-bélék-nya pakaian-nya.*]

TEMENGG.: [540]Apa fikir Ché' Mah detar baharu yang kawan pakai 'ni? [541]Kawan baharu terima terus dari Jawa. [542]Sajak rupa-nya kawan pakai, bukan?

SALMAH: [543]Oih! Saya nampak sajak betul, Dato'. [544]Padan benar-lah dengan rupa orang yang memakai-nya pula. [545]Hébat macham penglima.

[[546]*Temenggong membetul-betulkan destar-nya itu lagi dengan megah rupa-nya.*]

TEMENGG.: [547]Éh, belum juga-kah siap lagi kuéh 'tu? [548]Lama benar pula! [549]Kawan suka Ché' Mah mari-lah dudok di-sini dekat kawan, kita berbual-bual.

SALMAH: [550]Dekat 'dah 'nak siap.

[[551]*Bunyi orang mengetok pintu.* [552]*Temenggong terlompat bangkit.*]

TEMENGG.: [553]Siapa 'tu? [554]Ini ta' boléh jadi 'ni! [555]Kawan ta' hendak orang berjumpa kawan berdua-dua dengan Ché' Mah di-sini malam-malam bagini! [556]Ka-mana kawan 'nak lari 'ni? [557]Kok tidak pun, biar kawan bersembunyi.

SALMAH: [558]Ka-sini, Dato'! [559]Naik ka-atas para 'tu. [560]Dudok diam-diam di-situ, jangan berdechit!

[[561]*Temenggong memanjat naik, tergapai-gapai bukan main susah.* [562]*Habis seluar baju lawar-nya dengan destar baharu-nya itu kena arang. Terdengar suara orang berchakap di-luar pintu.* [563]*Susah sahaja bunyi suara-nya.*]

BENDAHARA [*di-luar*]: [564]Boléh-kah kawan masok, oi!

SALMAH [*pergi membukakan pintu*]: [565]Mengapa pula ta' boléh? [566]Sila-lah masok Tengku. [567]Dari tadi lagi paték ternanti-nanti. [*Masok Bendahara.*] [568]Paték tengah membuat kuéh sadikit 'ni, buat membasah-basah tekak Tengku.

BEND.: [569]Kawan ta' berapa gemar makan kuéh-kuéh.

SALMAH: Ah! [570]Kuéh paték ini tentu Tengku gemar. [571]Kuéh sepésal paték buatkan 'ni.

BEND.: [572]Ma' Engku awak di-rumah 'tu pun selalu juga membuat kuéh-kuéh sepésal. [573]'Tapi kawan ta' pernah makan.

SALMAH: [574]Mengapa ta' makan, Tengku?

BEND.: [575]Sebab kawan ta' suka Ma' Engku awak 'tu.

SALMAH: [576]Fasal apa ta' suka?

BEND.: Fasal apa! [577]Salmah tahu-lah — 'dah tua. [[578]*Kedengaran bunyi orang bersiul sayup-sayup di-tepi jalan; sa-kejap berpantun pula.* [579]*Bendahara tegak telinga-nya mendengar-nya*] Siapa 'tu?

SALMAH: [580]Mana? [581]Paték ta' kedengar apa-apa.

BEND.: Ia. [582]Kawan kedengar. [583]Ada bunyi orang bersiul-siul berpantun di-tepi jalan 'tu. [584]Jangan pula dia masok ka-mari!

SALMAH [*meninjau dari tingkap*]: Betul, Tengku. [585]Ada orang datang nampak-nya.

BEND.: [[586]*bangkit pergi meninjau sama*] [587]Éh! rupa-rupa-nya macham Raja Muda sétan 'tu, nampak-nya. [588]Apa di-mentekedarah-nya datang ka-sini, haram jadah 'tu!

SALMAH [*pura-pura ta' kenal*]: Ia-kah, Tengku? Raja Muda-kah 'tu?

BEND.: Ia! Ia! Dia-lah 'tu. *Ya Allah!* [589]Jangan dia terjumpa aku di-sini! [590]Malu besar aku, orang tua, di-chakap-chakapkan-nya kapada kawan-nya orang muda-muda. [591]Apa aku 'nak buat 'ni? [592]Tolong-lah aku, Salmah. Lekas! [593]Ka-mana aku 'nak lari?

SALMAH: [594]Mari sini, Tengku. [595]Kukor kelapa 'ni. [596]Membelakang arah ka-dia. [597]Tudongkan seléndang 'ni ka-atas kepala. [[598]*sambil melémparkan kain seléndang-nya ka-atas kepala Bendahara*] [599]Nanti paték katakan Tengku perempuan tua bekerja menolong-nolong paték di-dapor.

[*Masok Raja Muda*]

R. MUDA [*termalu-malu*]: [600]Terlekas saya sadikit agak-nya, ia?

SALMAH: Ia, Tengku. Tengku terlekas sadikit. [601]Belum pukul sa-puloh lagi. [602]Tapi apa salah-nya? [603]Paték tengah membuatkan kuéh sadikit tadi 'ni, 'nak beri Tengku santap. [604]Biar-lah orang tua dapor 'tu 'aja menyudahkan-nya. [[605]*Pergi berchakap kapada 'orang tua dapor' pura-pura suroh buat itu ini.*]

R. MUDA: [606]Baik benar Ché' Salmah 'ni. [607]Héboh membuatkan saya kuéh pula, pada hal dia tengah susah hati 'tu mengenangkan Ché' Salim.

SALMAH: Ia. [608]Tadi paték susah hati sadikit. [609]Tapi ini Tengku 'dah ada, 'dah suka rasa-nya. [610]Sila-lah, mari kita dudok berbual. [[611]*Kedua-nya dudok.*]

R. MUDA [[612]*memelok badan Salmah perlahan-lahan.* [613]*Salmah biarkan sahaja, ta' mengélak.*]: [614]Saya sa-hari-harian 'ni ta' lupa, ingatkan Ché' Salmah 'aja.

SALMAH: Ia?

R. MUDA: ⁶¹⁵'Ni kita 'dah berjumpa berdua-dua. ⁶¹⁶Bukan main lama rasa-nya menanti pukul sa-puloh tadi.

SALMAH: Ia. ⁶¹⁷Paték rasa pun bukan main lama.

R. MUDA [⁶¹⁸*memandang kapada 'perempuan tua' yang mengukor kelapa itu.* ⁶¹⁹*'Orang tua' itu mengukor bukan main chepat, macham 'nak patah kukoran itu.*]: ⁶²⁰Ta' boléh-kah Ché' Salmah suroh perempuan tua 'tu pergi keluar sa-kejap? ⁶²¹Ta' sedap-lah dia ada terponggok di-situ.

SALMAH: ⁶²²Sa-kejap lagi! ⁶²³Biar di-sudahkan-nya kuéh 'tu dahulu.

R. MUDA: ⁶²⁴Lama benar pula nampak-nya dia mengukor nyior.

SALMAH: Ia. ⁶²⁵Dia 'tu bekerja lambat. ⁶²⁶Ulit benar orang-nya.

R. MUDA: ⁶²⁷Bukan main besar pula perempuan-nya, ia?

[⁶²⁸*Bendahara terdengar.* ⁶²⁹*Dia chuba hendak mengechilkan badan-nya.*]

SALMAH [*berbisék*]: Ia. ⁶³⁰Dia 'tu orang Korinchi, dari Sumatera. ⁶³¹Jangan Tengku kata-kata dia besar, ⁶³²jadi rimau dia 'karang! ⁶³³Orang Korinchi selalu boléh mengubah rupa-nya jadi rimau.

R. MUDA: Ia? ⁶³⁴Ada-kah pernah sudah Ché' Mah téngok dia menukar rupa jadi rimau bagitu? [⁶³⁵*Kedengaran bunyi kaki orang berdepék-depék di-luar pintu.* ⁶³⁶*Kemudian bunyi suara Raja berteriak* ' O, Tuan rumah!'] *Ya Allah!* ⁶³⁷Ayah 'tu! ⁶³⁸Hai jahanam-lah aku! ⁶³⁹Chelaka orang tua bedebah 'tu...

[⁶⁴⁰*Raja mengetok pintu macham 'nak roboh bunyi-nya.* ⁶⁴¹*Salmah lekas menyorongkan lampu ka-dalam tangan Raja Muda, di-tolakkan-nya arah ka-tempat Temenggong itu.*]

SALMAH [⁶⁴²*berbisék kuat-kuat*]: ⁶⁴³Tengku jadi kaki lampu sekarang! ⁶⁴⁴Tatang lampu 'ni tetap-tetap. ⁶⁴⁵Berdiri tegak-tegak dekat orang tua betina 'tu. ⁶⁴⁶Diam-diam ta' usah bergerak-gerak!

[⁶⁴⁷*Masok Raja, terus menuju Salmah.*]

RAJA: Ha! Apa khabar Ché' Manja? Manja Tuanku-nya! ⁶⁴⁸Aku 'ni tiba terdahulu sadikit agak-nya. ⁶⁴⁹Aku ta' tersabar, 'nak lekas berjumpa kamu.

SALMAH: Ta' apa, Tuanku. ⁶⁵⁰Paték mémang sa-hari-harian 'ni ternanti-nantikan Tuanku tiba.

RAJA: ⁶⁵¹Ini aku 'dah tiba. ⁶⁵²Mari-lah dudok di-sini dekat aku. [⁶⁵³*Di-chuba-nya memelok Salmah.* ⁶⁵⁴*Salmah berdiri mengélak.*] Éh! Mengapa pula? ⁶⁵⁵Engkau hamba aku. ⁶⁵⁶Aku titah, engkau ta 'at peréntah aku.

SALMAH: ⁶⁵⁷Kita bertawar dahulu, Tuanku. ⁶⁵⁸Tuanku mesti beri paték satu permintaan dahulu, kalau Tuanku hendakkan paték. Boléh?

RAJA: [659]Apa benda-nya kamu hendak? [660]Apa-apa pun kamu minta, aku beri. [661]Hendak kerosang emas? Gelang kaki? Gelang tangan? Intan? Berlian? Kata-lah.

SALMAH: Tidak, Tuanku. [662]Ta' sampai bagitu mahal. [663]Permintaan paték murah 'aja.

RAJA: Apa? [664]Apa benda-nya?

SALMAH: [665]Paték minta sa-lama sa-tengah jam Tuanku jadi hamba paték. [666]Ikut apa yang paték suroh.

RAJA: Baik-lah. [667]Aku sa-tuju. [668]Sekarang tuanku chanték aku, apa yang tuanku 'nak suroh paték ini buat?

SALMAH: [669]Biar paték ingat-ingatkan dahulu. [[670]*Pura-pura berfikir 'Apa 'nak di-buat 'ni?'*]: Ah! Paték tahu! [671]Mari kita main tonggang-tonggang kuda.

RAJA [[672]*ta' berapa suka nampak-nya*]: Siapa jadi kuda? Aku-kah, engkau?

SALMAH: Tuanku-lah! [673]Ta' kan paték. [674]Kalau ta' mahu, paték titah-kan. [675]Tuanku 'dah janji 'nak ta'at.

RAJA: [676]Titah di-junjong, Tuanku Chanték. [677]Apa peréntah paték kerjakan. [[678]*Merendahkan badan lalu merangkak berkaki empat di-atas lantai.*]

SALMAH [[679]*memegang belakang Raja dari ékor baju-nya lalu naik menong-gang.*]: Jalan! Jalan! Berlari! Berlari!

[[680]*Raja merangkak menggiang-giut rupa-nya oléh berat. [681]Muka-nya mérah-mérah, tetapi merangkak juga ka-hujong ka-pangkal bilék itu. [682]Salmah suroh berlari. [683]Orang lain-lain yang bersembunyi itu tertawa diam-diam sapertikan pechah perut melihat-nya. [684]Kesudahan-nya Bendahara terlampau shoⁿk, di-hempaskan-nya sa-biji kelapa ka-atas kepala Raja Muda yang terpachak jadi 'kaki lampu' itu. [685]Raja Muda melolong. [686]Temenggong terjun dari atas para. [687]Kesemua orang itu meluru keluar, lari susup-sasap dalam gelap itu pulang ka-rumah masing-masing. [688]Hanya tinggal Tuan Kadhi sahaja dalam pak.*]

KADHI [[689]*dari dalam pak*]: [690]Lepaskan kawan! Lepaskan kawan!

[*Berbunyi pukul sa-belas. Masok Salim.*]

SALIM: Bagus Salmah! Bagus! [691]Aku tiba sa-baik-baik sempat menéngok kuda ranggong istana 'tu melompat keluar.

KADHI: Keluarkan kawan! Keluarkan kawan!

SALIM: [692]Siapa pula dalam pak 'tu? [[693]*Pergi dekat kapada pak.*]

SALMAH Tuan Kadhi.

SALIM: Bagus! Bagus! [⁶⁹⁴*Tergelak berdekah sapertikan 'nak runtoh rumah itu. ⁶⁹⁵Dia dengan Salmah dudok berdua-dua di-atas pak itu.*] ⁶⁹⁶Chuba-lah cheritakan Salmah apa hal yang sudah terjadi semenjak aku keluar pagi tadi.

SALMAH: ⁶⁹⁷Orang-orang-nya semua datang. ⁶⁹⁸Mah janjikan tiap-tiap sa-orang pukul sa-kian pukul sa-kian datang malam 'ni. ⁶⁹⁹Dia semua ikut jam janji 'tu masing-masing. ⁷⁰⁰Sekarang semua-nya 'dah lari pulang chuma tinggal Tuan Kadhi 'ni sa-orang sahaja.

SALIM: Hah! ⁷⁰¹Iblis besar Tuan Kadhi 'ni rupa-nya. ⁷⁰²Apa kita 'nak buat dia?

SALMAH: Apa pula? ⁷⁰³Dia-lah abang bawakan jadi musang berjanggut. ⁷⁰⁴Janggut-nya mémang panjang!

SALIM: Ia! ⁷⁰⁵Aku pun terfikir. ⁷⁰⁶Apa kata Mah tadi? ⁷⁰⁷Dia semua ada belaka di-sini tadi, ia?

SALMAH: Ia. ⁷⁰⁸Semua ada keenam-enam-nya 'tu.

SALIM: ⁷⁰⁹Siapa datang mula-mula?

SALMAH: ⁷¹⁰Tuan Kadhi-lah mula-mula sa-kali.

SALIM: Hⁿa! ⁷¹¹Élok-lah itu. ⁷¹²Nanti aku bawa dia mengadap ka-istana ésok. ⁷¹³Ia, fikiran 'Mah 'tu betul. ⁷¹⁴Dia-lah musang berjanggut yang Raja suroh chari 'tu, aku baharu dapat malam 'ni. Hah! Hah! Hah! [*Tergelak-gelak kedua-dua-nya.*]

Pertunjokan 2

[⁷¹⁵*Pagi ésok-nya, di Balai Penghadapan. ⁷¹⁶Raja bersemayam di-atas singgasana. ⁷¹⁷Di-hadapan-nya arah ka-sebelah kanan dudok Raja Muda dan Bendahara. Ka-sebelah kiri dudok Temenggong dan Laksamana. ⁷¹⁸Keempat-empat-nya kelihatan sangat resah dan serba salah. ⁷¹⁹Salim berdiri di-sebelah, menghadap kapada Raja dan orang besar-besar berempat itu. ⁷²⁰Muka-nya macham orang sedap hati lepas beroléh ke-menangan. ⁷²¹Hampir dengan dia ada sa-buah pak besar; ⁷²²di-dalam pak itu Tuan Kadhi.*]

RAJA: Salim. ⁷²³Aku suka benar menéngok engkau sudah balék bagini lekas. ⁷²⁴Dapat-kah barang yang aku suroh chari 'tu?

SALIM: ⁷²⁵Harap di-ampun, dapat, Tuanku. ⁷²⁶Senang benar paték menangkap-nya. ⁷²⁷Bukan paték susah-susah menchari. ⁷²⁸Dia datang sendiri menyerahkan diri ka-rumah paték.

RAJA [⁷²⁹*hairan, ta' berapa perchaya*]: ⁷³⁰Wah! Pelék 'tu! ⁷³¹Apa yang engkau dapat? ⁷³²Betul-betul-kah musang berjanggut, atau apa?

SALIM: [732a]Ia-lah, musang berjanggut-lah, Tuanku. [733]Chukup panjang janggut-nya!

RAJA: [734]Mana dia? [735]Di-mana engkau kurongkan? [736]Dalam pak besar yang engkau bawa 'ni-kah?

SALIM: Tuanku. [737]Dalam pak 'ni-lah dia. [738]Bukan main besar musang! [739]Berempat orang paték upah mengusong pak 'ni tadi dari rumah paték. [740]Chuba-lah Tuanku tinjau ka-dalam pak 'ni. [*741Di-bukakan-nya tudong pak itu.*]

RAJA [*742bertitah kapada Raja Muda*]: [743]Chuba anak kita pergi téngok apa ada dalam pak 'tu. [744]Téngok betul-kah Salim 'ni berchakap benar, atau main-main sahaja.

[*745Raja Muda pergi rapat kapada pak, membongkok memandang ka-dalam-nya lalu terperanjat, 746Dia tersentak ka-belakang apabila di-dengar-nya suara Kadhi.*]

KADHI [*berbisék*]: [747]Paték tahu di-mana Tengku malam tadi.

SALIM: [748]Élok betul musang-nya, bukan, Tengku?

R. MUDA: Ia — e — e — ia, élok.

RAJA: H[n]a. [749]Apa macham? [750]Ia-kah betul musang berjanggut?

R. MUDA: [751]Entah-lah, Tuanku. [752]Paték — paték — paték ta' tahu 'nak mengatakan. [753]Paték pun ta' berapa faham fasal binatang-binatang.

RAJA: *Ya Rabbi!* [754]Budak ini! [755]Ta' kenal-lah musang? [756]Ta' pernah menéngok musang? [*757Kapada Bendahara, saperti orang ta' sabar lagi bunyi suara-nya*] [758]Chuba Bendahara pergi téngok.

BEND. [*759pergi memandang ka-dalam pak, kemudian tersentak*]: *Allah!* [760]Apa bangsa musang-nya 'ni?

SALIM: [761]Apa Tengku fikir? [762]Raja musang betul, bukan? [763]Janggut-nya pun bukan main lebat. [*763Sambil membongkok mengurut-ngurut janggut kadhi.*] [764]Ta' terhabis buat ubat walau berapa banyak pun kelurut Tuanku. [*765Sambil memandang berkeliling kapada sekalian yang hadhir itu dengan muka mengéjék.*]

BEND.: Ia. [766]Fasal janggut-nya tentu sa-kali boléh di-harap. [767]Kawan ta' sangkal 'tu.

RAJA: [768]'Tapi ia-kah musang betul?

BEND.: Harap di-ampun, Tuanku. [769]Musang betul-kah, bukan, entah-lah. [770]'Tapi — 'Tapi — sah-lah suatu macham binatang!

RAJA: Suatu macham binatang! [771]Apa chakap Bendahara 'ni? [772]Ta'-kah kenal, musang-kah, kerbau-kah?

BEND.: [773]Kenal, Tuanku. Eh! — Tidak! — Paték 'nak kata — ia-lah. [774]Kerbau bukan! [775]Kalau kerbau, bertandok. [776]Ini ta' ada bertandok. RAJA [[777]*mendengus macham murka*]: Akh! Bangang! [778]Bendahara pun macham anak kita bodoh-nya! [*Kapada Temenggong*] [779]Chuba Temenggong pergi téngok. [[780]*Temenggong pergi mendekati pak lalu membongkok memandang kadalam-nya.* [781]*Ia pun terperanjat serta terlompat ka-belakang.*] SALIM: Aih! [782]Nampak-nya Dato' Temenggong terkejut besar 'ni. Mengapa? [783]Macham mana fikiran Dato', musang saya 'tu?

[[784]*Temenggong berdiri ta' dapat berkata-kata*]

RAJA: H[n]a. [785]Apa fikir Temenggong musang 'tu? Mengapa? [786]Di-gigit-nya-kah?
TEMENGG.: Tidak, Tuanku. [787]Bukan betul-betul di-gigit-nya.
RAJA: [788]'Dah 'tu, di-apakan-nya Temenggong, sampai terlompat ka-belakang bagitu jauh?
TEMENGG.: [789]Ta' ada apa, Tuanku. [790]Chuma — paték — paték —terlampau hairan menéngok-nya. [791]Lain benar rupa-nya.
RAJA: [792]Yang kita 'nak tahu satu fasal 'ni sahaja: [793]betul-kah musang atau bukan-nya?
TEMENGG.: [794]Fasal itu, Tuanku, paték — paték ta' tahu 'nak mengechamkan — ta' berani 'nak kata —
RAJA: Ta' berani 'nak kata? [795]Apa 'dah gila-kah awak semua 'ni? [*Kapada Laksamana*] Laksamana! [796]Pergi-lah awak chuba téngok pula. [797]Awak tentu ta' peranjat. [798]Kalau dia panjang janggut, awak panjang misai, berjodoh-lah!
[[799]*Laksamana pergi kapada pak, membongkok memandang ka-dalam-nya.* [800]*Tersentak balék dengan serta-merta ka-belakang.* [801]*Sambil undor itu ia menchebék-chebékkan muka kapada Kadhi dalam pak itu terlalu dahshat rupa-nya.*]
SALIM: Ah! [802]Ta' suka nampak-nya To' Laksamana menéngok musang saya. [803]Apa salah-nya? [804]Apa kurang?
RAJA: H[n]a. Laksamana! Apa macham? [805]Awak sa-kurang-kurang-nya tentu ada satu-satu fikiran yang putus fasal ini. [806]Jangan bangang macham orang-orang lain 'ni. [807]Apa keputusan awak? [808]Betul-kah musang jebat berjanggut?
LAKS.: [809]Fasal janggut, sah-lah ada, Tuanku. [810]Ta' usah gadoh-lah 'tu! [811]Panjang-nya pun ta' boléh di-umpat lagi. [[812]*Sambil mengachukan*

*panjang-nya janggut Kadhi dengan mengurut-ngurut ka-bawah dari
dagu-nya sendiri.* [813]*Dia sendiri tiada berjanggut.*]

RAJA: Bagus-lah 'tu.

LAKS. [*memekap hidong-nya*]: [814]Bau jebat-nya pun bukan main dahshat,
Tuanku. [*Sambil menjegil mata-nya memandang arah ka-Kadhi.*]
[815]Tidak-lah Tuanku terbau?

RAJA: Tidak. [816]Kita ta' terbau apa-apa. [817]Barangkali kita kena pergi dekat
menéngok-nya sendiri baharu terbau.

[[818]*Dia turun dari singgasana, pergi kapada pak.* [819]*Orang lain-lain itu berpandang-pandangan sama sendiri sambil berfikir masing-masing apa akan
di-buat oléh Raja apabila sudah di-lihat-nya benda dalam pak itu kelak.
Raja memandang ka-dalam pak.* [820]*Terkejut sadikit apabila di-dengar-nya
Kadhi berbisék.*]

KADHI [*berbisék*]: [821]Paték tahu Tuanku jadi kuda malam tadi!

[[822]*Raja memandang kapada Salim, kemudian memandang balék kapada
Kadhi.*]

RAJA: [823]Kita uchapkan selamat kapada awak, Ché' Salim, serta banyak-
banyak terima kaséh juga. [824]Betul-lah, bangsa baik benar musang-nya
awak dapat. [825]Chukup élok lagi dengan besar-nya pula. [826]Chuma kita
'nak minta awak tolong satu perkara 'aja lagi. [827]Tolong-lah bawa balék
tawanan awak 'ni pulang. [828]Simpan dahulu di-rumah awak barang sa-
hari dua. Boléh?

SALIM: Ta'at setia, Tuanku. Titah di-junjong.

[[829]*Bunyi orang mengeloh dari dalam pak.* [830]*Orang lain-lain itu hanya
mengangkat kening masing-masing serta bergenyit-genyitan sa-orang
dengan sa-orang. Raja balék bersemayam ka-atas singgasana-nya.*]

Pertunjokan 3

[*Pagi ésok-nya, di-rumah Salim.* [831]*Salim dengan Salmah laki isteri dudok
di-tikar minum kopi sambil berchakap tertawa-tawa.*]

SALMAH: [832]Apa kata Tuan Kadhi waktu abang lepaskan dia tadi?

SALIM: [833]Ta' banyak chakap-nya. Dia 'nak sembahyang suboh kata-nya.
[834]Malu benar-benar dia nampak-nya. [835]Ta' terpandang dék dia muka
aku. He[n]h! [836]Salmah kok menéngok rupa muka-nya masa itu! Puchat!
[837]Di-turis pun ta' berdarah. [838]Aku berani bertaroh apa dia tentu
bertobat, ta' tergamak lagi 'nak chuba-chuba main muda bagitu masa
yang ka-hadapan. [*Bunyi orang mengetok pintu.*] [839]Siapa pula 'tu agak-
nya? [840]Pagi-pagi lagi 'dah tiba! [*Pergi ka-pintu berchakap di-luar.*]

Hadiah daripada Tuan Kadhi? Banyak terima kaséh. [841]Sampaikan-lah kapada Tuan Kadhi terima kaséh kami berdua. [*842Dia masok menda-patkan Salmah membawa hadiah itu, sa-buah gelok pérak terlalu indah-indah perbuatan-nya berukir-ukir.*] Hadiah daripada Musang Berjanggut! [843]Kita 'dah dekat sa-bulan kahwin ada pula hadiah lagi! [844]Bukan hadiah kahwin! [*845Kedua-nya membélék gelok itu dengan gemar dan suka.*]

SALMAH: Chanték, ia? [*846Di-letakkan-nya di-atas méja perhiasan. Lagi orang mengetok pintu.*]

SALIM: Wah! Lagi sa-orang? [*Pergi ka-pintu. Berchakap di-pintu.*] Apa? Daripada To' Laksamana? [847]Baik-nya To' Laksamana! [848]Orang ber-budi, kita berbahasa; [849]orang memberi kita merasa. [850]Ta' terbalas dék aku. [851]Tolong sampaikan terima kaséh sahaja-lah banyak-banyak dari-pada kami berdua kapada-nya, ia? [*Masok balék membawa barang hadiah itu.*]

SALMAH [*852bertanya Salim masok itu*]: Apa barang-nya?

SALIM: Tépak siréh pérak, lengkap dengan cherana, chembul, pekapor, kachip, bagai. [*Kedua-dua-nya membélék-bélék tépak itu. 853Sa-bentar kedengaran pula orang mengetok pintu lagi. Salim pergi ka-pintu, sambil pergi sambil berchakap*]: [854]Itu tentu daripada Temenggong pula agak-nya. [*Berchakap di-pintu.*] Daripada Tem — Éh! Tengku Bendahara? Terima kaséh banyak-banyak. [855]Tolong sampaikan kapada-nya menga-takan kami kedua terhutang budi benar rasa-nya menerima pemberian-nya 'ni. [*Balék mendapatkan Salmah membawa barang hadiah Bendahara itu.*]

SALMAH: [856]Bukan-lah Temenggong, macham yang abang agak tadi?

SALIM: Bukan. Daripada Tengku Bendahara. [857]Terdahulu dia sa-kali ini, ta' mengikut giliran-nya. [858]Ma'alum-lah, orang 'nak lekas menutup tembelang-nya malam kelmarin. [859]Jangan sampai pechah, tahu orang semua.

SALMAH: [860]Apa barang-nya 'ni? [861]Buka-lah lekas, 'Bang. [*862Salim membuka bungkus; 863di-dapati-nya dua buah kaki lilin.*]

SALIM [*meletakkan kaki lilin di-atas méja*]: [864]Chuba kita dérétkan hadiah ini semua-nya di-atas méja 'ni. [865]Di-sini untokkan tempat hadiah Temenggong. [866]Kosongkan tempat-nya besar-besar sadikit. [867]Dia tentu besar barang yang akan di-kirimkan-nya 'tu. [868]Dia mé-mang sukakan besar pada apa-apa pun. [*Lagi bunyi orang mengetok pintu*] Ha. [869]Itu entah pun dia agak-nya 'tu? [870]Chuba Mah agak, apa barang-nya?

SALMAH: e — e — e — [⁸⁷¹*Bunyi ketok berulang.*]

SALIM: ⁸⁷¹Lekas-lah! ⁸⁷²Apa barang-nya Mah agak?

SALMAH: A — Mah kata — anu — [*Salim pergi ka-pintu.*]

SALIM [*di-pintu*]: *Allah!* Terima kaséh banyak-banyak. ⁸⁷³Tolong-lah sampaikan kapada Temenggong terima kaséh kami kedua banyak-banyak fasal hadiah-nya 'ni. ⁸⁷⁴Tuhan juga-lah 'kan membalas-nya. [⁸⁷⁵*Balék masok membawa suatu bungkus besar, belum tahu apa isi-nya.* ⁸⁷⁶Ini dia, Mah, daripada To' Temenggong. ⁸⁷⁷Entah apa-lah 'tu. Chuba buka.

SALMAH [*membuka, Salim memandang*]: Éh! Kain baju, ha!

SALIM: Ia. Kain baju. ⁸⁷⁸Chuba téngok, untok Mah 'aja-lah, atau untok aku pun ada?

SALMAH [*membuka kain-kain itu, memeréksa-nya satu-persatu*]: Ada kedua-dua-nya. ⁸⁷⁹Untok abang chukup dengan seluar baju, kain samping, detar, kasut sérét bagai. Untok Mah baju, kain baték seléndang, selipar, sikat... semua chukup. [*Kedua-nya tertawa, Masing-masing menchubakan pakaian-pakaian itu. Sa-bentar itu kedengaran pula lagi orang mengetok pintu.*]

SALIM [*membilang dengan pantas segala barang-barang yang telah di-terima itu*]: Satu, dua, tiga, empat. ⁸⁸⁰Dua lagi harus akan tiba. ⁸⁸¹Entah siapa-lah dalam raja dua beranak 'tu akan sampai perkiriman-nya dahulu. [*Pergi ka-pintu*] Daripada Tengku Raja Muda? Terima kaséh. ⁸⁸²Tolong-lah sampaikan sa-penoh-penoh terima kaséh daripada kami kedua kapada Tengku Raja Muda, ia? [*Balék masok membawa suatu kotak berbungkus,*] Ini daripada 'adék' Mah! Entah apa-lah 'tu! Chuba buka.

SALMAH [*membuka sambil tersenyum-senyum kulum, terlampau suka rupa-nya*]: Oh! Ayer wangi. Sapu tangan. ⁸⁸³Sapu tangan 'ni bertulis nama abang. Ayer wangi bertulis nama Mah.

SALIM: Wah! ⁸⁸⁴'Adék' Mah berkirim ayer wangi kapada Mah, ia?

SALMAH: ⁸⁸⁵Raja Muda 'tu, ia, élok budak-nya, 'Bang. ⁸⁸⁶Abang tentu gemar menéngok dia 'tu, ia tidak?

SALIM [*masam sadikit muka-nya*]: Ia. ⁸⁸⁷Bila dia 'dah besar bésok, lagi dia bertambah manis kapada anak bini orang!

SALMAH [*sengaja hendak mengusék Salim*]: ⁸⁸⁸Abang 'ni chemburu! ⁸⁸⁹Dengki hati 'kan anak raja 'tu.

SALIM [*bérang*]: Chemburu? Gila! ⁸⁹⁰Chemburu apa? ⁸⁹¹Kalau Mah 'dah suka 'kan dia, apa 'nak aku katakan? ⁸⁹²Mah sukakan 'adék'-nya, ter-champak-lah abang-nya 'ni! ⁸⁹³Biar-lah abang-nya 'ni hanyut membawa diri. [894]' Bunga bukan sa-kuntum, kumbang bukan sa-ékor' kata orang tua-tua.

SALMAH: Téngok-lah 'tu! [895]Abang 'dah 'nak membuat gila! [896]Mah bukan betul-betul! [897]Chuma bergurau-gurau 'aja. [898]Ta' usah-lah abang masokkan ka-hati. [899]Kalau Mah salah, ampunkan 'aja-lah. [*menggéséng-géséngkan pipi-nya kapada kepala Salim. Bunyi ketok yang kuat di-pintu.*]

SALIM: [899a]Itu tentu Raja engkau itu, Mah.

SALMAH: Bukan Raja Mah. Kuda Mah. [900]Bukan-kah Mah kudakan dia malam 'tu? [*Salim berlari pergi ka-pintu. [901]Di-terima-nya dengan hormat dan tidak berkata-kata suatu kotak besar berbalut kain kuning. [902]Di-junjong oléh Salim, di-bawa-nya masok kapada Salmah, di-buka-nya bersama-sama Salmah. [903]Dalam kotak itu di-dapati dua kotak lain, satu bertulis nama Salmah, satu lagi bertulis nama Salim.*]

SALMAH [[904]*mengambil kotak yang bertulis nama dia; di-buka-nya*]: Wah! Barang-barang peremasan ha! Intan berlian! [905]Ini apa pula surat-nya sa-chebis 'ni? [[906]*Di-ambil-nya surat, di-bacha-nya.*] 'Daripada 'paték' pachal yang hina, hamba 'Tuanku', kapada tuanku-nya yang chomél, muda belia, Ché' Salmah.' [*Salmah memandang Salim sambil tertawa, berseri-seri muka-nya. Salim tertawa sama.*]

SALIM [*mengambil kotak yang bernama dia; di-buka-nya pula*]: [907]Wah! Aku ada surat 'aja sa-keping! [908]Apa kata-nya 'ni? [*Di-ambil-nya surat, di-bacha-nya*] [909]'Kapada perjurit harapan kita yang sedia bertuah. [910]Ta' payah di-beri emas intan lagi, kerana intan gemala yang telah sedia dapat kapada-nya itu lebéh mahal daripada segala emas intan dalam dunia.' [[911]*Salim dengan Salmah berpandang-pandangan. Salmah memakai barang-barang intan kurnia Raja itu, kemudian datang memelok Salim.*] [912]Mah-lah intan gemala abang!

BERPANTUN MENCHARI UMPAN

¹Saya teringat masa saya kechil-kechil dahulu saya selalu di-suroh oléh emak saya pergi menangkap sepatong di-dalam sawah kerana hendak di-buat umpan merachun tikus. ²Masa itu umor saya ada-lah kira-kira lima atau enam tahun.

³Ada pun yang di-katakan sepatong itu ia-lah sa-jenis binatang terbang yang sa-akan-akan kapal terbang rupa-nya; ⁴Kepala-nya bulat penoh dengan mata saperti mata lalat, badan-nya bujor, ékor-nya panjang dan sayap-nya sentiasa terhampar walau pun pada masa ia hinggap di-rumput-rumput dan di-pokok-pokok padi itu. ⁵Binatang itu selalu di-dapati ter-lalu banyak dalam sawah kerana ia suka diam di-tempat-tempat yang berrumput panjang dan berayer. ⁶Maka ia-itu bermacham-macham pula jenis-nya, ada yang besar, ada yang kechil serta bermacham-macham warna-nya. ⁷Tetapi jenis yang besar itu-lah yang di-kehendakkan buat umpan merachun tikus; ⁸warna-nya hijau berbinték-binték kehitam-hitaman. ⁹Besar-nya kira-kira dua inchi sa-tengah dari kepala ka-hujong ékor dan buka badan-nya kira-kira sa-suku inchi.

¹⁰Maka pada masa-masa hari panas atau ketika hampir-hampir tengah hari kelihatan-lah ia beratus-ratus ékor berterbangan pada merata sawah itu, entah apa-apa yang di-makan-nya; ¹¹tetapi tidak-lah pula ia merosakkan padi. ¹²Ketika itu pergi-lah saya ka-sawah membawa suatu lidi kelapa yang di-ikatkan pada hujong-nya sadikit kekabu, kelihatan putéh sahaja di-hujong lidi itu. ¹³Saya pergi itu kadang-kadang sa-orang diri sahaja dan kadang-kadang berkawan-kawan dengan adék saya atau dengan budak-budak lain, semua-nya hendak menangkap sepatong juga. ¹⁴Sambil berjalan dalam sawah itu sambil kami chuit-chuitkan hujong lidi itu serta kami menyanyi demikian:

> Chuit-chuit patong!
> Anak 'kau timpa manggar
> Balék busut 'lah hulu 'tu.

¹⁵Demikian-lah di-ulang-ulangkan. ¹⁶Maka sepatong itu apabila di-lihat-nya sahaja kekabu putéh bergerak-gerak ka-atas ka-bawah itu ia pun

datang menyembar menangkap kekabu itu, di-sangka-nya makanan-nya.
[17]Maka melekat-lah gigi-nya atau kuku jari-nya yang halus itu pada urat-urat benang kekabu itu, lalu kami tangkap akan dia di-masokkan ka-dalam suatu chepu atau tin rokok kosong yang sedia kami bawa. [18]Dengan hal yang demikian sa-telah kira-kira sa-jam atau sa-tengah jam sahaja kami berjalan ka-hujong ka-pangkal di-dalam sawah itu sambil menyanyi saperti tadi dapat-lah hingga lima enam puloh ékor sepatong masing-masing dan tin kami pun penoh. [19]Maka pulang-lah kami di-berikan sepatong itu kapada emak. [20]Masa itu semua-nya sepatong itu sudah mati kerana bertutup di-dalam chepu itu tadi.

[21]Petang-petang itu bekerja-lah emak dan bapa kami di-rumah mem-belah belakang sepatong itu di-masokkan ka-dalam-nya rachun warangan yang telah di-lechah jadi serbok. [22]Kemudian di-chuchok atau di-apit-lah sepatong yang telah berachun itu dengan penchuchok-penchuchok lidi nyior, sa-ékor atau dua ékor pada satu-satu penchuchok. [23]Sa-telah dapat kira-kira tiga empat puloh penchuchok di-bawa-lah ka-sawah di-pachak-kan sa-chuchok dua chuchok di-mana-mana tempat yang di-agakkan tikus itu biasa lalu. [24]Dengan jalan ini banyak-lah tikus itu mati.

[25]Ada pun nyanyi itu yang sa-benar-nya hanya-lah sa-kadar menyu-kakan hati kami ketika berjalan ka-hujong ka-pangkal dalam panas itu; [26]tetapi pada masa saya menyanyikan dahulu saya perchaya betul-betul nyanyi itu-lah yang telah menipu sepatong itu dan menarék dia datang menangkap kekabu di-hujong lidi itu. [27]Saya sangkakan sepatong itu bodoh benar kerana perchaya sunggoh-sunggoh akan kekabu itu anak-nya yang telah di-timpa oléh manggar kelapa 'di-balék busut sa-belah hulu' dan itu-lah sebab ia datang menerkam hendak mengambil anak-nya itu.

MENYÉMAH

---

[1]Masa saya budak-budak dahulu saya ada juga berchampor dalam permainan 'bersengkéta batang keladi' itu ketika di-adakan isti'adat berpuar di-kampong saya ia-itu kampong Jempul, jajahan Kuala Pilah, Negeri Sembilan. [2]Tetapi di-sana isti'adat itu di-sebut orang 'menyémah'. [3]Pada masa itu saya ta' mengerti apa tujuan isti'adat itu, hanya saya suka kerana orang ramai dan semua-nya berjalan mengharong sawah dengan rioh rendah-nya, sambil berjalan itu sambil 'bersengkéta' melechutkan batang keladi sa-besar-besar lengan ka-atas belakang kawan-kawan dengan sa-kuat-kuat hati hingga bersepai-sepai batang keladi itu. [4]Maka sunggoh pun batang keladi itu tidak keras saperti kayu tetapi sakit juga oléh-nya. [5]Tiap-tiap orang yang kena itu membalas pula. [6]Jika budak-budak ada yang menangis oléh sakit lalu berkelahi.

[7]Batang keladi itu di-sediakan berikat-ikat hingga sa-pemelok sa-pemelok besar ikat-nya di-letakkan di-mana-mana dalam semak-semak di-tepi-tepi sawah tempat yang akan di-lalui itu. [8]Sambil lalu itu masing-masing orang pun mengambil beberapa kerat daripada ikatan itu di-buat sengkéta. [9]Sa-telah habis maka di-sebelah hadapan ada lagi ikat-ikat yang lain. [10]Demikian-lah sa-hingga sampai ka-hujong perjalanan itu. [11]Sekarang ini sudah jarang-jarang di-adakan isti'adat menyémah itu di-kampong Jempul sebab tidak di-perkenan oléh ahli-ahli agama.

TRANSLATIONS OF THE TEXTS

TEXT A: GHOST IN A SHROUD

Act I

Scene 1

[^{1}*In the Malabari's coffee shop.* ^{2}*Enter Kasim and Saleh. They sit down.*]

MALABARI: Coffee, sir?

KASIM: ^{3}Yes, please. ^{4}Two white coffees. ^{5}Put an extra bit of sugar in, will you, kaka?

MAL.: All right. What do you want to eat? Rolls? Biscuits? Cakes?

SALEH: ^{6}What cakes have you got? ^{7}Are there any fritters? ^{8}Wafers?

MAL.: Yes. ^{8a}Fresh ones. ^{8b}My wife has just brought them from the house. Still hot.

[*Enter Musa*]

KASIM: Ah! ^{9}Here's Musa. ^{10}Come and have some coffee, Musa. [*To the Malabari*]: ^{11}Oh, kaka, make three coffees, will you? ^{12}There are three of us now. ^{13}And bring those fritters along. Bring a good many of them.

MAL. [^{14}*as he goes off to make the coffee*] ^{14a}Very well.

MUSA [*to Saleh*]: ^{15}I knew you were here, Saleh. ^{16}That's why I came to find you.

SALEH: [17]How did you know?

MUSA: [18]I called in at your house just now, to look for you. [19]Your wife said you were sure to be here.

SALEH: Oh! [20]I was half hoping that my wife would be thinking that I was still in the paddy-field. [21]And now she knows, all the time, that I am in the coffee shop! [21a]I can't hang about any longer. [22]I promised to get back early. [23]She asked me to help her knock down some coconuts.

KASIM: [24]Why were you looking for Che' Saleh, 'Bang Musa?

SALEH: [25]Yes, what was it about?

MUSA: [26]Er...what's his name...my friend Che' Lah has just come back from Kuala Lui. [27]He says that in the jungle he came through yesterday he came across a monster clump of rattan. [28]Not very far away. [29]Only about a couple of miles in from the main road, in this direction. [30]He said that it occurred to him that he might ask me to go with him and get it. [31]But, as luck would have it, he had promised to go and help his father-in-law harvest his rice at Simpang Tiga. [32]You know how it is— harvesting your rice crop isn't a job that you can get through in four or five days. [33]But that rattan—if we don't go soon, there's the danger that somebody else will take it.

KASIM: [34]Che' Lah's father-in-law? Who is he? Oh! [35]Old Pa' Anjang, isn't it? [36]What! He hasn't finished getting in his rice yet?

MUSA: [37]Not yet. [38]He hurt his foot. [39]Four or five days ago, when he was coming back from the fields, he was trailing his changkul along behind him. [40]Somehow or other, as he was dragging it along, the blade landed on his heel and made a great gash. It all but severed the tendon. [41]And then the wound swelled up into a blister. [42]Now he can't walk. [43]How is he to get his harvest in? [44]That's why 'Bang Lah and his wife are going there to lend him a hand. [45]He's got a fine crop of rice, too.

KASIM: [46]Yes, I heard about Pa' Anjang cutting his foot on a changkul. [47]I wondered how he was going to finish cutting his rice, with an injured foot like that. [48]But it seems strange, all the same, that he should have been trailing his changkul along like a child, a man of his age. [49]What was wrong with carrying it over his shoulder?

SALEH: [50]Well, what has to be, has to be. [51]But what about this rattan, 'Bang Musa? [52]Are you thinking of going to get it?

MUSA: Yes. [53]That's why I've come to look for you. To see if you would be willing to go with me. [54]Rattan is fetching a good price just now, you know, $40 a pikul. [55]I'd be very glad to make a bit of extra money, if it can be done. [56]You know how it is. I have three children at the English school, all of them wanting pocket money, and food, and bicycles, and books, and clothes. [57]Where am I to find the money, unless I take every chance that comes my way.

SALEH [[58]*bowing his head, and pondering*]: [59]$40 a pikul you said, 'Bang Musa?

MUSA: Yes. [60]I was thinking that if you were willing to go with me we might make it a partnership.

SALEH: [61]I wouldn't mind having a go. Why not? [62]My own rice is all ready for storing now. [63]But I must talk it over with my wife first, and see what she says about it.

MUSA [*to Kasim*]: [64]And you, Che' Kasim, what do you think about it? [65]Will you go, or not?

KASIM: [65a]I'm thinking it over. [66]Because I too am in want of a bit of money. [67]This next month I'm getting my daughter married. I shall have to spend a hundred or two at the very least. [68]If we got five or six pikul of rattan each, that would be pretty good, wouldn't it? [69]Five pikul, that makes $200. Wouldn't that be a big help! [70]How long, do you think, should we have to stay in the jungle?

MUSA: [71]A week at the very longest. [72]That would be enough.

SALEH: Hmh!

MUSA: [73]Why do you say 'Hmh', Saleh?

SALEH: [74]I don't feel very happy when I think of having to spend the nights in the jungle. [75]'Bang Mat Zain met a Mother Kopek ghost when he spent a night in the jungle like that. [76]Couldn't we come home every evening? [77]It isn't very far. [78]You said just now that it was only about two miles from the main road.

MUSA: [79]Ach! [80]What nonsense! [81]I'm surprised to see you believing in all that rubbish. [82]Just old wives' tales! [83]Don't you know that ghost stories are all of them fibs? [84]You get frightened, and then you take everything to be a ghost.

SALEH: [85]Perhaps you're right. [86]But whether you are or not, I just don't want to take the chance of meeting a ghost.

MUSA: [87]Don't bother. [88]There aren't going to be any ghosts. [89]In any case, what is there to be frightened of? [90]We'll put up a hut for us to live in during that week. [91]You say come home every evening. We could do that, but what if somebody stole the rattan that we left behind?

KASIM: ⁹²Say we stay in the jungle for as long as a week. ⁹³How much money should we be able to make, do you think?

MUSA: ⁹⁴According to my reckoning, we should easily make $200 each.

KASIM: ⁹⁵I say! As much as that? ⁹⁵ᵃIf that's so, all right.

MUSA: ⁹⁶And what about you, Saleh?

SALEH: ⁹⁷Yes, I'd like to go...that is...I shall have to ask my wife first, whether she's willing for me to go.

MUSA: Ach! ⁹⁸Can't you make up your own mind? ⁹⁹When are you going to be able to walk on your own two feet, Saleh? ¹⁰⁰Are you going to have to hold on to your wife's apron strings all your days?

SALEH: ¹⁰¹It isn't like that, 'Bang Musa. ¹⁰²I just can't bear quarrelling. ¹⁰³There'll be a fuss if I don't ask her.

MUSA: ¹⁰⁴All right. ¹⁰⁵Ask your wife, then, Saleh. ¹⁰⁶But don't let it go so far that you get held up, and won't be able to go after all.

SALEH: ¹⁰⁷Oh, I'll manage it all right. ¹⁰⁸About when would we be going, 'Bang Musa?

MUSA: ¹⁰⁹I reckon that we could get off at about midday tomorrow. ¹¹⁰That would just give us time to get the hut put up before sunset.

KASIM: ¹¹¹I could manage that all right.

MUSA: ¹¹²What about you, Saleh? ¹¹³Can you manage that?

SALEH: ¹¹⁴Yes, I can. [¹¹⁵*Then, almost in a whisper*]: ¹¹⁶If my wife lets me go.

MUSA: Good! ¹¹⁷We'll meet at the corner, by Che' Manap's shop, shall we? ¹¹⁸After the noon prayer, tomorrow.

KASIM: Yes. ¹¹⁹I'm quite sure I can manage that.

SALEH: ¹²⁰And so can I.

MUSA: ¹²¹In that case we had better go home at once now, and get ready. ¹²²We shall need to take our parangs, and some thick rope, a ladder, some rice and dried fish to eat, and a cooking pot.

[¹²³*The three of them get up and go out.* ¹²⁴*At that moment the Malabari who owns the shop chases after them.*]

MALABARI: Hi! Enche'! You haven't paid me yet! Who's going to pay for the coffee, and the fritters, and the wafers?

[¹²⁵*The three men go back into the shop, apologising.*]

MUSA: ¹²⁶I'm sorry! ¹²⁷I quite forgot.

SALEH: ¹²⁸We were all so busy talking we didn't think about paying the bill.

KASIM: ¹²⁹How much altogether, kaka?

MAL.: Three coffees at ten cents each, thirty cents. Cakes, how many did
you eat? [*Looking at the cakes*]: Oh. You didn't eat a single one. You
just kept on talking and talking, planning to get rich by collecting rattan.
I certainly shan't be able to get rich if people just come in for a cup of
coffee now and then, and all I get is thirty cents, like this!

KASIM [*paying him*]: ¹³⁰Here you are, kaka.

MUSA: ¹³¹Don't worry! ¹³²We three will always be dropping in for a cup
of coffee. ¹³³And if we have any luck we'll invite crowds of our friends
to have coffee in your shop.

MAL.: I hope so. Don't forget to come! [*As they go out*]: 'Salam Aleikum.
With luck, you'll make some money. But I hope you don't meet any
ghosts!

MUSA: ¹³⁴Pooh! Ghosts! Ghosts indeed! ¹³⁵We're living in the year one
thousand nine hundred and forty-nine, I would have you know. ¹³⁶We
have no truck with ghosts, these days. We've abolished them.

[¹³⁷*The three of them go out.* ¹³⁸*The Malabari keeps nodding his head, as
much as to say that he does not believe Musa's words. Then he gathers
together the cups and the cakes on the table where they have been
sitting.*]

Scene 2

[¹³⁹*Inside the hut.* ¹⁴⁰*The evening of the next day.* ¹⁴¹*Kasim is standing with
his back to the audience.* ¹⁴²*He is tightening a tie-rope of the wall of the hut.*
¹⁴³*A lighted lantern stands on the floor, in the middle of the room.*]

KASIM [¹⁴⁴*pulling the knot tight*]: There! ¹⁴⁵That's it. ¹⁴⁶That's firm enough,
that is.

MUSA [¹⁴⁷*coming up the steps into the hut and throwing down his parang*]:
¹⁴⁸We've just managed to get finished in time. ¹⁴⁸ᵃI didn't dream it
would prove such a sticky business to get the hut up. ¹⁴⁹All because it
was so hard to find enough bind-roots. ¹⁴⁹ᵃBut now that we've managed
it, that's that.

KASIM: Yes. ¹⁵⁰Whatever happens, our hut is finished. ¹⁵¹Now if it gets
dark, let it. ¹⁵²We don't have to worry any longer about a place to
sleep in.

MUSA: ¹⁵³Not that I've any objection to working in the dark, mind you.
¹⁵⁴If this torch of mine were all right I could work even in the night.
[¹⁵⁵*He picks up his electric torch and flicks it on, but it does not light up.*]
¹⁵⁶Look at that! ¹⁵⁷And I gave $3 for it at Che' Manap's shop. [¹⁵⁸*He*

throws the torch on the floor.] [159]And Saleh, if you please, says that he's forgotten to bring his.

KASIM: [160]I've no faith in the things they make these days. [*[161]He picks up Musa's torch and has a good look at it. [162]Obviously he does not approve of it, and he tosses it away*.]: [163]I'd prefer a lantern, any day. [164]Give me a lantern like this, and I'm satisfied. [*[165]He picks up the lantern that he has brought with him and cleans the wick*.]

[*[166]Enter Saleh, leaping in, in a state of great perturbation. He shuts the door tight*.]

SALEH: *Ya Allah!* [167]I'm sure I saw two eyes following me about! [168]Was it a *wéwér* ghost, d'you think? [169]In the jungle like this there are always all sorts of ghosts. [170]The *hantu raya*, and the *hantu wéwér*, and the *hantu pemburu*, and the *hantu menjangan*, and the *langsuir*, and the *pontianak*, and the djinns, and all sorts of other things.

MUSA [*[171]patting Saleh's back, like an old lady soothing her grandchild*]: [172]There! There! Don't be silly, Saleh, believing such nonsense as that. [172a]Where are there any ghosts in this world! [173]You're a man. [174]You've no business to be a coward. [175]A will o' the wisp, say you! [176]All that sort of thing is just imagination. You're hungry. [177]That's why all sorts of nonsensical ideas like that come into your head. [178]Let's have a good tuck in. [179]I'm feeling jolly hungry myself. [180]What do you say, Kasim?

KASIM [*pulling another knot tight*]: [181]Yes, I'm coming. [*[182]He picks up his bundle from the end of the floor of the hut, and sits down to eat his food with Musa and Saleh. [183]Saleh too picks up his package of rice and sits down. [184]He looks around him, and feels reassured. [185]Musa is there, and Kasim is there, and the lantern is burning*.]

SALEH: [186]It's pleasant sitting here, with Che' Kasim's lantern, isn't it? [*[187]He opens his leaf-wrapped meal*]: [188]Let's see what my wife has given me to eat with my rice.

MUSA: [189]Not much, by the look of it. [190]Does she keep you short on food, too?

SALEH: [191]It's not much, but it's fair shares between us. [192]'Together we skin an elephant heart, together we dip the heart of a louse'. Isn't that how it goes? [193]Help yourself, 'Bang Musa, Che' Kasim.

MUSA: [194]No thank you. [195]No. [196]You've only got a little there. [197]You'd better have some of mine, and Che' Kasim's. [*[198]He opens his rice*]: [199]Here's mine. [200]You take some. [201]Kasim, you have some, too.

KASIM: No, thank you. [*He opens his rice packet.*] ²⁰¹ᵃHere's mine.
²⁰²Take some, 'Bang Musa, Che' Saleh. ²⁰³We'll sample it together.

MUSA
SALEH } No thank you.

[*They begin to eat*]

Act II

Scene 1

[²⁰³ᵃ*Still inside the hut.* ²⁰⁴*Three hours later.* ²⁰⁵*The lantern is still burning.*
²⁰⁶*The three men are asleep, lying close to each other across the middle of
the room.* ²⁰⁷*Musa is on the side nearest the wall, Kasim is on the side
nearest the audience, and Saleh is in the middle.* ²⁰⁸*Musa is snoring softly.*
²⁰⁹*Kasim begins to groan.* ²¹⁰*Saleh turns over.* ²¹¹*The groans get louder and
louder.* ²¹²*Saleh wakes up, then sits up and looks around him.* ²¹³*There's
no ghost anywhere, it's only Kasim groaning.* ²¹⁴*Saleh lies down again.*
²¹⁵*Kasim's groans get still louder.*]

SALEH [²¹⁶*sitting up, and looking at Kasim*]: Hi! ²¹⁷What's the matter,
Che' Kasim?

KASIM: ²¹⁸I've got a pain in my stomach. [²¹⁹*He groans, as if in agony.*
²²⁰*Musa hears it in his sleep, and turns over*]: O–o–h! O–o–h!

SALEH: ²²¹What sort of pain? ²²²A griping pain? ²²³Is it wind, perhaps?

KASIM [²²⁴*sitting up and then lying down again, several times over, with his
hands pressing against his stomach to ease the pain*]: O–o–h! O–o–h!
²²⁵Colic, it must be. ²²⁶The pain is dreadful! O–o–h! *Allah! Allah!*

MUSA [²²⁷*waking up, then sitting up and looking across at Kasim*]: ²²⁸What
is it?

KASIM [²²⁹*rolling about with the pain*]: *Allah!* ²³⁰I've got a terrible pain.

MUSA: ²³¹What sort of pain can this be? ²³²Where do you feel it?

KASIM [*pressing his hand on his stomach*]: ²³³Here. ²³⁴Here, on the left.

MUSA [*rubbing Kasim's stomach; to Saleh*]: ²³⁵Go and blow up the fire,
Saleh, and warm a stone, to hold against his stomach.

[²³⁶*Saleh gets up and goes to warm a stone.* ²³⁷*Kasim writhes on the floor, in
an extremity of pain, like somebody who has been bitten by a cobra.*
²³⁸*A moment or two later he becomes unconscious and lies there motionless,
like a dead man.* ²³⁹*Saleh is still standing at the door, afraid to go outside.
Musa calls to him*]: ²⁴⁰Kasim is gone, Saleh. ²⁴¹He's gone. ²⁴²There
wasn't time to do anything. ²⁴³Poor Kasim! ²⁴⁴What ever sort of stomach

ache is this? [²⁴⁵*Saleh comes back with all speed.* ²⁴⁶*He looks at Kasim with a face full of woe.*]

SALEH: Yes. He's gone.

[²⁴⁷*Musa and Saleh carefully cover up Kasim's corpse.*]

MUSA: ²⁴⁸One or other of us must go to the village and tell Kasim's wife.

SALEH: Yes. ²⁴⁹One or other of us must go.

MUSA: ²⁵⁰Who's to go? ²⁵¹Will you?

SALEH: ²⁵²Not me! ²⁵³I'm afraid of that will o' the wisp that I saw.

MUSA [*snorting*]: Will o' the wisp, indeed! ²⁵⁴Well, if it's like that, I'll go. ²⁵⁵You keep watch by the corpse.

SALEH [²⁵⁶*still more scared*]: ²⁵⁷No, 'Bang Musa! ²⁵⁸That won't do. ²⁵⁹That would be even more dreadful! ²⁶⁰I'm terrified of the ghost of a dead man!

MUSA: Well then. ²⁶¹Make up your mind. ²⁶²Which can you best face? ²⁶³*I* don't care, either way. ²⁶⁴A flickering ghost, or a dead man's ghost, I'll face either of them.

SALEH [²⁶⁵*dithering with fright*]: Flickering ghost. Dead man's ghost. [*as though weighing them, to decide which is the more horrifying*] Flickering ghost, dead man's ghost. [²⁶⁷*He swallows hard, and then comes to a decision*]: ²⁶⁸Let it be the flickering ghost. ²⁶⁹If it chases me, I'll run with all my might.

MUSA: Good! [*then changing his tone*]: ²⁷⁰But, to satisfy you, we'll draw lots. ²⁷¹Whichever of us pulls out the longer twig, he'll be the one to go.

SALEH: All right. ²⁷²But even if I pull out the short one, let me have the flickering ghost, all the same.

[²⁷³*They draw.* ²⁷⁴*Luckily, Saleh draws the longer one.* ²⁷⁵*So he is the one to go.*]

MUSA: Ah! ²⁷⁶Your wish has come true. ²⁷⁷There's no need to be frightened. ²⁷⁸Trust yourself to Allah. ²⁷⁹Now off you go, at once. ²⁸⁰May all be well with you. ²⁸¹The moon is not completely hidden. You'll be able to see the path. ²⁸²I'll keep watch here.

[²⁸³*Musa sits down at a little distance from the right of the 'corpse'.* ²⁸³ᵃ*Saleh goes towards the door.*]

SALEH [²⁸⁴*Turning from the door and tip-toeing back to get hold of the lantern, to light him on his way*]: ²⁸⁵Is this lantern giving a good light?

MUSA: Hi! ²⁸⁶Don't do that! ²⁸⁷That's Kasim's lantern. ²⁸⁸He's dead, and now you're going to take his belongings!

SALEH [*pretending to examine the wick*]: [289]No! [290]I wasn't going to take it! [291]I was just going to trim the wick, so that you shouldn't be left with a dismal light.

MUSA [*sarcastically*]: Yes! [292]You were going to trim the wick! [*changing his tone*]: [293]Go now, at once. [294]Don't loiter about any longer.

SALEH: Yes. [295]I'm going, this very minute.[[296]*He goes down the steps, his heart thumping with fright.*]

Scene 2

[[297]*Outside the hut.* [298]*A short time afterwards.* [299]*Saleh has covered about sixty yards from the hut.* [300]*He is very nervous.* [301]*The moon has just risen, but it is invisible because it is hidden by the jungle trees.*]

SALEH [[302]*He is charging along in headlong haste.* [303]*He bumps his head into a tree*]: *Allah!* [304]Another bump for my head! [[305]*He does it again*] *Allah!* And another! Wah! [306]If I go on crashing about like this, by the time I get out of the jungle my head will be one mass of bumps. [[307]*There is the sound of a branch snapping off.*] [308]What was that?... [309]Oh, nothing... [310]This won't do! [311]I must get away from here. [[312]*He has a sensation of something like a person swathed in white cloth brushing against him as it goes past. He screams.*] *La ilaha illa 'llah!* [[313]*Something else, he thinks, like somebody swathed in black cloth this time, brushes against him as it goes by.* [314]*He screams again.*] *La ilaha illa 'llah!* That was Ma' Kopek's ghost, I think. *Ya Allah!* [315]Help me! [316]I can't stand this any longer! [317]I'd better go back and ask 'Bang Musa to go with me. [[315]*He runs in this direction, then in that, not knowing where he is going. Then he stops.*] [319]But if I go back and ask him to come with me, he is sure to laugh at me and call me a coward. [[320]*He comes to a halt, and considers the situation.* [321]*At that moment he catches sight of a little sapling near the place where he is standing. It ends in a fork*]: Ha! [322]Two prongs! [323]I've got an idea. [[324]*He begins to hack off the little plant with his parang.*] [325]I'll play a trick on Musa! [326]By hook or by crook I'll surely have him running out of that hut. [327]He says he's not afraid, that he doesn't believe in ghosts! Just wait! [328]I'll see how far his bravery goes. [329]I bet anything he'll come running out, and he'll go on running till he gets to the village. [330]And I'll just follow him! [331]So that he'll think it's the ghost of Kasim's corpse that's chasing him. [[332]*He starts back to the hut.*]

Scene 3

[³³³*Back in the hut.* ³³⁴*A few minutes later. Musa is sitting beside the 'corpse' of Kasim, reciting the 'Qul huwa 'llah' without a moment's intermission.* ³³⁵*Then, he breaks off his reciting and stretches out his hand to reach the basket which contains the remains of his rice.*]

MUSA: ³³⁶That's enough. ³³⁷Corpse or no corpse, I'm hungry. ³³⁸I had quite a good meal this evening, and yet here I am, hungry again. [*He opens the basket.*] ³³⁹I think there was some rice left. [*He begins to pinch together a mouthful.* ³⁴⁰*The head of the 'corpse' moves, as Saleh fits the forked stick to it from under the house; then it rises, about two inches.* ³⁴¹*Musa blinks in amazement, then his eyes bulge and his mouth drops open as he stares at the corpse.* ³⁴²*His hand comes to a halt half-way between the basket and his mouth.*] *Astaghfiru'llah!* ³⁴³Did that head move? ³⁴⁴It looked to me as if it did. [³⁴⁵*He keeps his eyes fixed upon the corpse for a few seconds.* ³⁴⁶*It does not move.*] Ach! ³⁴⁷Just my imagination, it must be. ³⁴⁸I'm getting as bad as Saleh! [³⁴⁹*feeling amused*]: ³⁵⁰How is he getting on, I wonder? ³⁵¹I guarantee he's shrivelled up with fright, walking in the jungle all alone, and in the dark. [³⁵²*He puts the ball of rice into his mouth and swallows it.*] Ghosts! Rubbish! [³⁵³*The head of the 'corpse' rises again, higher than before.*] *La ilaha illa 'llah!* It moved again?...No! Ach! ³⁵⁴I must pull myself together. ³⁵⁵This is all nonsense! [³⁵⁶*He peers into the face of the 'corpse'.* ³⁵⁷*Then he sits back.* ³⁵⁸*He feels reassured.* ³⁵⁹*He presses together another mouthful.* ³⁶⁰*Just as he is going to carry it up to his mouth, the corpse rises until it is half-way to a sitting position, and then remains there.* ³⁶¹*Musa gazes at it in horror, his eyes starting out of his head.* ³⁶²*Then he speaks to it.*]: ³⁶³Lie down again! Lie down! ³⁶⁴It wasn't *my* fault. ³⁶⁵*I* didn't kill you. ³⁶⁶That food that you ate. There was something wrong with it. ³⁶⁷Lie down again! [³⁶⁸*The body of the 'corpse' falls back again.*] Oooh! [³⁶⁹*fanning himself*]: Ha! ³⁷⁰That's right. [*To the corpse*]: ³⁷¹You lie still there. ³⁷²Don't you budge again. [³⁷³*He looks around and sees a piece of strong cord. He picks it up.*]: ³⁷⁴I'll make you lie still. ³⁷⁵I'll tie you down. [³⁷⁶*He goes to tie the cord around the 'corpse'.* ³⁷⁷*He bends over it.* ³⁷⁸*He has only just begun to pass the cord round the flooring laths when the 'corpse' rises again, until it is sitting up straight.* ³⁷⁹*It rises with such force that the face collides with Musa's chin.* ³⁸⁰*Musa lets out a yell, then rushes headlong out of the hut and makes straight for the village.* ³⁸¹ Saleh*

[*comes out from under the hut and runs off too, following in Musa's footsteps.*]

Act III

Scene 1

[³⁸²*At Musa's house.* ³⁸³*Half an hour later.* ³⁸⁴*Fatimah, Musa's wife, is asleep in the bedroom.* ³⁸⁵*Musa is hammering at the door of the house. It sounds as if it must give way under the blows.*]

FATIMAH [³⁸⁶*Getting up hurriedly*]: ³⁸⁷Who is it?

MUSA: ³⁸⁸It's me, Musa. ³⁸⁹Open the door. Be quick!

[³⁹⁰*Fatimah opens the door.* ³⁹¹*Musa bursts in, in a paroxysm of terror, then slumps down, gasping, in front of Fatimah.*]

FATIMAH [³⁹²*greatly alarmed*]: *Ya Allah!* ³⁹³What's this? ³⁹⁴What is it? ³⁹⁵Why have you come back in the middle of the night like this? A tiger?

MUSA [³⁹⁶*gasping for breath, and pointing to the door*]: Kasim!

FATIMAH: ³⁹⁷What about Kasim? ³⁹⁸Has he come with you?

MUSA: Yes! ³⁹⁹Er...No! ⁴⁰⁰Kasim's dead...⁴⁰¹But he's chasing me. ⁴⁰²He's outside there.

FATIMAH: ⁴⁰³Kasim is chasing you? ⁴⁰⁴What's this gibberish that you're talking? ⁴⁰⁵But you said that Kasim was dead. ⁴⁰⁶Where have you left him?

MUSA: In the hut...Er...No!...⁴⁰⁷Outside there.

FATIMAH: ⁴⁰⁸If he's outside, I had better ask him to come in. [⁴⁰⁹*She goes to the door.*]

MUSA [⁴¹⁰*in a voice that gets shriller and shriller, like a scream*]: Don't! Don't! ⁴¹¹Don't ask him to come in!—⁴¹²It isn't Kasim outside. ⁴¹³It's the ghost of his corpse.

FATIMAH [⁴¹⁴*startled*]: The ghost of his corpse? Oh! Oh! [⁴¹⁵*In a changed voice*] ⁴¹⁶But you said you didn't believe in ghosts.

MUSA [⁴¹⁷*impatiently*]: ⁴¹⁸Don't bother about what I said! ⁴¹⁹Help me to keep him from getting in. [⁴²⁰*He begins to recite the verse 'al-kursi', and any sort of prayer that he knows for driving away evil spirits.* ⁴²¹*Soundlessly he mouths the words.*]

FATIMAH: ⁴²²I'll shut the door. [⁴²³*She goes to shut the door.*]

MUSA: ⁴²⁴That's no good! ⁴²⁵Even if you do shut the door, a ghost can still get in. ⁴²⁶Leave it open. ⁴²⁷If he does get in, it will be easier for us to run outside. [428]Come here and stand by the door. Recite any verses that you know. [429]Say them clearly. Shout them into his face if he tries to come in. [[430]*The two of them take up their stand on the right and left of the doorway and then, quietly but rapidly, begin to chant their verses.* [431]*They are both ready to burst into the 'La ilaha illa 'llah' verse if the ghost tries to come in.* [432]*After a while Fatimah's chanting gradually becomes slower and slower.* [433]*Musa tells her to speed up*]: [434]Quickly! Like me. [435]If we stop, he'll come in, I know. [[436]*The two of them chant more and more vigorously and peer through the doorway, prepared to burst into the' La ilaha illa 'llah' verse if the ghost should try to get inside.*]

Scene 2

[*Kasim's house.* [437]*A few moments later.* [438]*In the bedroom, Kasim's wife, too, is asleep. Her name is Meriam.* [439]*Somebody is heard knocking at the door, and then a voice calls, almost in a whisper.*]

SALEH: Che' Yam! Che' Yam!

MERIAM [[440]*opening her eyes, but without moving*]: What?

SALEH: Che' Yam! Che' Yam!

MERIAM [[441]*turning over, still half asleep*]: [442]It isn't light yet, 'Bang Chim. [443]Why do you want to get up so early? [[444]*Then suddenly she is fully awake.* [445]*She has just remembered that her husband is not there.* [446]*She sits up, her eyes blinking, and listens carefully to decide whether there really is somebody calling or not.*]

SALEH: Che' Yam! Che' Yam!

MERIAM: [447]Who is it?

SALEH: [448]It's me, Saleh. [449]Open the door. [450]It's Saleh. I've come to bring you some news.

[[451]*Meriam gets out of bed and goes to open the door.* [452]*She sees Saleh standing in the doorway.* [453]*In his hand he holds a forked branch.*]

MERIAM: Good heavens! It's Che' Leh! [454]Why have you come back in the middle of the night like this? [455]Didn't you go into the jungle yesterday with 'Bang Chim and 'Bang Musa? [456]Where are they now? [457]Is anything wrong?

SALEH: Yes. [458]There's been a bit of an accident. Che' Kasim has...has...

MERIAM: [459]Has what? [460]Where is he now?

SALEH: [461]He's staying in the jungle, in the hut where we slept last night.

MERIAM: [462]Staying with 'Bang Musa?

SALEH: No. [463]'Bang Musa has come home.

MERIAM: Come home? ⁴⁶⁴Why? ⁴⁶⁵What's wrong?

SALEH: ⁴⁶⁶I don't really know. ⁴⁶⁷I didn't ask the reason. ⁴⁶⁸He didn't say anything, but he came back in a great hurry. ⁴⁶⁹I expect he wanted to fetch something that he'd left behind.

MERIAM: ⁴⁷⁰Well in that case, why did you come too, and leave 'Bang Chim alone in the jungle?

SALEH: ⁴⁷¹I was afraid that 'Bang Musa might run into some danger, coming through the jungle all by himself in the middle of the night. ⁴⁷²That's why I followed him.

MERIAM: ⁴⁷³Oh yes? And 'bang Chim left all alone by himself in the jungle? ⁴⁷⁴No danger in that, I suppose? ⁴⁷⁴ᵃIf he should come to any harm, what would you say about that?

SALEH: ⁴⁷⁵Che' Kasim is safe, quite safe. ⁴⁷⁶There's nothing now for him to be afraid of. ⁴⁷⁷There's not a single danger that he can run into now. ⁴⁷⁸He's quite safe.

MERIAM: ⁴⁷⁹What do you mean by that, Che' Leh? ⁴⁸⁰How do you know? Maybe there is a tiger lying in wait for him, left all alone like that.

SALEH: ⁴⁸¹Even a tiger wouldn't matter.

MERIAM: Wouldn't matter? ⁴⁸²What are you talking about, Che' Leh?

SALEH: What, indeed? ⁴⁸³I'm simply telling you the truth. He is...He... He has—

[⁴⁸⁴*At this moment Kasim comes racing up to the house, as though he is in a great hurry.* ⁴⁸⁴ᵃ*In his hand he carries the lantern, still alight.* ⁴⁸⁵*Saleh gapes in astonishment then tries to hide behind some bushes near the door.*]

MERIAM: Ah! ⁴⁸⁶Here's 'Bang Chim! ⁴⁸⁷Are you really all right? ⁴⁸⁸Thank God!

KASIM [*to Saleh*]: ⁴⁸⁹You're a fine one, aren't you, Che' Saleh! ⁴⁹⁰You left me all alone in that hut, in the middle of the jungle. ⁴⁹¹What happened? ⁴⁹²I don't remember a single thing after I got that frightful stomach pain.

SALEH: 'Bang Musa and I thought that you...We saw that you looked just like a—

KASIM: ⁴⁹³I fainted, passed right out. ⁴⁹⁴When I came to myself again I saw that I was left there all alone. ⁴⁹⁵Why did you run away and leave me like that?

SALEH: ⁴⁹⁶'bang Musa and I thought that you—

KASIM: ⁴⁹⁷All the same, it was a good thing that you thought of leaving your food for me. ⁴⁹⁸When I came round, I saw the food basket near me.

⁴⁹⁹When I opened it I saw there was still some rice left in it, and some prawn paste. ⁵⁰⁰By that time I was feeling empty, and I just polished off whatever was there. ⁵⁰¹Your rice and Musa's I mean. ⁵⁰²My own I threw away, because I thought it was probably my food that had given me those pains. ⁵⁰³I wonder what was wrong with that food that you packed for me yesterday, Che' Yam?

MERIAM [⁵⁰³ᵃ*looking sideways at him and pretending to be angry*]: ⁵⁰⁴You threw it away? ⁵⁰⁵What a waste! ⁵⁰⁶Good food like that! ⁵⁰⁷In these days, too, when everything is so hard to get, and so dear.

KASIM [*sarcastically*]: Yes! Good food indeed! ⁵⁰⁸I all but died through eating that food that you packed for me. ⁵⁰⁹What did you put in it?

MERIAM [⁵¹⁰*after thinking a moment*]: ⁵¹⁰ᵃHm. Now what could it have been, I wonder? ⁵¹¹I hope it wasn't because the dried fish had gone off a bit yesterday. ⁵¹²It did cross my mind. But we've often eaten fish like that before, and nothing has happened. ⁵¹³Besides, don't you remember that verse our grandmothers used to sing?

> Screw-pine mats both fine and coarse ones,
>> Princes' wedding-mats she weaves.
> Fish that's tainted waste not—make it
>> Relish for your salad-leaves.

KASIM: ⁵¹⁴Oh, for goodness' sake don't quote pantuns at me! ⁵¹⁵Just take care another time. If the fish is tainted, throw it away, don't use it. ⁵¹⁶How is one to know? ⁵¹⁷If one's luck is out, maybe something poisonous has got into it, and that's why it has gone off. ⁵¹⁸This time, luck was with me. My end was not yet due, thanks be to God. [⁵¹⁹*Turning towards Saleh*]: ⁵²⁰But 'Bang Musa, where is he now?

SALEH: ⁵²¹He's gone home. ⁵²²He thought you were dead, too, just as I did.

KASIM: Oh yes? *Subhan Allah!* ⁵²³It appears that I have been dead and have come back to life!

SALEH: ⁵²⁴Yes. It was because he thought you were dead that he ran home at top speed. ⁵²⁵Judging by the way he ran, all wild and flustered, it seemed to me that he kept seeing the ghost of your corpse chasing after him.

KASIM: Ha! Ha! Ha! ⁵²⁶Like that, was it? ⁵²⁷That's a real joke, to hear that! ⁵²⁸I used to think that he really and truly did not believe in ghosts. [⁵²⁹*He has a sudden thought.*] ⁵³⁰Ah! Yes! I've got an idea! ⁵³¹We'll have a bit of fun with him! [⁵³²*He darts into the bedroom, takes a sheet off the bed, and wraps it round his head and body as he comes out again*]: ⁵³³I'm going to show him what a coward he is, so that he'll know himself better. [⁵³⁴*He starts off towards Musa's house, then turns his head back towards Saleh and Meriam*]: ⁵³⁵You come along too. We'll see how 'Bang Musa doesn't believe in ghosts! [⁵³⁶*He goes on.* ⁵³⁷*Meriam and Saleh follow him.*]

Scene 3

[*At Musa's house, a few moments later.* ⁵³⁸*The door of the house is, of course, standing open.* ⁵³⁹*Musa and Fatimah are there, inside, on the right and left of the doorway, chanting prayers, still waiting, in case Kasim's ghost should make its way in.*]

MUSA } [*over and over again*]: *La ilahi illa 'llah.*
FATIMAH }

[⁵⁴⁰*Something that looks like a flash of white cloth is seen at the edge of the doorway. Musa and Fatimah start in alarm.* ⁵⁴¹*They continue their chanting and reciting, getting faster and faster.* ⁵⁴²*A moment later, there appears something like a white wing, billowing out in a great fan outside the door.* ⁵⁴³*Musa and Fatimah turn pale, then, in their fright, they stop chanting.* ⁵⁴⁴*At that moment, Kasim, in his wrappings, comes in.* ⁵⁴⁵*When he reaches the end of the wall on one side of the room he faces Musa and Fatimah and keeps nodding his head towards them.* ⁵⁴⁶*They are both speechless, unable to utter a single word.* ⁵⁴⁷*Kasim slowly raises his right arm, draped in the white sheet, and points towards Musa, all the time nodding his head as if to accuse him.* ⁵⁴⁸*Musa gazes at him, his eyes starting out of his head.*]

MUSA [⁵⁴⁹*He is gasping with terror.* ⁵⁵⁰*He begins to mouth some words again, but his voice sounds like a whisper*]: *Ya Allah! Ya Allah!* Help! Help! *La ilahi illa 'llah.*

[⁵⁵¹*Fatimah is still speechless.* ⁵⁵²*Suddenly Kasim walks right up to Musa.* ⁵⁵²ᵃ*Musa moves backwards, not daring to take his eyes off the ghost, in case it should make a sudden spring at him.* ⁵⁵³*Kasim follows him all over the room as he keeps backing away from him.* ⁵⁵⁴*When he has got Musa flattened into a corner, he makes as if to throw his arms around him.* ⁵⁵⁵*Musa howls with fright, but Kasim does not actually embrace him; he merely throws the sheet over Musa's head.* ⁵⁵⁶*Musa thrashes about, this way and that, trying to free himself from the sheet, until he hears Kasim's* *voice taunting him.* ⁵⁵⁷*All this time Fatimah has remained rooted to the* *spot, unable to do a thing.* ⁵⁵⁸*But a moment later she suddenly realises that* *what she took to be a ghost has suddenly changed its appearance and is* *none other than Kasim himself in very truth.* ⁵⁵⁹*She edges her way along* *and goes to stand beside her husband.* ⁵⁶⁰*At that moment Saleh and Meriam* *come in and join in the laughter when they see what is happening.*]

KASIM: ⁵⁶¹So you thought I was dead, 'Bang Musa, did you?

MUSA [⁵⁶²*freeing his head from its wrapping, and then standing stock still,* *gazing at Kasim without being able to utter a word*]: er—er—er—

KASIM: ⁵⁶³No! ⁵⁶⁴I'm not dead yet. ⁵⁶⁵But to think that you could have the heart to leave me alone in the hut like that!

MUSA [⁵⁶⁶*finding his voice again*]: ⁵⁶⁷You scared me. ⁵⁶⁸You sat up, when you were lying there stretched out like a corpse.

KASIM [⁵⁶⁹*feeling mystified and not understanding at all*]: ⁵⁷⁰When did I sit up? ⁵⁷¹Did I really sit up? ⁵⁷²I don't remember a thing until I came to myself again, and found that you and Che' Leh were no longer there. ⁵⁷³Did I really sit up before that?

MUSA: ⁵⁷⁴Yes, you really did. ⁵⁷⁵First of all I saw your head come up a bit [⁵⁷⁶*showing with his hand how far it had come up.* ⁵⁷⁷*Saleh, standing* *behind him, looks on with a smile, then gives a demonstration with his* *forked branch of how he had thrust up Kasim's head from underneath the* *hut.*] ⁵⁷⁸Then you went down again and lay quite still. ⁵⁷⁹Then up again, higher than before. ^{579a}I began to feel all prickling with goose-flesh. ⁵⁸⁰So I got a rope, meaning to tie you to the flooring so that you couldn't come up again. ⁵⁸¹Just as I was going to tie it, suddenly your head and body came up with a rush until you were sitting bolt upright. ⁵⁸²Your face came crack against my forehead. [*He rubs his forehead*]: I've still got the bump there.

SALEH [*laughing*]: ⁵⁸³Yes, that's true. I saw it. ⁵⁸⁴It really was a comic sight, I thought. ⁵⁸⁵If you had been there to see it yourself, Che' Kasim, you would have burst your sides with laughing.

MUSA [⁵⁸⁶*turning sharply towards Saleh*]: Saleh! ⁵⁸⁷What do *you* know about it? ⁵⁸⁸*You* weren't with me at the time.

SALEH: ⁵⁸⁹Wasn't I indeed? ⁵⁹⁰I most certainly was. ⁵⁹¹It was you who didn't see me.

MUSA: ⁵⁹²Where were you at the time?

SALEH: ⁵⁹³Underneath the hut. [⁵⁹⁴*He fits his forked stick to Kasim's neck* *and shows how he thrust up Kasim's head until it rose in that violent fashion. Kasim laughs.* ⁵⁹⁵*Musa shakes his head, with mortification, it would seem.*]

KASIM: ⁵⁹⁶Oh, it's a real shame that I couldn't be there to see it all happening!

MUSA: *Astaghfiru'llah!* ⁵⁹⁷Was it really you, Saleh? ⁵⁹⁸You did play me up! ⁵⁹⁹I really was a simpleton. ⁶⁰⁰To think that you managed to fool me as easily as that! [*Still shaking his head*]: ⁶⁰¹So, what can I say? ⁶⁰²It's happened, and that's that. [⁶⁰³*Trying to cover his humiliation by putting a bold face on things*]: ⁶⁰⁴But, in any case, I was right. ⁶⁰⁵Where is there a ghost? ⁶⁰⁶There's only Kasim. ⁶⁰⁷The truth is that ghosts are all just imagination. ⁶⁰⁸When you feel frightened, and you're all alone, that's when all sorts of ideas spring up and tell you that there are ghosts. ⁶⁰⁹If you can manage to control your fear all the ghosts vanish. [⁶¹⁰*Kasim makes as if to wrap himself in the sheet again, but Musa stops him*]: Don't! Don't. ⁶¹¹I'm still not quite recovered. [*changing his tone*]: ⁶¹²This is all because we haven't had anything to eat. ⁶¹³The sun is already high. [*To his wife*]: ⁶¹⁴You go and put some water on to boil, Che' Mah, and make some coffee, and some pancakes, so that we can have something to eat.

FATIMAH: ⁶¹⁵Yes, I'll go and see to that. [*To Che' Meriam*]: Come along into the kitchen, Che' Yam.

MERIAM: Yes, that's it. ⁶¹⁶I'll help Che' Mah in the kitchen.

[⁶¹⁷*The two women go into the kitchen.*]

MUSA [⁶¹⁸*to Kasim and Saleh, waving his hand to invite them to sit down*]: ⁶¹⁹Let's sit down, Kasim, Saleh, and we'll chat about something else while Che' Mah makes the pancakes.

[⁶²⁰*The three men sit there chatting and smoking their cigarettes, and enjoying a good laugh.*]

TEXT B: THE BEARDED CIVET-CAT

Act I

Scene 1

[¹*It is morning.* ²*Two people, a young husband and wife, are seated on a mat in their home.* ³*Both are of high birth, and they are newly married.* ⁴*The wife is radiantly beautiful.* ⁵*The husband is looking very downcast.*]

SALMAH: ⁶Why do I see you looking so troubled, 'Bang? ⁷As though you had lost some dear one!

SALIM: ⁸Hm. *I* don't know. ⁹I really don't know how to tell you. ¹⁰An evil fortune has fallen upon us, our happiness goes soaring out of reach. ¹¹We are only just married, but it looks as if we are going to part. ¹²Perhaps be separated for ever, and never meet again.

SALMAH: ¹³Separated? ¹⁴Why separated? ¹⁵It's less than a month since we were married.

SALIM: ¹⁶Well what's to be done? ¹⁷I shall just have to go and leave you. There's no escape. ¹⁸And at once, too. ¹⁹Ah, my luckless fate! ²⁰It would have been better if I had never been born!

SALMAH: ²¹You've got to go *where*? ²²*Why* can't you escape it?

SALIM: ²³It's a royal command. How can I get out of it? ²⁴The old saying is that the Raja's business is carried on the head, but one's own business is tucked away under the arm.

SALMAH [*startled*]: ²⁵A royal command! ²⁶In that case, yes, you will have to go. ²⁷But it won't be for long, surely? ²⁸At the longest a week?

SALIM: ²⁹A week. ³⁰Ha! You little know!

SALMAH: ³¹If not a week, then a month?

SALIM [*mockingly*]: Yes! A month!

SALMAH: A year?

SALIM: ³²You don't know what you are talking about! ³³For ever, if you want to know. ³⁴I shan't be able to come back ever, until I die. ³⁵What's to be done, when the sky falls on your head?

SALMAH: ³⁶How can this be? ³⁷I don't understand, 'Bang. ³⁸Where are you going for all that long time?

SALIM: ³⁹I myself don't know where. ⁴⁰All I know is that I've been told to go this very morning, and that I can't linger about any longer.

SALMAH: ⁴⁰ᵃYou don't know! ⁴¹Don't pretend, 'Bang! ⁴²You certainly do know. ⁴³It isn't likely that the Raja hasn't told you where he is going to send you. ⁴⁴At any rate, he himself certainly knows where he's going to tell you to go. ⁴⁵If you don't know, why don't you ask him?

SALIM: [46]Not likely! [47]He doesn't know himself. [48]It isn't that he wants to send me to any particular place.

SALMAH: [49]Oh, this is sheer nonsense.

SALIM: [50]He's going to tell me to go and look for...

SALMAH: [51]Look for what?

SALIM: [52]To look for a bearded civet-cat.

SALMAH: A bearded civet-cat! [53]Where is there a bearded civet-cat in the world? [54]If that's true, it's quite clear that the Raja is mad.

SALIM: [55]It is quite true that he's mad. [56]That's just why I have to go and look for it.

SALMAH: [57]But why does he want a bearded civet-cat? [58]What is he going to do with it?

SALIM: [59]It isn't that he wants a civet-cat. [60]The truth is that he wants you.

SALMAH: What? Wants me? Stuff and nonsense! [61]That's enough, 'Bang. [62]Don't say any more. [63]Don't go. [64]Or if you do go, take me with you. [65]Don't leave me behind.

SALIM: [66]It isn't only the Raja who wants you, you know, Mah. [67]All the ministers of his court are mad about you, Mah, every single one of them.

SALMAH: Heavens above! Disgraceful! Madness! Rubbish!

SALIM: [68]Just listen! [69]Dato' Temenggong is one who wants you. [70]I saw him, round-eyed, just gazing at you the day when we sat in state at our wedding. [71]As though he were going to eat you.

SALMAH [[72]with a look of utter distaste on her face]: Hah! The evil old monkey! [73]Every time I look at him I want to be sick. [74]I hate to see the way he carries on, showing off, and boasting, with no sense of what is fit and proper.

SALIM: [75]To' Laksamana is another one. [76]He's madly in love with you, too.

SALMAH [[77]looking rather pleased]: To' Laksamana? Ha! [78]He's rather handsome, [79]with his stiff moustache, curving up at the ends, like wire. Very dashing! [[80]Shows with her hands how the Laksamana's moustache curves upwards.]

SALIM [[81]looking jealous]: [82]Mah! I don't think it's quite nice for you to be praising To' Laksamana like that! [[83]He strokes his own moustache, which is wispy and sparse.]

SALMAH [[84]with an apologetic air]: Oh! [85]You mustn't be hurt like that!

⁸⁶Of course I *prefer* a moustache that's not too thick. ⁸⁷I was only saying that To' Laksamana's moustache is a nice one for a man who is a laksamana.

SALIM [⁸⁸*looking displeased*]: ⁸⁹Oh, really!

SALMAH [*looking pleased*]: ⁹⁰Who else? [⁹¹*changing the tone of her voice when she catches sight of Salim looking at her out of the corner of his eye, with an aggrieved expression*] ⁹²I hope, that is to say, that there isn't anybody else wanting me...

SALIM: ⁹³Not anybody else, indeed! ⁹⁴That kadhi, what's to be done about him? ⁹⁴ᵃThat sham saint! That cheat of a scholar! ⁹⁵He's after you too.

SALMAH: Who? Tuan Kadhi? *Astaghfiru 'llah!* ⁹⁶The pantun is quite right,

> When elders err and judges sin,
> Shall we, their flock, not fall?

⁹⁷ Well, any more?

SALIM: ⁹⁸There's that worthless young Raja Muda. He...

SALMAH: What? The Raja Muda? *La ilahi!* [⁹⁹*with a little pouting smile*]: ¹⁰⁰Him, yes, he's rather sweet, isn't he? ¹⁰¹He's so boyish in his ways. ¹⁰²I quite like the look of him.

SALIM [*looking displeased*]: ¹⁰³You! Well, really, Mah! ¹⁰⁴If you feel like that I had better take myself off, and never come back again.

SALMAH [¹⁰⁵*in a repentant tone*]: 'Bang! 'Bang! ¹⁰⁶You mustn't be annoyed, 'Bang. ¹⁰⁷I didn't really mean it. ¹⁰⁸I just think it would be nice to have him for a younger brother.

SALIM [*in a sarcastic tone*]: Yes! Your young brother! ¹⁰⁹Go on with you! ¹¹⁰And there's another...Tengku Bendahara. ¹¹¹I suppose you'd like him for a little brother too?

SALMAH: Tengku Bendahara! *Ya Allah!* ¹¹²Heaven preserve me! That tough old thing with his puffing and blowing! [¹¹³*She screws up her face and shows how the Bendahara's moustaches sweep downward*]: ¹¹⁴His very face is enough to put you in mind of your grave!

SALIM: Well. ¹¹⁵That's enough of that. ¹¹⁶Now what are we going to do? ¹¹⁷What's to be our plan? ¹¹⁸Must I just go and look for that bearded civet-cat? ¹¹⁹Have you ever heard of a bearded civet-cat? ¹²⁰The truth is that the Raja's real purpose is to tell me to go away and never come back again, so that it will be easy for him to come to terms with you. ¹²⁰ᵃThat's clear.

SALMAH: Oh dear! ¹²¹What are we going to do? ¹²²What way out is there? [¹²³*She begins to cry. Her whole body is shaken with sobs.* ¹²⁴*Suddenly she stops crying,* ¹²⁵*and says, brightly*]: ¹²⁶I've got an idea!

SALIM [¹²⁷*pricking up his ears*]: ¹²⁸What is it?

SALMAH [¹²⁹*nodding her head up and down*]: ¹³⁰You just leave it to me. ¹³¹I know what to do. ¹³²They all know that you are going off this morning? [*She gets up suddenly.*] ¹³³Come on, 'Bang. ¹³⁴Get your things together. ¹³⁵And then off you go, at once.

SALIM [¹³⁶*looking disappointed*]: ¹³⁷Go where? ¹³⁸Where am I to go to?

SALMAH: ¹³⁹To the back of Beyond! ¹⁴⁰To anywhere you like. [*Then, with a mysterious little smile*]: ¹⁴¹But remember! You must be back before 11 o'clock tonight.

SALIM: ¹⁴²But what is it that you are going to do? ¹⁴³Do tell me, I want to hear...

SALMAH: ¹⁴⁴There's no need. ¹⁴⁵I mustn't tell you. ¹⁴⁵ᵃI know what to do. ¹⁴⁶There isn't time to tell you all about it. ¹⁴⁷If they all know that you must go this very morning, no doubt before very long they'll be coming here, one by one. ¹⁴⁸Then if they find you here, still not gone, our plan won't work. ¹⁴⁹Hurry up, 'Bang. ¹⁵⁰Here's your bundle. ¹⁵¹Go now, quickly.

SALIM [¹⁵²*He takes his bundle and goes out, then turns back*]: ¹⁵³I had better take something to eat. ¹⁵⁴If I'm going to be wandering about aimlessly until 11 o'clock, or else hiding in the brushwood, I shall certainly get hungry.

SALMAH: ¹⁵⁵Why yes, of course you will! ¹⁵⁶I didn't think of that. ¹⁵⁷This wife of yours is a forgetful creature! ¹⁵⁸No wonder! With my mind all in a whirl as it is. [¹⁵⁹*She goes to the shelf above the cooking-place and wraps up some rice and some dried fish.*] ¹⁶⁰Here you are! ¹⁶¹Some of yesterday's rice and some dried fish to go with it.

SALIM: ¹⁶²Thank you. [¹⁶³*He takes his package of food and goes off down the steps.*]

Scene 2

[¹⁶⁴*Midday.* ¹⁶⁵*Salmah is sitting on the floor, weaving a mat.* ¹⁶⁶*She is looking very sad.* ¹⁶⁷*The Kadhi arrives.* ¹⁶⁸*Salmah pretends not to see him.*]

KADHI: ¹⁶⁹May I come in? ¹⁷⁰You are left all alone?

SALMAH: Oh! Tuan Kadhi! ¹⁷¹Do come in, Tuan. ¹⁷²Yes. I'm left all alone. ¹⁷³Abang Salim isn't here.

KADHI: Ha! ¹⁷⁴Where is he?

SALMAH: ¹⁷⁵He's gone away. His Highness ordered him to go and look for a bearded civet-cat.

KADHI: A bearded civet-cat? ¹⁷⁶Where is there such a thing as a bearded civet-cat? ¹⁷⁷It's very peculiar. ¹⁷⁸What does His Highness intend to do with it, I wonder?

SALMAH: ¹⁷⁹Goodness knows! I don't know what the meaning of it all is.

KADHI: ¹⁸⁰Hm! Yes. It's certainly strange. ¹⁸¹And you're not afraid, left alone?

SALMAH: ¹⁸²In the daytime, like this, I'm not afraid. ¹⁸³But when it gets dark I really don't know how it will be with me.

KADHI: ¹⁸⁴In that case, let me stay here and keep you company, and comfort you, rather than that you should stay all alone like this. ¹⁸⁵Even if I have to stay until to-night, I shouldn't mind.

SALMAH: ¹⁸⁶Thank you, Tuan. Thank you very much indeed. ¹⁸⁷I cannot thank you enough for your kindness. ¹⁸⁸But while it's still daylight, forgive me if I decline your offer. ¹⁸⁹People would not approve. ¹⁹⁰And I'm not afraid now, because it's light. ¹⁹¹If you want to come, come tonight, at about 8 o'clock.

KADHI: ¹⁹²Yes, no doubt, people would think it not proper. ¹⁹³It's better that I shouldn't come in now. ¹⁹⁴This evening, at about 8 o'clock, I'll come back. ¹⁹⁵Good-bye then for now. [¹⁹⁶*He goes out and returns home.* ¹⁹⁷*Salmah laughs to herself.*]

SALMAH: Learned fraud! ¹⁹⁸Turban as big as a basket—and a crooked heart! ¹⁹⁹You're the one that I shall make into a bearded civet-cat this night! ²⁰⁰Your beard is long enough! [²⁰¹*She stops*]: ²⁰²After this, who'll come next, I wonder.

[²⁰³*A moment later, footsteps are heard.* ²⁰⁴*Salmah goes back to her weaving.* ²⁰⁵*There is a knock at the door.* ²⁰⁶*The Dato' Laksamana comes in, looking very distinguished.*]

LAKS.: *As-salam alaikum*, master of the house.

SALMAH: Oh! To' Laksamana! ²⁰⁷You startled me! ²⁰⁸I wondered who it could be.

LAKS.: ²⁰⁹I was passing this way. ²¹⁰I thought it would be a good idea to call in for a moment and see the newly-married couple. ²¹¹Where is Salim?

SALMAH [*pretending to be sad*]: ²¹¹ᵃAbang Salim isn't here. ²¹²He's gone away. His Highness told him to go and look for a bearded civet-cat. ²¹³There's no knowing when he'll be back. ²¹⁴I'm just left here all alone.

LAKS.: Oh dear, dear, dear! [215]A bearded civet-cat? Where is he to look for that? [216]If he doesn't find it, he'll certainly never come back again! He'll be afraid of His Highness' displeasure. [217]And you? Aren't you frightened, being left all alone?

SALMAH: [218]Yes, I do feel a bit nervous...but who is to keep me company? [219]My parents don't know about it yet.

LAKS.: [220]In that case, let *me* keep you company. How sad! [221]So lovely and so young, and left all alone!

SALMAH: [221a]On no, Dato'! [222]A man to keep a woman company! [223]What would people say! [224]Besides, when it's bright daylight like this, I don't feel nervous. [225]And I've got my work too. [226]Look! [227]What do you think of this mat that I'm weaving, Dato'? Do you like it?

LAKS. [*looking at her weaving*]: [228]It's very beautiful. [229]As it would be, considering who is making it! [230]Lovely to look at, and a clever weaver into the bargain! [231]This diamond-shaped bit here, what's the name of that weave? [*He points to that bit of the pattern.*]

SALMAH: [232]That's called the 'toasted rice-grain lozenge'.

LAKS.: [233]It looks as if your supply of mengkuang is going to run out, before long. [234]Have you got any more ready prepared anywhere? [235]Let me go and get it for you. [236]Or if you haven't got any left I can go and cut some for you, and help you parch it, and split it and dry it, and carry it in for you. Shall I?

SALMAH: *Allah!* [237]You do like to air your knowledge, don't you, Dato'? But don't you bother. There's no need. [238]I can do it myself.

LAKS.: [239]But I would like to help you. [240]I don't like the thought of your delicate hands doing all that rough work. [241]Let me go and get some for you, shall I? [[242]*He makes as if to go.*]

SALMAH: No, Dato'! [243]If you do really want to get some for me, don't do it now. [244]I don't want you to put yourself to that trouble.

LAKS.: [245]What trouble would it be? [246]I should be back here in no time at all.

SALMAH: [247]No, please don't, Dato'. [248]Wait! If you really do want to do it you can bring me some this evening. [249]Just now I have to go to Ma' Teh's house, to see that son of hers who has fever. [250]I promised her, yesterday. [251]I shan't be back until this evening. [[252]*She begins to pack up her weaving, as if about to set out*]

LAKS.: [253]Oh! I see. [254]Very well. [255]I'll go home then, now. [256]And this evening I'll come back with some mengkuang. Yes? ²⁵⁷What time would suit you?

SALMAH: ²⁵⁸Say, after you've had your meal. ²⁵⁹At half-past eight. ²⁶⁰Who knows, I may be delayed in getting back...

LAKS.: Ha! Yes, then, At half-past eight. ²⁶¹Be sure to wait for me, won't you? ²⁶¹ᵃGoodbye!

SALMAH: ²⁶²Wait! ²⁶²ᵃThere'll be no doubt about my waiting! Goodbye! [²⁶³*The Laksamana goes out.* ²⁶⁴*Salmah smiles, and goes on with her own thoughts*]: ²⁶⁵When the time comes, you'll learn a thing or two! [²⁶⁶*A moment later, there is the sound of footsteps.* ²⁶⁷*Salmah raises her eyebrows.*] ²⁶⁸Now which of them is it this time, I wonder? [*There is a knock at the door. Salmah opens it*]: Oh! Dato' Temenggong! Come in.

[²⁶⁹*The Temenggong enters. He sways affectedly from side to side as he walks. He carries a couple of durians, tied together with string, dangling from his fingers.*]

TEMENGG.: ²⁷⁰Here's a little present, Salmah, to comfort you, left all alone. ²⁷¹My durians are ripe. They are all falling now. ²⁷²I've brought two for you. I picked out my very best golden durians. ²⁷³I hear that Salim is away. ²⁷⁴That's why I have come to see you.

SALMAH: ²⁷⁵I am very grateful to you, Dato'. Thank you.

TEMENGG.: ²⁷⁶We had better split one now, and then we can eat it together. ²⁷⁷Let me split one for you. ²⁷⁸Where's the parang? [²⁷⁹*He looks around for it.*]

SALMAH: ²⁸⁰Oh, not just now. ²⁸¹Wait till this evening. ²⁸²Just at this moment I am off to Ma' Teh's house to see her son. He is ill. ²⁸³Will you come this evening, please, Dato'? ²⁸⁴I'll be back at about 9 o'clock.

TEMENGG.: Oh! ²⁸⁵In that case, yes, I will. ²⁸⁶At 9 o'clock I'll be back again. ²⁸⁷Wait for me! ²⁸⁸Don't split those durians before I arrive, will you? ²⁸⁹Wait till I come.

SALMAH: ²⁹⁰I wouldn't be as greedy as that! [²⁹⁰ᵃ*The Temenggong goes off, waving his hand vigorously in farewell. Salmah counts up on her fingers*]: One, two, three. The Kadhi, the Laksamana, the Temenggong. ²⁹¹That's three of them accounted for. ²⁹²That leaves three more. [²⁹³*A moment later, there is the sound of heavy footsteps.* ²⁹⁴*Salmah puts her head on one side and listens.*] That tough old Tengku Bendahara! ²⁹⁴ᵃHe doesn't know his place. ²⁹⁵Nasty old thing!

[²⁹⁶*Enter the Bendahara, puffing and blowing with exhaustion.*]

BEND.: Ha! ²⁹⁷How are you?

SALMAH: [298]I'm very well, Tengku.

BEND.: Where is Salim?

SALMAH: 'Bang Salim isn't here. He's gone away.

BEND.: [299]Gone away? [300]Where to?

SALMAH: [301]Goodness knows. [301a]I don't. [302]He didn't say where he was going. [303]But he did say that he was going for a long time.

BEND.: [304]You don't know? Hm!

SALMAH: No, I don't know, Tengku. [305]Did you want to see him?

BEND.: [306]No. [307]I didn't want to see *him*. [*He comes to a halt.*] I wanted to see you.

SALMAH: Allah! [308]I am honoured to hear it. [309]That a man of your exalted rank should choose to call upon me. [[310]*She pretends to be packing up her weaving as though she is just about to go out.*] [311]But here am I, just on the point of going out. [312]I shan't be able to detain you for long.

BEND.: [313]Where are you going? [314]And what for?

SALMAH: [315]I've been asked to go to Ma' Teh's house, down by the river. She says that her son Si Ajit, the one that has fever, has taken a serious turn for the worse. [316]That's why I am going to see him.

BEND.: That's a pity. [317]Couldn't you put it off?

SALMAH: [318]How could I possibly put it off, Tengku? [319]The boy's ill. [320]Maybe it will be the last time that I shall see him! [321]But you could come back tonight, couldn't you? [322]I shall be home at about 9 o'clock. [323]If you would be good enough to come at about half-past nine, I shall be able to make things ready for you. [324]As it is, I haven't anything prepared.

BEND.: At nine o'clock?

SALMAH: No. Half-past nine. [325]Give me a half-hour's grace. [326]I shall want to make a few preparations in readiness for you, Tengku. [327]Take a bath, and arrange my hair, and change my clothes, and put water on to boil. All sorts of things. [328]It isn't likely that I would entertain you without offering you any refreshment!

BEND.: Ha! That will be nice. [329]I like seeing you dressed up in your finery, with smart hair-prongs in your coiffure. [330]At half-past nine tonight, I'll be back. [331]For the present, then, I'll be going home. Goodbye!

SALMAH: Goodbye, Tengku. [332]I shall be going myself in a minute or two. [[333]*The Bendahara goes down the steps and returns home.* [334]*Salmah pretends to be doing a bit more tidying up before going out.*] ³³⁵I feel quite sick. ³³⁶Who's left now? [*Counting*]: The Kadhi, the Laksamana, the Temenggong, the Bendahara. Still two left. ³³⁷I wonder which of them will arrive first, father or son? [³³⁸*In a moment or two there is the sound of soft footsteps approaching.* ³³⁸ᵃ*Salmah looks out.* ³³⁹*She sees a young man, about eighteen years of age.*]: Oh, it's the son.

R. MUDA [³⁴⁰*peeping through the chink of the door*]: ³⁴¹My father isn't here, is he? Oh, no. ³⁴²May I come in?

SALMAH: Hey! ³⁴³You're already inside, and now you are pretending to ask permission! [³⁴⁴*They both laugh.*]

R. MUDA: ³⁴⁵You're right! ³⁴⁶I just hadn't realised that I had come inside.

SALMAH: ³⁴⁷/³⁴⁸Why did you ask whether your father was here, the very moment you arrived? Why was that?

R. MUDA: ³⁴⁹Because I heard him saying that he was going to come and see you. ³⁵⁰I saw him leaving the palace. ³⁵¹So I thought he would surely have arrived here.

SALMAH: Really! ³⁵²His Highness intends to come to my house? I can't believe it!

R. MUDA: Yes. ³⁵³I know that my father admires you. ³⁵⁴And when he went out just now he was alone. He had none of his suite with him. ³⁵⁵That shows that he was about some private business. ³⁵⁶It's quite likely that he'll be here before long. ³⁵⁷But if he admires you, so do I! ³⁵⁸Which will you choose, Che' Mah?

SALMAH: Oh! ³⁵⁹What a shame! ³⁶⁰If only he weren't on his way here, wouldn't it be pleasant, just the two of us? We could just sit and chat to our heart's content. ³⁶¹I've been wanting to have a nice long talk with you for some time now.

R. MUDA: ³⁶²Well then, why wait any longer? ³⁶³Now's the time! ³⁶⁴Don't bother about the old man. ³⁶⁵Let's sit close together and talk a lot of nonsense until it gets dark.

SALMAH: Oh! ³⁶⁶No, we can't do that, Tengku! That would be very dangerous. [³⁶⁷*Pretending that a sudden idea has flashed into her mind*]: ³⁶⁸I've thought of a way! ³⁶⁹You go home now. [³⁷⁰*The Raja Muda looks downcast.*] ³⁷¹But come back tonight, at ten o'clock. ³⁷²I'll be ready by that time. [³⁷³*There is the sound of very heavy footsteps outside.*]

R. MUDA: *Ya Allah!* That's my father! ³⁷⁴Let me go out this way. [³⁷⁵*He goes out by the back door, whispering as he goes*]: Ten o'clock, yes?

SALMAH [*answering in a whispher*]: Yes. Ten o'clock. ³⁷⁶Go, quickly!

[³⁷⁷*There is a loud knock on the door. It is repeated several times.* ³⁷⁸*Salmah goes to open it.* ³⁷⁹*She comes face to face with the Raja.* ³⁸⁰*She pretends to be startled.*]: *Ya Allah!* ³⁸¹Your Highness is it? ³⁸²I am indeed blessed by Fortune that Your Highness should choose to come to tread the dust of this humble dwelling! ³⁸³Of your grace, be pleased to enter. [*The Raja comes in.*]

RAJA: ³⁸⁴I've only come for a moment or two. ³⁸⁵All my ministers are waiting for me in the Council Chamber. ³⁸⁶But I have come, all the same, to tell you how sorry I am that I had to tell Salim to go and...to go and do something for me. ³⁸⁷If I was wrong to do so, forgive me. ³⁸⁸And don't be anxious.

SALMAH: ³⁸⁹Your gracious pardon, Highness, ³⁹⁰but this journey of his, it won't take long, will it?

RAJA [*as though heartily agreeing*]: No! No! ³⁹¹What would be the good of staying away for a long time? ³⁹²It's just a small job that I've given him to do. ³⁹³You know, Salmah? ³⁹⁴I've got a whitlow on the big toe of my right foot. ³⁹⁵The doctor who is treating it says that it will never be cured unless it is rubbed with ointment made from the beard of a civet-cat. ³⁹⁶That's why I want that bearded civet-cat.

SALMAH: ³⁹⁷It is true, as Your Highness says.

RAJA: ³⁹⁸It doesn't look at all the right thing, does it, for a great ruler such as I am to be walking with a limp, because of a whitlow?

SALMAH: ³⁹⁹Most certainly, Your Highness, it is not right. ⁴⁰⁰People would regard it as a shameful sight. ⁴⁰¹Like Pa' Pandir playing the fool.

RAJA: ⁴⁰²Ha! That's it exactly. ⁴⁰³So, willy-nilly, I had to send somebody or other to look for that bearded civet-cat. ⁴⁰⁴But I couldn't see anybody who could be trusted to carry out the task except Salim. ⁴⁰⁵I know that there's no other person in the land who is more skilful than he is. ⁴⁰⁶That's why I sent him.

SALMAH: Your Highness.

RAJA: ⁴⁰⁷It will be just a small job for Salim, I know. ⁴⁰⁸However it turns out, he's sure to be back within a day or two, bringing the bearded civet-cat with him. ⁴⁰⁹Before he went, I told him that there was no need for him to be worried about you while he was away. ⁴¹⁰I myself would take every care of you, I told him.

SALMAH: I thank you, Your Highness. ⁴¹¹Your abounding favour I carry upon the crown of my head.

RAJA: ⁴¹²And now I had better be getting back with all speed. ⁴¹³My subjects await me. ⁴¹⁴But tonight, I shall come again to see you. ⁴¹⁵Let us say, after my meal, round about nine o'clock, I'll be back here. ⁴¹⁶You will be ready, won't you?

SALMAH: ⁴¹⁷Your gracious pardon, Your Highness! ⁴¹⁸At 9 o'clock I shall not have returned home. ⁴¹⁹I have promised to go and lend a hand at a house down by the river, where there is a wedding going on. ⁴²⁰It will be ten o'clock before I am back, I expect.

RAJA: ⁴²¹Very well. I will come at ten o'clock.

SALMAH: Half-past ten, Your Highness. ⁴²²When I get back, I simply must make a few preparations to receive Your Highness. ⁴²³I am deeply honoured that Your Highness intends to come. ⁴²⁴'Since the palms of my hands are too small, I hold up my winnowing tray to receive your gracious favours.'

RAJA: Oh, Very well. Half-past ten.

[*The Raja goes out.* ⁴²⁵*Salmah clenches her fist and shakes it at his back.* ⁴²⁶*Then she gathers together her weaving and goes into the kitchen.*]

SALMAH [⁴²⁷*muttering to herself, and making faces, as she goes into the kitchen*]: Ha! ⁴²⁸Take care of me indeed! ⁴²⁹Just wait until this evening, I'll teach him!

Act II

Scene 1

[*In the kitchen. There are to be seen the following articles: a charcoal cooking-place with cooking-stones on it and a shelf above it; plates and bowls; pots and pans; a table; a bench; a lamp; and a coconut grater in the form of a low wooden stool, shaped like a horse, with a rasp fixed into its mouth, and a large chest.*]

SALMAH [⁴³⁰*She is kneading dough in a bowl.* ⁴³¹*She appears to be waiting for something*]: ⁴³²It's very nearly eight o'clock. ⁴³³Tuan Kadhi is sure to arrive in a minute or two. ⁴³⁴I do hope each one will keep to his proper turn and arrive at the time he promised. ⁴³⁵If they don't, I shall be in a fix! ⁴³⁶I'll just run over the list and remind myself who is coming, and at what time. At eight o'clock, the Kadhi, at half-past eight the Laksamana, at nine o'clock the Temenggong, at half-past nine—who? [*She thinks for a moment*]: Oh yes! [*in the voice of a crochety old man*]: the Bendahara! ⁴³⁷After that, at ten o'clock, the Raja Muda. [⁴³⁸*She* *smiles as she mentions his name.*]: [439]I must be sure to tuck him out of sight in some safe place before his father arrives. [440]I don't want him to get into any trouble. [441]The Raja arrives at half-past ten. Good! I'm waiting! [441a]I must pretend to be busy. [442]This time they'll know what's what! [[443]*A gong is heard, striking eight o'clock.* [444]*Salmah nods her head and purses her lips as she listens to it.* [445]*She keeps giving side-long glances towards the door.* [446]*There is the sound of footsteps coming up and nearing the door.*]: Ha! [447]That will be the Kadhi. [448]That slippery customer the Kadhi! [449]He doesn't know me yet! [[450]*She goes and opens the door.* [451]*The Kadhi comes in.*]

KADHI: Ha! [452]How is the young lady? [453]I've arrived punctually, exactly at the time I said I would, haven't I? [454]Not a moment late.

SALMAH: Yes! [455]Extra punctually! [456]Not a minute out!

KADHI: [457]How do you mean, 'extra punctually'? [458]Eight sharp means eight o'clock, not before, and not after. [459]As a matter of fact, I've been actually counting every minute since half-past seven. [[460]*Salmah glares at him.*] [461]Because I was really worried, thinking of you, left here all alone.

SALMAH: Hm.

KADHI: [462]Come and sit down and we'll have a little talk. [[463]*He tries to draw Salmah to the bench.*] You don't want to?

SALMAH: Wait! Not yet! [464]Look, I'm just beginning to make a few cakes to welcome you with. [[465]*She begins to mash some ripe bananas into the dough.*]

KADHI: [466]You're an expert housewife, Che' Mah. [467]Let me help you, will you?

SALMAH: Oh no. [468]I wouldn't dream of asking you to help. [469]You sit down for a bit. [470]I shan't be a minute. [[471]*The Kadhi sits there, blinking, waiting for Salmah to finish, but she never does.* [472]*There is the sound of somebody walking up and down outside.* [473]*The Kadhi starts in suprise, then stands up.*]

KADHI: [474]What's that? [475]There's somebody walking about outside by the sound of it. [476]Heavens! What am I going to do? [477]If anybody finds me here at this time of night—the fat will be in the fire!

SALMAH: [[478]*She pretends to be scared.* [479]*She looks out of the window.*]: Ya Allah! [480]There *is* somebody there! [[481]*She points to a large chest*]: [482]Get into that chest!

[[483]*The Kadhi gets into the chest.* [484]*Salmah shuts it and then puts some things on top of it. Enter the Laksamana.* [485]*He walks with mincing affectation and seems very pleased with himself.*]

LAKS.: [486]Ha! You're back, then? [487]Just as we arranged, Sweetheart. [488]I was a little before my time. [489]That's why I was walking up and down outside just now. [490]I thought you hadn't got back. [491]Then suddenly I saw you looking out of the window.

SALMAH: Yes. [492]It struck me that it would never do for you to arrive before me. [493]So I came back early.

LAKS.: Did you really? [494]That's a sign that our hearts were set on the same thing, isn't it? [495]We were having a race, each of us trying to get here first. [496]And you won. [[497]*He tries to put his arm round Salmah's waist.*]

SALMAH: Not yet! [498]Have a little patience! [499]Look! I'm in the middle of making some cakes to welcome you with, To' Lak. [500]Let me get these finished first. [501]You just sit down for a bit. [502]I shan't be long. [503]Whatever we do, it will be all the better for a little refreshment beforehand. [*The Laksamana sits down.*]

LAKS.: [504]Has anybody else been to see you today, Che' Mah?

SALMAH: Oh no! Who else would there be? [505]Only you. [506]I shouldn't want anybody else to come. [507]But you are different. [508]You are 'special'.

LAKS. [[509]*He stands up and goes close to Salmah.* [510]*He tries to put his arm round her shoulders.*]: Come and sit down. [511]Bother those cakes!

SALMAH [*pushing him away*]: Patience! Patience! [512]You've no patience. [[513]*The Laksamana goes towards the window.* [514]*He looks out, and gives a start of surprise.*]

LAKS.: [515]What's this? It looks as if...Oh *no*! It can't be!...What? Yes! It looks very much like the Temenggong coming this way!...Yes! It's him! It is! Oh! Quick! Quick! [516]Where can I escape? Help me! Yes! It's the Temenggong right enough! [517]He mustn't find me here at this hour of the night!

SALMAH: [518]Here! [519]Get into this cupboard. [520]Stay quite still. [521]Don't budge!

[[522]*The Laksamana goes into the cupboard and stands there, stiff as a ramrod.* [523]*The Temenggong enters, dressed up to the nines.*]

TEMENGG.: [524]I'm a bit early. [525]You won't be cross with me, will you?

SALMAH: [526]Why should I be cross? [527]I'm only too delighted that you have come early. [528]Except—there's just one thing—you'll have to wait a bit. [529]I'm making a few cakes, to offer you as refreshment. [530]But they aren't ready yet.

TEMENGG.: [531]Oh that doesn't matter. [532]It's a good idea, to make some cakes. [533]I'll help you. [534]I can make cakes too.

SALMAH: Oh no. [535]There's no need for you to help. [536]I wouldn't like to see your beautiful coat smeared with flour, and soot and all that. You just sit down. [537]I'll be through in a minute or two.

[*The Temenggong sits down.* [538]*He twists and untwists his moustaches.* [539]*Then he examines his clothes minutely.*]

TEMENGG.: [540]What do you think of this new turban that I'm wearing, Che' Mah? [541]I've just got it, straight from Java. [542]It looks smart on me, don't you think?

SALMAH: [543]My word! It looks very smart indeed to me, Dato'. [544]Quite in keeping with its wearer! [545]You look as fine as a commander in chief.

[[546]*The Temenggong re-adjusts his turban from time to time, looking very proud of himself.*]

TEMENGG.: [547]Hi! Have you still not finished those cakes? [548]You're taking a very long time over them! [549]I want you to come and sit by me here, so that we can talk.

SALMAH: [550]I'm very nearly ready now.

[[551]*There is a knock at the door.* [552]*The Temenggong jumps up from his seat.*]

TEMENGG.: [553]Who's that? [554]This isn't possible! [555]I don't want anybody to find me here alone with you, at this time of night! [556]Where can I go? [557]Or else, let me hide somewhere.

SALMAH: [558]Here, Dato'! [559]Climb up on the shelf. [560]Stay there and keep quite still, don't make the tiniest squeak!

[[561]*The Temenggong, with great difficulty, scrambles up on to the shelf.* [562]*His smart silk coat and trousers and his new turban get all covered with soot. Somebody can be heard speaking outside the door.* [563]*His voice sounds very doleful.*]

BENDAHARA [*from outside*]: [564]Oi! Can I come in?

SALMAH [*going to open the door*]: [565]Of course. Why not? [566]Please do come in, Tengku, [567]I've been waiting for you for a long time. [*The Bendahara enters.*] [568]I'm making a few cakes, to tempt your appetite.

BEND.: [569]I don't much like cakes.

SALMAH: Ah! [570]You're sure to like these cakes, Tengku. [571]I'm making some special ones.

BEND.: [572]My wife is everlastingly making special cakes. [573]But I never eat them.

SALMAH: [574]Why don't you eat them, Tengku?

BEND.: [575]Because I don't like *her*.

SALMAH: [576]Why don't you like her?

BEND.: Why? [577]I'll tell you, Salmah—she's getting old. [[578]*There is a faint sound of somebody whistling, coming along the road; a moment or two later there is a snatch of a song.* [579]*The Bendahara pricks up his ears and listens.*]: Who's that?

SALMAH: [580]What? [581]I didn't hear anything.

BEND.: Yes! [582]I heard something. [583]There's somebody whistling, and singing, coming along the road. [584]Heaven forbid that he should come in here!

SALMAH [*putting her head out of the window*]: You're right, Tengku. [585]There *is* somebody coming, by the look of it.

BEND.: [[586]*getting up and going to look out of the window with her*]: [587]Heavens! It looks very much like that son of Satan the Raja Muda. [588]Curse him! Why in the world should *he* be coming here, the misbegotten wretch!

SALMAH[*pretending not to recognize him*]: Is it, Tengku? Is it the Raja Muda?

BEND.: Yes! Yes! It's him! *Ya Allah!* [589]Don't let him find me here! [590]The shame of it, me at my age to become the common talk of him and his young friends! [591]What am I to do? [592]Help me, Salmah! Quick! [593]Where can I go?

SALMAH: [594]Come here, Tengku. [595]Grate this coconut. [596]Sit with your back to him. [597]Put this scarf over your head. [[598]*She throws her scarf over the Bendahara's head.*] [599]I'll tell him that you are an old woman who helps me in the kitchen.

[*Enter the Raja Muda*]

R. MUDA [*rather shyly*]: [600]I'm a bit early I think, am I?

SALMAH: Yes, Tengku, You are a bit early. [601]It isn't ten o'clock yet. [602]But what's wrong with that? [603]I was in the middle of making a few cakes for you to eat. [604]Just let my kitchen-woman finish them. [[605]*She goes and talks to the 'kitchen-woman', pretending to give her instructions about this and that.*]

R. MUDA: [606]You are very good, Che' Salmah. [607]Bothering to make cakes for me, when in reality your heart is heavy, thinking of Che' Salim.

SALMAH: Yes. [608]I was feeling rather sad just now. [609]But now that you are here I feel happy. [610]Come and sit down, and let's talk. [[611]*They sit down.*]

R. MUDA [[612]*gently putting his arm round Salmah's waist.* [613]*Salmah allows him to do so. She makes no move to avoid it.*]: [614]All day long I have kept remembering, I've been thinking only of you.

SALMAH: Yes?

R. MUDA: [615]And now, here we are, just the two of us together. [616]It seemed a long, long time, waiting for ten o'clock.

SALMAH: Yes. [617]It seemed long to me, too.

R. MUDA [[618]*looking at the 'old woman' who is grating the coconut.* [619]*She grates at a terrific speed. It looks as if the grater must surely snap off.*]: [620]Couldn't you tell the old woman to go out for a bit? [621]It makes me feel uncomfortable, having her stuck there like that.

SALMAH: [622]Just a minute or two longer. [623]Let her finish the cakes first.

R. MUDA: [624]She seems to be taking a terribly long time to grate that coconut.

SALMAH: Yes. [625]She takes a long time over things. [626]She's a sleepy-head, she is.

R. MUDA: [627]And yet she's a fine big woman, isn't she?

[[628]*The Bendahara hears this.* [629]*He tries to make himself small.*]

SALMAH [*in a whisper*]: Yes. [630]She's a Korinchi, from Sumatra. [631]Don't say anything about her size [632]or she'll turn into a tiger! [633]A Korinchi can always turn himself into a tiger.

R. MUDA: Yes? [634]Have you ever seen *her* turn into a tiger like that?

[[635]*There is a clatter of footsteps outside the door.* [636]*Then the Raja's voice is heard calling 'O mistress of the house!'*]: Ya Allah! [637]It's my father! [638]Hell! I'm done for! [639]Confound the old wretch!

[[640]*The Raja knocks on the door. It sounds as if it will come crashing in.* [641]*Salmah hastily thrusts the lamp into the Raja Muda's hand and pushes him in the direction of the Temenggong.*]

SALMAH [[642]*in an urgent whisper*]: [643]You're a lamp-stand now. [644]Hold the lamp steady. [645]Stand up quite straight near the old woman. [646]Keep still. Don't move!

[[647]*The Raja enters and goes straight up to Salmah.*]

RAJA: Ha! How's my darling? Her royal master's darling! [648]I've arrived a bit early, I think. [649]I just couldn't wait, I was so eager to see you.

SALMAH: That doesn't matter, Your Highness. [650]All day long I have not been able to do anything but look forward to Your Highness' arrival.

RAJA: [651]And now, here I am. [652]Come and sit here, by me. [[653]*He tries to embrace Salmah.* [654]*She stands up and slips away from him*]: Oh! What's this? [655]You are my subject. [656]When I command, you obey.

SALMAH: [657]We'll strike a bargain first, Your Highness. [658]If you want me you must first of all grant me one request. Will you?

RAJA: [659]What is it that you want? [660]Whatever you ask for, I will give you. [661]Do you want gold brooches? Anklets? Bracelets? Diamonds? Brilliants? Just say the word.

SALMAH: No, Your Highness. [662]Nothing as expensive as that. [663]What I ask for costs very little.

RAJA: What? [664]What is it?

SALMAH: [665]I ask that for one half-hour *you* become *my* subject. [666]And do whatever I bid you do.

RAJA: Very well. [667]I agree. [668]Now, my fair queen, what is it that my royal mistress is going to bid her subject do?

SALMAH: [669]Let me just think a moment. [[670]*She pretends to be pondering over what she will ask him to do.*]: Ah! I know! [671]Let's play horse-and-rider.

RAJA [[672]*not particularly pleased, by the look of it*]: Who's to be the horse? Me? Or you?

SALMAH: Your Highness, of course. [673]It couldn't be *me*. [674]If you refuse, I issue my royal command. [675]Your Highness has promised to obey.

RAJA: [676]Your command shall be obeyed, O Queen of Beauty. [677]Whatsoever order you issue, your humble subject will carry it out. [[678]*He lowers himself to the floor, then crawls along on hands and knees.*]

SALMAH: [[679]*She holds the end of the Raja's coat, then gets astride his back.*]: Gee up! Gee up! Faster! Faster!

[[680]*The Raja sways as he crawls along, because of the weight on his back. [681]His face gets red, but he goes on crawling up and down the room. [682]Salmah urges him on. [683]The other men, in their hiding places, are smothering their laughter at the sight, until they are ready to burst. [684]At last the Bendahara cannot contain himself any longer. He brings a coconut crashing down on the head of the Raja Muda who is standing there, rigid, being a lamp-stand. [685]The Raja Muda lets out a howl. [686]The Temenggong leaps down from the shelf. [687]All of them go rushing out, and run, ducking and diving through the undergrowth in the darkness, each to his own home. [688]There remains only the Kadhi, in the chest*].

KADHI [⁶⁸⁹*from inside the chest*]: ⁶⁹⁰Let me out! Let me out!

[*The 11 o'clock gong is heard. Enter Salim.*]

SALIM: Well done Salmah! Well done! ⁶⁹¹I arrived just in time to see that bandy old palace horse come leaping out.

KADHI: Let me out! Let me out!

SALIM: ⁶⁹²*Who's* that, inside the chest? [⁶⁹³*He goes towards the chest.*]

SALMAH: Tuan Kadhi.

SALIM: Oh! Splendid! Splendid! [⁶⁹⁴*He roars with laughter, loud enough to bring the house down.* ⁶⁹⁵*He and Salmah both sit down on the chest.*] ⁶⁹⁶Now just tell me everything that's happened since I left this morning.

SALMAH: ⁶⁹⁷Well, they all came. ⁶⁹⁸And I made an arrangement with each of them to come at such and such a time this evening. ⁶⁹⁹They all kept to their appointed times. ⁷⁰⁰And now they have all run off home, except Tuan Kadhi who is still here.

SALIM: Hah! ⁷⁰¹The father of evil himself, this Tuan Kadhi it seems. ⁷⁰²What are we going to do with him?

SALMAH: What, do you ask? ⁷⁰³*He's* going to be the bearded civet-cat that you take to the palace. ⁷⁰⁴His beard is certainly long enough!

SALIM: Yes! ⁷⁰⁵And I've got another idea too. ⁷⁰⁶What did you say just now? ⁷⁰⁷They were all of them here, every one of them?

SALMAH: Yes. ⁷⁰⁸All six of them.

SALIM: ⁷⁰⁹Who came first?

SALMAH: ⁷¹⁰The Kadhi came first of all.

SALIM: Ha! ⁷¹¹That's fine. ⁷¹²I'll take him to the palace tomorrow to pay his respects to the Raja. ⁷¹³Yes. You are right. ⁷¹⁴He's the bearded civet-cat that the Raja told me to find. I caught him this evening! Ha! Ha! Ha!

[*They both have a good laugh.*]

Scene 2

[⁷¹⁵*The next morning, in the Hall of Audience.* ⁷¹⁶*The Raja is seated upon his throne.* ⁷¹⁷*Below him, to the right, are seated the Raja Muda and the Bendahara; to the left are seated the Temenggong and the Laksamana.* ⁷¹⁸*All four of them seem to be restless and ill at ease.* ⁷¹⁹*Salim is standing at one side, facing the Raja and the four ministers.* ⁷²⁰*He wears a look of satisfaction, as of a man who has had the better of an opponent.* ⁷²¹*Near him there is a large chest.* ⁷²²*Inside the chest is the Kadhi.*]

RAJA: Salim. [723]I am very pleased to see that you have come back so soon. [724]Did you succeed in getting what I asked you to find?

SALIM: [725]With your gracious favour, I did, Your Highness. [726]I caught it with the greatest of ease. [727]I didn't have to bother about looking for it [728]It came to my house of its own accord and gave itself up.

RAJA [[729]*surprised, and not quite believing*]: [730]Well! Well! Well! That's an extraordinary thing! [731]What is it that you got? [732]Is it really and truly a bearded civet-cat, or what?

SALIM: [732a]Yes, a bearded civet-cat it is, Your Highness. [733]With a really long beard.

RAJA: [734]Where is it? [735]Where have you caged it? [736]In that big chest that you have brought with you?

SALIM: Yes, Your Highness. [737]In this chest it is. [738]A really whopping great civet-cat! [739]I had to hire four men to carry the chest from my house. [740]Just take a peep inside the chest, Your Highness. [[741]*He opens the lid of the chest.*]

RAJA [[742]*speaking to the Raja Muda*]: [743]You go, my son, and see what is in the chest. [744]See if Salim here is really speaking the truth, or playing a joke on us.

[[745]*The Raja Muda goes up to the chest, bends over it and looks inside, then gives a start.* [746]*He jumps back when he hears the Kadhi's voice*]

KADHI [*in a whisper*]: [747]I know where you were last night.

SALIM: [748]It's a fine civet-cat, isn't it, Tengku?

RAJA M.: Yes—er—er—Yes, a fine one.

RAJA: Ha. [749]Well? [750]Is it truly a bearded civet-cat?

R. MUDA: [751]I don't rightly know, Your Highness. [752]I—I—I don't know what to say. [753]I don't know much about animals.

RAJA: *Ya Rabbi!* [754]What a boy! [755]Don't you know what a civet-cat looks like? [756]Haven't you ever seen one? [[757]*To the Bendahara, in a tone of impatience*]: [758]You go and have a look, Bendahara.

BEND. [[759]*going and looking into the chest, and then jumping back*]: *Allah!* [760]What sort of civet-cat is this?

SALIM: [761]What do you think of it, Tengku? [762]A real king of civet-cats, isn't it? [763]And with a really thick beard, too. [[763a]*He bends over the chest and strokes the Kadhi's beard.*] [764]You could go on making ointment for ever, no matter how many whitlows His Highness has. [[765]*He looks round at them all with a jeering expression on his face.*]

BEND.: Yes. ⁷⁶⁶As far as the beard goes, there's no doubt about that. ⁷⁶⁷That I do not deny.

RAJA: ⁷⁶⁸But is it really a civet-cat?

BEND.: Your gracious pardon, Highness. ⁷⁶⁹Whether it is a genuine civet-cat or not, that I couldn't say. ⁷⁷⁰But—but—it's certainly some sort of an animal.

RAJA: Some sort of an animal! ⁷⁷¹What sort of talk is this, Bendahara? ⁷⁷²Don't you know a civet-cat from a buffalo?

BEND.: ⁷⁷³Yes, Your Highness—er—No!—I mean—yes. ⁷⁷⁴It isn't a buffalo! ⁷⁷⁵A buffalo has horns. ⁷⁷⁶And there aren't any horns.

RAJA [⁷⁷⁷snorting in his wrath]: Ach! Idiot! ⁷⁷⁸You're as stupid as that son of mine. [To the Temenggong]: ⁷⁷⁹You go and have a look, will you, Temenggong.

[⁷⁸⁰The Temenggong goes up to the chest and bends over it to look inside. ⁷⁸¹He gives a start, and jumps back.]

SALIM: Ah! ⁷⁸²It seems that you got a fright, Dato' Temenggong. Why was that? ⁷⁸³What do you think of this civet-cat of mine, Dato'?

[⁷⁸⁴The Temenggong stands speechless.]

RAJA: Ha! ⁷⁸⁵What do you think of the civet-cat, Temenggong? What about it? ⁷⁸⁶Did it bite you?

TEMENGG.: No, Your Highness. ⁷⁸⁷It didn't actually bite me.

RAJA: ⁷⁸⁸Well then, what did it do to you, to make you leap back so far?

TEMENGG.: ⁷⁸⁹Nothing, Your Highness. ⁷⁹⁰Except that I—I—was very surprised at its appearance. ⁷⁹¹It looks quite different.

RAJA: ⁷⁹²What I want to know is just this one thing. ⁷⁹³Is it a civet-cat or is it not?

TEMENGG.: ⁷⁹⁴On that point, Your Highness, I—I—wouldn't know how to recognize—I wouldn't venture to say—

RAJA: Wouldn't venture to say! ⁷⁹⁵Have you gone mad, the whole lot of you? [To the Laksamana]: Laksamana! ⁷⁹⁶Will you go and have a look please. ⁷⁹⁷You, I'm sure, won't take fright. ⁷⁹⁸If the creature has a long beard, you have long moustaches, so you'll make a good pair!

[⁷⁹⁹The Laksamana goes to the chest, bends over it, and looks inside. ⁸⁰⁰He jumps back hastily. ⁸⁰¹As he moves back he makes horrible grimaces at the Kadhi, in the chest.]

SALIM: Ah! ⁸⁰²You don't like my civet-cat it appears, To' Laksamana. ⁸⁰³What's wrong with it? ⁸⁰⁴What do you not like?

RAJA: Ha! Laksamana! What about it? ⁸⁰⁵You, at any rate, surely have some definite opinion on the subject. ⁸⁰⁶Don't be idiotic like these others. ⁸⁰⁷What's your verdict? ⁸⁰⁸Is it a genuine bearded civet-cat?

LAKS.: ⁸⁰⁹As for the beard, that's certainly there, Your Highness. ⁸¹⁰There's no need to dispute that! ⁸¹¹And there's no denying its length, either. [⁸¹²*He indicates the length of the kadhi's beard by downward strokes from his own chin.* ⁸¹³*He himself has no beard.*]

RAJA: That's good.

LAKS. [*pinching his nose together*]: ⁸¹⁴And the musky smell of it is really horrible, Your Highness. [*With his eyes glaring in the Kadhi's direction*]: ⁸¹⁵Can't you smell it, Your Highness?

RAJA: No. ⁸¹⁶I can't smell anything. ⁸¹⁷Perhaps I shall have to go near and have a look at it myself before I shall get the smell of it.

[⁸¹⁸*He comes down from the throne and goes to the chest.* ⁸¹⁹*The others exchange glances, each wondering what the Raja will do when he sees what is in the chest. The Raja looks into the chest.* ⁸²⁰*He gives a slight start when he hears the Kadhi's whisper.*]

KADHI [*in a whisper*]: ⁸²¹I know that Your Highness turned into a horse last night!

⁸²²*The Raja looks at Salim, then looks back at the Kadhi.*]

RAJA: ⁸²³We proffer you our good wishes, Che' Salim, together with our profound thanks. ⁸²⁴You are right. It's a very good specimen of a civet-cat that you've caught. ⁸²⁵Fine looking, and of a good size too. ⁸²⁶Only, we ask you to render us one more service. ⁸²⁷Please take your captive back home with you. ⁸²⁸Keep it at your own house for a day or two. Will you do that?

SALIM: My obedience is ever yours, Your Highness. Your command shall be obeyed.

[⁸²⁹*There is the sound of a sigh from within the chest.* ⁸³⁰*The others merely raise their eyebrows and exchange winks. The Raja goes back to his throne and sits down.*]

Scene 3

[*The next morning. In Salim's house.* ⁸³¹*Salim and Salmah are seated on a mat, laughing and talking together.*]

SALMAH: ⁸³²What did Tuan Kadhi say when you let him go just now?

SALIM: ⁸³³Nothing much. He said he was going to say his dawn prayer. ⁸³⁴He seemed truly ashamed of himself. ⁸³⁵He couldn't look me in the face. [836]If you could have seen him just then, Salmah! Pale! [837]A knife couldn't have drawn blood from him. [838]I bet anything he bitterly rues his prank. He won't go running after women in the future. [*There is a knock at the door.*] [839]Whoever can that be, I wonder? [840]Arriving as early as this! [*He goes to the door and talks to somebody outside.*]: A present from the Kadhi? Thank you very much. [841]Convey to the Kadhi our joint thanks. [[842]*He comes back and goes up to Salmah with the present, a silver bowl, very beautifully incised, of fine workmanship*]: A present from the Bearded Civet-cat! [843]We've been married nearly a month, and still the presents are coming in! [844]No wedding present this! [[845]*They both examine the bowl with pleasure and delight.*]

SALMAH: Lovely, isn't it? [[846]*She places it on a table which has other beautiful things on it. There is another knock at the door.*]

SALIM: Ho! Ho! Somebody else? [*He goes to the door and talks to somebody there.*]: What's that? From To' Laksamana? [847]How kind of him! [848]'Service earns its due requital. [849]A gift is to enjoy.' [850]I cannot thank him enough. [851]Please convey to the Laksamana our deepest gratitude, will you? [*He brings the present in.*]

SALMAH [[852]*questioning Salim as he comes in*]: What is it?

SALIM: A silver sireh set, complete with everything—salver, tobacco box, lime box, scissors, and all the rest. [*The two of them examine every article in the betel-nut set. [853]A moment or two later somebody else is heard knocking at the door. Salim goes to open it, talking as he goes*]: [854]This will be from the Temenggong, I'm sure. [*Speaking to someone at the door*]: From the Tem— Oh! Tengku Bendahara? Many many thanks. [855]Please tell him that we are both of us deeply grateful to receive this gift of his. [*He comes back to Salmah with the Bendahara's present.*]

SALMAH: [856]It wasn't the Temenggong, as you thought?

SALIM: No. It's from Tengku Bendahara. [857]He's too soon this time. He hasn't kept to his turn. [858]I can well understand. He's in a hurry to cover up his yesterday's performance. [859]He doesn't want the story to get out, and everybody know about it.

SALMAH: [860]Whatever is it? [861]Open it quickly, 'Bang. [[862]*Salim opens the parcel. [863]He finds a pair of candlesticks in it.*]

SALIM [*putting the candlesticks on the table*]: [864]Let's put all the presents out in a row on the table. [865]Keep this place for the Temenggongs'. [866]Leave a fairly big space for it. [867]He's sure to send something large. [868]He likes everything to be on the big side. [*There is another knock at *the door.*] Ha! [869]Is this him, I wonder? [870]Guess what it's going to be, Mah.

SALMAH: er—er—er—[*The knock is repeated.*]

SALIM: [871]Hurry up! [872]What do you guess?

SALMAH: A—I'll say a—you know, a—[*Salim goes to the door.*]

SALIM [*at the door*]: *Allah!* Many many thanks. [873]Please be good enough to convey to the Temenggong sincerest thanks for his present on behalf of us both. [874]Heaven alone can requite him. [[875]*He comes back carrying a large package. He does not yet know what is in it.*] [876]Here it is, Mah, from To' Temenggong. [877]I wonder what it is. You open it.

SALMAH [*opening it, while Salim looks on*]: Oh! Clothes.

SALIM: So it is. Clothes. [878]Have a look, Mah, See if they are only for you, or are there some for me as well?

SALMAH [*opening out the garments and examining them one by one*]: For both of us. [879]A complete set for you, trousers, baju, sarong, turban, slippers, everything. For me, baju, a batik sarong, scarf, slippers, comb—everything complete. [*They both laugh and begin trying on the garments. But at that moment another knock is heard.*]

SALIM [*quickly counting the things that have already been received*]: One, two, three, four. [880]Two more to come. [881]I wonder whose present will arrive first, the Raja's, or his son's. [*He goes to the door.*]: From Tengku Raja Muda? [882]Please give our heartiest thanks to Tengku Raja Muda, will you? [*Salim returns, bringing a box wrapped in cloth.*] This is from your little brother, Mah! I wonder what it is. Do open it.

SALMAH [*She opens it with a little smile playing about her lips, and looking very pleased*]: Oh! Perfume. And a handkerchief. [883]The kerchief has your name on it, and the perfume has my name on it.

SALIM: Hm! [884]So your young brother has sent you some perfume, has he?

SALMAH: [885]That Raja Muda, he's a handsome young man, isn't he, 'Bang? [886]You do think he's good-looking, surely? Or don't you?

SALIM [*looking a bit sour*]: Yes. [887]When he grows up, you women will find him even more of a charmer.

SALMAH [*deliberately teasing him*]: [888]You're jealous! [889]You're being spiteful about him.

SALIM [*flaring up*]: Jealous? You must be mad. [890]Why should I be jealous? [891]If you've fallen for him, what is there for me to say? [892]You like your 'younger brother' better, and this elder brother of yours is thrown aside. ⁸⁹³I'll drift away on my own. ⁸⁹⁴'There's more than one flower in the garden, There's more than one bee on the wing.' as the old folks used to say.

SALMAH: Just look at you! ⁸⁹⁵Now you're being silly! ⁸⁹⁶I didn't really mean it! ⁸⁹⁷I was only joking. ⁸⁹⁸You mustn't take it to heart. ⁸⁹⁹If I did wrong, please forgive me. [*She rubs her cheek against Salim's head. There is a loud knock at the door.*]

SALIM: ⁸⁹⁹ᵃThat's that Raja of yours, for certain, Mah.

SALMAH: Not my Raja. My steed. ⁹⁰⁰Didn't I turn him into a horse last night? [*Salim hurries to the door. ⁹⁰¹He receives, in respectful silence, a large box wrapped in yellow cloth. ⁹⁰²He lifts it on to his head and brings it in to Salmah. Together they open it. ⁹⁰³Inside the box there is another one, inscribed with Salmah's name, and still another one, with Salim's name on it. ⁹⁰⁴Salmah takes the box which has her name on it and opens it.*]: Oh! Gold! Diamonds and brilliants! ⁹⁰⁵And what's this little note here? [⁹⁰⁶*She picks up the letter and reads it*]: 'From your subject and humble servant, his mistress' slave, to his fair queen, the young and lovely Che' Salmah.' [*Salmah laughs, and looks at Salim. Her face is alight with pleasure. Salim joins in her laughter.*]

SALIM [*taking the box that has his name on it, and opening it in his turn.*]: ⁹⁰⁷Oh! I've only got a sheet of paper! ⁹⁰⁸What's this, written on it? [*He takes up the note and reads it.*]: ⁹⁰⁹'To my trusty knight, whom Fortune has already blessed. ⁹¹⁰No need to send him gold or diamonds more, for the sparkling jewel which is in his possession is more precious than all the gold and diamonds in the world.' [⁹¹¹*Salim and Salmah look across at each other. Salmah puts on her diamonds, the Raja's gift, then goes and puts her arms round Salim's neck.*]: ⁹¹²You are my sparkling jewel!

TEXT C: SINGING FOR YOUR BAIT

¹I remember that when I was a little boy my mother used often to tell me to go and catch dragonflies in the rice-fields, because they were wanted for making bait to poison the rats. ²At that time I was about five or six years old.

³The name *sepatong* is given to a type of insect which looks something like an aeroplane. ⁴Its head is quite round, and its eyes are like the eyes of a fly; it has an oval body and a long tail, and its wings are always outspread even when it alights on grasses and rice plants. ⁵This insect is

always found in large numbers in the rice-fields because it likes to live in wet places where the grass is long. [6]There are many varieties, some large, some small, and they are of different colours. [7]But it is the large sort that is needed for making poisoned rat-bait. [8]It is green, with blackish spots. [9]In size it is about two and a half inches from the head to the end of the tail, and the width of the body is about a quarter of an inch.

[10]When the sun was hot, or, when it was getting towards noon, hundreds and hundreds of them would be seen flying about all over the paddy-fields, finding food of some sort or other, [11]yet they did not seem to do any harm to the rice. [12]At such times, off I would go to the paddy-fields, carrying a coconut-frond vein (*lidi*) to the end of which a bit of tree-cotton had been tied. It showed up, white and clear, at the end of the *lidi*. [13]Sometimes I would go alone, and sometimes with my brother, or with other children, all of them bent on catching dragonflies. [14]As we walked, we kept jerking the end of the *lidi* up and down, and chanting these lines:

> Flip-flap-flip, you dragonfly,
> The palm-flower fell, and your baby was crushed,
> 'Way back there, behind the knoll.

[15]Over and over again we sang it. [16]And the dragonflies, the moment they saw the white kapok dancing about, would come swooping down to get it, thinking that it was food. [17]Then their teeth, or their fine claws, would get tangled in the fine threads of the tree-cotton, and we would catch them and put them in a box or an empty cigarette tin that we had brought with us. [18]In this way, after we had been going up and down in the paddy-fields for about an hour, or only half an hour, singing the little song, we had each got as many as fifty or sixty dragonflies and our tins were full. [19]Then we would go home and give the dragonflies to our mother. [20]By that time they were all dead, because of having been shut up in the tin.

[21]At home that afternoon my mother and father would split the insects along the back and insert some arsenic that had previously been worked to a powder. [22]Then they would thread, or else clip together, the poisoned insects with skewers made of coconut-frond veins, one or two to each skewer. [23]When they had got about thirty to forty skewers ready they took them to the paddy-fields and stuck them in the ground, a few here, a few there, in whatever places they judged to be in the path of the rats. [24]In this way, large numbers of the rats were killed.

[25]As for the jingle, in reality its only purpose was to keep us happy

while we walked backwards and forwards from end to end of the paddy-fields in the hot sunshine. ²⁶But at that time I really did think that it was our singing that had tricked the dragonfly, and enticed it to come and snatch at the kapok on the end of the *lidi*. ²⁷I thought it was a very silly creature because it really believed that the kapok was its baby which had been crushed under the coconut blossom that had fallen on top of it ''way back there behind the knoll', and that that was why it came swooping down, to carry off its child.

TEXT D: A MOCK BATTLE IN
THE RICE-FIELDS

¹Long ago, when I was a child, I myself have taken part in the game of *keladi*-stalk fighting, at a time when the ceremony of *berpuar* was carried out in my own village, that is to say, the village of Jempul, in the Kuala Pilah district of Negeri Sembilan. ²But there the ceremony is called *menyémah*. ³At that time I did not understand what the purpose of the ceremony was; I was just delighted because there were crowds of people about, and because they went wading through the rice-fields, shouting at the tops of their voices. As they went along they shot arm-long *keladi*-stalks at each other's backs as hard as ever they could, until at last the spikes broke into bits. ⁴Although the *keladi*-stalks were not rigid like wood, nevertheless they did hurt quite a bit. ⁵Everyone who got hit, hit back at his attacker. ⁶Some of the children, indeed, would cry with the pain, and then start quarrelling.

⁷The *keladi*-stalks were made ready beforehand in bundles, of a size that could be carried on the arm, and they were placed here and there in the rough grass at the edges of the fields that were to be traversed. ⁸As he passed, each man took a few bundles, ready for the fray. ⁹When they were finished, there were other bundles further on. ¹⁰And so it went on, until they came to the end of the course. ¹¹Nowadays the *menyémah* ceremony is very seldom carried out in the village of Jempul, because the religious leaders do not approve of it.

LIST OF WORKS CONSULTED

A. Bakar Hamid. Articles in *Dewan Bahasa*, Kuala Lumpur, May, July, 1964.

Asmah Haji Omar. Articles in *Dewan Bahasa*, Kuala Lumpur, Oct., Nov., Dec., 1962; Nov., Dec., 1963; Jan., March, April, Nov., 1964; April, 1966; Feb. 1967.

Bloch, B. and Trager, G. L. *Outline of Linguistic Analysis*, Baltimore, 1942.

Buse, J. E. *Rarotongan Sentence Structures*, Bulletin of the School of Oriental and African Studies, Univ. of London, vol. XXVI, part 3, 1963.

Chomsky, N. *Syntactic Structures*, Mouton, The Hague, 1957.

Fokker, A. A. *Inleiding tot de Studie van de Indonesische Syntaxis*, B. Wolters, Groningen, Djakarta, 1951.

Gonda, J. (1) *Prolegomena tot een Theorie der woord soorten in Indonesische Talen*, Bijdragen tot de taal- land- en volkenkunde van Nederl.-Indie, vol. 105.

    (2) *Een onbevredigend behandeld punt in de Maleise Grammatika*, Bijdragen, vol. 97.

Honey, P. J. *Word Classes in Vietnamese*, Bulletin of the School of Oriental and African Studies, Univ. of London, vol. XVIII, part 3, 1956.

Lewis, M. B. (1) *Teach Yourself Malay*, English Universities Press, 1947.

    (2) *Translation and Composition Exercises for Malay Students*, Macmillan, 1952. (References in the footnotes given as *TCE*.)

Lewis, M. B. and Sulaiman bin Hamzah. *Learn to Talk Malay*, Macmillan, 1954. (References in the footnotes given as *LTTM*.)

Postal, P. *Constituent Structures*, Indiana University Research Centre in Anthropology, Folklore and Linguistics, Mouton, The Hague, 1964.

Robins, R. H. (1) *Formal Divisions in Sudanese*, Transactions of the Philological Society, London, 1953.

    (2) *General Linguistics. An Introductory Survey*, Longmans, 1964.

Slametmuljana, R. B. *Kaidah Bahasa Indonesia*, Djambatan, Djakarta, 1960.

Teeuw, A. *Some Problems in the Study of Word-Classes in Bahasa Indonesia*, Lingua, vol. xi, Amsterdam, 1962.

Wilkinson, R. J. *A Malay-English Dictionary*, Salavopoulos and Kinderlis Mytilene, 1932. (References in the Index given as Wlk.)

Winstedt, R. O. *An Unabridged Malay-English Dictionary*, Kelly and Walsh, Singapore, 1954.

Wojowasito, S., Poerwadarminta, W. J. S. and Gaastra, S. A. M. *Kamus Indonesia-Inggeris*, 3rd edition, Versluys, Djakarta, 1959.

GLOSSARY FOR THE TEXTS

NOTE 1. This word-list is intended to cover only the usages which occur either in the Texts or in other examples quoted in footnotes or text. Where possible entries are minimal, e.g. *ikan*: fish. For further information the reader is referred to the dictionaries mentioned in the 'List of Works Consulted' on p. 284. Fuller entries are given where *ad hoc* meanings, if given unsupported, might prove to be misleading to the reader.

NOTE 2. A word is given under its root form, followed by such affixed forms as are relevant. For the benefit of the reader who is not conversant with the Malay language the following brief guide to the mechanics of the verbal prefix *me-* is offered. The same rules apply substantially for the prefix *pe-*. The prefix *ber-* presents no difficulty since the root form is left when the prefix is detached, e.g. for *berjalan* see *jalan*.

To look up a word which begins with the prefix *me-*:

1. If *me-* is followed by *mb*, look up the word under 'b'
   e.g. me + m + bacha: see bacha
2. If *me-* is followed by *nd*, or *nj* or *nch*, look it up under d, j, or ch
   e.g. me + n + dengar: see dengar
        me + n + jahit: see jahit
        me + n + chari: see chari
3. If *me-* is followed by *m* + vowel, look it up under 'p'
   e.g. me + m + ukul: see pukul (but also *memasak* from *masak*)
4. If *me-* is followed by *n* + vowel, look it up under 't'
   e.g. me + n + angis: see tangis (but also *menanti* from *nanti*)
5. If *me-* is followed by *ngg* or *ngh*, look it up under 'g' or 'h':
   e.g. me + ng + geletar: see geletar
        me + ng + hadap: see hadap
6. If *me-* is followed by *ng* + vowel, look it up under 'k'
   e.g. me + ng + awin see kawin
        me + ng + ukor see kukor (but also, from *ukor* measure)

If there is no entry under 'k', look it up under the vowel, or under *ng*

    e.g. me + ng + ikat   see ikat

    me + ng + ukir   see ukir

    me + nganga   see nganga

7. If *me-* is followed by *ny*, look it up under 's'

    e.g. me + ny + impang see simpang

    If there is no entry under 's', look it up under *ny*

    e.g. me + nyanyi   see nyanyi

8. If *me-* is followed by any other consonant, look it up under that consonant

    e.g. me + luru   see luru

ABBREVIATIONS USED: *Ar.* = Arabic; *Ch.* = Chinese; *coll.* = colloquial; *Dut.* = Dutch; *Eng.* = English; *esp.* = especially; *fam.* = familiar; *Hind.* = Hindustani; *Ind.* = Indonesian; *Jav.* = Javanese; *kpd.* = kapada; *lit.* = literally; *N.S.* = Negeri Sembilan; *Pers.* = Persian; *pol.* = polite; *Skr.* = Sanskrit; smbdy, smthg = somebody, something; *Tam.* = Tamil; *writt.* = used in writing, not in speech.

abang, 'bang: elder brother; form of address from a man to an older man, from wife to husband

achu, mengachu(kan): to make a feint of doing something, make as if to

ada: exist, be present; *mengadakan* make to exist, carry into effect; *mengada2* show off, be conceited

adap: *see* hadap

adék: younger brother or sister; form of address from husband to wife

Adohi!: exclamation expressing pain; wonder

agak: guess; approximately, fairly, rather; *agak-nya* probably, I should think, perhaps; *agak2* roughly, approximately

agama, ugama *Skr.*: religion

agut-agut: gasping (as a fish out of water)

Ah!: exclamation implying mild remonstrance

ahli *Ar.*: specialist; member of a group; *ahli rumah* wife

Ai!, Aih!: exclamation implying surprise; impatient protest

'aib *Ar.*: shame, slur, disgrace

'aja: *see* sahaja

ajak, mengajak, 'ngajak: invite (to accompany, or to do something)

ajal *Ar.*: destined hour of death

Ajit: abbreviation of the name Majid

akal, 'akal *Ar.*: intelligence: *coll.* scheme for getting out of a difficulty, bright idea

akan, 'kan: going to, about to; with regard to, towards, to; *ta' akan, ta' kan* not likely (to happen)

akar: root, fibre; creeping plant

aku, ku-, -ku: I, me (used between intimates, and in prayer); *mengaku* admit, confess; *mengaku salah* admit to being in the wrong

alang: medium, in the middle; moderate; *alang-kah (baik)*! lit. Is it (only) moderately (good)? an understatement for 'Wouldn't that be fine!'

alas: protective base or lining (e.g. tray, saucer)

aléh, mengaléh: move, change, shift (something); *beraléh* change one's position; *aléh-aléh* suddenly (denoting change of circumstances)

'alim *Ar.*: pious, learned (esp. in religious matters)

amat: very

ambil, mengambil: take, fetch, bring, get; pick up; *ambil (di-)hati* take to heart

ampun: pardon (in Text B, form of request for permission to speak, addressed to the Ruler)

anak: child, offspring; young (of creatures); part (of a composite whole); *beranak* to bear a child; to possess a child; *Raja dua beranak* the Raja and his son; *anak pokok* seedlings

angan-angan: thoughts, imaginings, fancies

anggok, menganggok: bob up and down; *menganggokkan* make to bob up and down; *menganggok-nganggokkan kepala* to keep nodding the head

angin: wind, air; *masok angin* to do a thing in vain

angkat, mengangkat: raise, lift up, take away: *terangkat* raised; *berangkat* to set out (orig. of the ruler only, but now becoming generally used)

angkit, mengangkit: lift or carry (light objects)

anglo *Ch.*: brazier

anjing: dog

antara *Skr.*: between

antok, berantok: knock against (something); *terantok* crashing against, in collision

anu: used when a speaker has momentarily forgotten the name of a person or thing, 'er..., you know, what's his name...'

anyam, menganyam: to weave; *anyaman* a piece of weaving

apa: what? *apa2* anything at all, whatsoever; *ta' apa, ta' mengapa* it's all
right, never mind

apabila: when

apit, mengapit: squeeze between two surfaces

arah: direction; *(meng)arah* be in the direction of; *ta' tentu arah* aimlessly,
uncertainly; *ta' ketahuan arah* not knowing where one stands; *membelakang arah ka-* to have one's back towards...

arang: charcoal, soot

asak, mengasak: stuff into, insert by pressure; *terasak* 'flattened' (e.g. into
a corner)

As-salam 'alaikum *Ar.*: Peace be unto you

Astaghfiru'llah *Ar.*: God forbid!

atas: the top (of something); *(di-)atas* on top of, on; *(ka-)atas* to the top,
up

atau: or

awak: *lit.* body; you (polite)

ayah: father

ayahanda: honorific form of *ayah*, father

ayat *Ar.*: verse (esp. of the Koran); sentence

ayer: water, liquid, juice; *berayer* wet (of fields); *ayer lior* saliva

ba' = bagi: give

bacha, membacha: recite, read; *membacha-bacha* keep on reciting,
chanting; *bachaan* recital, reading, chanting

badan *Ar.*: body

bagai: sort, kind; *coll.* (at end of a list) 'and so on', 'and all the rest',
sc. of the same kind

bagini: in this fashion, like this

bagitu: in that fashion, like that

bagus: good, beautiful, fine, satisfactory

baharu: new; newly, only just

bahasa *Skr.*: language, good manners; *berbahasa* courteous, polite,
cultured; *bahasa kebangsaan* the National Language

bahaya *Skr.*: danger

baik: good; well; *Baik-lah* Very well! All right; *baik-baik* properly, with
care; *sa-baik-baik (sempat)* just exactly (in time to)

baju *Pers.*: Malay coat (short, of thin material)

bakar, membakar: to toast, roast, burn; make hot

bakul: basket

balai: hall; raised open pavilion; *balai penghadapan* hall of audience

balas, membalas: requite; *ta' terbalas* beyond repayment

balék: reverse, back; return, go back, go home; again; *ka-balék Bukit Qaf* to the back of Bukit Qaf (= 'to Jericho!'); *berjalan pergi balék* walk up and down

banchoh: knead (dough); mix, mash

bandar *Pers.*: port, town

'bang *see* abang

bangang: ? = *bengang*, wide open, agape; dumbfounded

bangkit: arise, rise up; *bangkit berdiri* stand up; *bangkit dudok* sit up; *terbangkit* rise up without volition

bangku: bench, seat

bangsa *Skr.*: race; sort, kind

bangun: get up (from chair, floor, bed)

banyak: many, much; *sa-banyak itu* as much as that

bapa: (*fam.*) father

barang: thing, goods, something; (before a numeral) approximately; *barang tiga batu* some three miles or so; *barang sa-hari dua* for a day or two; *barang ka-mana* (to) where-soever

barangkali: perhaps

baring: lying down, to lie down (with face upwards)

baroh: lower-lying land, nearer river or sea-shore

basah: wet; *membasah(kan)* to make wet; *membasah-basah tekak* to serve small cakes as appetizers

batang: stem, stalk; trunk

baték, batik *Jav.*: cloth patterned by painting unwaxed portions in traditional designs

batu: rock, stone, mile-stone; mile; *batu kepala* (from *batok* (*Jav.*) coconut) skull and scalp

bau: smell, odour; *terbau* to get a whiff of

bawa, membawa: convey, conduct, bring, take

bawah: the underneath, lowest part; (*di-*)*bawah* at the bottom, underneath, *dari bawah* from underneath

baya, sa-baya (dengan): of the same age as

bayang: vague outline, shadow; *terbayang* vaguely outlined; *Saya ta' terbayang*... It wouldn't occur to me to...

bayar, membayar: to pay

bedebah *Pers.*: ill-fated

bekal: food, or other provision, intended for consumption or use away from one's base; *bekalkan* to put together such provisions or equipment

belah, membelah: split lengthways; (*di-*)*sa-belah kanan* on the right, *di-sebelah belakang* at the back; *sa-belah hulu* higher up the river

belaka: to the last one, entirely, altogether

belakang: back, rear; *mengikut dari belakang* follow in someone's wake

belanga: shallow cooking pot (for meat)

belanja: expenditure, spending money

-belas: -teen; *sa-belas* eleven; *dua belas* twelve

bélék, membélék: to examine closely

beli, membeli: to buy

belia *Skr.*: (*writt.*) fresh, in the bloom of youth

beliak: rolling up the eyes to show the whites; *mata terbeliak* with eyes popping out of one's head

belit, membelit: to coil, wind round

belum: not yet; *sa-belum* before (some time or occurrence)

benang: thread, yarn, cotton

benar: true, genuine; truly; (*mem*)*benarkan* give permission for...; *kebenaran* permission, permit; *yang sa-benar-nya* the truth of the matter is, as a matter of fact

benchi: hate

benda *Skr.*: thing, article; *harta benda* property

bendahara *Skr.*: treasurer; First Lord of the Treasury, Prime Minister

bendang: rice-fields

bengkak: swollen, inflamed; *membengkak* to swell up

bentar: a moment; *sa-bentar lagi* a moment later

bérang: flaring up in a spurt of anger

berani: brave, bravery; *memberanikan hati* to summon up one's courage

berapa: how much, how many; *ta' berapa baik* not very good; *beberapa* several

beras: husked rice

beri, memberi: to give; *memberi tahu* to inform; *pemberian* gift

berlian *Eng.*: brilliants, diamond paste

berok: the coconut monkey

berséh: clean; (*mem*)*berséhkan* to make clean

besar: big, important, large, thick (of rope); *jalan besar* main road; *membesarkan* to make big; *kebesaran* greatness; insignia of greatness;

presumption; *sa-besar* as big as; *sa-besar2* roughly as big as; *besar-nya* size; *besar hati* proud, elated; *orang besar-besar* (in Text B) chiefs

bésok *see* ésok

betina: (*fam.*) female

betul: correct, accurate, true, straight, co-inciding; truly; (*mem*)*betulkan* to put straight, adjust; *kebetulan* happening to be in line with, exactly coinciding, i.e. at the very moment when...; *yang betul-nya* the truth of the matter is...

biar: allow, permit

biasa *Skr.*: wonted, usual; be accustomed, be in the habit of...

bibir: lip, edge

biji *Skr.*: seed, pip; a numeral coefficient for small things; *sa-biji kelapa* a coconut; *dua biji mata* two eyes

bikin: make, do (used in the towns)

bila: when? when; *bila2* at any time whatsoever

bilah: narrow strip (of cane, bamboo); used as a numerical coefficient for weapons, knives, etc.; *sa-bilah parang* a wood knife

bilang, membilang: count, enumerate

bilék: room

binatang: creature, animal, insect

binchang, membinchangkan: to discuss

binchul: bump (on the forehead); *binchul2* covered with bruises and bumps

bini: (*fam.*) wife

binték: spot; *berbinték2* spotted

biru: blue

bisa *Skr.*: poison, venom

bisék, berbisék: to whisper

bising: noise, noisy

biskut *Eng.*: biscuit

bodoh: foolish, silly

bohong: lie, untruth; *pembohong* untrue; liar

boléh: be able, can; *coll.* will

bomor: Malay doctor

bongkok: bent over, bowed; *membongkok* to stoop, bend

bongsu: youngest, last

buah: fruit; used as a numerical coefficient before an increasingly large range of nouns; *sa-buah periok* a cooking pot; *sa-buah pak besar* a large wooden chest

bual: bubbling up; *berbual2* to chat, gossip

buang, membuang: discard, throw away, get rid of; *membuang-buang* discarding wastefully

buat, membuat: do, make; for (a certain purpose), in order to, acting as; *buatkan* make (for somebody), do (to somebody); *buatan* manufacture, manufactured; *perbuatan* workmanship, manufacture, manufactured article; *buat2* pretence, pretending

buboh, memboh: put (into some place, or into food)

budak: child, young person

budi *Skr.*: kindness, graciousness, kindly disposition; *berbudi* courteous, kindly

bujor: lengthwise; longer than wide, oval; *terbujor* stretched out at full length

buka, membuka: to open, unfasten; remove (coat, hat); *terbuka* open, opened; *buka badan-nya* the width of the body

bukan: not (implying the existence of an alternative); *bukan? bukan-kah?* isn't it so? *bukan-nya* it isn't that..., it wasn't that...; *bukan2* imaginary, non-existent; *bukan main* (followed by an adj.) genuinely, exceedingly

bukit: hill; *membukit* be hilly (of land)

buku: *Eng.* book

bulan: moon; month

bulat: round

bunga: flower

bungkus: bundle, package; *berbungkus* wrapped up; *nasi bungkus* cooked rice in a leaf-wrapper; *bungkus nasi* a leaf-packet of cooked rice

bunoh, membunoh: to kill, murder

buntang: protruding (of eyes)

bunyi: sound, noise; *berbunyi* to sound (e.g. of a musical instrument)

burok: in disrepair, worn out (of clothes), rotten (of wood), shabby, plain, unworthy (of people)

buru, memburu: to hunt; *pemburu* hunting (adj.); hunter

busok: decaying, rotten, 'going off' (of fish, eggs, etc.)

busut: ant-hill

chabang: fork, bifurcation; *berchabang dua* two-pronged, with two branches

chabut(kan): pull out, draw out, extract; *(ber)chabut undi* to draw lots;

terchabut péndék finding oneself with the short stalk (after drawing for 'long or short')

chaching: worm

chadar *Hind.*: *kain chadar* sheet (for bed)

chakap: undertake responsibility for; talk, speak; *berchakap* converse, talk; *berchakap2* keep on chatting; *chakap2kan* to make somebody the subject of gossip

cham, mengecham: recognise by sight

champak, (men)champakkan: throw down, throw away; *terchampak* thrown aside, abandoned

champor, berchampor: mix, mingle

chanai, menchanai *Tam.*: to grind, sharpen; roll out (pastry)

changkah: ? = changgah: a two-pronged fork; to thrust up with a forked instrument

changkul: square-bladed hoe used mainly for digging; *menchangkul* to hoe, dig over; *mata changkul* the blade of the hoe

chanték: pretty

chapai, menchapai: to reach out for, grasp with stretched arm

chara *Skr.*: fashion, method, way

chari, menchari: seek, look for, go to get

chawan *Ch.*: tea-cup

Ché': abbreviation of *enche'* when used in conjunction with a name

chebék (chemék), menchebék: to pout, stick out the lower lip either in discontent or in mockery; *menchebék2kan muka kpd.* making faces at, grimacing

chebis: torn at the edge; *sa-chebis* a scrap (of cloth or paper)

chechah: dip (smthg) into liquid

Chéh!: exclamation implying slight disapproval

chelah: cleft, chink, crevice

chelaka *Skr.*: accursed

chemar: dirt; dirty, soiled

chemas: nervousness, anxiety; harassed, upset; *chemas-chemas(mati)* narrowly escaping (death), all but (dead)

chembul: round-lidded metal box for tobacco or gambir, one of the receptacles in a betel-nut set

chemburu: jealous, suspicious

chemék see chebék

chengang: bewilderment; *terchengang* struck with amazement

chenggang, berchenggang: part, be separated

chepat: quick; *chepat2* very quickly

chepu: round-lidded box (for betel requisites, etc.), of metal or wood

cherai, bercherai: asunder, parted; divorced

cherana: a pedestal bowl or salver for holding betel-nut equipment

cherdék: resourceful, clever

cherita *Skr.*: story, tale, relation; *cheritakan* to tell, relate

chika: severe colic

Chim: abbreviation of the name Kasim

Chis!: exclamation implying impatient remonstrance

chita *Skr.*: thought-concentration; feeling

chomél: dainty, charming

chuba, menchuba: try; (as a polite introduction to an imperative) 'please', 'will you'

chuchok: pierce with a pointed instrument, 'thread' (e.g. beads); *penchuchok* 'piercers', spikes, skewers

chuchu: grandchild

chuit: jerky movements; gesticulate with fingers; *chuitkan* to make something flutter about

chukor, berchukor: to shave

chukup: enough; *coll.* quite; *coll.* complete (with)...

chuma: only, merely

chungap, menchungap: pant, blow; *terchungap2* gasping (e.g. with fright)

churi, menchuri: steal

Chus!: exclamation implying strong disapproval

daging: flesh; meat

dagu: chin

'dah *see* sudah

dahi: forehead

dahshat: *Ar.* alarm; alarming, horrifying

dahulu: before, formerly; early; *terdahulu* earlier than expected

dalam: the inside of a thing or place; (*di-*)*dalam* inside, in; *dalam sa-hari dua 'ni* within this next day or two

dapat: manage to, be able; succeed in getting, obtain; come to fruition; come into one's possession; *mendapatkan* go to find, meet, see smbdy; *dapati* come across, find (e.g. a certain situation)

dapor: cooking place, stove; kitchen

darah: blood; *berdarah* blood-stained, bleeding

dari: from; than

daripada, pada: than

datang: come; *mendatangkan* cause to come, cause; *orang mendatang* 'arriving' people, immigrants

dato', datok, To': grandfather; chief; a title of respect

daun: leaf

dawai: wire

daya *Skr.*: resource, stratagem; *dayakan* to play a trick (on smbdy); *ta' berdaya* without resources, powerless

debar, berdebar2 hati: with heart thumping (from fear or excitement)

dechit: squeak, twitter; *berdechit* to squeak

dék: (in conversation, replacing *oléh*) by; because of; belonging to

dekah, berdekah: guffaw; *tertawa berdekah2* loud chuckling laughter

dekat: near; nearly; *mendekati* to go near to, to approach; *mendekatkan* to bring smthing close; *dekat2* close together

delapan, 'lapan: eight

demam: fever; have fever, be feverish

demikian: (*writt.*) thus; *dengan hal yang demikian* in this way

denda *Skr.*: a fine

dengan: with, by means of; by reason of; in company with

dengar, mendengar: hear, listen to; *kedengaran* heard, there is heard; *terdengar, kedengar* heard, overheard; catch the sound of

dengki: envy, spite; *dengki hati* spiteful, ungenerous

dengkor, mendengkor: to snore

dengus, mendengus: to snort

denting, berdenting: (of a moustache) ?upturned, ?stiff and bristling see Text B 79, (usually used of a chinking sound. Wlk. has: '1. cf. *lenting*, i.e. curved up at the end. 2. twang; taut)'

depan (= di-hadapan): in front; *bulan depan* next month

depék, berdepék2: (? = *depak*) clattering (of footsteps)

dérét, berdérét: in a line, one behind the other; *dérétkan* to arrange in a line

destar *Pers.*: turban; *N.S. detar* a Malay headdress

detar *see* destar

déwan, diwan *Pers.*: audience hall; council of state; official department or institution

di-: 1. in, at, on.

    2. verbal prefix

dia: he, she, it, they, him, her, them

diam: still, silent; remain quiet; dwell, live, stay; *terdiam* ceasing to move, falling silent; *diam2*, perfectly still

dinding: partition; dividing wall, wall

diri: 1. self, oneself; *sa-orang diri* by oneself, alone; *membawa diri* take oneself off; *tahu (a)kan diri* come to one's senses, know what's what. 2. erect position; *berdiri* stand, be standing; *terdiri* erected, set up, standing; brought to a standstill

do'a *Ar.*: prayer (for some definite purpose)

dosa *Skr.*: sin; *berdosa* sinful

dua: two; *berdua2* together; *yang kedua* the second; *kedua-nya, kedua2-nya* the two of them, both

dudok: position; be seated, sit; live, be in (a place), remain, stay; *terdudok* in a sitting position; *kedudokan* position, situation

duit *Dut.*: cash, money

duka *Skr.*: sadness; *duka chita* sad, feeling sad

duli *Skr.*: dust; *berchemar duli* to soil (your feet) with dust ('in entering my humble abode')

dunia *Ar.*: this world

durian: durian (a large fruit with a thick thorny husk; *duri* thorn)

Éh!: an ejaculation indicating surprised attention

Eh, e: an interpolation indicating hesitation, corresponding to Eng. er...er...er

Ehem: an exclamation expressing discreet surprise

éjék, mengéjék: tease, taunt (by mimicking)

ékor: tail; end (of a coat); corner (of the eye); used as a numerical co-efficient for living creatures other than human beings; *sa-ékor kuda* a horse

élak, mengélak: to dodge aside

élok: fine, beautiful; in good order

emak, mak: mother

emas, mas: gold; *peremasan* goods made of gold

empat: four

enam: six; *ke-enam2-nya* all six of them

enché': a respectful title to a Malay of either sex who does not possess a distinctive title (equivalent to Mr etc.), usually shortened to *Ché'* in front of a name

engkau, -kau, 'kau, kau-: (intimate, or to inferiors) you

engku: a title of high rank

éngsut, beréngsut: making a slight movement, edging towards or away from smthg

entah: a verbal word implying uncertainty: may be, I don't really know, is it perhaps...?

erang, mengerang: to groan in pain

erti, herti, mengerti: to understand; *erti-nya* the meaning of it

ésak(or isak), mengésak: to sob; *terésak2* sobbing

ésok, bésok: the morrow; tomorrow, some time in the future

faham (*coll.* paham) *Ar.*: understand, know about

fasal (*coll.* pasal) *Ar.*: topic, section; affair, business; because of; *apa fasal?* why?

feduli, fadzuli (*coll.* peduli, perduli) *Ar.*: care about, heed

fikir, berfikir (*coll.* pikir) *Ar.*: think, think about, reflect; *berpikir2* keep thinking about smthg; *terpikir* find oneself thinking about smthg, have an idea; *pikiran, fikiran,* opinion, way of thinking; thought; *memutuskan pikiran* come to a decision

gadoh: fuss, row, dispute; *bergadoh* dispute noisily, argue, quarrel, make a fuss

gajah: elephant

gamak, menggamak: take something in the hand to guess at the weight; guess, reckon; take in hand to...

ganjil: odd (of numbers); peculiar, unusual

ganyut: tough, hard (not ripening, of fruit; not softening in cooking, of vegetables); *orang tua ganyut* an old man who tries to look young

gapai, menggapai *Ind.*: throw one's hands about seeking for a support; *tergapai2* clutching at anything within reach

gaya *Skr.*: grand manner, air, mode, appearance, style; *bergaya* with a jaunty air; *menggayakan* to indicate the manner of; *menggayakan tangan* to indicate by a gesture of the hand

gébang, bergébang: to chat, gossip

gedé *Jav.*: big

gelak: laughing out loud; *tertawa gelak2* with peals of laughter

gelang: bracelet; *gelang kaki* anklets

gelap: darkness; dark

gelegak, menggelegak: bubbling, on the boil, seething

géléng, menggéléng(kan): shake (the head) from side to side

geletar, menggeletar: tremble, shudder

geli, geli hati: amused, tickled

gelok: a water-vessel made of a coconut shell with the top part cut off and used as a lid; any water vessel of this shape

gemala *Skr.*: luminous bezoar stone fabled to appear in the head of a dragon; lustrous gem

gemar: liking, preference; to like

géndéng: go sideways, heel over; *menggéndéngkan kepala* to put the head on one side

genggam, menggengam: grasp in the fist; *menggengam tangan* to clench the fist

gentar: trembling

genyit: a wink; *bergenyit-genyitan* exchanging winks

gerak: small movements; *bergerak2* to move slightly, to stir

gerbang: opening out as a fan; loose, dishevelled

gésél, menggésél: brush against smbdy

géséng: rub against; *menggéséng2kan pipi kpd.* rubbing the cheek against...

giang-giut, menggiang-giut: ? = *Ind. giat* active, energetic. See Text B 680 where it is followed by *oléh berat* 'because of the weight'. Perh. 'swaying'

gigi: tooth, teeth

gigit, menggigit: to bite

gila: mad, unbalanced; infatuated

gilir, giliran: one's turn (in rotation)

golék, bergolék, golék-gelentang: roll over and over

gopoh: haste, hurry; *gopoh2* extreme haste

goring, goréng: dry frying, dry roasting

gosok, menggosok: to rub, massage

gugor: fall through ripeness (of fruit), fall prematurely or unexpectedly (of miscarriages, stars, aeroplanes); *rahat gugor* fall in a glut (of durians)

gula: sugar

gulai: wet curry

guling: roll about; *berguling2* rolling over, this way and that

guna *Skr.*: usefulness, value; *berguna* of use, useful

gurau, bergurau2: to jest, joke, be playful

guru: *Skr.* teacher

Ha! H^na!: exclamation implying agreement with an existing situation

habis: finished, used up, none left; utterly, to the limit of possibility; and then? (i.e. when that was over?); *ta' terhabis* inexhaustible; *habis lama-nya* at the very longest; *habis binchul2* nothing but bumps and bruises

hadap, menghadap: to face, confront; *hadapan* front; *di-hadapan* in front, in front of; *terhadap kpd.* coming face to face with smbdy; *mengadap* have audience with a superior

hadhir, hadzir, hathir *Ar.*: present, in attendance

hadiah *Ar.*: gift

Hah!: exclamation implying distaste

Hai!: exclamation to call attention; to express surprise, resignation (B 8), alarm (B 638)

Haih!: exclamation indicating lively concern

hairan, héran *Ar.*: surprised, astonished

hak, hakk *Ar.*: property

hal *Ar.*: condition, situation; affairs, business; *apa hal?* why?; *pada hal* in actual fact (contrary to one's first impression)

halau, menghalau: to chase away, drive away

halus: fine, delicate

hamba: *orig.* slave, but used of any unpaid servant in the old-time royal courts

hampar, terhampar: spreading out horizontally, outspread

hampir: near, nearly; *hampir2* round about, approximately

hantu: evil spirit, demon, ghost; *hantu wéwér* a ghost which misleads its victims with a fugitive flickering light; *hantu menjangan* or *manjang* familiar spirit of a wizard; *hantu bungkus* the ghost of a dead man which rolls after its victim, wrapped in grave clothes

hanya: merely, only

hanyut: drift, adrift

haram *Ar.*: forbidden by religion

harap: hope, expectation; confidence; reliable, trustworthy

harga *Skr.*: price

hari: day, the period of 24 hours; *sa-hari2an ini* all this day long

harong, arong, mengharong: to ford, wade through

harta *Skr.*: property, belongings

harus: proper, fitting; probably, likely

hati: heart, liver; core; disposition

hébat, haibat *Ar.*: awe-inspiring; (*coll.*) smart, striking (of appearance);
  menghébat to be dressed up in all one's finery

héboh: commotion, stir

Heⁿh!: exclamation implying disparagement, disagreement, displeasure

Héh!: exclamation indicating surprise

helai: a numeral coefficient for thin things, in sheets or threads; *sa-helai
  tali* a rope

hempas, hempaskan: dash down with violence; *berhempas2. berhempas
  pulas* thrashing about (e.g. when in pain or distress)

hendak, 'nak: intend; desire to; will, shall; going to be; *hendak(kan)*
  want (smthg); *kehendak (hati)* wish, desire, longing

hentak, entak, menghentak: ram down; pound; stamp, tramp, tread
  heavily

henti, berhenti: to stop, halt; *ta' berhenti2* without a moment's pause;
  terhenti brought to a halt, coming to a halt

hias, menghiasi: adorn, decorate; *perhiasan* decoration, ornament

hiba, iba: anxious; anxious love, solicitude

hibor: solace; *menghiborkan* to comfort

hidong: nose

hidup: alive, be alive; *hidupkan, menghidupkan* to make alive, to kindle
  (a fire)

hijau: green; *mengijau* to turn green

hilang: vanished, disappeared, lost; dead; *menghilangkan* make to
  disappear, get rid of; *kehilangan* lost; having suffered loss; loss

hina *Skr.*: humble, lowly, mean

hingga, sa-hingga: as far as, up to, until

hinggap: come to rest (on smthg), perch, alight

hitam: black; *kehitam2an* blackish

hormat *Ar.*: respect, honour

Huh!: exclamation, a gasp of relief, or of apprehension

hujan: rain; be rainy, be wet; *kehujanan* rained on, caught in the
  rain

hujong: end; (*berjalan*) *ka-hujong ka-pangkal* (to walk) up and down,
  backwards and forwards, from end to end (of a room)

hulor, menghulor(kan): pay out (a rope), stretch out (a hand, an arm)

hulu, ulu: head (esp. of a river); hinterland, 'up-country'

hutan: jungle, forest

hutang: debt; *terhutang budi* indebted for kindness received ia: 1. he, she, it, they; *ia-lah, ia-itu* see Index.

    2. yes; *Ia ta' ia* Yes or no (which ever way you take it, what you say is true)

Iblis *Ar.*: Satan; devil, demon

ibu: mother; *ibu kaki* the big toe

ikan: fish

ikat, mengikat: tie, bind; *tali pengikat* a rope which ties something together; *ikatan* knot; bundle; *berikat tali* tied with string; *berikat2* tied in bundles

ikhtiar *Ar.*: decision, plan, course of action chosen

ikut, mengikut: to follow

imam *Ar.*: leader of the congregation in a mosque

inchi *Eng.*: inch

indah: fine, beautiful, impressive

ingat, mengingat: be mindful of, remember; *teringat*, to have a sudden idea, or memory; to call to mind; *ingat2kan* to think about, give thought to

inggeris: English

ingin: long to, want to

ini: this

intai, mengintai: to look at something without being seen, peep, spy; *terintai2* taking a peep at smthg (e.g. through a chink)

intan: diamond

ipar: (brother or sister)-in-law

iring, mengiring: be at the side of, accompany, follow in procession (as one of the ruler's suite)

isap, hisap, mengisap: suck, suck in, inhale; *mengisap rokok* to smoke a cigarette

isi: contents

istana, astana *Skr.*: ruler's palace

isteri *Skr.*: (*pol.*) wife

isti'adat *Ar.*: ceremony, customary ceremonial

itu: that

jadah, zadah *Pers.*: child of; *haram jadah* unlawfully begotten, misbegotten

jadi: come into being, come about, happen, become; and so...; *menjadikan* to cause to be; *terjadi* that has happened, come about; *kejadian* happening, occurrence, incident jaga *Skr.*: be awake; be on watch; be careful; *terjaga* suddenly waking, awake

jahat: wicked; (of a child) naughty

jahil *Ar.*: ignorant (esp. on matters of religion)

jahit, menjahit: to sew; *tukang jahit* tailor, seamstress

jajahan: territories; (official) district

jalan: way, road, method; (ber)*jalan* to move, walk, travel; *menjalankan* to cause to move, to drive (a car); *jalanan* journey, way

jam *Pers.*: clock; hour

jambatan: quay, bridge

jamin: guarantee; (men)*jamin* go bail for

jamu, menjamu: to entertain, give hospitality

jangan: let it not be, so that...not, lest; do not

janggal: discordant, inharmonious

janggut: beard; *berjanggut* having a beard, bearded

jangka: callipers, compasses; *jangkakan* to measure off with compasses; to split a *mengkuang* leaf into strips using a tool fitted with several parallel cutting edges

janji: agreement, arrangement; *berjanji* to agree, promise

jantan: (*fam.*) male, masculine

jarang: wide apart, at wide intervals; rare; *jarang2* seldom

jari: finger, toe

jauh: distant, at a distance

jawab, menjawab *Ar.*: answer

jebat *Ar.*: civet, musk

jegil, terjegil: sticking out, bulging (of eyes, with malevolence)

jehanam, jahanam *Ar.*: gehenna, hell; utterly destroyed, ruined

jelak: surfeit; sated, sick of

jeling, menjeling: give a sideways glance

jemor: drying in the sun; *berjemor* basking in the sun; (men)*jemorkan* to dry smthg in the sun

jemput, menjemput: press between thumb and finger; pressure of hand in greeting a guest; greet; welcome

jéngkét, jéngkit: tilting up; *berjalan berjéngkét2* walk on tiptoe

jengok, menjengok: peep out of or into, in order to see what is going on

jenis *Ar.*: kind, sort, genus

jerang, menjerang(kan): to put a vessel containing food over a source of heat; *jerangkan ayer panas* = 'to put the kettle on' jerit, menjerit: to shriek

jin *Ar.*: genie, goblin

jinjing, menjinjing: to carry smthg light in the hand

jodoh *Tam.*: match, affinity; *berjodoh* making a perfect pair

jolak, menjolakkan: to thrust something upward from underneath, e.g. with a stick

jolok, menjolok, menjolokkan: to knock down ripe fruit from the tree by thrusting upwards with a long pole

jual, menjual: to sell

juga: a post-position particle which implies guarded assent and can seldom be directly translated. See Index

juma'at, juma't *Ar.*: *hari juma'at* Friday

jumpa, berjumpa: to meet with; *terjumpa* happen to come across

junjong, menjunjong; carry on the head; *menjunjong titah* carry out a royal behest

jurus, sa-jurus: a brief interval

ka-: to (a place)

kachau: mixed up, confused; fuss, trouble

kachip: betel-nut slicers

kadang-kadang: sometimes

kadar *Ar.*: *lit.* power; up to the extent of, roughly to the extent of; *kadar dua inchi* about 2 inches; *sa-kadarkan* only to the extent that... See Texts B 528, C 25

kadhi, kadzi, kathi *Ar.*: judge (of Canon Law)

-kah: a post-position particle denoting interrogation

kain: cloth; a sarong; *kain baju* clothes

kaka: respectful form of address to a Malabari

kaki: foot, leg; *berkaki empat* four-legged; on all fours; *kaki lilin* candlestick

kalau: if; *kalau2* if by chance, lest by chance

kali: time, occasion; *sa-kali* once; *sa-kali sa-kali* occasionally, now and then; (*tidak*) *sa-kali-kah* (not) by any means; *yang baik sa-kali* very good, the best; *mula2 sa-kali* at the very beginning, the very first

kalimah *Ar.*: short utterance

kambing: goat

kami: we (excluding the hearer)

kampong: a gathering together; a group of houses comprising a village; a large homestead; a 'compound' kamu: you (to children or inferiors)

kanan: right; *arah ka-kanan* on the right of, towards the right

'kang *see* sekarang

kapada: to (a person)

kapal *Tam.*: ship

kapor: lime; *pekapor* lime-container in a betel-nut set

'karang *see* sekarang

karut: confused, muddled, foolish; *mengarut* to talk foolishly

kasar: coarse, rough

kaséh: favour, affection, love; *kaséhan* compassion, pity; *Kaséhan!* Dear!
Dear!, Poor thing!; *kekaséh* the loved one; *Terima kaséh* Thank you!
or No, thank you!

kata: saying, remark, word; *kata, mengata(kan), berkata* say

kawan: friend; I, you (between speakers of roughly equal age and status);
berkawan2 dengan in company with

kawin, kahwin: marriage, wedlock; marry; *kawinkan, mengawinkan* to
give in marriage

kaya *Skr.*: rich, great

kayu: wood, timber; *pokok kayu* tree; *daun kayu* leaf of tree

kebun: plantation, estate; garden; *kebun bunga* park, garden

kechil: small; *mengechilkan* to make small(er); *kechil hati* annoyed, hurt

kechut: shrivelling up; *terkechut* frightened, startled; *pengechut* cowardly,
a coward

kedai: shop (small)

kejap: flick of an eye, a blink; *sa-kejap* a moment

kejar, mengejar, berkejar: to chase, run after; *terkejar2* moving at great
speed

kejut, terkejut: stiffening with fear, terrified

kekabu, kabu-kabu: tree-cotton, kapok

keladi: calladium; *mengeladi* to be as slippery as a calladium leaf, to be
'a slippery customer'

kelahi, berkelahi *Tam.*: to quarrel, dispute

kelak: (*writt.* frequently in final position) in the future (usually to be
rendered in translation merely by an appropriate tense form)

kelapa: coconut

kelarai: diamond-shaped (of patterns)

kélék, kilék: armpit; *kélék, mengélék* to carry under the arm

kelibat, sa-kelibat: a flash, a moment

keliling: situation around; *sa-keliling* all around; *berkeliling* being, or going, all around

kelip: twinkle (of stars), blink (of eyes); *berkelip2*, *terkelip2* twinkling, blinking

kelmarin: yesterday; the other day; some time in the past

keloh: deep breathing; *mengeloh* to sigh

kelu: struck speechless

keluar: to go out (*see* also *luar*)

kelurut: a whitlow; inflamed sore on finger or toe

kemamar, terkemamar: blinking in amazement

kemas: tidy, in good order; *berkemas* make oneself ready; *kemaskan*, *mengemaskan* to make tidy, to put in order

kemudian: then, afterwards, later

kemunchak: summit, top

kena, mengena: come in contact (with smthg), hit against; incur, run into, be obliged to (do smthg); *kenakan* to fit smthg into its place (e.g. a light-bulb into its socket); to get the better of somebody, catch somebody out

kenal, mengenal: recognize by sight, know

kenan, berkenan: to like, find agreeable; *(mem)perkenan* to approve of

kenang, mengenang(kan): think of with gentle affection, remember in absence, recall with happy memories

kenchang: strong (of winds, currents); vigorous (of movement)

kening: eyebrow

kenyang: satisfied (with food), replete

kepala *Skr.*: head

keping: piece, slice; used as a numeral coefficient for pieces of wood, paper etc.; *sa-keping surat* a letter

kepok: rice bin (in the paddy field)

keputak, berkeputak: ?for *putar* q.v. See Text B 290a

kerana, karena, karna *Skr.*: because, because of

keras: hard; severe

kerat, mengerat: cut (smthg) across, cut off, amputate; *sa-kerat* a piece, a part, one; sometimes used as a numeral coefficient: *beberapa kerat daripada ikatan itu*... a certain number of the bundles

kerbau: buffalo

kerékéh: making small amounts of money in any way that presents itself

kerépék: *kuéh kerépék* fritters made with sago and bananas

keréta *Port.*: carriage, car

kering: dry

kerja *Skr.*: work, business, affair; *bekerja* to work; *kerjakan* to work at a thing, to carry a thing through; to ruin something

kerling, mengerling: to give a sidelong look

kerosang: set of three brooches, often connected by thin gold chains, used for fastening the front of a Malay woman's *baju*

ketap, mengetap: to shut tight (e.g. the lips); *mengetap-ngetapkan bibir* to keep pursing the lips

ketawa: to laugh; *ketawakan* to laugh at (smbdy)

kéték: the long pair of legs of a grasshopper; *terkéték2* moving jerkily

ketiga *see* tiga

ketika *Skr.*: a moment; time, a period or point in time; *sa-ketika itu* at that moment

keting: back of ankle; *urat keting* Achilles tendon

ketok, mengetok: rap, tap, knock

khabar *Ar.*: news; *khabarkan* to tell

khuatir *Ar.*: anxious, apprehensive, worried

kian: thus much; *sa-kian* once as much as this, i.e. so much

kibar, berkibar: to flap, *mengibarkan tangan* to wave the hand

kipas: a fan; *mengipas-ngipaskan* to keep fanning

kira, mengira: to calculate; *berkira* to think that...; *berkira 'nak* to intend to...; *kira2* about, approximately; *sa-kira-nya* if perchance

kiri: left; *sa-belah kiri* on the left; *di-kiri kanan* on left and right, on both sides

kirim, mengirim, berkirim: to send; *(surat) kiriman* (a letter) sent; *perkiriman* something sent, present

kita: we

kok: (*coll.*) if

kongsi *Ch.*: partnership, society; *berkongsi* work in partnership

konon: it is said

kopék: limp, flaccid

kopi *Eng.*: coffee

kosong: empty, meaningless; *kosongkan* make empty, clear a space

kotak: small box; compartment (in a larger piece of furniture)

ku-, -ku v. aku

kuala: estuary, river-mouth or confluence

kuasa *Skr.*: power, authority; (*coll.*) *ta' kuasa 'nak* feel disinclined (to do smthg)

kuat *Skr.*: strong, vigorous; vigorously; *dengan sa-kuat2 hati* with all one's might

kubor *Ar.*: grave, tomb

kuching: cat

kuda: horse

kuéh: cake, sweetmeat

kukoh: strong, firm

kukor, mengukor: to rasp (e.g. a coconut); *kukoran* a coconut rasp

kuku: claw, nail

kulum: sucking at something in the mouth

kuman: parasite; minute creature; atom

kumat-kamit: moving the lips and cheeks (e.g. when reading), mouthing words with little or no sound

kumbang: carpenter-bee; flying beetle

kumpul, berkumpul (*intr.*), mengumpulkan (*tr.*): gather together, assemble; *terkumpul* gathered together

kuning: yellow

kuntum: a bud; used as a numeral coefficient for flowers; *sa-kuntum bunga* a flower; *bunga sa-kuntum* one flower

kunyong, sa-kunyong2: suddenly, unexpectedly

kurang: less; too little; *habis kurang(-nya)* the least possible, the minimum; *sa-kurang2-nya* at the very least

kurnia *Skr.*: grace, favour, bounty (from a superior)

kurong: confining in an enclosed space; trap; cabin; *kurongkan, mengurongkan* to shut up in a small space

lagi: still; more, more still; *sa-kali lagi* once again; *lagi pun* moreover; what's more...; *ta' susah lagi* no longer troubled; *pagi-pagi lagi* still early in the day

-lah: a suffixed particle which gives weight to the word (or, sometimes, longer unit) to which it is attached

lain: other, different; *melainkan* (*lit.* making different) other than, except, except that; but (offering the 'correct' alternative to the preceding proposition)

Lak: abbreviation for *Laksamana*

laki: husband; *laki bini* husband and wife; *laki2* (*pol.*) male, masculine

laksamana *Skr.*: admiral; high court dignitary

laku: conduct, behaviour; *kelakuan* behaviour; *sa-laku* with the air of, like

lakun *Jav.*: role; *lakunan* an act (in a play)

lalat: house-fly

lalu: go past, pass by; then, afterwards; *lalui* go past (a place)

lama: long (of duration in time); *sa-lama2-nya* for ever; *ta' lama lagi* in a short time, before very long; *sa-lama sa-tengah jam* for one half-hour

lambat: slow, late

lambong, melambong: to be tossed up, to bounce

lampau: passing over and beyond, too much; *terlampau* exceedingly, too, very; exceeding

lampu *Port.*: lamp; *lampu peték* electric torch; *kaki lampu* lamp-stand

langit: sky

langsong: forthwith, proceeding directly

langsuir: vampire which preys on women in childbirth

lantai: flooring, floor

lanting *Eng.*: lantern

lapah: to skin (an animal)

'lapan *see* delapan

lapar: hungry

larang, melarang: to forbid; *larangan* forbidden, reserved (for smbdy)

lari: run away; *lari, berlari* run; *terlari2* running helter-skelter, without heeding one's path

lata, melata: creep, crawl; wander; *terlata2* wandering aimlessly

latéh, berlatéh: practice; practise

lauk: food (fish, meat, eggs, etc.) eaten with rice

laut: sea

lawak, melawak *Hind.*: to clown, play the fool

lawar: smart, elegant (of clothes); *melawar* look smart, be smartly dressed

layor, melayorkan: to parch, scorch

lebat: luxuriant (of foliage, hair)

lebéh: more (than); excess; *lebéh2* the remains (of food)

lechah: muddy and wet

léchéh *Ind.*: sticky

lechut: slip out easily (as pips from fruit); *melechutkan* to let fly (e.g. a stick, from the hand)

Léh: abbreviation of the name *Saléh*

léhér: neck

léka: utterly absorbed (in some pursuit)

lekas: immediately, without delay; earlier than usual, or than expected; quickly; *terlekas* too early, before an appointed time

lekat, melekat: stick, stick fast, be fixed

lembut: soft

lémpah, melémpah: to flow out, to overflow

lémpar, melémpar (kan): throw, hurl, toss away, throw down

léngah: linger, dawdle, loiter; *terléngah balék* be late back (unavoidably)

lengan: arm

lénggang, melénggang, berlénggang2: swaying

lengkap: fully equipped, complete with...

lénték, melénték: to curve up at the tips

lepas: free from restraint, loose; after; *lepaskan* to set free; *melepaskan diri* to free oneself

letak, letakkan, meletakkan: to place, set in position, lay down, put; *terletak* placed in position, situated

léwat: late, behind time

lidi: veins of coconut palm fronds

lihat, melihat: see, look at; *kelihatan* be visible, be seen, appear

lilin: candle

lima: five

lindong: shade, shelter; *terlindong* hidden, concealed

lintang, melintang: lie across, athwart

lintas, melintas: dash across; *terlintas* flash across (the mind, of an idea)

lior *see* ayer

lohor, dzohor *Ar.*: noon: *sembahyang lohor* the midday prayer

lolong, melolong: to howl like a dog

lompat, melompat: to leap; *terlompat* with a leap

luar: the outside (of smthg); *di-luar* on the outside of..., outside; (*ka-*)*luar* to the outside, outside; *keluar* to go out

luat, meluat: to feel nauseated

luka: wound, cut; wounded

lukis, melukis: delineate, draw

lumba, (lomba) berlumba: race, compete

lupa *Skr.*: forget; *terlupa* (I) quite forgot; *pelupa* forgetful,

luroh *see* seluroh

luru, meluru: to rush at something; to rush along; *terluru-luru* rushing on (and taking no heed); *lari meluru* run headlong

lurus: straight; *meluruskan* to straighten

Ma': abbreviation of *emak*, used before a proper name

ma'af *Ar.*: forgiveness; *ma'afkan* to forgive

ma'alum, ma'lum *Ar.*: known, know; *ma'alum-lah* it is well known, you know, it is understandable

macham: sort, kind, manner; (*coll.*) as if, like; (*ber*)*macham2* of all sorts

Mah: abbreviation of the names Fatimah, Salmah, etc.

mahal: precious, rare; dear, expensive

mahu: want, wish

main: play, to play: *main2* to play about, pretend; *bukan main* genuinely, truly; *main2kan* play a trick on smbdy; *permainan* game

maka: (*writt.*) a connective which does not need translation

makan: eat, consume; food; *makanan* food, meal

makin: more, the more, more and more; *makin...makin* the more...the more

Malabari: a native of Malabar, in India

malam: darkness, night; dark; *sa-malam* last night, yesterday; *bermalam* spend the night; *kemalaman* benighted; *malam2an* in the depth of the night

malang: thwarting, unfortunate; misfortune; be unfortunate; *kemalangan* run into bad luck; misfortune; accident

malim, ma'alim *Ar.*: one learned in religion

malu: shame; ashamed; shy; *termalu2* overcome by shyness, shyly

mana: which? (of a selection); (*di-*)*mana?* where?; (*ka-*)*mana?* whither?; *dari mana?* whence?; (*yang*) *mana?* which one?; *macham mana?* how?; *macham mana pun* however things may be, in any case; (*macham*) *mana tahu?* how can one know?, who knows?; *ka-mana2 pun* to wheresoever, to anywhere at all; *sa-banyak mana* to what extent, how much

mandi: bathe, take a bath

manggar: fallen blossom of a palm

mangkok: bowl, cup

manis: sweet; likeable (of a person)

manja: special fondness; *memanjakan* to spoil (a child)

marah: anger; angry

mari: for *ka-mari* hither. See Index

masa *Skr.*: time, epoch; when

masak: ripe; cooked; *masak, memasak* to cook

masam: sour, unripe

maséh: still, up to this/that time

mashhor *Ar.*: famous, renowned

masin: salty; *termasin* over-salted

masing-masing: each one separately, severally

masok: enter, go in; set (of sun); *masokkan* to put something in; *masokkan ka-hati* to take to heart, be hurt; *termasok* included; included by mistake

mata: eye; centre; blade (of knife)

matahari: sun

mati: dead; stopped (of engine, clock); *kematian* having suffered bereavement by death

mayat *Ar.*: corpse

megah: famous, distinguished; proud

méja *Port.*: table

melainkan *see* lain

mémang: in the nature of things, true to type, as would be expected, naturally, of course

menang: be successful in competition, win; *kemenangan* a victory

mengah, termengah2: panting, puffing

mengapa: why?; *ta' mengapa* it doesn't matter

mengkuang: the larger screwpine (pandanus), used for plaiting mats, etc.

menjangan *see* hantu

menong, termenong: plunged in thought

mentah: raw, uncooked; unripe; inexperienced

mentekedarah: a syncopated form of the original curse *muntahkan darah* (May you die) vomiting blood. In Text B 588 it is made into a passive verb, *lit.*: 'What is-being-cursedly-done by him in coming here!'

mentua: parent-in-law

mérah: red; *mérah2* reddish; very red

meréka: (*writt.*) they, them; persons

mesti: needs must, must

mimpi: dream

minggu *Port.*: week

minit *Eng.*: minute (unit of time)

minta, (pinta), meminta: to ask for (smthg); *permintaan* request minum: to drink; *minum ayer* to take light refreshments

minyak: oil, grease

misai: moustache

muafakat *Ar.* (*coll.*) mupakat, pakat: agreement, arrangement; *berpakat* make an agreement, discuss arrangements

muda: young; *muda2* youngish; very young; *Raja Muda* Heir Apparent

mudah: easy; easily, lightly; *mudah2an* may it be that...

muka: face, front; page; surface; *di-muka simpang* 'on the corner' (i.e. at the 'face' of the branch road); *muka masam* looking displeased

mula *Skr.*: beginning; *mulaï, memulaï* to begin; *mula2* at first, to begin with; *sa-mula* once again, over again

mulut: mouth

murah: generous, cheap

murka *Skr.*: wrath (of God, or of a ruler)

musang: civet-cat, pole-cat

mustahil *Ar.*: unbelievable, incredible

nabi *Ar.*: prophet

nafas *Ar.*: breath

naik: to rise, come up, go up

'nak *see* hendak

nama *Skr.*: name; *bernama* having as name, named

nampak, tampak: be visible; see; *nampak-nya* apparently, it seems

nanti, menanti: to wait; *menanti2* keep on waiting; *ternanti2* waiting (on the alert for something)

nasi: cooked rice

nasib *Ar.*: destiny, fate; *nasib baik*... fortunately...

negeri *Skr.*: land, country; state

nganga, menganga: to be agape; to yawn; *mulut ternganga* gaping (with astonishment, fear)

nikah *Ar.*: marriage (the religious ceremony)

-nya: 1. a post-position pronoun. After a noun it may usually be translated 'of him', 'of it', etc., or else 'the', implying 'in the case', e.g. *Ini hotel-nya* 'This is the hotel'; after a *me-* verb-form (and after *kapada*) it may usually be translated 'it', 'him', etc.; after a *di-* verb-form it may usually be translated 'by him' etc.

2. a nominalising suffix, when used after an adj., e.g. *besar-nya* size

nyala, menyala: flare up, light up, be alight

'nyalang: by the time that. See Index

nyanyi, menyanyi: to sing

nyaring: shrill, high-pitched

nyata *Skr.*: clear, manifest

nyior: coconut

nyiru: basket-work tray for winnowing rice

O: vocative-piece preceding a name or title

Oh!: exclamation, denoting sudden recollection: 'Ah yes, before I forget...'

Oi!: exclamation intended to draw attention: Hi!

Oih!: exclamation denoting appreciation, approval

olah: manner, way of doing things, whim; *sa-olah2* as if, as though

oléh: by (a person), by reason of, because of (a situation), *beroléh* have, possess, get

orang: person, people, one; *orang rumah* wife; $200 *tiap2 sa-orang* $200 each; *sa-orang2* all on one's own; *anak bini orang* wives and daughters (of other men, i.e. women). Used as a numeral coefficient: *sa-orang tukang* a craftsman

Pa': abbreviation of *bapa*, used as a respectful title before a proper name; *Pa' Pandir* the foolish 'hero' of Malay folk-lore

pachak, memachak: to stick something upright into the ground; *ter-pachak* stuck upright like a post

pachal: (archaic) humble slave

pada: at, in, on (before non-place words, but see Index); *pada pikiran saya* in my opinion; *pada perasaan-nya* he thinks that...; *pada sa'at itu* at that moment; *pada hal* whereas, in reality

padan: fitting, in keeping, suitable

padi: rice in the husk

pagi: morning

pagut: bite (of snakes), peck (of birds)

pak *Ch.*: wooden box, chest

pakai, memakai: to use, wear; (*coll.*) accept as normal, do habitually; *pakaian* clothes

pakat *see* muafakat

paksa *Skr.*: force, compulsion; *paksa, memaksa* to force, compel

paku: nail, spike; *terpaku* transfixed

paling, berpaling: to turn the head, look round

panas: heat; hot (of temperature, not of spices); *hari panas* a fine day

pandai: skilled, expert, clever

pandang, memandang: to turn one's eyes towards, look at; *terpandang* catch sight of; *terpandang2* find oneself looking at; *memandang-mandang* keep looking in a certain direction; *berpandang2an* looking at each other; *ta' terpandang* not able to be looked at

pandu: trial, testing; guidance; *pandu, memandu* to guide

panggil, memanggil: summon, call, invite

pangkal: beginning, origin, first part of (a road, a limb, a tree)

pangkat: rank, grade; *berpangkat* of high rank

panjang: long; *berchakap panjang2* discuss at great length

panjat, memanjat: to climb (e.g. a rope), to swarm up

palit, memalit: to smudge, smear; *palit2* all smeared with...

pantai: shore, beach

pantas: active, nimble, swift; *dengan pantas* swiftly

pantun: a four-lined verse of which the first couplet, though often apparently unconnected in meaning, foreshadows the second couplet by medial and final assonances. It is the second couplet which carries the message; *berpantum* to improvise or quote such quatrains, to sing verses

para: shelf or rack above the cooking-place in a Malay kitchen

parang: a heavy wood-knife with a blade that is broadest at the end

paroh: half; *sa-paroh dudok* half sitting (and half lying)

pasal *see* fasal

pasang, memasang: set in motion (a machine), bring into working order; light (a lamp); *lanting terpasang* a lighted lantern; *lanting pun berpasang* (Text A 185) and the lantern is alight

pasar *Pers.*: market

patah: broken; break off, snap (of a twig)

paték: I, me (in addressing a ruler)

patut: seemly, proper

payah: difficult (of work), hard; serious (of illness); *ta' payah*: lit. it is not (worth) the trouble, i.e. 'Don't!' (as a polite prohibition)

pechah: broken, shattered (e.g. of a cup); *pechah perut* 'burst one's sides' (with laughing)

peduli *see* feduli

pegang, memegang: hold

pekap, memekap: cover (mouth, ear) with the hand; 'hold' the nose, to avoid an unpleasant smell

pekék, memekék: cry out shrilly, scream; *terpekék* screaming (involuntarily)

pelék: strange, unexpected, surprising, 'funny'

pelesu, falsu *Port.*: counterfeit

pelok, memelok: put one's arms round; embrace; *sa-pemelok* an armful, as much as one can hold in the arms

penat: tired, exhausted; *kepenatan* exhausted; weariness, exhaustion

péndék: short

penglima: military commander

péngsan: lose consciousness, faint

penjuru: corner, angle

penoh: full; *sa-penoh2 terima kaséh* heartiest thanks

penting *Jav.*: important, worthy of consideration

pérak: silver

perang: war, warfare

peranjat, terperanjat: startled

perchaya(kan) *Skr.*: believe, trust

peréksa, meméréksa *Skr.*: examine carefully, look into; *(saya) kurang peréksa* I don't know

perempuan: woman

perenchah: flavouring; highly seasoned food eaten as a relish

peréntah: order, direction; *meméréntah* to rule, govern, command

pergi: to go

periok: deep cooking pot (for rice); *periok belanga* pots and pans

perjurit, perajurit *Jav.*: warrior

perkara *Skr.*: affair, thing, matter

perlahan, perlahan2: softly, gently

pernah: ever, at some time; *ta' pernah* never

perut: stomach, abdomen, uterus

petang: evening, afternoon: *petang 'karang* this evening

peték, memeték: pluck, pick (flowers); switch on (a torch); *lampu peték* electric torch; *petékan* selection, selected passage (from a book)

peti: box

pikir *see* fikir

pikul, memikul: to carry over the shoulder; *sa-pikul* a measure of weight (133⅓ lb)

piléh, memiléh: to choose

pilin, memilin: to twist, twine (as in making ropes)

pinggan *Tam.*: plate; *pinggan mangkok* crockery

pinggang: waist

pintar: clever, wily

pintu: door, gate

pipi: cheek

pisat, pesat *Ind.*: quick: *pisat2an* hurriedly

pisau: knife

pokok: plant, shrub, tree

pondok: hut, shed

ponggok, punggok: stumpy, squat; *burong punggok* the short-tailed hawk-owl; *memonggok, terponggok* sitting in one position for a long time, like the owl

pontianak: vampire; evil spirit which preys on women in childbirth and on babies

puar: wild ginger; *berpuar* (in *N.S.*) to fight a mock battle in the rice-fields to exorcise evil spirits

puas: satisfied; *puas2* to one's heart's content

puasa *Skr.*: fast, abstinence; the Fast of the month of Ramadzan

puchat: pale

puchok: shoot, tip, bud (of plants)

Puh!: exclamation implying scorn

puji, memuji: to praise; *memuji2* to keep on praising, to flatter; *pujian* praise, praises

pujok, memujok: to coax

pukul, memukul: to strike, hit; *pukul sembilan* 9 o'clock; *pukul berapa?* what is the time? at what time?

pula: a post-position particle which implies a sequence of ideas and can therefore sometimes be translated 'in turn', 'then', 'next'. When the sequence is unexpected, or unwelcome, the note of surprise, puzzlement or indignation which the particle introduces is usually best translated by appropriate intonation.

pulang: to return (to a base); go home

pulas: wringing, twisting; *sakit memulas* colic

puléh: recovered (from illness, fright), restored to original state

puloh: a ten; *sa-puloh*, ten; *empat puloh* forty

pun: a post-position particle which highlights the preceding word (or longer unit) and can seldom be directly translated

punya: possession; possess. (Note: *baharu punya* for 'new' in Text A 8*a* is bazaar Malay commonly used, as here, by non-Malays. So also in A 8*b* *Saya punya bini* for 'my wife' where a Malay would usually say *bini saya*)

pura-pura: shamming, pretending

putar, berputar: rotate

putéh: white

putus: severed (of a rope), broken, broken off, settled (of dispute, discussion); *putuskan, memutuskan* to make a decision; *putus harap* disappointed; *keputusan* final decision, outcome

raba, meraba: feel about (e.g. in one's pocket), grope, run one's fingers over (e.g. bumps on the forehead)

Rabbi!: *Ar.* O Lord!

rachun: stomach-poison; *merachun(kan)* to poison

rahat: fallen (of durians), see *gugor*

ramai: in large numbers (of people); *orang ramai* the populace, the public; the audience

ranggong, meranggong: squat with knees wide apart; walk on all fours

rangkak, merangkak: crawl on hands and knees

rantai: chain; *tiga rantai* three chains (measurement)

ranting: twig, small branch; *meranting* be like a twig, ?wispy. See Text B 83

rapat: in contact, close to, close together; *tutup rapat2* shut tight; *merapat kapada* move close to

rapék, merapék: to talk nonsense, chatter inconsequently

rasa *Skr.*: sensation, feeling, experience; to taste; *rasa-nya* it seems, apparently, I think; *merasa* taste, savour, enjoy; *berasa* feeling... (e.g. surprised); *terasa* have the sensation of..., feel...; *perasaan* sensation, feeling, idea; *perasaan saya* in my opinion, I think; *ta' perasan* (to do a thing) without realising that you are doing it

rata: level, flat; *sa-rata2, merata* all over (an area)

ratus: hundred; *sa-ratus* one hundred; *berratus2* in hundreds

raung, meraung: cry out in pain or distress

raya: great; *jalan raya* main road

rebah: fall to the ground, collapse (e.g. of a person fainting)

rendah: low; *merendahkan* to make low

renong, merenong: look fixedly at smthg

resah: fidgety, restless, nervous

riang: gay, in high spirits

ribu: thousand; *sa-ribu* one thousand

rimau, harimau: tiger

ringgit: dollar

rioh: tumult, hubbub; *rioh rendah* uproarious din

roboh: crash down, fall heavily, collapse (e.g. of a house)

rosak: spoilt, damaged; *merosakkan* to damage (smthg)

rotan: rattan

roti *Hind.*: bread, cakes, biscuits; *roti chanai* flat bread

rugi *Skr.*: loss (financial, but frequently used colloquially to imply a missed opportunity of any sort)

rumah: house, building

rumpun: a clump (e.g. of bamboo)

rumput: grass, weeds; *berrumput* covered with grasses

rundok, merundok: bend, bow the head (but in Text B. 113 used of a long flowing moustache which sweeps downward)

rungut, merungut: to mumble, grumble

runtoh: to crash down (of heavy objects)

rupa *Skr.*: appearance, form, shape; *rupa-nya* apparently, so it seems, evidently; *rupa2-nya* it looks very much as if...; *berupa* having the form of, in the shape of

sa- *see* satu

sabar *Ar.*: patience; be patient; *ta' sabar*, impatient, impatiently; *ta' tersabar* unable to restrain one's impatience

sadikit: a little, not much; a few

sah *Ar.*: genuine, valid

sahaja, 'aja: only, merely

sajak *Ar.*: assonance, harmony, rhythm; poem; in harmony, well-suited

sakit: sickness, hurt; sore, hurt, ill; *kesakitan* afflicted with pain; pain, illness

salah: fault, wrong-doing; wrong, in the wrong, at fault; *apa salah-nya?* why not?; *salah sa-orang kita* one or other of us; *salahkan* to put in the wrong, to accuse

salam *Ar.*: peace; *Salam 'alaikum!* Peace be with you!

salin, menyalin: change (one thing for another of the same kind); *bersalin kain* change one's clothes sama *Skr.*: same, equal; *(ber)sama, bersama2* together with, along with

sambal: spiced dishes eaten with curry and rice

sambil: together with (doing smthg); simultaneously

sambut, menyambut: to receive with formality (a guest or a gift)

sampai: reach as far as, attain to, arrive; up to, until; *sampaikan, menyampaikan* make to arrive, deliver; *sampai hati* to have the heart to...

samping, kain samping *Jav.*: a one-width sarong worn over the trousers

sanding, bersanding: to sit side by side, used of the ceremonial sitting in state ('enthronement') of the bride and bridegroom at the wedding reception

sangat: exceedingly, excessively, very; serious, severe (of illness)

sanggul: hair ornaments, large decorated hair pins; coiffure; *bersanggul* wearing hair ornaments, with hair carefully dressed

sangka: opinion; to think that..., be under the impression that... (usually mistakenly)

sangkal, menyangkal: deny, contradict

sangkut: catch on something, be held back; *tersangkut* caught (on something), held up

santap: take food, eat or drink (of princes)

sa-peninggal *see* tinggal

saperti, sapertikan: like, as if; as for, concerning

sapu, menyapu(kan): to smooth on (e.g. ointment); to wipe off (e.g. dust); *sapu tangan* handkerchief

satu, suatu, sa-: one, a; *satu2* each separate one; *satu persatu* one at a time (of things); *sa-* is used before a numeral coefficient: *sa-ékor sepatong* a dragonfly, *lepas sa-orang sa-orang* one after the other. See Index

sawah: rice-fields

saya, sahaya: I

sayang: affection, a feeling of gentle regret; unfortunately; *Sayang!* A pity! How sad!

sayap: wing (of bird or insect)

sayup, sayup2: faintly (audible or visible)

sebab *Ar.*: reason, cause; because

sebut, menyebut: to say, pronounce, give a name

sedang: medium; in the middle of (doing smthg)

sedap: pleasant, comfortable, at ease (of heart, mind); good to taste (of food); *sedap hati* feeling pleased

sedar: conscious, aware of...; *sedarkan diri* regain consciousness, (*fig.*)
  come to one's senses; *tersedar* recovering consciousness

sedia *Skr.*: already, before; ready, prepared

segala *Tam.*: all, the whole

sejok: cold, cool

sekalian, sakalian, sekelian: all together, all

sekarang, 'karang, 'kang: presently, now; *sekarang ini* in a moment or two,
  at this moment; *malam 'karang* this evening

sekat, menyekat: obstruct, restrict

sekolah *Port.*: school

selalu: always, frequently, constantly

selam, menyelam: to dive

selamat *Ar.*: safety; safe; *selamatkan* to make safe, save; *Selamat jalan* (to
  the one who goes), *Selamat tinggal* (to the one who remains) Goodbye

seléndang: shoulder scarf, head scarf

selimut: wrap, rug, blanket; *selimutkan* to put a coverlet over smbdy

selipar *Eng.*: slippers

seliséh: varying, not coinciding, failing to meet

seluar *Ar.*: trousers; *seluar baju* suit

selubong: a veil; *berselubong* wearing a veil or wrapper; *selubongkan* to
  wrap (smthg) around head and shoulders

seluroh: all, the whole of

sémah, menyémah: to make offerings to spirits; to propitiate spirits

semai: planting in a nursery plot; *semaian* nursery for seedlings

semak: undergrowth

semangat: the spirit of life, the vital spark

semayam, bersemayam: sit in state (of a ruler)

sembahyang: prayer; to pray

sembar, sambar: pounce on and carry off (in teeth, claws)

sembilan: nine

sembunyi: concealment; *bersembunyi* hide oneself; hidden; *menyembunyikan* to hide (smthg)

semenjak: period after; since, ever since

sementara: while, during; *sementara itu* in the meanwhile

sempat: having (only just) time or space (to do smthg); *sa-baik-baik
  sempat* just in the nick of time to...

sempurna *Skr.*: perfect; complete, satisfactory

semua *Skr.*: all; *kesemua(-nya)* all of them

semut: ant

sén: cent

senam, bersenam: stretch the muscles; do physical exercises

senang: easy, without difficulty; leisured; *senang2* with ease; *menyenang-kan hati* to set (someone's) heart at ease

sendiri: self, oneself, him-, her-, itself

sengaja: deliberately, purposely

sengkéta *Skr.*: contest, feud; *bersengkéta* (in *N.S.*) wage mock-battle in rice-fields to drive out evil spirits

senja *Skr.*: early evening, dusk

sentak, menyentak(kan): pull at with a jerk; *tersentak ka-belakang* stepping back hurriedly

sental: scrub, scrub out, erase, (*coll.*) 'polish off' (of food)

sentiasa *Skr.*: always, perpetually

senyap: still, motionless, silent, quiet

senyum: smile; *tersenyum2* breaking into a little smile; *senyum simpul* a slightly rueful apologetic smile; *senyum kulum* a pouting smile

sepai, bersepai2: broken up into bits

sepatong: dragonfly

sepésal *Eng.*: (*coll.*) special

sepit: catch between two surfaces; *kuéh sepit* thin wafers cooked between gofering irons

serah(kan), menyerah(kan): surrender, give up; *berserah* give oneself up

seram, seram2: goose-flesh, feeling on edge, hair on end

seraya *Skr.*: along with, at the same time as (doing smthg else)

serba *Skr.*: all, of all sorts; *serba salah* (*lit.* wrong whichever course one takes) ill at ease, feeling awkward

serban *Pers.*: turban

serbok: powder

sérét, menyérét: to trail (smthg) along the ground; *kasut sérét* backless slippers

sergah, menyergah: to startle with a sudden movement or sound

seri *Skr.*: charm; bright splendour; the pick of...; *berseri2* bright, shining

sérong: askew, sideways, slanting

serta *Skr.*: together with, along with, and; *serta-merta* suddenly, at once

sétan *see* shaitan

shaitan, sétan: devil, fiend, spirit of evil

shoⁿk: ?excited (? = shak *Ar.*: suspicion. See Text B 684)

shukor *Ar.*: thanks

si-: a friendly prefix for personal names, applied usually to children and in fables, to personified animals

sial: ill-omened, bringing bad luck

siang: daylight, the daytime; early; *siang2* early morning; broad daylight

siap: ready, prepared; *bersiap* make oneself ready; prepared; *siapkan* make (smthg) ready

siapa: who?

sigai: a light ladder for tree-climbing

sikat: comb; *bersikat* comb one's hair

sila, silakan *Skr.*: Be pleased to... (used in welcoming a guest to enter, to be seated, to partake of food)

simpan, menyimpan: to keep; to put away

simpang, menyimpang: turn off at an angle; *simpang tiga* crossing place of three roads

simpul: a knot

singgasana *Skr.*: throne

sini: here, this place

singgah, menyinggah: to call in at (a house, a port)

siréh: betel-vine, betel-leaf

situ: there, that place

siul, bersiul: to whistle

sorok, menyorok: be under cover, crouch out of sight; *menyorokkan* thrust (smbdy or smthg) out of sight

sorong, menyorong: push (smthg) forward

suami *Skr.*: (*pol.*) husband

suap: a mouthful of food, taken with the fingers; *menyuap* to convey the 'pinch' of food to the mouth

suara *Skr.*: voice

suatu *see* satu

suboh *Ar.*: dawn

sudah, 'dah: completed, ended; already come about; already; *menyudah-kan* bring to completion, finish; *Sudah-lah!* That's enough! *kesudahan-nya* the conclusion of it, finally, at length

sudi: willing, content to...

sugul (= mashghul) *Ar.*: mournful

suka *Skr.*: pleasure; pleased; to like to...; *menyukakan* to make happy suku: a quarter, a section

sulit: secret; *bersulit2* in secret

suloh: torch

sumber *Jav.*: spring, source

sumbu: wick

sungai: river

sunggoh: true, genuine, truly; *sunggoh pun...tetapi* although...(yet)

sungkor, tersungkor: scrabbling about on the earth; grovelling on the ground

surat *Ar.*: a writing; document, letter

suroh, menyuroh: tell smbdy to do smthg, bid

susah: troubled; difficult; trouble, difficulty; *bersusah2* to take trouble over smthg

susor: outer edge; *menyusor* to skirt the edge of (e.g. a shore)

susu: breast; milk; *susui* to suckle

susup: passing low underneath something; *susup-sasap* tumbling along, scrambling along (as in headlong flight through undergrowth)

ta' *see* tidak

ta'at *Ar.*: obedient

tadah, menadah: to catch smthg from below on outstretched palms, on a tray

tadi: just now, recently

tagéh, ketagéh: a craving

tahan, menahan(kan): restrain, hold back, detain, control; bear, put up with; *tahan, bertahan* to last long, endure

tahu, mengetahui: to know; *ta' ketahuan*: *lit.* not able to be known; not able to be described

tahun: year

takut: afraid; *takutkan* (= *akan*) to be frightened of (smthg); *takutkan, menakutkan* to frighten; *ketakutan* frightened; fear, fright; *penakut* cowardly; coward

tali: cord, string

talu, bertalu2: continuous, without intermission; one after the other

tambah: increase (by repetition); *bertambah* to increase, be increased

tanah: earth, soil

tanam, menanam: to plant, bury

tanda: sign, token

tandok: horn; *bertandok* having horns

tangan: hand

tanggoh: postponement; *tanggohkan* to put smthg off

tangis, menangis: to weep

tangkap, menangkap: to seize, catch, capture

tanjong: cape, promontory; *menanjong* be in the shape of a promontory

tanya, bertanya: to ask, to question

tapak: palm of hand, sole of foot

'tapi *see* tetapi

tarék, menarék: pull, drag, draw; *menarék nafas* draw breath, breathe

taroh, menaroh: to put, place; stake; keep, possess; *bertaroh* to place a bet

tatang, menatang: carry on the palm of the hand

taukéh *Ch.*: employer; proprietor

tawan: take captive; *tawanan* captive, prisoner

tawar, bertawar: to bid, offer a price; to bargain

tawarikh *Ar.*: annals, history

tedong *see* ular

tegah: prohibition; prohibit

tegak: erect, vertical; *tegak2* bolt upright

tegok, menegok: to gulp down

tekak: back part of the mouth, gullet

tekan, menekan: exert pressure on smthg; press hard

telah: a word which implies completion in the past; *sa-telah itu* after that; *sa-telah sa-tengah jam* after half an hour

telan, menelan: to swallow

telinga: ear

teman: companion; *temankan* to keep someone company

tembaga *Skr.*: brass

tembelang: rotten, addled (of eggs); unseemly conduct; gaffe

Temenggong: a high-ranking minister of state

témpang: limping, lame; *tertémpang2* limping about all over the place

tempat: place; *tempat tidor* bed

témpoh *Port.*: extension of time allowed; length of time, period

tengah: middle; mid; be in the middle (of doing smthg); *tengah hari* midday; *sa-tengah* a half

Tengku: title and form of address used in some Malay states for members of the ruling family. In Text B (a Malay adaptation of a traditional Indian story) it is used for high-ranking ministers of state

téngok, menéngok: to see, look at

tentang: over against, facing; concerning; a 'place' in a book, in a piece of weaving

tentu: sure, certain; assuredly

tépak: an oblong metal box, container for a betel-nut set

tepat: exact, precise, 'on the dot' (of an appointment kept)

tepi: edge, brim; *menepi* to edge away, keep to the edge

tepok, menepok: to pat with the hand

tepong: flour

terang: clear, bright

terbang: to fly; *berterbangan* flying about in all directions; *kapal terbang* aeroplane

terbit: rise into view (from below), come up, come out; rise (of sun or moon)

terék: severe (of illness), excessive (of heat), tight (of a knot); *menerékkan tali* to pull a cord tight

teriak, berteriak: to cry out, to call, to shout

terima, menerima: to accept

terja, menerja: ?rush forward. ?Cf. *terjun* leap down, ?and *terjak* fly up into the air (of a startled chicken, Wlk.)

terjun: to leap down, fall from a height

terkam, menerkam: to rush at, spring upon, dash forward

terlalu: very, exceedingly, surpassing

terok: serious, severe (of illness)

tertawa: to laugh

terus: right through, straight on, direct; *menerusi* to go straight on through (a place)

tetak, menetakkan: hack, chop at

tetap: firm, fixed, secure; *tetapkan, menetapkan* to make firm; *tetap2* firmly, steadily

tetapi, -tapi: but

tiap-tiap: each, every

tiba: to arrive; *tiba2* suddenly

tidak, ta', tiada: not, *see* Index

tidor: sleep; to sleep

tiga: three; *bertiga* (being) three, three together; *ketiga* the three (as a group)

tikar: a (plaited) mat; *tikar mengkuang* a mat woven from coarse pandanus leaf; *tikar puchok* a mat woven from the finest pandanus leaf tikus: rat, mouse

timbang, menimbang: to weigh

timpa, menimpa: strike by falling down upon

tinggal: be left over, be left behind, remain; dwell, live; *tinggalkan, meninggalkan* leave (something) behind; *meninggal(kan dunia)* to die; *peninggal* time of absence; *sa-peninggal-nya* during his absence. *Tinggal-lah!* (for *Selamat tinggal*) Goodbye (to the one who remains behind)

tinggi: high

tingkap: window (of the Malay type, without glass)

tinjau, meninjau: crane the neck in order to see something

tipu, menipu: to deceive

titah: speech, command (of a ruler); to speak, command

To': abbreviation of *dato'*, used before a proper name

tobat, taubat, bertobat *Ar.*: repentant

tolak, menolak(kan): push, push away, reject; *bertolak* set off (on a journey), start out

tolong, menolong: to help; *menolong-nolong* lend a hand; *pertolongan* help, assistance; 'please', as a polite introduction before an imperative: *Tolong sampaikan...* Please convey...

tonggang, tunggang: sitting astride; *menonggang kuda* on horseback; *tonggang2 kuda* playing horses

tua: old (in years); *orang tua* father, parents; old person; *orang tua2* ancestors; *ketua* elder, minor headman

tuah: a stroke of luck; *bertuah* blessed with luck

tuai, menuai: to harvest rice with the *tuai*, a small reaping tool held in the palm of the hand

tuam: apply warmth for the relief of pain (e.g. a wrapped heated stone)

tuan: master, owner; sir; a generally applied title

tuanku (=tuan-ku): Your Highness, His Highness (form of address to a ruler)

tudong: lid, cover

Tuhan: God

tuju, menuju: aim towards, move towards; make for; *tujuan* objective, aim; *sa-tuju, bersetuju* be in agreement

tukang: craftsman

tukar, menukar: change, exchange

tulang: bone

tulis, menulis: to write; *bertulis* having writing on it, inscribed

tumbok, menumbok: to pound (e.g. rice); *penumbok* a pounder

tumit: heel

tundok: bow one's head, look down

tunggu: keep watch; wait

tungku: cooking-stones (three) on which the cooking pot rests

tunjok, menunjok('kan): to point to, show; *pertunjokan* a 'showing', scene (in a play)

turis: long shallow cut made with a knife, e.g. on bark; *menuris* to tap (rubber tree)

turun: go down; become lower; go out (of a Malay house, i.e. down the entrance steps); *turunkan* to make lower; *menurun* to have a downward slope

turut, menurut: to follow

tutup, menutup: to cover, close, shut; *bertutup* shut up, enclosed

ubah, berubah: to change, become different; *tiada berubah lain hanya*... (Text A 558) is none other than...

ubat: medicine; *mengubat(kan)* to treat medically

uchap, menguchap(kan): utter, express; *menguchap-uchap* keep repeating (e.g. prayers)

udang: prawn, shrimp

ukir, mengukir: to incise, engrave; carve; *berukir2* engraved with a pattern

ulang: repetition; repeat; *berulang2* over and over again

ular: snake; *ular tedong* cobra

ulat: worm, maggot

ulit, mengulit: to croon a lullaby

umor, 'umor *Ar.*: life; *sa-umor hidup* all one's life; *berumor delapan-belas tahun* eighteen years of age

umpan: bait

umpat: defame, slander, speak against

undi: lot, die

undor, mengundor: retreat, draw back

untok: allotted share, portion; for, in order to; *untokkan* to allot as a share

untong: fate, destiny, good luck; profit

upah, mengupah: to give payment for the performance of a specific task

urat: sinew, tendon, vein, artery; strand, thread

urut, mengurut: massage by drawing the hand along; husk grain by pulling it through the closed hand; *mengurut-ngurut* stroking

usah: *lit.* need, but usually a colloquial abbreviation of *ta' usah*: *lit.* there is no need (a polite prohibition). *Usah-lah!* Please don't!

usong, mengusong: to carry in a litter slung from poles

Wah!: exclamation indicating lively surprise, whether of pleasure or consternation

waktu *Ar.*: time, occasion; appointed time

walau *Ar.*: and if, though; *walau pun* even if

wang: money

wangi: fragrant; *ayer wangi* perfume

wara' *Ar.*: to abstain from things which are *haram* (i.e. forbidden by religion); abstemious

warangan: arsenic

warna *Skr.*: colour

wayang *Jav.*: a theatrical show; *wayang bangsawan* a show with live actors, as opposed to *wayang kulit* the shadow play (with leather puppets) and *wayang gelap* the cinema

wéwér *see* hantu

Ya! *Ar.*: Oh!, verily!

Yam: abbreviation of the name *Meriam*

yang: a connecting particle which is sometimes to be translated 'who', 'which'

INDEX TO FOOTNOTES

LIST OF SENTENCES ANALYSED
OR DISCUSSED